Springer Proceedings in Business and Economics

Springer Proceedings in Business and Economics brings the most current research presented at conferences and workshops to a global readership. The series features volumes (in electronic and print formats) of selected contributions from conferences in all areas of economics, business, management, and finance. In addition to an overall evaluation by the publisher of the topical interest, scientific quality, and timeliness of each volume, each contribution is refereed to standards comparable to those of leading journals, resulting in authoritative contributions to the respective fields. Springer's production and distribution infrastructure ensures rapid publication and wide circulation of the latest developments in the most compelling and promising areas of research today.

The editorial development of volumes may be managed using Springer's innovative Online Conference Service (OCS), a proven online manuscript management and review system. This system is designed to ensure an efficient timeline for your publication, making Springer Proceedings in Business and Economics the premier series to publish your workshop or conference volume.

More information about this series at http://www.springer.com/series/11960

Marietta Janowicz-Lomott ·
Krzysztof Łyskawa · Persefoni Polychronidou ·
Anastasios Karasavvoglou
Editors

Economic and Financial Challenges for Balkan and Eastern European Countries

Proceedings of the 10th International Conference on the Economies of the Balkan and Eastern European Countries in the Changing World (EBEEC) in Warsaw, Poland 2018

Springer

Editors
Marietta Janowicz-Lomott
Department of Risk and Insurance
Warsaw School of Economics
Warsaw, Poland

Krzysztof Łyskawa
Collegium of Management and Insurance
Poznań University Economics and Business
Poznań, Poland

Persefoni Polychronidou
International Hellenic University
Serres, Greece

Anastasios Karasavvoglou
International Hellenic University
Kavala, Greece

ISSN 2198-7246 ISSN 2198-7254 (electronic)
Springer Proceedings in Business and Economics
ISBN 978-3-030-39926-9 ISBN 978-3-030-39927-6 (eBook)
https://doi.org/10.1007/978-3-030-39927-6

This Springer imprint is published by the registered company Springer Nature Switzerland AG
The registered company address is: Gewerbestrasse 11, 6330 Cham, Switzerland

Preface

This volume of "Springer Proceedings in Business and Economics" includes papers presented at the 10th International Conference *The Economies of the Balkan and Eastern European Countries in the Changing World—EBEEC 2018*. The conference was organized jointly by the Technological Educational Institute (TEI) of Eastern Macedonia and Thrace, Department of Accounting and Finance (Greece), the Warsaw School of Economics (Poland) and the Poznań University of Economics and Business (Poland) and took place in Warsaw, Poland, on May 11–13, 2018.

The objectives of the conference were to discuss and to evaluate the results of the economic policy that have been applied during the last two decades in Balkan and Eastern European countries. Another goal was to suspend the prospect challenges and to investigate the policies in the sector of economy which are considered necessary, so that the countries are to be integrated getting as much benefit as possible. This aim brought together more than 120 papers prepared by more than 250 authors from 20 countries from the region and all over the world.

Consequently, the presented collection of articles is a proof that in many areas of science (international economies, European integration, economic growth, finance, banking, insurance, international trade, health care, agriculture, energy, innovation, management and marketing) we can find examples of research that identify the risks of the modern world. But participants of the EBEEC Conference offer concrete solutions in their fields. Our experience and new ideas are proofs that the countries of Balkans and Eastern Europe are developing very dynamically and in a modern way. There are many problems that we can find in other parts of the world. Our proposed solutions have arisen from the cultural specificity of our region, but they may have a universal character.

Warsaw, Poland — Marietta Janowicz-Lomott
Poznań, Poland — Krzysztof Łyskawa
Kavala, Greece — Anastasios Karasavvoglou
Serres, Greece — Persefoni Polychronidou

Contents

Political Risk Complementarity Between Business Economics and International Relations

Ioannis Psychogyios, Efstathios Fakiolas, and Nikitas Spiros Koutsoukis

Abstract Political risk is a term with multiple contexts. From an economic viewpoint, it is associated mainly with risks in business operations and private or public investments affected by politics; from an International Relations viewpoint, it is used to "risk" as a concept, but without the "business" or "investment" perspectives. In this work, we aim to match International Relations theory constructs with the constructs of widely used Political Risk Indices and thus identify how the perspectives relate and complement each other. Our objective is to elicit the suitability of political risk frameworks, from an economic standpoint, for decision-making purposes under alternate International Relations standpoints and vice versa.

Keywords Political risk · Political Risk Indices · International Relations theory

1 Introduction

In this paper, we consider the relationship between frameworks used to measure political risk from an economic and enterprise risk management (ERM) viewpoint and main theories of International Relations (Realism, Constructivism, Liberalism).

Our analysis is made in two parts: In the first one, we present key points of the International Relations theories and review their perception of political risk in relation to that found in economics and ERM. In the second part, we review how the

I. Psychogyios · E. Fakiolas · N. S. Koutsoukis (✉)
Political Technology Research Group, Department of Political Science and International Relations, University of Peloponnese, Corinth, Greece
e-mail: nkoutsou@uop.gr

I. Psychogyios
e-mail: ipsychogios@cosmote.gr

E. Fakiolas
e-mail: fakiolas@uop.gr

I. Psychogyios
OTE Group of Companies, Athens, Greece

M. Janowicz-Lomott et al. (eds.), *Economic and Financial Challenges for Balkan and Eastern European Countries*, Springer Proceedings in Business and Economics,
https://doi.org/10.1007/978-3-030-39927-6_1

components in well-known political risk frameworks may interact with the International Relations theories. In other words, we ponder whether the context of political risk context may shift, in a meaningful way, if interpreted from an IR perspective.

The purpose of this analysis, in addition to its interdisciplinary interest, is to enrich the analysis of political risk, from an ERM perspective, with insights from International Relations so that political risk can be more effectively achieved.

2 Key Theories of International Relations

We consider the key points of the three "schools" of International Relations theories, namely on Realism, Constructivism and Liberalism. More specifically:

Realism The core of the Realistic theory is that sovereign states are the key players in world politics. The international system is "anarchic" in a structural sense; it depicts the effort of each state to achieve security, power and wealth in the realms of the world. In this environment, the states may even resort to war, either to confront rivalries or in an effort to obtain more power. A scenario made possible by the absence of a world government (Griffiths and O'Callaghan 2002; Nye 1988).

Constructivism Constructivists presume that the states have certain goals to achieve: It can be physical security of the state, stability, recognition by other states, economic development. The international system is ungoverned but not structural; namely, its content is differently defined by each state individually, or "...Anarchy is what states make of it..." (Wendt 1992). Constructivism focuses on international institutions and their interaction with the state in matters of international legislation, diplomacy and sovereignty (Jackson and Sørensen 2006; Griffiths and O'Callaghan 2002; Wendt 1992).

Liberalism For the Liberals, the international system is a realm of progress. Individual freedom is a key principle of the realm. States must comply with this freedom and set constraints to protect it, in their roles as political actors of the international system. States may achieve their goals and interests (e.g., power, wealth) with peaceful means (i.e., economic growth) rather than military confrontation and focus on the role of international institutions. Hence, the key concept of the theory is a concern for liberty (Griffiths and O'Callaghan 2002; Nye 1988; Doyle 1988).

3 Political Risk in International Relations Theories

We proceed to seek the notion of "political risk" in these theories, based on constructs of political risk that we have identified in previous work (Psychogyios and Koutsoukis 2018). Namely:

- Political risk conceived as government actions interfering with business operations (i.e., governmental interference).
- Political risk is defined in terms of other events of political nature.

Overall, we note that "political risk" in the context of International Relations seems to have a generic interpretation. The emphasis is more on the notion of risk at large and less in its political aspects, as perceived in ERM.

The concept of risk is present in Realism. Classic Realists find alternative "manifestations of risk." For example, Thucydides considers that the exercise of foreign policy for a state is made in the environment full of dangers but also opportunities—i.e., risks. Machiavelli expects a leader to always seek for advantages, whereas Morgenthau considers power as a mean to maximum gain. Schelling perceives threats when examining strategies based on Games Theory (Jackson and Sørensen 2006). These interpretations blend well with the duality of "upside" and "downside" notions of risk.

From a Constructivist viewpoint, risks are manifestations of the real world and are simply "out there" independently of the participating actors (Clapton 2011; Rigakos and Law 2009).

Liberalists ascertain (Nye 1988):

- the pacific effects on trade (commercial),
- the pacific effects of republican government (democratic),
- the importance of rules and regulations between countries (regulatory),
- the transformative effect of transnational contacts and coalitions on national attitudes and definitions of interests (sociological).

This resembles a reversed risk analysis, since Liberals perceive the effects rather than the causes, as risks.

In order to build on these alternative approaches to risk and, hence, political risk as found in International Relations, we take into consideration the levels of analysis (LOAs), namely the actors of a political system (Segbers et al. 2006). In the LOA approach, there are five levels of actors, from the individual actor (e.g., a person or a decision maker) to more complex actors of the global/international system, as depicted in Table 1.

Table 1 Levels of analysis and International Relations theories

IR theory	L1	L2	L3	L4	L5
Realism	X		X		X
Constructivism			X		X
Liberalism		X	X	X	

Key L1 individual actor/agent/decision maker, *L2* societal/social/group/transnational/subnational actors ("domestic" sphere), *L3* unit/state/government, *L4* supranational entities, *L5* global/international system

All three selected theories of IR share a common ground in the 3rd LOA, which encompasses the entities "state" and "government." (Neo)Realists and Constructivists share a common interest in the global international system. Liberals are further interested in the second and fourth level, namely domestic societal, social groups and supranational entities.

Keeping in mind, that all the theories find common ground at the 3rd LOA, we note that it fits well to the definition of a political risk as decisions and actions of the state or government interference fit well in the arena of national and international politics and draw an analogy to the concept of political risk as government actions interfering with business operations.

With the exception of the 1st LOA, in 2nd and 4th LOAs, the key actors can be defined on both the national and supranational or international level, as either society-relevant actors on the domestic or supranational level. Hence, these levels contextualize political risk in its broader sense: the effects of the interaction between governmental and non-governmental actors and thus focuses on events of political nature.

We proceed to match the above findings to the components of key political risk frameworks, namely the Political Risk Services Index (PRS), the International Country Risk Guide (ICRG) Index, the Business Environment Risk Intelligence (BERI) Index and its variants, BERI-Political Risk Index (BERI-PR) and BERI-Operations Risk Index (BERI-OR), often used from an economics and enterprise risk management viewpoint.

3.1 The Political Risk Services (PRS) Index

The PRS Index considers political risk in two distinct time horizons, a "short" term of 18 months (PRS-18m) and a longer term of 5 years (PRS-5y). Within each time horizon, there are different political risk elements to consider. Hence in Table 2, we match each PRS Index with one or more LOAs (The PRS Group 2017a).

Based on PRS's breakdown of political risk, we notice that in the 18-month horizon, components 2–12 are largely based on governmental actions, except for turmoil which, in this case, refers to events in the political environment, such as strikes, demonstrations and terrorism (Coplin and O'Leary 1983).

Turmoil is also present in the 5-year horizon and again matched to L1. With the exception of international economic issues, the remaining 5-year horizon components also tend to fit the L2 LOA, namely the actions of formal state entities or government. Naturally the 17th component, international economic problems fit well to the L5 LOA.

Overall, the majority of components in the PRS Index are based on the actions of formal [state] entities, essentially suggesting that PRS is state-oriented.

Table 2 PRS Index components versus LOAs

Time horizon	Political risk component	Level of analysis				
		1st	2nd	3rd	4th	5th
18 months (PRS-18m)	1. Turmoil		•			
	2. Equity restrictions			•		
	3. Operations restrictions			•		
	4. Taxation discrimination			•		
	5. Repatriation restrictions			•		
	6. Exchange controls			•		
	7. Tariff barriers			•		
	8. Other import barriers			•		
	9. Payment delays			•		
	10. Fiscal and monetary expansion			•		
	11. Labor policies			•		
	12. Foreign debt			•		
5 years (PRS-5y)	13. Turmoil		•			
	14. Investment restrictions			•		
	15. Trade restrictions			•		
	16. Domestic economic problems			•		
	17. International economic problems					•

3.2 The International Country Risk Guide (ICRG) Index

Continuing our analysis in the same manner, we match the ICRG Index components with the LOAs, based on the context of ICRG (The PRS Group 2017b) as depicted in Table 3.

It is clearly seen that ICRG fuses a more comprehensive viewpoint and matches more LOAs. We notice that in this case, corruption lends itself well to L1—individual actors, like corrupt politicians. We also notice that it includes interstate relations, L4 in the form of conflicts between states. The remaining components refer to the political environment and the interaction between society and government (i.e., L2) and state actions (L3).

On aggregate, the ICRG Index is weighted mostly L2 and L3, but naturally expands to L1 and L4 which makes it a flexible on one hand but, when considered as an analytical tool, it should be used in a carefully defined LOA context on the other.

Table 3 ICRG Index components versus LOAs

Political risk components	Level of analysis				
	1st	2nd	3rd	4th	5th
1. Government stability			•		
2. Socioeconomic conditions		•			
3. Investment profile			•		
4. Internal conflict		•			
5. External conflict				•	
6. Corruption	•				
7. Military in politics			•		
8. Religious tensions		•			
9. Law and order			•		
10. Ethnic tensions		•			
11. Democratic accountability			•		
12. Bureaucracy quality			•		

3.3 *The Business Environment Risk Intelligence (BERI) Political Risk Index*

As mentioned previously, we consider the original BERI and its variants BERI-PR and BERI-OR in the context of the LOAs (Howell and Chaddick 1994; Howell 2014).

3.3.1 The BERI Index in Relation to the LOAs

The BERI Index divides political risk components into three groups, namely internal and external causes and symptoms of political risk. We match these to the LOAs in Table 4.

We notice that for the large part, ICRG refers to the societal sphere (L2) and less so to other LOAs. An exception to this is the component "Restrictive (coercive) measures required to retain power" easily seen as a government-instigated activity, hence fitting the L3 LOA.

Both components of external causes, "Dependence on a Major power" and the role as a regional political actor (influencer) are assigned to the L4 LOA, namely supranational actors.

On aggregate, the BERI seems to favor mostly the 2nd level of analysis and is closer to societal perception of political risk.

Table 4 BERI components versus LOAs

Dimensions	Political risk components	Level of analysis				
		1st	2nd	3rd	4th	5th
Internal causes	Fractionalization of the political spectrum and the power of these factions		•			
	Fractionalization by language, ethnic and/or religious groups and the power of these factions		•			
	Restrictive (coercive) measures required to retain power			•		
	Mentality, including xenophobia, nationalism, corruption, nepotism, willingness to compromise		•			
	Social conditions including population density and wealth distribution		•			
	Organization and strength of forces for a radical left government		•			
External causes	Dependence on and/or importance to a hostile major power				•	
	Negative influences of regional political forces				•	
Symptoms of political risk	Societal conflict involving demonstrations, strikes, and street violence		•			
	Instability as perceived by non-constitutional changes, assassinations and guerrilla wars		•			

3.3.2 BERI-PR and BERI-OR in Relation to the LOAs

Things shift when considering the variants, BERI-PR and BERI-OR, as depicted in Tables 5 and 6, respectively. Our interpretation is based on Howell (2014).

For BERI-PR, we notice the identical "External factors" components and hence assigned to identical LOA, i.e., L4. The "Nature of government and politics" components are evenly balanced across LOAs L1, L2 and L3. Finally, the "Societal character" components clearly fall under L2 LOA. Hence, on aggregate, BERI-PR seems to favor a societal interpretation, but other interpretations may influence its character overall.

Table 5 BERI-PR components versus LOAs

Index BERI-PR		Level of analysis				
Political risk components		1st	2nd	3rd	4th	5th
External factors	Influence of major powers				•	
	Negative regional influences				•	
Nature of government and politics	Stability			•		
	Authoritarianism	•				
	Political parties			•		
	Political opposition forces		•			
	Religion in politics		•			
	Corruption	•				
Societal character	Ethnic tension		•			
	Socioeconomic conditions		•			
	Domestic violence civil conflict		•			
	Nationalism		•			
	Attitudes toward foreigners		•			
	Culture		•			

Table 6 BERI-OR components versus LOAs

Index BERI-OR		Level of analysis				
Political risk components		1st	2nd	3rd	4th	5th
Nature of government and politics	Stability			•		
	Judicial/legal system			•		
	Political intrusion on economic management	•				
Societal character	Bureaucracy quality			•		
	Infrastructure		•			
	Professional services and contractors		•			
	Local management and partners		•			
	Culture		•			

In BERI-OR, the groups of components are reduced to two—external factors are removed. However, the context of the remaining groups differs from that of BERI-PR. We depict in Table 6.

With the exception of political intrusion on economic management, largely an individual affair, BERI-OR seems to balance between L2 and L3 or the societal and state LOAs.

4 Putting It Altogether

We use the LOAs framework as a binder to put together the two analyses. Therefore, in order to establish out how each political risk framework corresponds to an International Relations interpretation, one can aggregate both the political risk components and the IR schools based on their LOA correspondence. So, the score of each political index will "weigh" the index in relation to each IR school. We illustrate this approach in Table 7.

The aggregation works in the following way: For each IR school, we consider the counts of components present in the LOAs addressed by each school.

For example, Realism focuses on L1 and L3 and L5 LOAs but not in L2 or L4. So, to determine how much "Realist" is the PRS-18m Index we can add the number of PRS-18m components present in $L1 + L3 + L5 = 0 + 11 + 0 = 11$. Repeating the process for the other IR schools, we notice that the PRS-18m scores, respectively, add up to "11" in the Constructivist viewpoint and "12" in the Liberal viewpoint. This suggests that the PRS-18m Index can be readily used as a Political Risk Index in all three IR schools and vice versa; insights from each IR school can be readily applied to a PRS-18m-based political risk analysis. The situation is even more balanced for the PRS-5y with a score of 4-4-4.

In contrast, the BERI Index score heavily favors the Liberal school, with a score of 1-1-10. Again, this suggests that the BERI Index can be readily applied or used in a Liberal context but not in a Realist or Constructivist context. Accordingly, a BERI-based political risk analysis can utilize insights from IR analysts in the Liberal school. A similar reasoning can be applied to the remaining political risk frameworks.

We understand that this is a rather simple scoring method and that more sophisticated or detailed approaches may be conceived, such as a weighted scoring model. However, given that the LOAs are rather high-level analytical framework, we believe that the simplicity of this approach lends itself better for the initial fusing of ERM to IR.

5 Conclusions

Matching political risk and International Relations theories, with the assistance of frameworks of political risk measurement from an economic standpoint, is not as straightforward as we thought it would be. This is mostly due to the fact that both political risk frameworks and International Relations theories are rather high-level approaches and susceptible to a wide range of interpretations. In turn, this poses a significant challenge, when analysts seek to merge the insights from these to analyze the realm of political risk.

In an effort to add more specificity in this synergy, in this paper, we adopt the levels of analysis approach. We are pleased to say that it has proven useful in establishing this "proto-" fusion between political risk frameworks, in the context of economics

Table 7 Political risk components and IR schools, matched on LOAs

Risk Index	Component count	Levels of analysis					International Relations		
		1st	2nd	3rd	4th	5th	Realism (= L1 + L3 + L5)	Constructivism (= L3 + L5)	Liberalism (= L2 + L3 + L4)
PRS-18m	12		1	11			11	11	12
PRS-5y	5		1	3		1	4	4	4
ICRG	11	1	4	6	1		7	6	11
BERI	10		7	1	2		1	1	10
• BERI-PR	14	2	8	2	2		4	2	12
• BERI-OR	9	1	4	3			4	3	7

and mostly enterprise risk management, and the schools of International Relations, the "go-to" methods of comprehending politics in an international context.

Clearly, more research is necessary, both in the direction of political risk frameworks and in the direction of political risk in an International Relations context in order for this synergy to bear fruit to both enterprise risk analysts and International Relations analysts focusing on risks in International Relations. This work is one step in this direction, and we look forward to collaborating and exchanging views with our peers to take this challenge to the next level.

References

Clapton, W. (2011). Risk in international relations. *International Relations, 25*(3), 280–295.

Coplin, W. D., & O'Leary, M. K. (1983). Systematic political risk analysis for planners. *Planning Review, 11*(1), 14–17.

Doyle, M. W. (1988). Liberalism and world politics. *The American Political Science Review, 80*(4), 1151–1169.

Griffiths, M., & O'Callaghan, T. (2002). *International relations: The key concepts*. London: Routledge.

Howell, L. D. (2014). Evaluating political risk forecasting models: What works? *Thunderbird International Business Review, 56*(4), 305–316.

Howell, L. D., & Chaddick, B. (1994). Models of political risk for foreign investment and trade: An assessment of three approaches. *The Columbia Journal of World Business*, 70–91.

Jackson, R., & Sørensen, G. (2006). Social constructivism. In *Introduction to international relations: Theories and approaches* (pp. 161–177). Oxford University Press.

Nye, J. S. (1988). Neorealism and neoliberalism. *World Politics, 40*(2), 235–251.

Psychogyios, I., & Koutsoukis, N.-S. (2018). Political risk frameworks: A literature review. In S. Roukanas, P. Polychronidou, & A. Karasavvoglou (Eds.), *The political economy of development in southeastern Europe*.

Rigakos, G. S., & Law, A. (2009). Risk, realism and the politics of resistance. *Critical Sociology, 35*(1), 79–103.

Segbers, K., Dyllick-Brenzinger, P., Hoffmann, K., & Mauersberger, C. (2006). *Global politics: How to use and apply theories of international relations*. Berlin: Osteuropa-Institut der Freien Universität Berlin.

The PRS Group. (2017a). *Our two methodologies/PRS*. Retrieved November 03, 2017, from http://www.prsgroup.com/about-us/our-two-methodologies/prs.

The PRS Group. (2017b). *Our two methodologies/ICRG*. Retrieved November 03, 2017, from http://www.prsgroup.com/about-us/our-two-methodologies/icrg.

Wendt, A. (1992). Anarchy is what states make of it: The social construction of power politics. *International Organization, 46*(2), 391–425.

The Impact of Public Debt on Economic Growth: Empirical Analyses for Western Balkan Countries

Abdylmenaf Bexheti, Luljeta Sadiku, and Murat Sadiku

Abstract This paper intends to empirically analyze the impact of public debt on economic growth of Western Balkan countries using yearly data for the time period 2003–2016. The study employs panel regression techniques, such that fixed and random effects, 2SLS, as well as a causality test after a panel VAR. The short-run estimation results, in almost all specifications and models, indicate that public debt is weakly negatively correlated with economic growth of the sample countries, but the coefficient is only statistically significant in random effects as well as in 2SLS model. The quadratic term of debt is also included in the model, reflecting the nonlinear relationship of debt and growth. Its results disclose a maximum debt threshold of 50.87%. While the causality test reveals a uni-directional relationship, meaning that public debt does not cause real GDP growth, whereas GDP growth causes public debt. The policy implications for the region are that governments should take actions for a fiscal sustainability and active debt management as the rise of the level of debt above the found threshold of 50.87% of GDP will deteriorate the economic growth. In addition, fiscal policies need to be designed, through cyclical adjusting fiscal policies based on business cycles.

Keywords Public debt · Economic growth · Random effects · 2SLS · Causality analysis

---

A. Bexheti · M. Sadiku
South East European University, Tetovo, North Macedonia
e-mail: a.bexheti@seeu.edu.mk

M. Sadiku
e-mail: m.sadiku@seeu.edu.mk

L. Sadiku (✉)
International Balkan University, Skopje, North Macedonia
e-mail: luljeta.sadiku@yahoo.com

M. Janowicz-Lomott et al. (eds.), *Economic and Financial Challenges for Balkan and Eastern European Countries*, Springer Proceedings in Business and Economics,
https://doi.org/10.1007/978-3-030-39927-6_2

1 Introduction

Recently, the issue of public debt and its effects on economic development has gained a huge prominence among all, the public, policymakers, and academic researchers. Even more, it became one of the hottest topics among research community, notably after the last global financial crisis that led to an extraordinary increase of public debt crossways developed countries. It has been revealed that large public debts have adverse effect on capital accumulation and productivity that in turn affects negatively the economic growth. Indeed, high public debt adversely impacts the economic growth in the long run through several channels, such that higher long-term interest rates (Baldacci and Kumar 2010), higher future distortionary taxation (Barro 1979; Dotsey 1994), higher inflation (Barro 1995; Cochrane 2010), greater uncertainty and vulnerability to crises (cited in Kumar and Woo 2010).

Researchers economists econometrically estimated that high deficits and growing public debts cause reduction of available capital funds. The high deficit in the 1980s in the USA has caused decline of gross national income (GNP). Particularly, economists with liberal orientation and perspective argue that public debt growth, as a result of rising public spending, undermines the vitality of a nation. The crowding-out effect caused by the growing debt is predetermined by rising interest rates and inflation as a result of rise of the deficit! Thus, it discourages domestic saving and investment through the crowding-out effect causing debt overhang in the long run.

Economists have long recognized the fiscal policy as an instrument for boosting the economy, especially in the waves of economic stagnations. Alongside that, the permanent increase of government expenditures makes it puzzling for countries to finance them from current government revenues, which leads to budget deficits. The public debt is one of the alternatives that relief governments to finance their projects and stabilize the economies. In fact, the majority of developing countries have a weak tax revenue structure and as such the persistent borrowing became a typical practice. In this regard, the Western Balkan region is no exception to borrowing. So, despite the economic and the political significance of the problem, so far there has been very limited research of the underlying key issue for the sample countries. Indeed, most of the studies have been descriptive and do not use rigorous methods of analysis. Thus, the main purpose of this paper is to empirically analyze the impact of public debt on economic growth by an econometric perspective. Therefore, this research is of academic and practical interest for the region.

The reminder of the paper is as follows: Sect. 2 affords a brief literature review, Sect. 3 provides some stylized facts concerning the economic growth and public debt of Western Balkan region, Sect. 4 describes data and the methodology, Sect. 5 provides the empirical results while Sect. 6 concludes.

2 Brief Review of the Literature

A great number of theoretical and empirical studies exist in the literature that analyzes the public debt and its impact on economic growth. Yet the empirical evidence provides mixed and conflicting results and predictions. In fact, the majority of studies find an adverse effect of high public debt on economic growth, especially for developed countries and the debt levels above a threshold. In this regard, the most cited findings are those of professors of Harvard University, Reinhart and Rogoff (2010a, b) that analyze the developments of public (gross central government) debt and the long-term real GDP growth rate in a sample of 20 developed countries over a period spanning about two centuries (1790–2009). They found that "the linkage between growth and debt seems relatively weak at 'normal' debt levels, median growth rates for countries with public debt over roughly 90 per cent of GDP are about one per cent lower than otherwise, and (mean) growth rates are several per cent lower" (Reinhart and Rogoff 2010a, p. 573). The authors also found that economic growth was 3–4% when the debt was in moderate levels, below 60%, and growth was only 1.6% when debt was above 90%. Their research afforded attention-grabbing results for spacious other researchers, meaning that the obtained evidences were questionable and the same were very criticized. Thus, a group of authors from the University of Massachusetts, Herndon et al. (2013) replicated Reinhart and Rogoff (2010a, b) work and find coding errors and unconventional weighting of summary statistics that lead to errors that erroneously represent the relationship between public debt and GDP growth. Their finding suggests that average GDP growth at public debt/GDP ratios over 90% is not dramatically different than when debt/GDP ratios are lower. Challenged from their results and conclusions, Reinhart et al. (2012) reviewed the previous estimations and again confirmed that in advanced economies, levels of sovereign debt above 90% of GDP ("debt overhangs") lead to a decline in economic growth. The magnitude of the debt threshold has only been partially confirmed by other studies. Some economists, among others Paul Krugman (Nobel Prize), argue that the low economic growth causes debt growth and not the opposite.

While an earlier study of Pattillo et al. (2002) analyzes the external debt effect on per capita GDP growth for the time period (1969–1998) using a panel dataset of 93 developing countries. Their empirical results indicate that the effect of external debt on per capita GDP growth is negative for the net present value of debt levels above 35–40% of GDP. Also, Clements et al. (2003) reported a negative correlation between external debt and growth for a panel of 55 low-income countries for a period that spanned from 1970 to 1999. Checherita and Rother (2010) evaluated the effect of government debt on economic growth for 12 European countries over the period of 1970–2010 using a panel fixed effects estimation technique. The study reported a nonlinear impact of debt on economic growth, indicating that the government debt-to-GDP ratio has a negative effect on long-term growth when debt is about 90–100% of GDP. Kumar and Woo (2010) studied the long-run effect of public debt on economic growth using time series data that spans four decades of some developed and emerging countries. They concluded that there is a long-run negative relationship between debt and growth and the possibility of some nonlinearity effects of debt on growth.

In recent researches, Woo and Kumar (2015) and Cecchetti et al. (2011) find a linear inverse relationship between initial debt and subsequent growth in a sample of emerging and advanced economies, with the impact being somewhat smaller in the latter group. Both of them claim that beyond a certain threshold about 80–90% of GDP higher public debt lowers potential growth. Woo and Kumar (2015) find that higher debt starts affecting growth at a lower threshold (40% of GDP), but the effects become statistically significant only at about 90% of GDP. According to these results, countries with high debt should address their fiscal problems to avoid a deterioration in their growth perspectives. The creation of fiscal buffers might be an appropriate strategy to compensate for extraordinary shocks. Also, Panizza and Presbitero (2012) examined the impact of public debt and economic growth for a sample of OECD countries using the instrumental variable approach and causality analysis. They rejected the hypothesis that high debt causes lower growth. The study concluded that there is a negative relationship between debt and growth, but revealed that debt does not have any causal effect on growth.

On the other hand, Schclarek (2004) assessed the impact of gross government debt on economic growth for a sample of 24 industrial countries over the period 1970–2002. The study found no robust relationship between debt and growth. Additionally, Baum et al. (2012) investigated the relationship between public debt and economic growth using the dynamic threshold panel methodology for 12 European countries for the period 1990–2012. The study reported a positive and high statistically significant impact of debt on GDP when the debt-to-GDP ratio was less than 67%; after which point, there was no relationship between debt and GDP. Another study for the twelve Euro area countries conducted by Checherita-Westphal and Rother (2012), for the time period 1970–2010, concludes that government debt negatively affects the economic growth starting from the threshold between 70 and 80%. They also found that total factor productivity growth, private saving, and public investment are the channels where public debt is found to have a nonlinear effect on growth.

Mencinger et al. (2014) investigate the short-term effects of public debt on the economic growth rates of 25 EU countries affected by the European sovereign debt crisis, for the period 1995–2010 (for the "new" EU Member States) and 1980–2010 (for the "old" EU Member States). They find evidence of a nonlinear (inverted U-shape) relationship, the debt turning point being higher for the "old", more developed EU Member States (of about 80–94% of GDP) and lower for the "new" EU Member States (of about 53–54%). One year later, Mencinger et al. (2015) further expand their analysis for a panel of 36 countries (31 OECD countries and five non-OECD member states) and achieved similar conclusions. The same concave relationship is confirmed, with a debt-to-GDP threshold of about 44–45% in emerging market countries, about half the value of developed countries.

In addition, Afonso and Jalles (2013) have analyzed the impact of public debt on the real per capita GDP growth, as well as the existence of nonlinearity effects of debt on growth, both annually and with five-year average growth rates, for 14 European countries for the time spin 1970–2012. They confirmed the negative relationship between debt and growth, both in the short and long term by considering interactions of debt with monetary, public finance, institutional and macroeconomic variables. Concerning the interactions with macroeconomic variables, it was proved that taxation on capital and profit and growth rate of credit to the private sector are negatively related with growth, whereas growth rates of gross fixed capital formation, trade openness and current account balance are positively related. They also revealed the existence of inverted U-shape relationship between debt ratio and economic growth. Another study that confirms the nonlinear relationship between debt and growth is that of Bilan (2015). She finds a maximum debt threshold of 45–55% of GDP for Central and Eastern European countries over the period 1994–2013, that is lower for less developed countries (Romania and Bulgaria) and higher for more developed ones; however, it is much lower than developed EU countries.

Misztal (2010) uses a panel VAR methodology over the period 2000–2010, for the EU Member States, and finds that the increase of public debt by 1% resulted in the reduction of GDP by 0.3%, while a 1% increase in GDP led to the reduction of public debt by 0.4%.

Gnegne and Jawadi (2013) examine public debt and its dynamics for the UK and the USA, which also evidenced to be asymmetric and nonlinear, concluding that public debt seems to be based on several threshold effects, which helps to understand its dynamics with more accuracy. Certain, macroeconomic events such as economic slowdowns, debt, and financial crisis, as well as oil shocks, have proved to be important factors linked with structural breaks in public debt dynamics.

Contrary to all these findings for developed countries, Greiner and Fincke (2014) analyzed the effects of public debt on economic growth for emerging market economies using panel data estimation techniques and procedures and found a significant positive relationship between public debt and the subsequent growth of per capita GDP.

From all the previous findings, one can be concluded that this issue is highly debatable and there is not still any conclusive consensus among researchers concerning the threshold of negative impacts of public debt on economic growth. Even more, it differs considerably for developed and less developed economies.

3 Economic Growth and Public Debt of the Western Balkan Countries

In the period of 2005–2008, the average annual growth rate of Western Balkan countries was around 6% that was higher than that of the EU countries. However, the global financial crisis affected the economy of the region, causing severe negative consequences such that, increase in public debt levels, decline in European and international market demand for products and raw materials (lower exports), decrease of foreign direct investment (FDI) and a decline of remittance inflows. As a result of the above repercussions, in 2009, all countries of Western Balkan except Albania fell into recession (see Fig. 1). Even Albania had a decline of economic output, although was less impacted compare to other countries of the region. The economies slowly started to recover in 2010 and 2011, as real GDP grew by an average of 2.2 and 2.1%, respectively. However, the negative effects of the Eurozone debt crisis were felt in 2012, as the economies of countries fell again in recession. Almost a decade after the global financial crisis, the pre-crisis growth levels are not still restored. Based on Western Balkan Regular Economic Report (World Bank 2017), regional growth in 2016 was 2.9%, whereas in 2017 it was estimated to be 2.4%, and it is projected to rise to 3.3% in 2018 and 3.6% in 2019.

Prior to the 2008 global financial crisis, the Western Balkan region as a whole had government budget deficit levels below the EU average. However, since the crisis, the region faced with slower economic activity, reduced government tax revenues, and increased government expenditures to deal with the consequences of crisis. These created pressures to the debt levels as percentage of GDP to rise. In almost all countries after 2009, the debt rapidly increased (see Fig. 2). In several cases, the IMF provided emergency credits to shore up government balances and protect the national currencies from depreciation.

In all countries of the region, except Albania, the external debt is higher than the internal debt. However, since the crisis, the external debt rapidly increases in the whole region (see Fig. 3). The governments of the countries use the advantages of

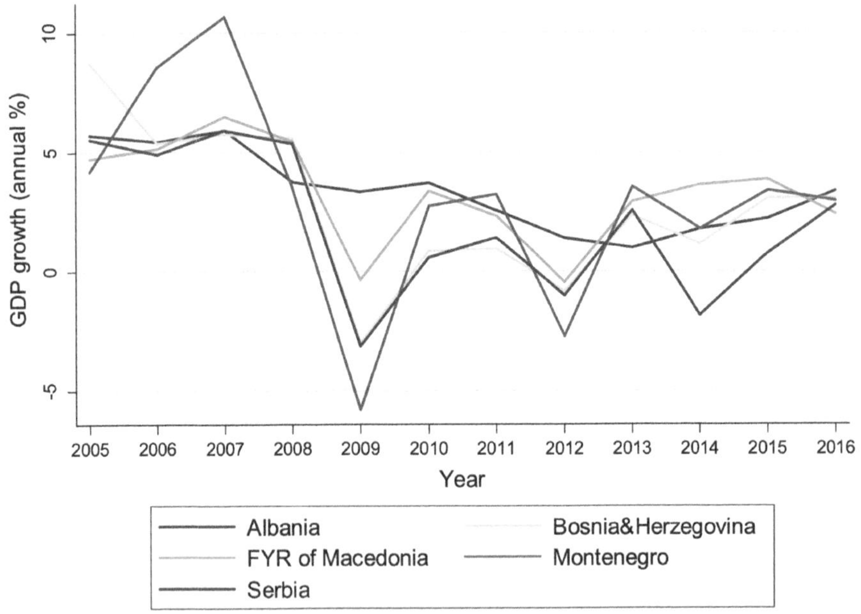

Fig. 1 Economic growth of Western Balkan countries. *Source* World Development Indicators, World Bank

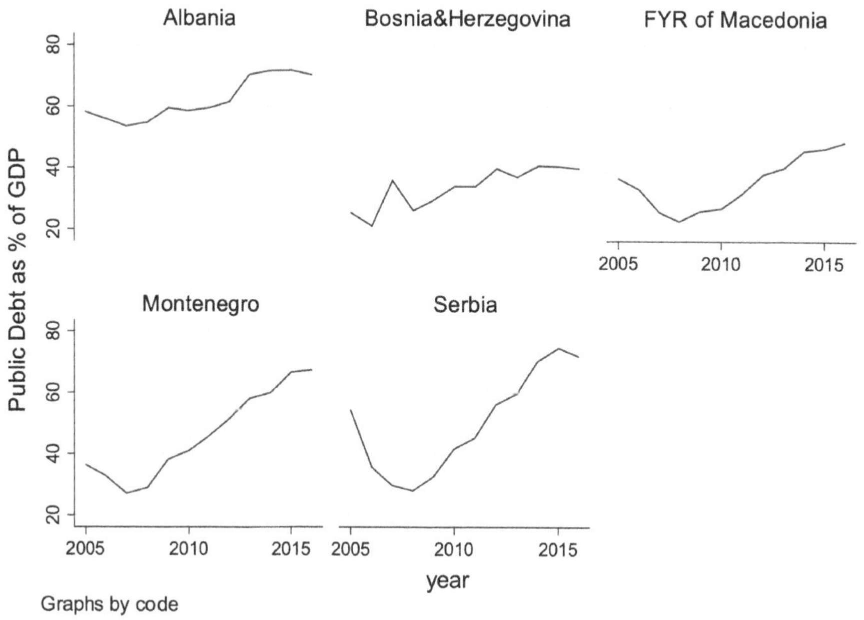

Fig. 2 The level of public debt of Western Balkan countries. *Source* Countries' Central Banks

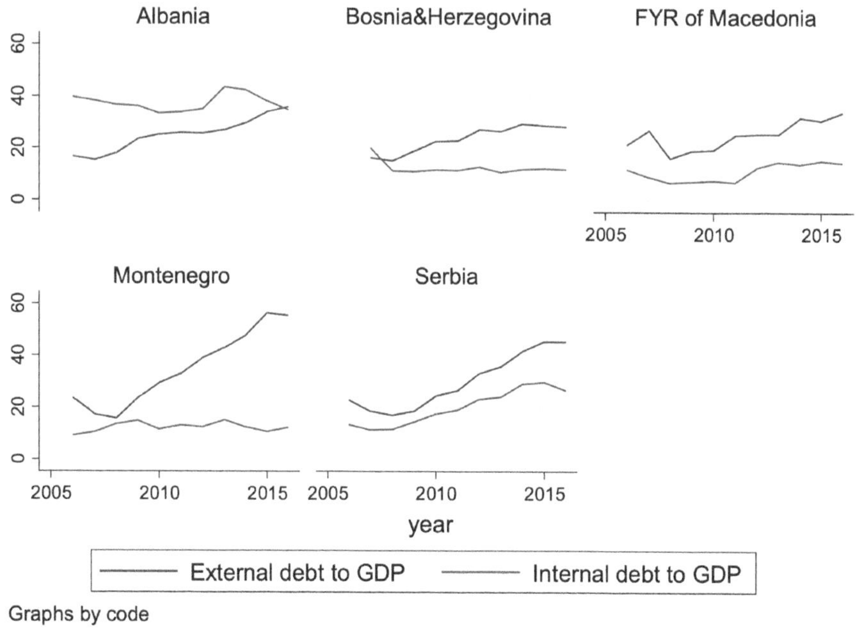

Fig. 3 The level of external and internal debt of Western Balkan countries. *Source* Countries' Central Bank

relatively favorable interest rates and the improved access to global capital markets. However, many economists see this increased level of debt as unsustainable.

4 Methodology and Data

The research methodology of this paper consists of panel regression analysis; first, examining the models for both fixed and random effects and using the Hausman's test for determining the appropriate and consistent model for the sample countries; second, two-stage least square (2SLS) estimator for panel data is used for solving the problem of endogeneity; and third, a panel VAR model, in order to test after the causality between growth and debt.

Initially, the methodology of panel regression analysis is presented and after panel VAR. In fact, data sets that combine time series and cross sections (countries) are called longitudinal or panel data sets. Panel data sets are more orientated toward cross-sectional analyses—they are wide but typically short (in terms of observations over time). Heterogeneity across countries is central to the issue of analyzing panel data. The basic framework is a regression of the form:

$$Y_{it} = X_{it}\beta + Z_i\pi + \varepsilon_{it}$$

X has k columns and does not include a constant term. The heterogeneity or individual effect is $Z_i\pi$ where Z contains a constant term and a set of individual or group-specific variables. It will be considered two cases:

Fixed Effects Z_i is unobserved, but correlated with X_{it} then OLS estimators of β are biased. However, in this case where $\alpha_i = Z_i\pi$ embodies all the observable effects and specifies an estimable equation, in which $\alpha_i = \alpha_1, \ldots, \alpha_n$ are treated as unknown intercepts to be estimated, one for each country.

Random Effects If the unobserved heterogeneity, however, formulated can be assumed to be uncorrelated with X_{it} then:

$$\begin{aligned} Y_{it} &= X_{it}\beta + E[Z_{i\pi}] + \{Z_{i\pi} - E[Z_{i\pi}] + \varepsilon_{it}\} \\ &= X_{it}\beta + \alpha + u_i + \varepsilon_{it} \end{aligned}$$

Random effects approach specifies that u_i is a group-specific random element which although random is constant for that group throughout the time period.

The specification test devised by Hausman is used to test for whether the random effects are independent of the right-hand side variables. This is a general test to compare any two estimators. The test is based on the assumption that under the hypothesis of no correlation between the right-hand side variables and the random effects, both fixed effects and random effects are consistent estimators but fixed effects are inefficient. (This is the assumption with random effects.) Whereas under the alternative assumption (i.e., that with fixed effects), fixed effects are consistent but random effects are not. The test is based on the following Wald statistic:

$$W = [\beta_{FE} - \beta_{RE}]'^{\Psi^{-1}}[\beta_{FE} - \beta_{RE}], \text{ where}$$

$$Var[\beta_{FE} - \beta_{RE}] = Var[\beta_{FE}] - Var[\beta_{RE}] = \Psi$$

W is distributed as X^2 with $(K - 1)$ degrees of freedom where K is the number of parameters in the model. If W is greater than the critical value obtained from the table, then we reject the null hypothesis of that both estimators are consistent, i.e., of "no correlation between the right-hand side variables and the 'random effects'" in which case the fixed effects model is better.

On the other side, the endogeneity is one of the main problems that panel data analysis features. The main challenge is to fix and solve this problem, in order to obtain unbiased estimators. In a panel context, most studies on growth regressions have made use of the instrumental variable (IV) approach to deal with the issue of simultaneity bias. The two-stage least squares estimator (2SLS) enables the correction of the problem of endogeneity even for multiple endogenous explanatory variables; thus, it is used to estimate the parameters and to avoid the problem of endogeneity.

Panel VAR model is also used in order to estimate the dynamic effects of total public debt on the economic growth and after that the causality test. The estimation and inference of panel VAR are done in the framework of generalized method of moment (GMM). Panel VAR analysis is predicted upon choosing the optimal lag order in both panel VAR specification and moment condition. The following panel VAR model is used in the empirical analysis:

$$\Delta \Upsilon_{it} = \Phi_0 + \Phi(L)\Delta \Upsilon_{it} + X_{it}\Psi + u_i + \varepsilon_{it}$$

where i represents each country, i.e., the cross-sectional dimension; t represents the time dimension; $\Delta \Upsilon_{it}$ is the vector of dependent variables; X_{it} is a vector of control variables; L is the lag operator; Φ, Ψ represent the matrices of parameters; u_i is a vector of dependent variable-specific panel fixed effects; ε_{it} is the idiosyncratic error term.

4.1 The Data

In this, empirical research used the annual data from 2003 to 2016 for five Western Balkan countries, namely Albania, Bosnia and Herzegovina, FYR of Macedonia, Montenegro, and Serbia, whereas Kosovo is omitted from the sample due to data availability on public debt. The GDP per capita growth and other control variables were collected from World Development Indicator (WDI) database provided by World Bank, whereas the data for total public debt from the respective countries' National Banks, and from CEIC Data that provides economic country data for whole world. The time span of the analysis is limited because of the lack of the data of public debt for the first decade of transition. The summary statistics of the variables used in the empirical research are presented in Table 1. Over the period of analysis, the average of GDP per capita growth of the region has been 3.14%, whereas the average total debt-to-GDP level is 45.49%. However, these averages do not exhibit large discrepancies between WB countries. Bosnia and Herzegovina and FYR of Macedonia have lower average total debt-to-GDP levels compare to the other countries.

Table 1 Summary statistics of the data

Variable	Mean	Std. dev.	Min	Max	Observations
GDP per capita growth	Overall 3.1398	2.917733	−5.99698	10.50518	$N = 70$
	Between	0.5037077	2.46187	3.795673	$n = 5$
	Within	2.882144	−5.73561	10.76655	$T = 14$
Real GDP per capita (2010 prices)	Overall 4999.12	1199.945	2709.143	7378.345	$N = 70$
	Between	963.3914	3969.385	6400.495	$n = 5$
	Within	827.5221	2273.244	6171.638	$T = 14$
Debt to GDP (%)	Overall 45.49	15.25005	21.25	74.7	$N = 70$
	Between	11.6236	33.7633	62.15167	$n = 5$
	Within	11.07455	23.70583	70.10583	$T = 14$
GFCF to GDP (%)	Overall 23.476	5.655161	16.68177	39.21585	$N = 70$
	Between	4.235654	19.97251	30.48241	$n = 5$
	Within	4.169529	17.15282	39.17913	$T = 14$
Trade openness	Overall 93.102	15.69195	69.59133	132.3403	$N = 70$
	Between	13.91726	75.95557	110.2609	$n = 5$
	Within	9.41588	74.71116	115.1818	$T = 14$
Population growth rate	Overall −0.2543	0.377475	−1.19124	0.214529	$N = 70$
	Between	0.341239	−0.60424	0.127119	$n = 5$
	Within	0.218526	−0.84133	0.356338	$T = 14$
Human development index	Overall 0.7473	0.029514	0.696	0.807	$N = 70$
	Between	0.026107	0.723272	0.78736	$n = 5$
	Within	0.017769	0.707509	0.775509	$T = 14$

Source Authors' calculations

4.2 Specification of Econometric Models

The econometric models that estimate the effects of public debt on economic growth in the Western Balkan (WB) countries are basically based on the alternative versions of models employed by Kumar and Woo (2010), Cecchetti et al. (2011) and Checherita-Westphal and Rother (2012). Thus, the first model is specified as in the following form:

$$Y_{it} = \alpha_0 + \beta_1 lnGDPC_{it-1} + \beta_2(DEBT)_{it-1} + \phi_k X_{k,i,t-1} + \lambda_i + \mu_t + \varepsilon_{it} \quad (1)$$

where Y_{it} is the dependent variable that represents the GDP per capita growth for country i at time t. The independent variables are: the initial stock of income that is proxied by the logarithm of GDP per capita of country i at the beginning of each period ($GDPC_{it-1}$, initial GDP per capita); *DEBT* consists of total public debt as % of GDP; X_k is a vector of control variables that affect the economic growth, considering the conventional growth literature and growth determinants, such that trade openness (OPENNESS) that corresponds to the ratio of the total value of exports and imports to GDP, gross fixed capital formation (GFCF) as % of GDP to reflect the impact of physical capital accumulation, population growth rate (POP), and human development index (HDI) that assess the level of development of countries in three dimensions, knowledge, long and healthy life and decent standard of living. Whereas as instrumented variable with public debt in the 2SLS is considered the public debt with one-time lag. While, λ_i is the unobserved country-specific effect; μ_t is the unobserved time-specific effect which captures global shocks; and ε_{it} is the error term.

For estimating Eq. (1), the annual GDP per capita growth is used in order to maximize the number of observations, instead of five-year GDP growth, as the sample size is limited due to availability of data for public debt for the sample countries. This approach may lead to estimates that are fully driven by business cycle fluctuations but can suffer from endogeneity problems as debt is only lagged by one year with respect to economic growth. On the other hand, the models conducted by Cecchetti et al. (2011), and Checherita-Westphal and Rother (2012) include five-year forward GDP growth rate to alleviate these problems.

In the second equation, the quadratic term, debt squared ($DEBT^2$) is included to study the nonlinearity effect. Some recent studies find a nonlinear relationship between growth and debt; these include among others (Checherita and Rother 2010; Mencinger et al. 2014, 2015; Afonso and Jalles 2013). Also, an interaction variable is considered between public debt and a dummy variable that takes the value 1 for debt level above 50% of GDP and value 0 for the debt level below 50% of GDP.

$$\begin{aligned} Y_{it} = \alpha_0 + \beta\, lnGDPC_{it-1} + \delta_1(DEBT)_{it} + \delta_2\left(DEBT_{it}^2\right) \\ + \delta_3(DEBT * D) + \phi_k X_{k,i,t} + \lambda_i + \mu_t + \varepsilon_{it} \end{aligned} \quad (2)$$

In addition, several control variables are considered in order to examine the effect of debt-to-GDP ratio in real per capita GDP growth as well as interacting variable with public debt is taken into consideration.

5 Empirical Results

According to the OLS fitted line, the relationship between public debt and economic growth shows that there is a weak negative correlation between them. Figure 4 shows a scatter plot of their linkage. It suggests that a 1 percentage point increase of public debt is associated with a decrease of subsequent economic growth of 0.04 percentage points, holding other factors unchanged (constant). The countries with higher average growth rates over the sample period tend to have a higher average level of indebtedness as well as a higher rate of increase in the level of relative indebtedness.

What in Fig. 4 can be observed is that there are countries with higher debt which experience sound growth rates, like Albania. Reversely, there are countries with lower debt levels and that exhibit higher economic growth. Spearman's correlation coefficient was also estimated to determine the relationship between debt and growth and it shows that there is a relatively low negative monotonic correlation between the two variables ($\rho = -0.269$).

The estimation results of models for the sample of 5 Western Balkan countries are summarized in the following tables. Considering all the results in Table 2, it can confirm the existence of convergence course. The expected negative coefficient for the initial real per capita GDP is attained, and in all cases, the coefficient is statistically

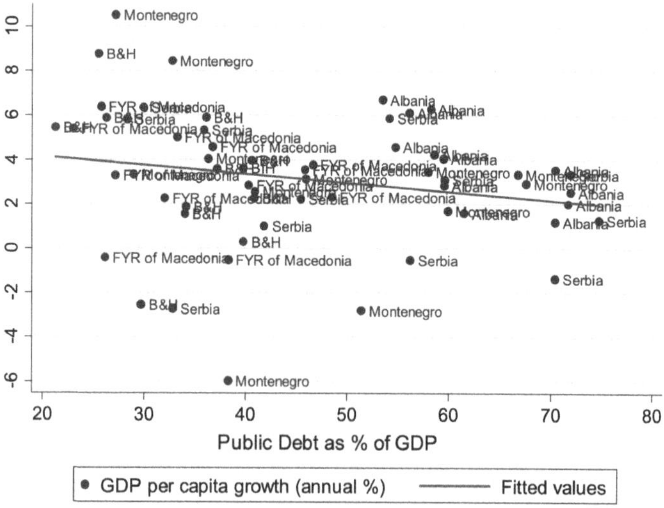

Fig. 4 The relationship between public debt and economic growth of Western Balkan countries. *Source* Authors' calculations

Table 2 Panel regression results

Variables	Fixed effects model (1)	Random effects model (2)	Fixed effects model (3)	Random effects model (4)	2SLS model (5)
$lnGDPC_{it-1}$	−12.144*** (1.741992)	−7.0029*** (1.29135)	−14.126*** (2.50703)	−14.248*** (2.1501)	−13.379*** (2.2782)
DEBT	−0.0823662** (0.033595)	−0.0395925* (0.0245786)	−0.018182 (0.038741)	−0.04519** (0.002438)	−0.06653* (0.03652)
GFCF	–	–	0.049949 (0.097503)	0.037536 (0.05403)	0.07859 (0.06425)
TRADE	–	–	0.052072 (0.035024)	0.063205** (0.02194)	0.05667** (0.02239)
POP	–	–	−1.87804 (1.34535)	−2.14557** (0.90478)	−0.23119** (0.11264)
HDI	–	–	55.00751 (33.1076)	77.83497*** (22.101)	4.4434 (2.9104)*
Constant	6.88663** (1.572137)	4.94086** (1.178241)	75.87006** (18.3836)	−3.0579 (3.3841)	35.30041 (74.4838)
N	65	65	65	65	65

Note Standard errors are in parentheses; heteroscedasticity and autocorrelation robust standard errors. For the specification tests, p values are reported. *, ** and *** indicate that the coefficients are significant at the 10%, 5% and 1% level of significance, respectively
Source Author's calculations

significant at 1% level of significance, revealing that WB countries converge for their own steady state in the analyzed time period.

In all five models, the coefficient of debt is with negative sign as it was expected, but it is statistically significant only in the random effects models. Concerning the fixed effects model, the coefficient of debt is statistically significant in the model where only the initial GDP per capita and debt are considered as independent variables, whereas when other control variables are included in the model (see Model 3 in Table 2), its statistical significance disappears. However, after performing the fixed and random effects models, it was conducted the Hausman test for deciding between them and which one is more efficient. It basically tests whether the unique errors (ui) are correlated with the regressors; the null hypothesis suggests that they are not. Based on the results of the test, the null hypothesis cannot be rejected, revealing that random effects are more preferred compare to fixed effects model. Thus, the random effects model suggests that public debt negatively affects the economic growth of the Western Balkan countries and also controlling by the other growth determinants. Yet, in two-stage least square (2SLS) model that to some extent mitigates the problem of endogeneity, the coefficient of public debt is again statistically significant at 10% level. Considering its results as more reliable, it can be endorsed that public debt has a weak negative effect on the growth of WB region in the analyzed time span. However, the model may suffer from omitted variable bias. Concerning the other control variables, gross fixed capital formation (GFCF) is with positive sign but statistically insignificant in all models. This result reveals that the region is less equipped with capital in relation to population and resources. The region needs to raise the saving rate in order to reach the Golden Rule steady state that requires a fall in consumption and a rise in capital investment, so over time higher investment causes the capital stock to rise and the real output to enhance. On the other side, the coefficient of population growth rate is negative at the 5% level of significance, as predicted by Solow growth model, that an increase in the rate of population growth reduces the steady-state level of capital. Regarding the coefficient of trade openness, it is with positive sign and statistically significant at 5% level, in random effects and 2SLS models. Human development index is positively linked with economic growth and statistically significant at 1% level in random effects model and 10% level at 2SLS model.

In this section, we extend the preceding analysis to study the nonlinearity between debt and growth, including the quadratic term. This is done by estimating the instrumental variables regression for panel data estimating fixed and random effects, where the lag of debt-to-GDP ratio is considered as instrumental variable. Unlike the previous models, in these regressions, the saving rate is included as a control variable beside the others, whereas the gross fixed capital formation is omitted from the models since it was statistically insignificant.

Table 3 presents results for 2SLS panel regressions of the nonlinear effects of public debt on economic growth. As in the preceding models, the coefficients on initial GDP per capita are negative and statistically significantly different from zero at the 1% level in all models, which again confirm the existence of β-convergence. It can be seen from regressions in Table 3 that the nonlinear quadratic-type relationship is only obtained in random effects panel regressions. Still, after performing the fixed and random panel regressions, again the Hausman test suggests that random effects model is more efficient and appropriate for this set of data and variables. Thus, the coefficients of DEBT and DEBT^2 in models labeled as (3) and (4) are both statistically significant at 10% level. Regarding the sign of the coefficient of DEBT is with positive sign, while the quadratic term (DEBT^2) has a negative sign, revealing that the functional relationship that connects the growth rate of GDP and public debt is somehow of concave shape, disclosing the existence of a maximum value. Based on these results, it is confirmed the hypothesis that when public debt is lower, the effects on growth are positive, but these effects steadily decline as public debt is rising, meaning that after a debt threshold the effects are opposite. Accordingly, the turning point is estimated by the formula: $-\delta_1/2\delta_2 = -1.298113/2\cdot(-0.012759) = 50.87$. This result shows that the debt-to-GDP turning point for Western Balkan countries is 50.87% of GDP, which is much lower than the one found in the existing literature for developed countries. The majority of empirical studies on this issue find a maximum public debt-to-GDP threshold of about 90–100% of GDP for developed countries, including among others Reinhart and Rogoff (2010a), Checherita and Rother (2010), Baum et al. (2012), Mencinger et al. (2014), Woo and Kumar (2015). Yet this result is in line with the results of authors that analyzed this situation for developing countries and found that the public debt-to-GDP threshold is about half the value of developed ones (see Pattillo et al. 2002; Bilan 2015; Mencinger et al. 2015). According to Bilan

Table 3 Panel regression results of nonlinearity

Variables	2SLS fixed effects model (1)	2SLS fixed effects model (2)	2SLS random effects model (3)	2SLS random effects model (4)
$GDPC_{it-1}$	−19.2369*** (6.86216)	−19.39764*** (7.60862)	−15.14086*** (3.746906)	−15.37848*** (3.836914)
DEBT	1.493181 (1.11392)	1.647401 (1.468641)	1.298113* (0.7444941)	1.285231* (0.748101)
$DEBT^2$	−0.0138757 (0.010413)	−0.01567 (0.0144)	−0.012759* (0.007451)	−0.0124672* (0.2856)
TRADE	0.068229** (0.059484)	0.062368*** (0.066427)	0.096495*** (0.0371)	0.096397*** (0.037219)
SAVING	−0.3892809 (0.340069)	−0.451718 (0.47258)	−0.187756** (0.08526)	−0.191414** (0.086355)
POP	−0.287729 (2.049416)	–	−0.1096075 (1.226692)	–
HDI	15.19246 (55.7533)	–	36.04859 (34.33305)	–
DDEBT	–	−0.157779** (0.069361)	–	−0.1545347** (0.0763733)
Constant	129.2071 (41.52788)	130.078 (45.66668)	95.24832 (20.55915)	96.91198 (21.31672)
R-squared	0.4932	0.3962	0.5706	0.4123
N	65	65	65	65

Note Standard errors are in parentheses; heteroscedasticity and autocorrelation robust standard errors. For the specification tests, p values are reported. *, ** and *** indicate that the coefficients are significant at the 10%, 5%, and 1% level of significance, respectively. Maximum value of the quadratic model in public debt: $max_{debt} DEBT = \frac{-\delta_1}{2\delta_2}$

Source Author's calculations

(2015), the possible reasons are that developing countries enjoy lower credibility compare to developed ones from potential lenders and investors, which makes the negative effects of a large public debt to appear sooner, as well as developing countries are more vulnerable and depend to a large extent on foreign capital.

Concerning the other explanatory variables, the coefficient of trade openness is positive and statistically significant in all models, revealing that openness to international trade is an important determinant of economic growth of WB countries.

The most surprising result is concerning the sign of the coefficient of the saving rate that is negative and statistically significant in random models. Therefore, this means that the decrease of public savings as a result of a higher budget deficit has not been compensated by an increase in private savings. It has implied the national savings to decrease, resulting in lower total investment, either domestically or internationally. Thus, lower investment has a negative effect on GDP, as it leads to a smaller capital stock, higher interest rate, lower labor productivity and wages (Elmendorf and Mankiw 1999).

In the models labeled as (2) and (4) in Table 3, the variables of population growth and human development index are both dropped since they were not statistically significant, instead is added the dummy variable. The coefficients on the other regressors do not change substantially when this modification is made, indicating that the results are not so sensitive to these variable's omissions. The coefficient of the dummy variable that takes the value 1 for the debt level above 50% of GDP is negative and statistically significant at 5% level, validating the threshold of 50.87%. Accordingly, from both results, the debt level above 50% of GDP affects negatively the economic growth of WB countries. However, the results should be treated with caution because of the short time span, as well as the rise of debt and the slow economic growth might have been as a result of global financial crisis and Eurozone debt crisis. This concern is particularly relevant when considering the short-term correlation between growth and debt as in this case, since recessions obviously lead to an instantaneous increase in the debt ratio. In this case, almost all WB countries fell into recession in 2009 that resulted with decline of tax revenues, particularly marked for taxes on goods and services and international trade and transactions, as a result the public debt sharply increased. Aftermath, there was a very sluggish economic recovery while public debt was persistently increasing.

All in all, the results confirm that the public debt impacts negatively the economic growth after a threshold that differs for developed and developing economies. Having in mind the economic development and position of Western Balkan countries, a further increase of public debt raises the concerns about its sustainability and the future stance of monetary and fiscal policies. Such a situation causes the distrust to the citizens by deteriorating the private savings and investments that in turn will affect negatively the economic growth. Moreover, the high public debt spurs governments to implement severe fiscal consolidation measures, either by increasing taxes or by cutting down public expenditures such as productive capital investments, impacting depressingly the output growth.

5.1 Results of Panel VAR and Granger Causality Tests

Before performing the panel VAR model, the lag selection order is conducted, thus based on the Akaike information criterion (AIC), the optimal lag order for the used variables is 3. As it is common in most of the VAR models and studies, we report the results in the form of impulse response functions. Figure 5 is displayed the impulse response functions after the two-variable panel VAR. The responses are estimated over eight-period horizon. According to the results, the growth is not much affected from a shock of public debt, meaning that for one standard deviation shock given to public debt, GDP per capita growth reacts very slowly. In other words, the response of GDP growth by a shock of public debt is positive in the first two periods, whereas at the other periods, it is negative but very close to zero. The explanation behind this stands in the fact that in the aftermath of the crisis, the Western Balkan countries faced with difficulties in regaining control over public finances. Even the increased public

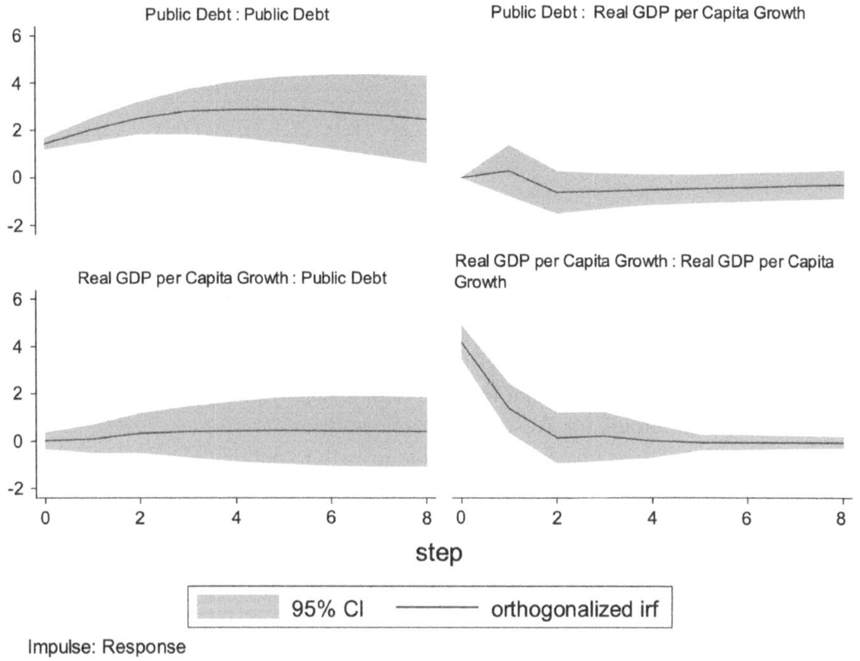

Fig. 5 Impulse response functions. *Source* Author's calculations

debt served to finance a great portion of the current government expenditures, rather than capital investment. In particular, public sector salaries and pensions constitute a larger share of overall spending in the Western Balkans.

Another explanation might be, as public debts increased, interest payments also drifted up. Mandatory governmental expenditures (salaries, pensions, and interest payments) are now much higher in the Western Balkans than in the new Member States or the EU-15, in particular in Albania, FYR of Macedonia and Montenegro, thus severely constraining the flexibility of the budget (Koczan 2015).

A panel VAR stability test was also run in order to check for stability conditions, so the results confirmed that the estimations are stable, as all moduli of the eigenvalue of the estimated models are strictly less than unity and all the units lie in the circle.

In order to define the causality between GDP per capita growth and public debt, a Granger causality analysis is performed after the two-variable panel VAR model. The ordering of the variables is GDP per capita growth rate and the total debt-to-GDP ratio; however, the estimation results remain unaffected by a change in the ordering of the variables. Table 4 shows the results, through which can be observed that the null hypothesis cannot be rejected, meaning that public debt does not cause economic growth. While the null hypothesis that GDP per capita growth does not cause public debt is rejected at 10% level of significance. This result implies weak causality from the real per capita GDP growth rate to the public debt but not vice versa. As Krugman (2011) argues that the linkage between debt and growth could be driven by the fact

Table 4 Granger causality test

Equation\excluded		chi2	df	Prob > chi2
RGDPCG				
	PublicDebt	2.005	1	0.157
	ALL	2.005	1	0.157
PublicDebt				
	RGDPCG	4.019	1	0.061
	ALL	4.019	1	0.061

Source Author's calculations

that it is low economic growth that leads to high levels of public debt, which claim is characteristic and holds for Western Balkan countries.

A uni-directional causality from economic growth to public debt was found by a number of authors. For instance, Lof and Malinen (2014) conclude that the negative correlation between both variables is mainly driven by the impact of economic growth on sovereign debt, not the other way around.

5.2 *Limitations of the Study*

Summing up, based on the obtained results of all models, the effect of public debt on the economic growth for this set of countries is still ambiguous. Although we obtained evidence of a nonlinear concave relationship, the results are only statistically significant at 10% level. Moreover, the time span is too short and the number of observations is only 70, which is too short for a robust panel estimation. Furthermore, it restricts the analysis to short-run estimation, whereas the medium-term and long-term analysis is impossible with this number of observations. Thereby, the future econometric estimations should expand the time period by providing also data for the first decade of transition as well as adding in the sample the other transition countries of Southeast Europe, that will also increase the number of observations.

Nevertheless, the paper contributes to the existing empirical literature since it is among the first attempts that empirically investigates the effects of public debt on economic growth for Western Balkan countries through several estimation procedures.

6 Conclusions

The global financial crisis and Eurozone debt crisis have fueled and intensified the debate concerning the effectiveness of fiscal policy and the consequences of escalating public debt. Thus, a number of authors were enthused to empirically investigate the effects of debt on growth, especially for EU member and OECD countries. Fewer studies were focused on analyzing this issue for developing countries. Thereby, the intention of this research paper was to examine the effects of public debt on economic growth of Western Balkan countries over the period 2003–2016, using panel regression techniques. The results revealed that the random effects model is appropriate for the used variables. The negative influence of public debt on economic growth was evident in almost all models; however, the coefficient was only statistically significant in random effects and 2SLS. Also, through panel 2SLS were estimated the fixed and random effects of a nonlinear relationship, including the quadratic term of public debt. The results revealed the existence of an "inverted U-shape" relationship between public debt and GDP per capita growth rate, with a debt turning point of about 50.87%. Beyond this threshold, a further increase of public debt is expected to negatively affect the economic growth. This result was also confirmed through adding the dummy variable in the model, which takes the value 1 for debt levels above 50% of GDP and 0 below. Its coefficient was negative and statistically significant.

However, compared to the results of other empirical studies on developed countries, the threshold appears to be much lower for Western Balkan countries, on the other hand very similar to the findings for Central and Eastern European countries. It was also found a uni-directional causal relationship from GDP per capita growth to public debt but not vice versa, as well as a slow response of GDP per capita growth by a shock of public debt.

The findings of this study suggest that policymakers should take serious actions toward ensuring fiscal sustainability, and active debt management, as the rise of the level of debt above the found threshold of 50.87% of GDP will deteriorate the economic growth. In addition, fiscal policies need to be designed, through cyclical adjusting fiscal policies based on business cycles.

References

Afonso, A., & Jalles, J. T. (2013). Growth and productivity: The role of government debt. *International Review of Economics and Finance, 25*, 384–407.

Baldacci, E., & Kumar, M. (2010). *Fiscal deficits, public debt and sovereign bond yields* (IMF Working Paper). Washington: International Monetary Fund (forthcoming).

Barro, R. (1979). On the determinants of the public debt. *Journal of Political Economy, 85*(5), 940–971.

Barro, R. (1995). *Inflation and economic growth* (NBER Working Paper No. 5326).

Baum, A., Checherita-Westphal, C., & Rother, P. (2012). *Debt and growth: New evidence for the euro area* (European Central Bank Working Paper Series No. 1450).

Bilan, I. (2015). Economic consequences of public debt: The case of Central and Eastern European countries. In *EURINT, Proceedings*. ISSN 2393-2384.

Cecchetti, S., Mohanty, M., & Zampolli, F. (2011). *Achieving growth amid fiscal imbalances: The real effects of debt*. In Achieving maximum long-run growth, a symposium sponsored by the Federal Reserve Bank of Kansas City, Jackson Hole, Wyoming.

Checherita, C., & Rother, P. (2010). *The impact of high and growing government debt on economic growth: An empirical investigation for the euro area* (IMF Working Paper No. 10/1237).

Checherita-Westphal, C., & Rother, P. (2012). The impact of high government debt on economic growth and its channels: An empirical investigation for the euro area. *European Economic Review, 56,* 1392–1405.

Clements, B., Bhattacharya, R., & Nguyen, T. Q. (2003). *External debt, public investment, and growth in low-income countries* (IMF Working Paper No. 03/249).

Cochrane, J. (2010). *Understanding policy in the great recession: Some unpleasant fiscal arithmetic* (Working Paper). Chicago: University of Chicago Press.

Dotsey, M. (1994). Some unpleasant supply side arithmetic. *Journal of Monetary Economics, 33,* 507–524.

Elmendorf, D. W., & Mankiw, G. N. (1999). Government debt (Chap. 25). In J. B. Taylor & M. Woodford (Eds.), *Handbook of macroeconomics* (Vol. 1, pp. 1615–1669). Elsevier.

Gnegne, Y., & Jawadi, F. (2013). Boundedness and nonlinearities in public debt dynamics: A TAR assessment. *Economic Modelling, 34,* 154–160.

Greiner, A., & Fincke, B. (2014). *Public debt, sustainability and economic growth: Theory and empirics.* Berlin: Springer Science + Business Media.

Herndon, T., Ash, M., & Pollin, R. (2013). *Does high public debt consistently stifle economic growth? A critique of Reinhart and Rogof.* Political economy research institute. University of Massachusetts. Working papers series No. 322.

Koczan, Z. (2015). *Fiscal deficit and public debt in the Western Balkans: 15 years of economic transitions* (IMF Working Paper WP/15/172).

Krugman, P. (2011, July 7). Self-defeating austerity. *New York Times.*

Kumar, M., & Woo, J. (2010). *Public debt and growth* (IMF Working Paper 10/174).

Lof, M., & Malinen, T. (2014). Does sovereign debt weaken economic growth? A panel VAR analysis. *Economics Letters, 122*(3), 403–407.

Mencinger, J., Aristovnik, A., & Verbic, M. (2014). The impact of growing public debt on economic growth in the European Union. *Amfiteatru Economic Journal,* ISSN 2247-9104, The Bucharest University of Economic Studies, Bucharest, *16*(35), 403–414.

Mencinger, J., Aristovnik, A., & Verbic, M. (2015). Revisiting the role of public debt in economic growth: The case of OECD countries. *Engineering Economics, 26*(1), 61–66.

Misztal, P. (2010). Public debt and economic growth in the European Union. *Journal of Applied Economic Sciences, 5*(3), 292–302.

Panizza, U., & Presbitero, A. F. (2012). *Public debt and economic growth: Is there a causal effect?* (MoFiR Working Paper No. 65).

Pattillo, C., Poirson, H., & Ricci, L. (2002). *External debt and growth* (IMF Working Paper No. 02/69).

Reinhart, C., & Rogoff, K. (2010a). Growth in a time of debt. *American Economic Review, 100*(2).

Reinhart, C., & Rogoff, K. (2010b). Growth and debt revisited. VoxEU, 11 August.

Reinhart, C. M., Reinhart, V. R., & Rogoff, K. S. (2012). Public debt overhangs: Advanced-economy episodes since 1800. *Journal of Economic Perspectives, 26*(3), 69–86.

Schclarek, A. (2004). *Debt and economic growth in developing industrial countries.* Mimeo. Available at: http://www.nek.lu.se/publications/workpap/Papers/WP05_34.pdf3–78.

Woo, J., & Kumar, M. S. (2015). Public debt and growth. *Economica, 82*(328), 705–739.

World Bank. (2017). *Western Balkan regular economic reform* (No. 12).

Inflation and Economic Growth in Turkey: Evidence from a Nonlinear ARDL Approach

Özcan Karahan and Olcay Çolak

Abstract The relationship between inflation and economic growth is one of the most debated issues within the different schools of economics. Keynesian economists claim that there is a positive relationship between inflation and economic growth while Classical economists assert that inflation negatively affects economic growth. In order to extend the existing evidence concerning the inflation–growth nexus, this study aims to examine the Turkish case. We use the newly developed Nonlinear Autoregressive Distributed Lag (NARDL) model for the quarterly data set between 2003 and 2017. Estimation results indicated the existence of a nonlinear negative relationship between inflation and economic growth in the long-run. Thus, empirical findings support the Classical approach arguing an adverse relationship between inflation and economic growth. Accordingly, price stability should be considered as the basic prerequisite for assuring long-term economic growth in Turkey. In order to promote long-term economic growth, the Turkish economy needs anti-inflationary policies rather than making a sacrifice by enduring a high-level inflation as pointed out by the Keynesian approach. Hence, it can be also concluded that the Central Bank of the Republic of Turkey (CBRT) has still a significant justification in order to maintain the Inflation Targeting (IT) Monetary Policy implemented since 2001.

Keywords Inflation · Economic growth · Nonlinear ARDL

Ö. Karahan (✉)
Faculty of Economics and Administrative Sciences, Bandırma Onyedi Eylül University, 10100 Bandırma, Balıkesir, Turkey
e-mail: okarahan@bandirma.edu.tr

O. Çolak
Faculty of Economics and Administrative Sciences, Uşak University, Ankara Izmir Yolu 8. Km, Uşak, Turkey
e-mail: olcay.colak@usak.edu.tr

M. Janowicz-Lomott et al. (eds.), *Economic and Financial Challenges for Balkan and Eastern European Countries*, Springer Proceedings in Business and Economics,
https://doi.org/10.1007/978-3-030-39927-6_3

1 Introduction

It is mostly accepted that the sound functioning of economic systems largely depends on the stability of the macroeconomic variables. Any instability of the macroeconomic variables could negatively influence the operation of economic structure. However, every school of economics has handled and prioritized the stability of different macroeconomic variables for the sustainability of balances in an economy. Economists advocating the Classical approach considered price stability as the basic condition for ensuring sound economic structure. The Keynesian view mostly deals with the macroeconomic variables related to deficiency of total demand as a basic source of instability affecting permanent economic growth.

In the literature, economists supporting the Classical view produce sample researches indicating the adverse effects of inflation on economic systems. Namely, increasing inflation creates significant uncertainties for the producers and consumers that are the basic actors of economic life. Thus, the Classical approach strongly argued that fundamental economic activities cannot be carried out properly due to the problems caused by uncertainties from price instability. From this perspective, price stability or an anti-inflationary environment is considered as the prerequisite for sustainable economic growth.

The Keynesian view focuses on the factors related to the deficiency of total demand that arise from some structural problems of capitalist economy. Therefore, this approach advocates that interventionist public policies increase aggregate demand in order to promote economic growth permanently. Thus, the only precondition for sustainable growth in terms of the Keynesian approach is to promote the volume of the total demand without considering whether this process creates price instability or not. Furthermore, while public policies toward increasing aggregate demand promote economic growth, inflation can also increase because of inflationary pressures created by expansionary public policies implemented.

In summary, concerning the relationship between inflation and economic growth, the Classical approach argues that increased inflation negatively affects economic growth by creating uncertainty while Keynesian view asserts that there is a positive relationship between economic growth and inflation. Over the years, a number of economists have tried to test the hypotheses of Keynesian and Classical views. However, there is still much controversy about the causality relationship between inflation and economic growth in the literature.

Considering the starting point above, the aim of this paper is to examine the relationship between inflation and economic growth for the Turkish economy. The rest of this paper proceeds as follows. Section 2 provides a brief overview of the literature on the relationship between inflation and economic growth. Section 3 presents the data, methodology, and empirical results. Section 4 concludes and makes some policy implications.

2 Literature Review

The relationship between inflation and economic growth has been the major issue of many empirical studies. Over the years, a number of economists have tried to interpret the relationship between inflation and economic growth. Looking at the literature, it seems that the studies examining the relationship between inflation and economic growth gain huge importance after inflation-targeted stabilization programs have been implemented by many countries over the last decades. However, the debate on the nature of the relationship between inflation and economic growth continues.

In the framework of the Classical approach, the negative relationship between inflation and economic growth is one of the most popular arguments. In this context, inflation has a negative impact on economic growth by causing uncertain environments in the economy. Price stability has important influences on investment and consumption and hence ensures steady and sustainable growth. However, inflation distorts relative prices and creates uncertainty for basic economic activities. In other words, an increase in inflation reduces the effectiveness of the price mechanism to coordinate economic activities and thus dampens the economic growth rate. For example, high inflation causing increased price variability can lead to uncertainty about the future profitability of investment projects. Inflation uncertainty is also a significant factor affecting consumers' decision-making due to the value of future nominal payments and gains to be unknown. Thus, inflationary environments make it difficult to build up prospective production and consumption decisions. Therefore, inflation creating uncertainty for economic agents has an adverse impact on the basic dynamics of national income like consumption and investment.

Many studies have indicated that inflation disrupts the effective operation of the economic system and consequently dampens economic growth. In this line of the literature, Ma (1998) estimated vector autoregression (VAR) models using quarterly data between 1977 and 1997 for the Colombian economy. The results showed that the rise of inflation had a negative impact on economic growth by causing increased uncertainty. Thus, findings highlight the negative effects of inflation on the Colombian economy and imply stronger anti-inflationary policies for the monetary authorities. Fountas et al. (2002) used bivariate generalized autoregressive conditional heteroscedasticity (GARCH) model to examine the relationship between inflation and output growth rates in the Japanese economy over the term 1961–1999. Empirical results showed that a higher rate of inflation and the associated inflation uncertainty lead to lower output growth in Japan. Thus, findings support the argument of a price stability objective for the monetary authority. Bittencourt (2012) investigated the role of inflation in determining economic growth in four Latin American countries. Panel data analysis during 1970–2007 confirmed that inflation is the main macroeconomic determinant of growth in the region. Moreover, inflation has detrimental effects on economic growth. Finally, Mohseni and Jouzaryan (2016) examined the role of inflation on economic growth in Iran during 1996–2012. Using ARDL model, the significant and negative effect of inflation on economic growth in the long-run was indicated. This finding revealed that policy-makers should pay closer attention to the importance of inflation and plan to reduce inflation in order to achieve economic growth. Baharumshah et al. (2016) explored the relationship between inflation, uncertainty, and economic growth in a panel of 94 emerging and developing countries. Based on the system—generalized method of moments (GMM), they found that there exists an inflation threshold beyond which inflation and output growth are negatively correlated. The negative effect of inflation on economic growth is felt especially at excessively high levels of inflation. The empirical results support the adoption of policies geared toward achieving lower inflation rates in the framework of IT monetary regime. Aydın et al. (2016) also investigated the role of inflation threshold level in the relationship between inflation and economic growth for 224 emerging market countries during the period 1980–2013. Findings indicated that inflation has a statistically significant and negative effect on economic growth above the threshold level.

On the contrary to the Classical approach, the Keynesian view argues a positive relationship between inflation and economic growth. According to this view, economic growth basically depends on total demand in the framework of a multiplier mechanism. Thus, the precondition for economic growth is to promote the total demand. However, while demand-side policy stimulates economic growth, it can also cause to excess demand for commodities in goods market. That means inflation is considered as a natural phenomenon of promoting economic growth rather than a macroeconomic problem. Economists advocating the Keynesian view also suggest that several channels through inflation positively affect economic growth. For example, in the inflationary environment overall prices have risen but producers feel that only the prices of their products have increased. Thus, the firms produce more since they assume that only their prices or profit increase. Consequently, increasing prices result in output growth. Besides, it is well known that increasing inflation reduces the real money balances. In order to accumulate the desired wealth, economic agents may need to save much more which causes faster output growth by augmenting capital accumulation. Inflation also causes economic agents to substitute out of money into reel investment. Consequently, inflation leads to greater capital intensity and promotes economic growth (Gokal and Hanif 2004, 6–12). All of these arguments advocating the Keynesian view show that it is possible to achieve the goal of economic growth by high inflation.

In line with the Keynesian view, some studies in the literature empirically proved that there may be a positive relationship between inflation and economic growth. Mallik and Chowdhury (2001) investigated the relationship between inflation and economic growth for four South Asian countries that are Bangladesh, India, Pakistan, and Sri Lanka. Using cointegration and error correction models based on annual data, authors found an evidence of a long-run positive relationship between inflation and economic growth. However, authors also indicated that moderate inflation is helpful to economic growth while faster economic growth also feeds back into inflation, which shows that these countries are on a knife-edge. That means these countries need inflation for economic growth, but if the growth rate is too fast, it may accelerate the inflation rate and bring them downhill. Rapach (2003) estimated the long-run real output responds to a permanent increase in the inflation rate using a structural VAR framework for 14 individual industrialized countries over the postwar era. The results indicate that permanent increase in inflation augments the long-run real output level. Benhabib and Spiegel (2006) examined the long-run relationship between inflation and economic growth by allowing for inflation and economic performance to follow a nonlinear relationship. Thus, they allow for inflation and growth to have a nonlinear specification dependent on inflation levels. For a cross section of countries with historical data, it is indicated that the relationship between inflation and economic growth is nonlinear. Results also confirm a positive relationship between inflation and economic growth at moderate inflation levels. Hwang and Wu (2011) analyzed the nonlinear effects of inflation on economic growth in China by using provincial data from 1986 to 2006. Findings of the study show that inflation threshold effect is highly significant and robust in China. Accordingly, it is indicated that moderate inflation rate, below threshold, stimulates growth. It is suggested that policy-makers in China should maintain a moderate inflation rate for a long-run growth. Finally, Behera and Mishra (2016) investigated the inflation–growth nexus in the context of Brazil, Russia, India, China, and South Africa (BRICS) countries. ARDL Bound Testing approach employed on the data covering the period from 1980 to 2012. The empirical results indicated a long-run positive relationship between inflation and economic growth for China and South Africa.

As can be seen from the studies focusing on the relationship between inflation and economic growth, some studies indicate the validity of the Classical approach while others confirm the Keynesian approach. Similarly, the results of the studies focusing on the relationship between inflation and economic growth in Turkey are inconclusive to advocate a single approach. Concerning the studies supporting the Classical approach, Karaca (2003) firstly examined the inflation–growth nexus in Turkey using quarterly data provided during the period 1987–2002. The results of regression analysis indicate that inflation affects economic growth negatively. More specifically, every 1-point increase in inflation decreases growth rate by 0.37 points during the examined period in Turkey. Artan (2006) investigated the impact of inflation on economic growth using GARCH model with data covering the period from 1987 to 2003. Empirical findings show that inflation has negative impact on economic growth. Namely, 1% increase in inflation rate decreases economic growth by 0.56%. Thus, it is concluded that inflation in Turkey is not a cost to be incurred for the realization of rapid growth. Karaçor et al. (2009) explored the nature of relationship between inflation and economic growth by using cointegration and causality analysis with quarterly data covering the period from 1990 to 2005. Empirical results detect that inflation is a variable affecting economic growth negatively. It also asserts that uncertainty coming along with inflation leads to growth decline. Lastly, some of the studies examining the inflation–growth nexus focus on the investigating the threshold value effect of inflation on the economic growth. Akgül and Özdemir (2012) searched a nonlinear relationship between inflation rate and economic growth during 2003–2009 using a two-regime threshold autoregressive (TAR) model. Findings present that high inflation has a significant negative effect on economic growth above the threshold level. Finally, Korkulu and Yilmaz (2017) investigated the impact of inflation on economic growth in Turkey using Granger causality analysis for historical data from 1939 to 2013. It is determined that a 1% increase in inflation decreases the growth rate by 0.15%. Overall, it is concluded that rising inflation is an obstacle to economic growth due to negative effects.

Contrary to findings advocated Classical view, some studies relating to Turkey investigate the positive relationship between inflation and economic growth. Süleymanov and Nadirov (2014) analyzed the relationship between inflation and economic growth in Turkish economy by using the data provided between 2003 and 2013. The results of Granger causality and the regression analysis investigate the positive relationship of economic growth on inflation. More specifically, every 1-point increase in economic growth is found to increase inflation rate by 7.78 points during the examined period. Özpence (2016) determined the causal relationship between inflation and economic growth in Turkey. Using VAR model and Granger causality test based on data for the term 2003–2015, it is concluded that there is one-directional positive causal relationship of economic growth on inflation. This finding is also explained by the domestic-demand-based policies implemented after economic crises in 2001. Kanca (2017) explored whether inflation and the rate of economic growth influence each other, and if they are influenced in what way this happens in the case of Turkey. Toda-Yamamoto's causality test is conducted to detect the causality among the variables for the years between 1980 and 2014. The results of the causality test indicated that there is a one-sided causality from economic growth to inflation. Tatlıyer (2017) analyzed the relationship between inflation and economic growth in Turkish economy from 1950 to 2015. Empirical findings indicate that higher moderate inflation can accompany with higher economic growth. Thus, it is concluded that there is no negative relationship between economic growth and moderate inflation. To sum up, it seems that there is no consensus on the nature of relationship between inflation and economic growth in Turkey, just as the results of the studies focusing on other countries' experiences in the world.

3 Data, Methodology, and Empirical Results

In this section, we empirically analyze the impact of inflation on economic growth in Turkey. Looking at the literature, studies focusing on the relationship between inflation and economic growth in Turkey generally use standard time series techniques of cointegration, error correction modeling, and the Granger causality. It also seems that most of these studies assume symmetric relations between inflation and economic growth while evaluating their long-run and as well as short-run interactions. Thus, they are inadequate to capture potential long-run and short-run asymmetries in the relationship between inflation and economic growth. In order to eliminate these shortcomings, we adopt an alternative econometric framework, namely NARDL model. Shin et al. (2011) advance a NARDL cointegration approach as an asymmetric extension to the well-known ARDL model of Peseran and Shin (1999) and Peseran et al. (2001). The NARDL model explores the long-run and short-run asymmetrical

Table 1 Summary statistics

Statistics	GR_t	INF_t
Number of observations	58	58
Mean	2.26	2.05
Maximum	14.07	5.44
Minimum	−18.7	−0.37
Standard deviation	10.37	1.2777
Skewness	−0.61	0.24
Kurtosis	1.95	2.67

relationship between the time series. Therefore, the NARDL model is suitable for the analysis of the asymmetries in the relationship between inflation and economic growth. Accordingly, the rest of the section is structured as follows. Firstly, data used in this study is described. Secondly, we specify the NARD model for the relationship between inflation and economic growth. Lastly, the estimation results of NARDL model are presented.

3.1 Data Description

By utilizing the quarterly series of inflation (INF) and real gross domestic product (GDP) growth rate (GR) adjusted for seasonal and calendar effects, we analyze the inflation–growth nexus for the Turkish economy during 2003–2017. Both series are obtained from the Electronic Data Distribution System (EDDS) database of the CBRT. The series of INF is compiled by the percentage change of the Consumer Price Index (CPI). The series of real GDP growth rate is gathered by the percentage change of real GDP that is calculated according to the expenditure approach. Summary statistics related to both series are displayed in Table 1. Standard deviation of INF series is relatively low while it gets higher value since the difference of maximum and minimum values in former is less than the latter. Maximum values for both series are observed in the second quarter of 2010 and fourth quarter of 2011 while the minimum values are observed in the first quarter of 2009 and in the third quarter of 2007, respectively.

3.2 Model Specification

The basic aim of our empirical investigation is to examine the impact of inflation on economic growth in Turkey. The general form of the model is as follows:

$$GR_t = \mu_0 + \mu_1 INF + e_t \tag{1}$$

where GR is the growth rate used as a dependent variable and INF is the inflation rate used as an independent variable. Previous studies considering with the Turkish case generally assumed that inflation has symmetric effects on the economic growth. However, we aim to explore the asymmetric nexus between inflation and growth. Accordingly, we follow the methodology of NARDL recently advanced by Shin et al. (2011) based on standard ARDL model. We first consider the following asymmetric long-run regression

$$GR_t = \alpha_0 + \alpha_1 INF_t^+ + \alpha_2 INF_t^- + \varepsilon_t \tag{2}$$

where GR is the growth rate, INF_t^+ and INF_t^- constitute the partial sums of positive and negative changes in inflation, respectively. That means inflation series is decomposed into two parts which represent the partial sums of positive and negative parts of inflation series. In the equation, α (α_0, α_1, α_2) is a vector of long-term parameters to be estimated. Consequently, Eq. (2) shows the long-run impact of inflation on the economic growth. INF^+ stands for the positive changes in inflation. Thus, α_1 indicates the long-run impact of inflation increases on the economic growth. Meanwhile, INF^- stands for the negative changes in the inflation and α_2 indicates the long-run impact of inflation reduction on economic growth. Thus, α_1 and α_2, respectively, capture the long-run impact of the positive and negative changes in inflation on economic growth. INF_t^+ and INF_t^- are calculated as follows:

$$INF_t^+ = \sum_{i=1}^{t} \Delta INF_t^+ = \sum_{i=1}^{t} \max(\Delta INF_i, 0) \tag{3}$$

$$INF_t^- = \sum_{i=1}^{t} \Delta INF_t^- = \sum_{i=1}^{t} \min(\Delta\, INF_i, 0) \tag{4}$$

Equation (2) shows a model of static asymmetric regression and indicates the nonlinear relationship between inflation and economic growth in the long-run. However, the presence of nonlinearity links among the variables also exhibits dynamic characters. An unrestricted NARDL model can estimate this underlying dynamic nonlinear connection between inflation and economic growth. In order to produce an unrestricted NARDL model, Eq. (2) can be integrated into a standard ARDL setting as follows:

$$\begin{aligned} GR_t = {} & \Upsilon + \beta_0 GR_{t-1} + \beta_1 INF_{t-1}^+ + \beta_2 INF_{t-1}^- \\ & + \sum_{i=1}^{p} \delta\Delta\, GR_{t-1} + \sum_{i=0}^{q} \left(\lambda_i^+ \Delta INF_{t-1}^+ + \lambda_i^- \Delta INF_{t-1}^-\right) + u_t \end{aligned} \tag{5}$$

Thus, Eq. (5) as a specification of dynamic asymmetric regression shows an unrestricted NARDL model. From this equation, the long-term coefficients in Eq. (2) can also be defined as $\alpha_1 = -\beta_1/\beta_0$ and $\alpha_2 = -\beta_2/\beta_0$. Besides, it is also possible from the estimation of Eq. (5) to determine the nonlinear short-run relationship between inflation and economic growth. Namely, $\sum_{i=1}^{p} \lambda_i^+$ measures the short-term impacts of the increase in the inflation on the economic growth while $\sum_{i=1}^{p} \lambda_i^-$ captures the short-term impacts of inflation reduction on the economic growth. Thus, the estimation of the unrestricted NARDL model based on Eq. (5) exhibits the dynamic characters of underlying relationship between inflation and economic growth.

Estimation of unrestricted NARDL model also lets us test both asymmetric cointegration relationship and long- and short-run symmetries among the variables. In order to detect the presence of nonlinear cointegration between inflation and economic growth, the null hypothesis with no asymmetric cointegration ($\beta_0 = \beta_1 = \beta_2 = 0$) is tested using the Wald F-test. For the long-run symmetry, the null hypothesis $\alpha_1^+ = \alpha_2^-$ (i.e. $\beta_1/\beta_0 = \beta_2/\beta_0$) is tested by means of a standard Wald test. For the short-run symmetric, the null hypothesis $\sum_{i=1}^{n} \lambda_i^+ = \sum_{i=1}^{n} \lambda_i^-$ is also tested by a standard Wald test. The rejection of the null hypothesis, which indicates the equality of the positive and negative partials of inflation, shows the nonlinearity relationship between inflation and economic growth.

3.3 *Empirical Results*

In the first step of NARDL methodology, it is necessary to ensure the lag order number of the time series used in the model since NARDL approach cannot operate in the presence of one or more I(2) variables. Accordingly, we check for the stationary status of the series by performing the ADF unit root tests. The results of ADF unit root test displayed in Table 2 show that the series of inflation is stationary at level, I(0) while the series of real GDP growth rate is stationary at first difference, I(1). Thus, it is indicated that all variables are integrated into an order less than two. Therefore, we can easily continue to estimate for the long- and short-term relationships among the variables with the NARDL model.

After confirming that all variables are integrated into an order less than two, we estimate the unrestricted NARDL model outlined by Eq. (5) in order to investigate the dynamic character of the relationship between inflation and economic growth. We first obtain results by setting up the maximum lags of each variable according to Akaike information criterion (AIC) at which no serial correlation, heteroskedasticity

Table 2 ADF unit root test

Variables	ADF test	ADF test (trend)	Decision
INF_t	−4.317 [0.0004]*	−4.256 [0.0037]*	I(0)
GR_t	−2.504 [0.1146]	−2.435 [0.3614]	I(1)
ΔINF_t	−6.461 [0.0000]*	−6.366 [0.0000]*	I(1)
ΔGR_t	−6.584 [0.0000]*	−6.583 [0.0000]*	I(1)

Note *indicates the significance level at 1%. Panel means included while time trend is not included and over-identification of variables exist. In this context, the best nonlinear model to identify the nexus between inflation and growth is selected to be NARDL (3, 4). Table 3 displays the full information estimate of correctly specified NARDL (3, 4) model in the four different panels.

Panel A presents the outcomes of the dynamic asymmetric estimation. To save for place, we do not show all coefficients for the rest of lag lengths for partial sums of inflation series. It is clear that one period lag of the partial sums of inflation (INF_t^+ and INF_t^-) are negative and statistically significant. These findings prove the asymmetry effects of any inflation rate changes on the economic growth in the long-run. Differenced series of the partial sums of inflation (ΔINF_t^+ and ΔINF_t^-) are

Table 3 Full information estimate of NARDL model

Panel A: dynamic asymmetric regression results				
Variables	Coefficient estimate		Standard error	
Constant	−15.6498*		6.4778	
GR_{t-1}	−2.2179*		0.4213	
INF_{t-1}^+	−8.1206**		2.8722	
INF_{t-1}^-	−8.2876**		2.8835	
ΔGR_{t-1}	0.8866*		0.2755	
ΔGR_{t-2}	0.3179*		0.0016	
ΔINF_t^+	0.1587		1.2590	
ΔINF_{t-1}^+	2.7963		2.0581	
ΔINF_t^-	−1.5096		1.4372	
ΔINF_{t-1}^-	−0.0426		1.0985	
Diagnostic tests				
R^2 0.97	Adj. R^2 0.94	F_{RESET} 0.10 [0.9617]	χ^2_H 0.38 [0.5351]	χ^2_{SC} 0.98 [0.8886]
Panel B: cointegration test				
Null hypothesis			Wald F-test	
H: $\beta_0 = \beta_1 = \beta_2 = 0$			3.49 [0.0373]**	
Panel C: asymmetry statistics				
Null hypothesis			Wald test	
$H_{LR}: \alpha_1 = \alpha_2$			3.3450 (0.084)***	
$H_{SR}: \sum_{i=1}^{n} \lambda_i^+ = \sum_{i=1}^{n} \lambda_i^-$			0.7994 (0.383)	
Panel D: normalized long-run estimates				
Variables	Coefficient estimate		F-statistics (*p*-value)	
INF_t^+	−3.661		6.851 (0.017)**	
INF_t^-	−3.737		7.110 (0.016)**	

Note *, **, *** indicate the significance levels at 1%, 5%, and 10%, respectively. χ^2_H, χ^2_{SC}, and F_{RESET} denote heteroscedasticity, serial correlation, and over-identification of variables positive but statistically insignificant. That means inflation changes do not have any asymmetric effect on the economic growth in the short-run.

Panel B shows the results of the test for nonlinear cointegration between inflation and economic growth. The null hypothesis with no asymmetric cointegration ($\beta_0 = \beta_1 = \beta_2 = 0$) is tested using the Wald F-test. The test results reveal that there is an asymmetric cointegration relation between inflation and economic growth at the level of 5% significance.

Panel C provides the test outcomes of the null hypothesis of symmetry in long-term and the short-term by using the Wald test statistics. Regarding the long-term relationship, the null hypothesis with no symmetry ($\alpha_1^+ = \alpha_2^-$) is tested. The results suggest the rejection of null hypothesis at the level of 10% significance. As for the asymmetry in short-run, null hypothesis with no symmetry $\left(\sum_{i=1}^{n} \lambda_i^+ = \sum_{i=1}^{n} \lambda_i^-\right)$ is tested. Findings cannot reject the null hypothesis in the short-run.

Panel D presents the normalized long-run positive (INF_t^+) and negative (INF_t^-) coefficients that indicate the impacts of 1% increase and 1% decrease in the inflation on the economic growth. Long-run coefficients of decomposed inflation series are negative and significant at the level of 5% significance. Thus, in the period studied the positive changes in inflation in Turkey cause to decreasing economic growth while the negative changes in inflation lead to increasing economic growth. The coefficient of positive partial sum is −3.661 and negative partial sum is −3.737, respectively. More specifically, 1% increase in the inflation level leads to 3.661% decrease in the economic growth rate while 1% decrease in the inflation level causes to 3.737% increase in the economic growth rate.

Overall, the findings indicate that inflation asymmetrically affects the economic growth in the long-run but not in the short-run. Thus, empirical results assert in the long-run that economic growth rate responds negatively to both increases and decreases in the inflation level. It can be argued that inflationary environment in Turkey makes it difficult to build up prospective production and consumption decisions by increasing uncertainty environment, which prevents economic growth in the long run. In other words, as pointed out by the Classical approach, ongoing inflation increases in Turkey lead to negative effects by causing uncertainty on the long-term economic growth. That means, in order to promote long-term economic growth, the Turkish economy needs the stability in the prices rather than making a sacrifice by enduring high-level inflation as pointed out by the Keynesian approach. To put it another way, policy-makers should keep a close eye toward inflation in order to enhance economic growth in the long run. As a result, findings of this study support the aim of price stability for the monetary authority in Turkey.

4 Conclusion

The nature of the relationship between inflation and economic growth is one of the most controversial issues among the schools of economics. The Classical approach asserts that inflation negatively affects growth by causing uncertainty that dampens the well-functioning operation of an economic system. On the contrary, the Keynesian view argues that inflation is considered as a natural phenomenon of promoting economic growth based on demand-side policies. Although the inflation–growth nexus is a popular research topic empirically investigated, there is no consensus on the direction and sign of the relationship between them. The purpose of this paper is to extend the existing evidence on the impact of inflation on economic growth by adopting an alternative econometric methodology. Namely, previous empirical studies have used the linear framework and therefore have largely ignored the possible characteristics of nonlinear relationship between inflation and economic growth. This paper analyzes the relationship between inflation and economic growth in Turkey during 2003–2017 using NARDL model to capture the long-run and short-run nonlinear connections among the variables.

Estimation results affirm the presence of nonlinear negative causality from inflation to economic growth in the long-run but not in the short-run. The coefficients of the positive and negative components of inflation have statistically significant impact on the behavior of the economic growth in the long run. Thus, it can be detected as a negative asymmetric long-term economic growth reaction to inflation. It is highly probable that inflation removing the leading role of prices by creating uncertainty disrupts the effective operation of the economic system. Consequently, this inflationary process dampens the economic growth in Turkey. This finding of course supports the Classical approach arguing an adverse relationship between inflation and economic growth. Therefore, inflation in Turkey, as indicated by the Keynesian approach, is not a natural phenomenon that would have to endure for the promotion of economic growth. In other words, to promote long-term economic growth, the Turkish economy needs anti-inflationary policies rather than making a sacrifice by enduring a high-level inflation. Hence, the CBRT still has significant justification in order to maintain the IT Monetary Policy implemented since 2001.

Acknowledgements This work was supported by the Scientific Research Projects Coordination Unit of Bandırma Onyedi Eylül University. Project Number: BAP-18-İİBF-1009-010.

References

Akgül, I., & Özdemir, S. (2012). Inflation threshold and the effects on economic growth. *Economics, Business and Finance, 27*(313), 85–106.

Artan, S. (2006). *Inflation, inflation uncertainty and growth in Turkey*. Turkish Economic Association Discussion Paper, 2006/4.

Aydın, C., Akıncı, M., & Yılmaz, O. (2016). When does inflation hinder the dynamics of economic growth? A dynamic panel threshold model upon emerging markets. *Gazi University, Journal Faculty of Economics and Political Sciences, 18*(3), 748–761.

Baharumshah, A. Z., Slesman, L., & Wohar, M. E. (2016). Inflation, inflation uncertainty, and economic growth in emerging and developing countries: Panel data evidence. *Economic Systems, 40*, 638–657.

Behera, J., & Mishra, A. K. (2016). Inflation and economic growth nexus in BRICS: Evidence from ARDL Bound Testing approach. *Asian Journal of Economic Modelling, 4*(1), 1–17.
Benhabib, J., & Spiegel, M. M. (2006). Moderate inflation and the deflation-depression link. *Journal of Money, Credit and Banking, 41*(4), 787–798.
Bittencourt, M. (2012). Inflation and economic growth in Latin America: Some panel time-series evidence. *Economic Modelling, 29,* 333–340.
Fountas, S., Karanasos, M., & Kim, J. (2002). Inflation and output growth uncertainty in their relationship with inflation and output growth. *Economic Letter, 75,* 293–301.
Gokal, V., & Hanif, S. (2004). *Relationship between inflation and growth.* Economic Department Working Paper/Reserve Bank of Fiji, 2004-04.
Hwang, J., & Wu, M. J. (2011). Inflation and economic growth in China: An empirical analysis. *China & World Economy, 19*(5), 67–84.
Karaca, O. (2003). Inflation-growth relationship in Turkey: Time series analysis. *Doğuş University Journal, 4*(2), 247–255.
Karaçor, Z., Saylan, Ş., & Üçler, G. (2009). Cointegration and causality analysis for the relationship between inflation and economic growth in Turkish economy. *Niğde University, Journal Faculty of Economics and Political Sciences, 2*(2), 60–74.
Kanca, O. C. (2017). Domestic debt, inflation, economic growth: An econometric application for Turkey. *Finans Politik ve Ekonomik Yorumlar, 54*(627), 47–58.
Korkulu, A., & Yılmaz, B. (2017). Growth-inflation relationship in Turkey: Granger causality analysis. *International Journal of Academic Value Studies, 3*(13), 85–93.
Ma, H. (1998). *Inflation, uncertainty and growth in Colombia* (pp. 1–28). IMF working paper, WP/98/161.
Mallik, G., & Chowdhury, A. (2001). Inflation and economic growth: Evidence from four South Asian countries. *Asian-Pacific Development Journal, 8*(1), 123–135.
Mohseni, M., & Jouzaryan, F. (2016). Examining the effects of inflation and unemployment on economic growth in Iran. *Procedia Economics and Finance, 36,* 381–389.
Özpence, A. I. (2016). Analysis of the relationship between inflation and economic growth in Turkey. *Journal of Economics, Finance and Accounting, 3*(3), 190–191.
Pesaran, M. H., & Shin, Y. (1999). An autoregressive distributed lag modelling approach to cointegration analysis. In S. Strom (Ed.), *Econometrics and economic theory in the 20th century* (pp. 371–413). London: Cambridge University Press.
Pesaran, M. H., Shin, Y., & Smith, R. J. (2001). Bounds testing approaches to the analysis of level relationships. *Journal of Applied Econometrics, 16,* 289–326.
Rapach, D. E. (2003). International evidence on the long-run impact of inflation. *Journal of Money, Credit and Banking, 35*(1), 23–48.
Shin, Y., Yu, B., & Nimmo-Greenwood, M. (2011). Modelling asymmetric cointegration and dynamic multipliers in a nonlinear ARDL framework. In R. Sickles & W. Horrace (Eds.), *Festschrift in Honor of Peter Schmidt* (pp. 281–314). New York: Springer.
Süleymanov, E., & Nadirov, O. (2014). The relationship between inflation and economic growth in the case of Turkey. *Journal of Qafqaz University-Economics and Administration, 2*(2), 119–125.
Tatlıyer M (2017) Inflation and economic growth in Turkish economy. *International Journal of Management Economics and Business, Special Issue,* 173–188.

Distance as Determinant of FDI in Transition Countries. The Case of Serbia

Dimitrios Kyrkilis and Natasa Grujic

Abstract The aim of this paper is to define the meaning and the role of distance in determining cross-border investment transactions. Specifically, it aims to use Serbia as an individual country case demonstrating the implementation of a model based on Ghemawat's culture, administrative, geographic, and economic distances (CAGE) framework for testing the key distance-related determinants of the foreign direct investment (FDI) inflows to a country. Since 2000, Serbia has embarked on an extensive political and economic reforms program, having achieved democratic stability by now. Its economic growth has been mainly driven by foreign direct investments. This paper analyzes how each one of distance dimensions, i.e., cultural, administrative, geographic, and economic, affects FDI inflows to Serbia. The empirical application of the model shows that cultural distance affects FDI flows negatively, while administrative, geographic, and economic distances have a positive effect on FDI inflows to Serbia.

Keywords Foreign direct investment · Distance · Transition countries

1 Introduction

Ghemawat (2001) argues that despite globalization, borders still matter for evaluating cross-border moves and the world is in a stage of semi globalization and will remain as such in decades to come. Ghemawat underpinned that differences between countries still have large effect on international business, and he grouped those differences in four broad categories—i.e., cultural, administrative, geographic, and economic—formulating the CAGE model framework at country and industry levels.

This paper represents an attempt to test Ghemawat's basic argument in the case of foreign direct investment (FDI) to Serbia, a transition country by industrial sector.

D. Kyrkilis (✉) · N. Grujic
University of Macedonia, Thessaloniki, Greece
e-mail: kyrkilis@uom.edu.gr

N. Grujic
e-mail: natasagrujicgr@gmail.com

M. Janowicz-Lomott et al. (eds.), *Economic and Financial Challenges for Balkan and Eastern European Countries*, Springer Proceedings in Business and Economics,
https://doi.org/10.1007/978-3-030-39927-6_4

FDI literature focuses on the interpretation of FDI through mainly market imperfections and the theory of industrial organization, the product cycle model, the eclectic theory (paradigm), and the market transaction cost approach (TCA). The configuration of ownership, location, and internalization (OLI) determinants sets up the main framework to explain FDI decisions (Dunning 2000, 2001). However, the underlying interpretation of location in the eclectic paradigm is much broader than in TCA. TCA approach sets up the framework which explains how international expansions occur. Thus, once motivated to expand internationally, companies confront challenges and risks which they need to mitigate and overcome. The most well-known risk is the liability of foreignness, which is defined as an additional cost for firms when they do business abroad. Uncertainty is another important risk undertaken by companies when they expand abroad. One social aspect of this challenge is suggested by the concept of "physic distance," which concerns the cultural, linguistic, institutional levels and other differences between home and host countries. In terms of institutional aspects, scholars have found that high regulatory control affects firms negatively in the host countries, thus influencing the incoming company strategy. Although firms need to deal with the local requirements and cope with these regulations, the unexpected additional costs may offset the benefits of internationalization. Therefore, since TCA connects firm-specific characteristic mechanisms with environmental factors, it has a limited and more illiberal focus on the intangible knowledge advantages of MNEs and subsequently is able to demonstrate the heterogeneity of firm-level behavior within any industry.

2001 is considered to be the starting year of transition to market in Serbia. The scenario of inflows of direct investments was the same as for the other countries in transition. Firstly, investments were coming through privatization of the state enterprises. Until 2006, FDIs in Serbia were increasing, but not significantly. Amid all internal political problems, investments were suffering the most. Furthermore, the assassination of the prime minister interrupted the process of reforms until the last half of 2003. During that period, privatization and selling of companies and banks were the main sources of FDI in Serbia. Then, as the political and economic stability were increasing, foreign partners were investing in a couple of sectors, mainly food and tobacco. Finally, FDIs expanded into trade, automotive industry, electronics, telecommunications, and financial services (Filipovic et al. 2006). In 2011, Serbia was the best performer in attracting FDIs in Southeastern Europe according to UNCTAD. This growing trend remains up to date.

2 The Concept of Distance, Theory, and Hypothesis Building

The concept of distance has important implications for strategic firm decisions, such as the location choice (e.g., Johanson and Vahlne 1977; Dunning 1988), transfer of organizational practices (Kostova and Roth 2002), and the entry mode strategy (Kogut and Singh 1988). Among different approaches of distance (Beckerman 1956; Hymer 1960, 1976; Johanson and Vahlne 1977; Nordstrom and Vahlne 1994; Hennart and Larimo 1998; Dunning 1988), the most prominent is mostly attributed to Ghemawat (2001).

Ghemawat (2001) supports that companies erroneously utilize an inadequate and incorrect modality when deciding on foreign expansion: the country portfolio analysis (CPA). The CPA focuses on national GDP, levels of consumer wealth, and people's propensity to consume, but ignores "the costs and risks of doing business in the market." These costs are grouped into a category classified as distance which itself is subdivided into four dimensions: cultural, administrative, geographic, and economic distances.

2.1 Culture Distance

"Culture as used here refers to the attributes of a society that are sustained mainly by interaction among people, rather than by the state" (Ghemawat 2007, p. 40). One of the most common cultural differences is language. Furthermore, differences in ethnic, religion or values, norms, and dispositions tend to reduce the interaction.

Cultural distance (CD) and its proxies were used in a lot of business areas, in both fields domestic and international. However, FDI is the most popular sphere for the application of the CD theory. According to Shenkar (2001), the first use of CD in FDI literature meant to explain the foreign market investor location. Theory claimed that there will be a less chance for MNCs to invest in culturally distant markets (e.g., Porter et al. 2000; Yoshino 1976; Ozawa 1979; Dunning 1988). The second use of CD in FDI literature meant to predict the mode of entry into foreign markets. A lot of studies have examined the influence of CD to FDI entry modes: wholly owned subsidiary (WOS) and partly controlled international joint venture (IJV), as well as on the establishment mode: Greenfield, acquisition, and JV. However, the empirical results of the studies are ambiguous (e.g., Kogut and Singh 1988; Kim and Hwang 1992; Erramilli 1996; Hennard and Larimo 1998). Finally, the third use of CD in FDI literature meant to explain the performance of the MNCs in international markets. Yet, for this application of CD, empirical results have been mixed as well (e.g., Li and Guisinger 1991; Johnson et al. 1991; Park and Ungson 1997).

Perhaps the best-known study that measures the CD among countries is Hofstede's (1980) survey of more than 100,000 employees of the multinational IBM in more than 60 countries. Using the survey, Hofstede has developed four dimensions of national culture: power distance, that shows until what level individuals are comfortable with inequality in relationships; individualism/collectivism, that demonstrates how much individuals focus on their own problems and needs; uncertainty avoidance, that explains to which extent people in a group feel threatened by uncertain or unknown situations and masculinity/femininity, that presents the role of sex in society. In 1991, Hofstede added one more dimension of national culture: "Confucian Dynamism," also known as long-term orientation (Hofstede et al. 1991). Even though Hofstede's model is one of the most used frameworks to compare cultural distances, it was heavily criticized (e.g., McSweeney 2002; Schwartz 1994; Shenkar 2001; Steenkamp 2001). Thus, several other cultural frameworks appear along with Trompenaars (1993), Schwartz (2008), and GLOBE (House et al. 2004).

Most studies have measured the cultural distance between the home market of MNCs and the target country of the expansion by using Kogut and Singh's (1988) index, which is based on Hofstede (1984) dimensions of national culture. Though a lot of scholars have become critical of this index and of Hofstede's model, studies have continued to rely on them, since little progress has been made in developing reliable alternatives (Drogendijk and Slagengen 2006).

The impact of cultural distance on cross-border transactions and FDI is currently the subject of considerable debate (Brouthers and Brouthers 2001; Shenkar 2001). In general, increasing cultural distance between countries increases the adaptation cost of foreign operations in the host country. The results of available empirical studies confirm that a large cultural distance will generally reduce FDI flows from home country to host country (Tihanyi et al. 2005). Based on this argumentation, we posit the following hypothesis:

Hypothesis I Considering Hofstede's cultural index, it is expected that the greater the cultural distance between home country and host country, the lower the inward FDI flows to the host country.

2.2 *Institutional Distance*

Institutional distance is a measure of differences in the institutional environment between the home country and the host country of MNEs. During the last decades, it is receiving a lot of attention from international business (IB) researchers and has also been conceptualized and operationalized in many different ways in IB studies. Scientists have used and applied institutional distance as one of the factors that companies are examining before entering into new international markets (Kostova 1997; Kostova and Zaheer 1999; Kostova and Roth 2002; Xu and Shenkar 2002; Arslan and Larimo 2010).

In past studies, scientists were using Scott's (1995) institutional framework in order to refer that institutional distance can be different for each institutional pillars: regulatory, normative, and cognitive (termed as cultural cognitive in some studies) (Xu et al. 2004; Gaur and Lu 2007; Xu and Shenkar 2002). Some researchers applied North's (1990) classification of formal and informal institutions to analyze the impact of institutional distance on strategies of MNEs (e.g., Peng 2003; Estrin et al. 2009; Dikova and Van Witteloostuijn 2007). Even though institutional distance has been conceptualized and operationalized differently in the past, Scott's (1995) institutional pillars are predominant classification used in IB studies.

The impact of institutional distance on FDI location and entry mode choices of MNEs can be found in the studies of Xu and Shenkar (2002), Yiu and Makino

(2002), Xu et al. (2004), Gaur and Lu (2007), Estrin et al. (2009), Trevino and Mixon (2004), Arslan and Larimo (2010), and others. Yet, in some of the studies researchers were examining the differences in just one aspect of institutional environment (e.g., Brouthers 2002; Xu et al. 2004; Gaur and Lu 2007; Gaur et al. 2007; Arslan and Larimo 2010; Chao and Kumar 2010). For example, Trevino and Mixon (2004) were concentrated on differences in legal reforms across countries in order to understand strategic FDI decisions.

FDIs are seen as an important determinant of economic growth of developing countries and are considered to be a vehicle for technological progress. Not surprisingly, the FDI promoting effect of good institutions might be an important channel of their overall effect on growth and development. Therefore, there are a few reasons why the quality of institutions should be taken into account for attracting FDI. In the beginning, good governance infrastructures may attract foreign investors. Furthermore, poor institutions can bring additional costs to FDI. Finally, FDIs are vulnerable to any kind of uncertainty, such as uncertainty stemming from poor government efficiency, policy reversals, graft or weak enforcement of property rights and legal system, etc.

Kaufman et al. (1999) stated five out of six government indicators that seem to have an influence on foreign investors: political instability and violence, government effectiveness, regulatory burden, rule of law, and graft. The sixth one, the voice and accountability indicator, was not significant determinant of FDI. La Porta et al. (1998) used International Country Risk Guide as independent variable and found out that the risk of repudiation of contracts by government, risk of expropriation, and shareholder rights were significant.

Using Kaufman et al. (1999) six government indicators, Globerman and Shapiro (2002) got found out that the good governance impacts positively both FDI inflows and outflows. The only limitation of this study is that the institutional quality of the home country and the host country of FDI cannot be included in the regression, because the authors did not use the bilateral flows. However, Levchenko runs the study of the effect of institutional distance between home country and host country of FDI by using bilateral data and suggested that institutional differences may be a source of comparative advantages. More precisely, some sectors could be more "sensitive" than others and that could be a source of more trade flows. Busse and Hefeker (2007) emphasized that government stability, law and order, bureaucratic quality, democratic structure, and lower levels of corruption are positively associated with FDI. Similarly, Daude and Stein (2007) found that a credible and efficient government and market friendly regulations have a positive relationship with FDI. Mengistu and Adhikary (2011) found that political stability, good public and political service, an improved legal system, and low levels of corruption promote FDI, while Buchanan et al. (2012) discovered a positive relationship between good governance and foreign investments.

Most studies tried to examine the link between democracy and FDI. Harms and Ursprung (2002) and Jensen (2003) discovered that MNEs are more likely to be attracted to host countries that have democratic structure, while non- or less democratic countries are connected with the greater risk of policy reversals and therefore attract less FDI. Kolstad and Villanger (2008) got the same results for developing countries only.

Political stability was also examined in several studies. Tuman and Emmert (1999) found a negative relationship between political instability in countries of Latin America and FDI from Japan. Quazi (2007) confirmed this finding, stating the positive relationship between political stability and foreign investments for Asian countries.

The study of the linkage between corruption and FDI has received a lot of intention. From a theoretical perspective, corruption can have both positive and negative impacts on foreign investments. Corruption increases uncertainty; therefore, it causes the additional cost of doing business, which can be a major discouragement for foreign investors (Rose-Ackerman 1975; Shleifer and Vishny 1993). On the other side, some scholars (Leff 1964; Huntington 1968) argued that when a host country has an excessive regulation and inefficient legal system, the interaction between corrupt autocrats and foreign investors can be helpful for MNE to enter a market. Some studies found out that corruption has a significant, negative impact on FDI (e.g., Wei 2000; Habib and Zurawicki 2002; Mauro 1995; Voyer and Beamish 2004), while some others do not confirm such a negative relation (e.g., Wheeler and Mody 1992; Egger and Winner 2005).

Hypothesis II MNCs coming from countries that have different institutional systems than the host country will invest less than companies coming from countries which share the same institutional system with the host country.

2.3 Geographic Distance

Geographic distance (GD) is known as one of the most important obstacles for trade, FDI, and other cross-border economic activities (Berry et al. 2010). Ghemawat (2001) sees GD not just as the actual distance (in kilometers or miles) between two countries, but as distance in terms of the physical size of the country, average within-country distances to borders, access to waterways and the ocean, and topography.

In economic geography literature, GD is considered to be an important cause of the choice of location of the production activity, since market accessibility is one of the basic motivations for MNCs to invest abroad. Thus, geographic distance is negatively related to FDI inflows to the host country. Solocha and Soskin (1994) emphasized that geographic proximity reduces informational and managerial uncertainty, lowers monitoring costs, and allows firms to become less exposed to risk. In addition, they stated that some raw material and intermediate products are often supplied from home country sources and that is what makes geographic proximity an important determinant.

Moreover, geographic distance makes the transfer of knowledge more difficult between different entities because personal contacts and interaction of teams will be less frequent (Hansen and Lovas 2004; Shenkar 2001). Therefore, one can assume that geographic distance is likely to reduce the willingness of companies to enter into geographically distance markets. Hence, we hypothesize as follows:

Hypothesis III The greater the geographic distance between home country and host country, the less FDI is undertaken between the countries.

2.4 Economic Distance

"Economic distance" (Ghemawat 2001) implies differences in the level of economic development between the home country and the host country. As stated by Tsang and Yip (2007), economic distance (ED) between two countries demonstrates differences in factor costs (e.g., wages) and in technological capability; both factors influence FDI decision and performance. These two authors also argued that behind every FDI and its location are exploration and exploitation motives. More specifically, in the resource exploration perspective, the role of FDI is to gain strategic assets (e.g., technology, management, and marketing expertise) available in the host country, whereas in the resource exploitation perspective, the idea of FDI is to relocate MNC's resources over borders. Thus, they emphasized that "economic distance is an important factor affecting not only whether the motive for FDI is resource exploitation or resource exploration, but also FDI survival" (Tsang and Yip 2007, p. 1157).

A lot of other studies have examined the impact of economic distance on the choice of both the host foreign market and the mode of entry (Iyer 1997; Yeung 1997; Zaheer and Zaheer 1997). Ghemawat (2001, p. 145) emphasized that "the wealth or income of consumers is the most important economic attribute that creates distance between countries." Thus, it can affect the levels of trade and the trading partner countries. According to this author, rich countries will undertake more cross-border economic activities with countries of a comparable economic size. However, the case will not be the same between poor countries. They will trade more with rich countries rather than with poor ones. Furthermore, MNCs that by investing abroad rely on economies of experience, scale, and standardization should choose countries that have the same or similar economic profiles.

The rich–poor interaction often involves arbitrage, which is "the way of exploiting differences" that does not derive from cultural, administrative, and geographic distances (Ghemawat 2007, p. 169). The well-known category of economic arbitrage is the exploitation of cheap labor, which is frequent for countries that are labor-abundant or they are in lower development phases than home countries. Apart from cheap labor, differences may be in capital, as well as in variations in more industry-specific inputs (e.g., knowledge) or in the availability of complementary products. As a consequence of economic arbitrage, companies that operate in industries where primary cost ingredients differ widely across countries or labor costs are important, it is highly probable to target countries with different economic profiles.

Moreover, Berry et al. (2010) said that, considering economic distance, countries vary in terms of their income, inflation, and trade balance (as a percentage of GDP). They added that those factors are important, because they are in direct correlation with consumer purchasing power and preferences, macroeconomic stability, and the openness of the economy to external influences. Thus, in international business literature those indicators have been found to influence the choice of foreign market and foreign market entry mode.

Considering the above, economic distance may operate both ways, either to increase FDI inflows in cases of exploiting country differences or to reduce such flows in cases of exploiting similarities.

Hypothesis IV (a) The bigger the economic distance between home country and host country, the lower the level of FDI inflows is expected to be.

Hypothesis IV (b) The bigger the economic distance between home country and host country, the greater the level of FDI inflows is expected to be.

FDI occurs when it is more beneficial for the foreign firm to exploit its ownership advantages in conjunction with the host country location advantages internally, i.e., by establishing a subsidiary in the foreign market, rather through alternative modes of entry, e.g., licensing. That means, given the host country's location advantages the foreign firm evaluates alternative ways of exploiting its ownership advantages or given its ownership advantages seeks the most efficient way of exploiting the foreign country's location advantages (Dunning 2000). In any case, the critical point is the coexistence of ownership, internalization, and location advantages the configuration of which differs among countries and industries (Dunning 2001). Cultural and institutional settings may be treated as parts of a country's location advantages that lower both investment and operational costs. Sectoral characteristics augment this function of culture and institutions. For instance, a strong system of intellectual protection deters imitation of technologies and/or know-how; hence, it facilitates foreign investments in sectors of technological intensity, especially if the technologies used are of intangible nature, i.e., information-intensive technologies (see Javorcik 2004). At the same time, FDIs in such sectors are motivated by strategic resource acquisition. Therefore, cultures and institutional settings that promote the development of such assets, e.g., business law and law enforcement system, economic governance and regulation system and quality, policy design and implementation quality, educational and vocational training systems, etc., are expected to influence the level and type, i.e., the technological intensity of incoming FDI. In addition, work ethics, and social norms and values affect the type of business and economic development, and thus, it influences the level and type of agglomeration economies generated in a country. In general, agglomeration economies are more important determinants in medium and high technology industries than in low technology ones; hence, countries of agglomeration economies developed in such industries, i.e., are expected to host FDIs in medium-high technology sectors. Therefore, cultural and institution settings similar to those of industrially developed nations are expected to promote FDI in medium and high technology.

Hypothesis V Overall, it is expected both the statistical significance and the sign of the distance dimensions to vary along different industrial sectors in the same host country.

3 The Model, Methodology, Data Sets

3.1 The Dependent Variable

The dependent variable of the model refers to annual FDI inflows to total manufacturing and four manufacturing subsector, namely low, medium-low, medium-high, and high technology as well as total services and two services subsectors, i.e., low knowledge-intensive services and high knowledge-intensive services for the period between 2004 and 2015. The classification of both manufacturing and services in subsectors by technological and knowledge intensity, respectively, follows the Eurostat's NACE Rev. 2 2-digit level classification system (see Appendix 1).

3.2 Independent Variables

3.2.1 Culture Distance

To measure cultural distance, the paper adopts the Hofstede's four cultural dimensions, i.e., *Power Distance, Individualism/ Collectivism, Masculinity/Femininity, and Uncertainty Avoidance.* Then, on these four dimensions factor analysis has been applied in order to construct a composite index approximating the culture distance variable. Results of the factor analysis exercise are shown in Table 1.

Table 1 Factor analysis/correlations

Method: Principal factors				
Rotation: Unrotated				
Number of observations: 42				
Retained factors: 2				
Number of parameters: 6				
Factor	Eigenvalue	Difference	Proportion	Cumulative
Factor 1	1.59481	1.43712	1.0942	1.0942
Factor 2	0.15769	0.22128	0.1082	1.2024
Factor 3	−0.06359	0.16786	−0.0436	1.1588
Factor 4	−0.23145		−0.1588	1.000

LP test Independent versus saturated: chi2 (6) = 43.04 Prob > chi2 = 0.0000
Source Stata 9.1, results

Table 2 Factor loadings (pattern matrix) and unique variance

Variable	Factor 1	Factor 2	Uniqueness
Power distance	0.8073	0.1440	0.3275
Individualism/collectivism	−0.7925	0.0903	0.3638
Masculinity/femininity	−0.0389	0.3546	0.8728
Uncertainty avoidance	0.5599	−0.0552	0.6834

Source Stata 9.1, results

The factor analysis yields one distinct factor whose eigenvalue is greater than 1, i.e., Factor 1 (see Table 1). Therefore, Factor 1 has been used for constructing the composite index (Tables 2, 3, 4, and 5). Table 6 shows the extraction of Squared Sums

Table 3 Factor analysis/correlations

Method: principal factors				
Rotation: orthogonal varimax (Horse off)				
Number of observations: 42				
Retained factors: 2				
Number of parameters: 6				
Factor	Variance	Difference	Proportion	Cumulative
Factor 1	1.58800	1.42649	1.0896	1.0896
Factor 2	0.16450		0.1129	1.2024

LP test Independent versus saturated: chi2(6) = 43.04 Prob > chi2 = 0.0000
Source Stata 9.1, results

Table 4 Rotated factor loadings (pattern matrix) and unique variances

Variable	Factor 1	Factor 2	Uniqueness
Power distance	0.8153	0.0881	0.3275
Individualism/collectivism	−0.7844	0.1447	0.3638
Masculinity/femininity	−0.0143	0.3564	0.8728
Uncertainty avoidance	0.5548	−0.0937	0.6834

Source Stata 9.1, results

Table 5 Factor rotation matrix

	Factor 1	Factor 2
Factor 1	0.9976	−0.0688
Factor 2	−0.0688	0.9976

Source Stata 9.1, results

Table 6 Scoring coefficients (method regression, based on varimax rotated factors)

Variable	Factor 1	Factor 2
Power distance	0.46979	0.31559
Individualism/collectivism	−0.37967	0.29149
Masculinity/femininity	−0.00073	0.28742
Uncertainty avoidance	0.15797	−0.09577

Source Stata 9.1, results

of Loadings % of variance for Factor 1 and indicates that the first dimension, i.e., *power distance,* accounts for 46.979% of the variance, the second dimension, namely *individualism-collectivism,* accounts for 37.967%, and the fourth dimension, namely *uncertainty avoidance,* accounts for 15.797%. The dimension *masculinity/femininity* is not taken into account because it contributes a rather very close to zero percentage to the total variation of Factor 1.

Finally, the composite index has been constructed according to the formulae below:

$$
\begin{aligned}
&Hofstede\,Type\,Cultural\,Index \\
&\quad = [power\ distance\ (difference\ between\ home\ and\ host\ country) * 0.46979 \\
&\qquad - individualism - collectivism\ (difference\ between\ home\ and\ host\ country) * 0.37967 \\
&\qquad + uncertainty\ avoidance\ (difference\ between\ home\ and\ host\ country) * 0.15797]^2
\end{aligned}
$$

Country scores are the Hofstede's country culture scores by each dimension for the countries involved, adopted from the Hofstede Centre https://www.hofstede-insights.com/country-comparison/.

3.2.2 Institutional Distance

The institutional distance variable is approximated by a composite index constructed as follows: by using the World Bank governance indicators which aggregate the views of a large number of enterprises, citizens, and experts responding to surveys run in industrial and developing countries alike. The individual data underlying the aggregate indicators are sourced from a diverse variety of survey institutes, think tanks, non-governmental organizations, and international organizations (World Bank 2005).

For the purposes of the current analysis, *government effectiveness, regulatory quality, and rule of law* define the **regulative** pillar of institutional distance, while *voice and accountability, quality of political stability, and absence of violence and control of corruption* describe the **normative** pillar of institutional distance. In a variety of international business research, cultural distance is used as a substitute for the cognitive pillar of institutional distance, because it has similar effects, as "mental programming" (Hofstede 1980) and it is closely related to cognitive systems (Xu

2001). Cultural distance is treated as a separate independent variable in this research; therefore, in order to avoid overlapping with the cognitive pillar of institutional distance, the former is excluded from the latter, and the institutional distance variable is approximated by the normative and regulative pillar alone.

The composite index for measuring ID has been constructed using the Kogut and Singh (1988) methodology for quantifying cultural distance. The precise formula is the following:

$$\mathrm{RD/ND} = \Sigma[(I_k - I_s)^2/V_i]/n$$

where I_k refers to the institutional indicator (I) for a home country k, I_s refers to the institutional indicator (I) for Serbia (s), and V_i is the variance of indicator I. RD and ND are regulative and normative distances of home country k to Serbia. The symbol n refers to the number of indicators for a particular measure. RD includes first three indicators, whereas ND includes the rest.

3.2.3 Geographic Distance

Weighted distances are calculated as distance between two countries based on bilateral distances between the biggest cities of those two countries, those inter-city distances being weighted by the share of the city in the overall country's population. Head and Mayer (2002) developed the general formula for calculating distances between country i and j:

$$D_{ij} = \left(\Sigma(pop_k/pop_i) * \Sigma\left(pop_l/pop_j\right) d_{kl}^{\theta}\right)^{1/\theta}$$

where pop_k designates the population of agglomeration k belonging to country i. The parameter θ measures the sensitivity of trade flows to bilateral distance d_{kl}. For the *distw* calculation, θ is set equal to 1. The *distances* calculation sets θ equal to -1, which corresponds to the usual coefficient estimated from gravity models of bilateral trade flows.

In this research, data for geographic distance have been acquired by the GeoDist dataset (http://www.cepii.fr/CEPII/en/bdd_modele/presentation.asp?id=6). Mayer and Zignago (2005) formulated the exhaustive set of gravity variables that GeoDist made available in order to analyze market access difficulties in global and regional trade flows.

3.2.4 Economic Distance

Economic distance is approximated in this research by the differences of GDP purchasing power parity (PPP) per capita between the host and the home countries. Data for this variable are in current US dollars, and it is taken from the World Bank's official website (http://data.worldbank.org/indicator/NY.GDP.PCAP.CD). GDP per capita is based on purchasing power parity (PPP). GDP PPP is gross domestic product converted to international dollars using purchasing power parity rates. An international dollar has the same purchasing power over GDP as the US dollar has in the USA. GDP at purchaser's prices is the sum of gross value added by all resident producers in the economy plus any product taxes and minus any subsidies not included in the value of the products. It is calculated without making deductions for depreciation of fabricated assets or for depletion and degradation of natural resources. Data are in current international dollars based on the 2011 ICP round.

The following formula has been used for generating the index approximating the economic distance variable.

$$ED = GDP\ PPP\ per\ capita\ of\ home\ country\\ -\ GDP\ per\ capita\ of\ host\ country\ (Serbia)$$

The model may be summarized in the following algebraic form:

$$\underset{\quad\;\; - \quad\; - \quad\; - \quad -/+}{\mathrm{FDI} = f(\mathrm{CD}, \mathrm{ID}, \mathrm{GD}, \mathrm{ED})}$$

where the signs below the independent variables designate the expected relationship between each one of them and the dependent variable.

The model has been estimated by applying the logarithm transformation of the above-stated form and consequently using the panel OLS econometric technique for each one of the following industrial groups: total manufacturing, low, medium-low, medium-high and high technology manufacturing subsectors, total services, and high technology-intensive services, and low technology-intensive services subsectors.

A sample of six countries, i.e., Austria, Germany, France, Italy, Slovenia, and USA, has been selected. These six countries together are the source of 50% of total direct investments inflows to Serbia. The remaining countries of an initial sample of one town, Hong Kong, and 42 countries, i.e., 25 members of the European Union (Austria, Belgium, Bulgaria, Croatia, Czech Republic, Denmark, Estonia, Finland, France, Germany, Greece, Hungary, Ireland, Italy, Latvia, Lithuania, Luxemburg, the Netherlands, Poland, Portugal, Romania, Slovakia, Slovenia, Spain, and Sweden) nine other European countries (Albania, Bosnia and Herzegovina, FYROM, Montenegro, Norway, Switzerland, Turkey, Ukraine, and UK), while the rest seven are from other continents (Australia, Canada, China, Israel, Russia, United Arab Emirates, and USA), were excluded because values of FDI annual inflows do not exist for several years of the investment period. The data come from the Vienna Institute for International Economic Studies, WIIW, http://data.wiiw.ac.at/. Data on FDI to Serbia by industry for the same countries are selected by the dataset FDI Markets, https://www.fdimarkets.com.

However, data for both high and medium-low technology manufacturing subsectors do not offer sufficient observations for taking unbiased and robust estimation results; the relevant regression analyses were not run. Therefore, estimations were run for medium-high and low technology industrial subsectors only.

4 Empirical Results

Results for total manufacturing are shown in Table 7. Only institutional distance is statistically significant role at 5% level of significance, and its coefficient is negative, meaning that Hypothesis II is verified.

Table 8 presents the results for total services. Only economic distance is statistically significant at the 1% level of significance, and the coefficient sign is positive, meaning that different economic environment between home countries and Serbia is the major determinant of foreign investment in the sector.

Table 7 Linear regression for manufacturing sector

Dependent variable: FDI to manufacturing sector, independent variable: CD, ID, GD, ED				
Usable observations: 78, Degrees of freedom: 74				
Centered R^2: 0.0888355				
Uncentered R^2: 0.3812167				
Durbin–Watson statistic: 1.9252				
Variables	Coefficient	Std error	T-stat	Significant
Cultural distance	−0.000052999	0.000213037	−0.24787	0.80422116
Institutional distance	−1.669919779	0.665178735	−2.51048	0.01424108
Geographic distance	−0.078636868	0.246614173	−0.31887	0.75072646
Economic distance	0.891309910	0.649257484	1.37281	0.17395623

Source Linear regression, Rats 8

Table 8 Linear regression for services sector

Dependent variable: FDI to services sector, Independent variable: CD, ID, GD, ED				
Usable observations: 78, Degrees of freedom: 74				
Centered R^2: 0.0557174				
Uncentered R^2: 0.7118476				
Durbin–Watson statistic: 2.0904				
Variables	Coefficient	Std error	T-stat	Significant
Cultural distance	0.000124935	0.000149602	0.83511	0.40634211
Institutional distance	−0.426728146	0.467113032	−0.91354	0.36392361
Geographic distance	−0.239245787	0.1737181565	−1.38147	0.171290.7
Economic distance	1.184292199	0.455932542	2.59752	0.01132341

Source Linear regression, Rats 8.0

Table 9 shows results for the medium-high technology industrial subsector. All independent variables are statistically insignificant but with the expected coefficient signs in the cases of culture and institutional distances. The positive sign of both economic and geographic distances comes as a surprise because in the case of medium-high technology industries the economic environment of the host country should be similar to the one of the home country supplying agglomeration economies, i.e., location advantages foreign subsidiaries need in order to profit from their ownership specific advantages. The positive sign of geographic distance may be explained that source countries for such industry investments are not located in Serbia's neighborhood. In any case, that agglomeration economies suitable for foreign investments in medium-high technology manufacturing do not exist in Serbia may explain the low level of FDI inflows in such industries and augment the statistical significance of the model in the same pool of manufacturing subsectors.

Results for the low technology industrial subsector are presented in Table 8. Institutional, geographic, and economic distances are statistically significant at 5%, 1%, and 5% level of significance, respectively. The coefficients for both the institutional and geographic distances are negative, while the coefficient of economic distance has a positive sign meaning that as economic distance increases, FDI inflows to the host country low technology industrial subsector increases.

Tables 10 and 11 show the results for low knowledge-intensive service subsector and high knowledge-intensive service subsector of Serbia. Three independent variables, i.e., cultural, geographic, and economic distances, are statistically significant at the 10%, 1%, and 1% level of significance, respectively, in the case of low knowledge-intensive service subsector. The coefficient of both cultural and geographic variables is negative, while for economic distance is positive. For cultural and geographic distances that means that as cultural differences and kilometers between countries increase, FDI inflows decrease. The findings for economic distance suggest

Table 9 Linear regression for medium-high technology industrial subsector

Dependent variable: FDI to medium-high technology industrial subsector, Independent variable: CD, ID, GD, ED				
Usable observations: 36, Degrees of freedom: 32				
Centered R^2: 0.0496469				
Uncentered R^2: 0.3446167				
Durbin–Watson statistic: 1.9084				
Variables	Coefficient	Std error	T-stat	Significant
Cultural distance	−0.411896333	0.721714859	−0.57072	0.57217651
Institutional distance	−1.022646132	0.902667185	−1.13292	0.26566690
Geographic distance	0.005312309	0.354154393	0.01500	0.98812533
Economic distance	0.940120226	1.295019424	0.72595	0.47314554

Source Linear regression, Rats 8.0

Table 10 Linear regression for low technology industrial subsector

Dependent variable: FDI to low technology industrial subsector, Independent variable: CD, ID, GD, ED				
Usable observations: 30, Degrees of freedom: 25				
Centered R^2: 0.3560463				
Uncentered R^2: 0.4538967				
Durbin–Watson statistic: 2.1015				
Variables	Coefficient	Std error	T-stat	Significant
Cultural distance	0.011787302	0.705078738	0.01672	0.98679452
Institutional distance	−1.703743110	0.832348423	−2.04691	0.05132561
Geographic distance	−1.1544137557	0.526664505	−2.93192	0.00710686
Economic distance	4.153086896	1.715391765	2.42107	0.02306619

Source Linear regression, Rats 8.0

Table 11 Linear regression for low knowledge-intensive service subsector

Dependent variable: FDI to low knowledge-intensive service sector, Independent variable: CD, ID, GD, ED				
Usable observations: 36, Degrees of freedom: 32				
Centered R^2: 0.3450689				
Uncentered R^2: 0.6723224				
Durbin–Watson statistic: 2.0178				
Variables	Coefficient	Std. error	T-stat	Significant
Cultural distance	−0.933737793	0.536654700	−1.73992	0.09148367
Institutional distance	0.323895246	0.671207722	0.48256	0.63269584
Geographic distance	−1.109867842	0.263343088	−4.21453	0.00019098
Economic distance	4.175441582	0.962954069	4.33608	0.00013507

Source Linear regression, Rats 8.0

that same economic arbitrage takes place since higher economic distance increases FDI inflows to the selected sector of the host country.

In the case of the high knowledge-intensive service subsector, Table 12 all independent variables are statistically insignificant, except institutional distance. The latter is statistically significant at 8% level of significance. Its coefficient has a negative sign, which means that as institutional differences between home countries and Serbia increase, FDI inflows to this subsector decrease.

Table 12 Linear regression for high knowledge-intensive service subsector

Dependent variable: FDI to knowledge-intensive service sector, Independent variable: CD, ID, GD, ED				
Usable observations: 30, Degrees of freedom: 25				
Centered R^2: 0.2719859				
Uncentered R^2: 0.8901112				
Durbin–Watson statistic: 1.9582				
Variables	Coefficient	Std error	T-stat	Significant
Cultural distance	0.132478858	0.315860392	0.41942	0.67848986
Institutional distance	−0.795059858	0.423109970	−1.87909	0.07193986
Geographic distance	0.031109913	0.233381950	0.13330	0.89502301
Economic distance	0.560803696	0.719287081	0.77967	0.44290647

Source Linear regression, Rats 8.0

5 Conclusion

The aim of this paper is to define the role of the concept of distance in determining cross-border investment transactions using the case of a transition country namely Serbia. In the paper, a model is constructed on the basis of Ghemawat's culture, administrative, geographic, and economic distances (CAGE) framework. The model used in this paper modifies CAGE by substituting administrative with institutional distance. For the purposes of this research, institutional distance is treated as consisting of two dimensions, i.e., regulative distance: anti-trust law, intellectual property rights and legal system, and normative distance: adaptability of government policy, bribe and bureaucratic corruption, independence of local authorities, government effectiveness, risk of political stability and transparency. The cognitive dimension of institutions, i.e., social aspects, is considered as part of culture. The latter contains four dimensions following Hofstede, namely: power distance that shows until what level individuals are comfortable with inequality in relationships; individualism/ collectivism that demonstrates how much individuals focus on their own problems and needs; uncertainty avoidance that explains to which extent people in a group feel threatened by uncertain or unknown situations; and masculinity/ femininity that presents the role of sex in society. In addition, geographic distance equals to kilometer distance between the capitals of source and host countries, and economic distance is measured as differences in GDP per capita between home and host countries determining differences in development levels, especially in agglomeration economies that characterizes development.

The model in its loglinear transformation has been estimated using panel OLS to illustrate how each of the above distance dimensions, i.e., cultural, institutional, geographic, and economic, correlates with FDI at total manufacturing and at different manufacturing subsectors categorized by technological level, i.e., high technology, medium-high technology, medium-low technology, low technology subsectors, and in services sectors and in two services subsectors, i.e., low knowledge-intensive and high knowledge-intensive service subsectors.

Empirical results differentiate substantially between sectors and subsectors showing different impacts of the concept of distance and its dimensions influenced mainly by the technological characteristics of each industry and consequently the type of agglomeration economies required for the efficient implementation of the ownership specific advantages of foreign subsidiaries.

In particular for manufacturing, institutional distance is the only statistically significant independent variable at the 5% level of significance. The sign of its coefficient is negative, which means that MNEs coming from countries with different institutional systems from Serbia will invest less in manufacturing sector than companies coming from countries which share the same institutional system with the host country. This result shows that Serbia, as a country in transition, should focus on developing its institutions since the cost of adapting to distant institutions poses great challenges for MNEs usually operating in rather more advanced institutional environments. However, over the last years, the Serbian market has shown significant development in institutions that minimize bureaucracy for foreign direct investment, increase transparency in business–government communication, protect intellectual property, and minimize corruption in business transactions. This progress is also confirmed by the growing number of FDI inflows in the manufacturing sector.

Regarding services, economic distance is the only statistically significant distance. The sign of coefficient is positive, which is an indication of economic arbitrage. This kind of result should be expected, because exploiting differences in services sector—through outsourcing and offshoring—is probably the most common form of economic arbitrage, especially in cost structures, i.e., labor cost. It is also important to mention that the service sector has been one of the fastest-growing sectors during the last years in Serbia. It has a direct contribution in employment creation and wealth, and its importance in promoting the competitiveness and prospects of other sectors is evident. Hence, it contributes indirectly to job and wealth creation across a broad range of economic activities. Therefore, cheap labor force in Serbia is a magnet for MNEs to invest in this sector.

In the case of medium-high technology manufacturing subsectors, there are no statistically significant independent variables, although R^2 is 34.46% and the Durbin–Watson statistic shows no presence of autocorrelation. This may be explained by the fact that there are missing observations for some years of the period of investigation, i.e., 2004–2015. However, the coefficients have the expected signs. Results for low technology manufacturing subsector demonstrate that three distances, i.e., institutional, geographic, and economic, are statistically significant at the 8%, 1%, and 1% level of significance, respectively. Economic distance coefficient has a positive sign, and the other two statistically significant variables have the expected coefficient. The low technology manufacturing subsector is rather more sensitive to labor cost than other costs stemming from other distances. However, an institutional environment that safeguards profitability is required.

Results for FDI inflows to low knowledge-intensive services subsector show that geographic and economic distances are strongly statistically significant, while cultural distance is statistically significant at the 10% level of significant. The coefficients of both cultural and geographic distances are negative, as expected. Economic distance has a positive coefficient, meaning that MNEs are searching for economic arbitrage. In the case of the knowledge-intensive services subsector, the only statistically significant independent variable is institutional distance.

Overall, foreign subsidiaries in Serbia are seeking for economic arbitrage, i.e., to take advantage of relatively low labor cost given that there is an efficient institutional environment, i.e., government effectiveness, regulatory quality, rule of law, voice and accountability, political stability and absence of violence and control of corruption close to the one experiencing in their home countries.

Appendix 1

Aggregation of the manufacturing industry according to technological intensity and based on NACE Rev.2
High technology
• Manufacture of basic pharmaceutical products and pharmaceutical preparations • Manufacture of computer, electronic, and optical products • Manufacture of air and spacecraft and related machinery
Medium-high technology
• Manufacture of chemicals and chemical products • Manufacture of weapons and ammunition • Manufacture of electrical equipment • Manufacture of machinery and equipment n.e.c. • Manufacture of motor vehicles, trailers, and semi-trailers • Manufacture of other transport equipment excluding building of ships and boats and excluding manufacture of air and spacecraft and related machinery • Manufacture of medical and dental instruments and supplies
Medium-low technology
• Reproduction of recorded media • Manufacture of coke and refined petroleum products • Manufacture of rubber and plastic products • Manufacture of other non-metallic mineral products • Manufacture of basic metals • Manufacture of fabricated metal products, except machinery and equipment excluding manufacture of weapons and ammunition • Building of ships and boats • Repair and installation of machinery and equipment

(continued)

(continued)

Low technology
• Manufacture of food products • Manufacture of beverages • Manufacture of tobacco products • Manufacture of textiles • Manufacture of wearing apparel • Manufacture of leather and related products • Manufacture of wood and of products of wood and cork, except furniture; manufacture of articles of straw and plaiting materials • Manufacture of paper and paper products • Printing and reproduction of recorded media excluding reproduction of recorded media • Manufacture of furniture • Other manufacturing excluding manufacture of medical and dental instruments and supplies

Source Eurostat, http://ec.europa.eu/eurostat/statisticsexplained/index.php/Glossary:High-tech_classification_of_manufacturing_industries

High tech knowledge-intensive services
· Motion picture, video and television program production, sound recording, and music publishing activities · Programming and broadcasting activities · Telecommunications · Computer programming, consultancy, and related activities · Information service activities · Scientific research and development

Source Eurostat, http://ec.europa.eu/eurostat/statistics-explained/index.php/Glossary:Knowledge-intensive_services_(KIS)

Appendix 2

World Bank Governance Indicators to measure ID

	Name of the WGI	Definition	Component of ID
1.	Government effectiveness	The quality of public services; the capacity of the civil service and its independence from political pressures; and the quality of policy formulation	Regulative

(continued)

(continued)

	Name of the WGI	Definition	Component of ID
2.	Regulatory quality	The ability of the government to provide sound policies and regulations that enable and promote private sector development	Regulative
3.	Rule of law	The extent to which agents have confidence in and abide by the rules of society, including the quality of contract enforcement and property rights, the police, and the courts, as well as the likelihood of crime and violence	Regulative
4.	Voice and accountability	The extent to which country's citizens are able to participate in selecting their government, as well as freedom of expression, freedom of association, and a free media	Normative
5.	Quality political stability and absence of violence	The likelihood that the government will be destabilized by unconstitutional or violent means, including terrorism	Normative

Source Kaufmann et al. (1999)

References

Arslan, A., & Larimo, J. (2010). Ownership strategy of multinational enterprises and the impacts of regulative and normative institutional distance: Evidence from finnish foreign direct investments in Central and Eastern Europe. *Journal of East-West Business, 16*(3), 179–200.

Beckerman, W. (1956). Distance and the pattern of intra-European trade. *The Review of Economics and Statistics, 28*, 31–40.

Berry, H., Guillén M. F., & Zhou N. (2010). An institutional approach to cross-national distance. *Journal of International Business Studies, 41*(9), 1460–1480.

Brouthers, K. D. (2002). Institutional, cultural and transaction cost influences on entry mode choice and performance. *Journal of International Business Studies, 33*(2), 203–221.

Brouthers, K. D., & Brouthers, L. E. (2001). Explaining the national cultural distance paradox. *Journal of International Business Studies, 32*(1), 177–189.

Buchanan, B. G., Le, Q. V., & Rishi, M. (2012). Foreign direct investment and institutional quality: Some empirical evidence. *International Review of Financial Analysis, 21,* 81–89.

Busse, M., & Hefeker, C. (2007). Political risk, institutions and foreign direct investment. *European Journal of Political Economy, 23*(2), 397–415.

Chao, M. C. H., & Kumar, V. (2010). The impact of institutional distance on the international diversity–performance relationship. *Journal of World Business, 45*(1), 93–103.

Daude, C., & Stein, E. (2007). The quality of institutions and foreign direct investment. *Economics and Politics, 19*(3), 317–344.

Dikova, D., & Van Witteloostuijn, A. (2007). Foreign direct investment mode choice: entry and establishment modes in transition economies. *Journal of International Business Studies, 38*(6), 1013–1033.

Drogendijk, R., & Slagengen, A. (2006). Hofstede, Schwartz, or managerial perceptions? The effects of different cultural distance measures on establishment mode choice by multinational enterprises. *International Business Review, 15,* 361–380.

Dunning, J. H. (1988). The eclectic paradigm of international production: A restatement and some possible extensions. *Journal of International Business Studies, 19,* 1–31.

Dunning, J. H. (2000). The eclectic paradigm as an envelope for economic and business theories of MNE activity. *International Business Review, 9,* 163–190.

Dunning, J. H. (2001). The eclectic (OLI) paradigm of international production: Past, present and future. *International Journal of the Economics of Business, 8*(2), 173–190.

Egger, P., & Winner, H. (2005). Evidence on corruption as an incentive for foreign direct investment. *European Journal of Political Economy, 21*(4), 932–952.

Erramilli, M. (1996). Nationality and subsidiary ownership patterns in multinational corporations. *Journal of International Business Studies, 26,* 225–248.

Estrin, S., Baghdasaryan, D., & Meyer, K. E. (2009). The impact of institutional and human resource distance on international entry strategies. *Journal of Management Studies, 46*(7), 1171–1196.

Eurostat Statistics Database. (2017). http://ec.europa.eu/eurostat/statistics-explained/index.php/Foreign_direct_investment_statistics. Accessed June 1, 2017.

FDI Markets database. (2017). Available https://www.fdimarkets.com/. Accessed April 11, 2017.

Filipovic, M., Hadzic, M., & Pavic, M. (2006). Privatisation process and the role of foreign direct investment (FDI) in Serbia-montentegro. *Agora Without Frontiers, 12*(2), 218–246.

Gaur, A. S., Delios, A., & Singh, K. (2007). Institutional environments, staffing strategies and subsidiary performance. *Journal of Management, 33*(4), 611–636.

Gaur, A. S., & Lu, W. (2007). Ownership strategies and survival of foreign subsidiaries: Impacts of institutional distance and experience. *Journal of Management, 33*(1), 84–110.

Ghemawat, P. (2001). Distance still matters. *Harvard Business Review, 79*(8), 137–147.

Ghemawat, P. (2007). *Redefining global strategy: Crossing borders in a world where differences still matter*. Harvard Business School Press.

Ghemawat, P. (2010). The globalization of markets. In *Globalization note series*. Available http://www.ghemawat.com/management/files/AcademicResources/Globalization%20of%20Markets.pdf.

Globerman, S., & Shapiro, D. (2002). Global foreign direct investment flows: The role of governance infrastructure. *World Development, 30*(11), 899–1919.

Habib, M., & Zurawicki, L. (2002). Corruption and foreign direct investment. *Journal of International Business Studies, 33,* 2.

Hansen, M., & Lovas, B. (2004). How do multinational companies leverage technological competencies? Moving from single to interdependent explanations. *Strategic Management Journal, 25*(8:4), 801–822.

Harms, P., & Ursprung, H. W. (2002). Do civil and political repression really boost foreign direct investments? *Economic Inquiry, 40*(4), 651–663.

Head, K., & Mayer, T. (2002). *Illusory border effects: Distance mismeasurement inflates estimates of home bias in trade*. CEPII working paper 2002-01.

Hennart, J. F., & Larimo, J. (1998). The impact of culture on the strategy of multinational enterprises: Does national origin affect ownership decisions? *Journal of International Business Studies, 29*(3), 515–538.

Hofstede, G. (1980). *Culture's consequences*. Beverly Hills, CA: Sage.

Hofstede, G. (1984). *Culture's consequences, international differences in work- related values*. Abridged edition, SAGE Publications.

Hofstede, G., Hofstede, G. J., & Minkov, M. (1991). *Culture and organizations: Software of the mind*. USA: McGraw-Hill.

House, R. J., Hanges, P. J., Javidan, M., Dorfman, P. W., & Gupta, V. (2004). *Culture, leadership, and organizations. The GLOBE study of 62 societies*. Thousand Oaks, CA: Sage.
Huntington, S. P. (1968). *Political order in changing societies*. New Haven: Yale University Press.
Hymer, S. (1976, 1960 dissertation). *The international operations of nation firms: A study of foreign direct investments*. Cambridge: MLP Press. Available at: http://teaching.ust.hk/~mgto650p/meyer/readings/1/01_Hymer.pdf.
Iyer, G. R. (1997). Comparative marketing: An interdisciplinary framework for institutional analysis. *Journal of International Business Studies, 28*(3), 531–561.
Javorcik, B. S. (2004). The composition of foreign direct investment and protection of intellectual property rights: Evidence from transition economies. *European Economic Review, 48*(1), 39–62.
Jensen, N. M. (2003). Democratic governance and multinational corporations: Political regimes and inflows of foreign direct investment. *International Organization, 57*(3), 587–616.
Johnson, J. L., Cullen, J. B., & Sakano, T. (1991). Cultural congruency in international joint ventures: Does it matter? In *Proceedings of the Eastern Academy of Management Fourth Biennial International Conference*. Nice, France, June 1991.
Johanson, J., & Vahlne J. E. (1977). The internalization process of the firm: A model of knowledge development and increasing foreign market commitments. *Journal of International Business Studies, Spring/Summer, 8*, 23–32.
Kaufmann, D., Kraay, A., & Zoido-Lobaton, P. (1999). Aggregating governance indicators. In *Policy research paper 2195*, The World Bank.
Kim, W. C., & Hwang, P. (1992). Global strategy and multinational entry mode choice. *Journal of International Business Studies, 23*(1), 29–53.
Kogut, B., & Singh, H. (1988). The effect of national culture on the choice of entry mode. *Journal of International Business Studies, 19*(3), 411–432.
Kolstad, I., & Villanger, E. (2008). Determinants of foreign direct investment in services. *European Journal of Political Economy, 24*(2), 518–533.
Kostova, T. (1997). Country institutional profiles: Concept and measurement. In *Academy of Management Proceedings* (pp. 180–184).
Kostova, T., & Roth, K. (2002). Adoption of an organizational practice by subsidiaries of multinational corporations: Institutional and relational effects. *Academy of Management Journal, 45*(1), 215–233.
Kostova, T., & Zaheer, S. (1999). Organizational legitimacy under conditions of complexity: The case of the multinational enterprise. *Academy of Management Review, 24*(3), 64–81.
La Porta, R., Lopez de Silanes, F., Shleifer, A., & Vishny, R. (1998). Law and finance. *Journal of Political Economy, 106*(6), 1113–1155.
Leff, N. H. (1964). Economic development through bureaucratic corruption. *American Behavioral Scientist, 8*(3), 8–14.
Li, J. T., & Guisinger, S. (1991). Comparative business failures of foreign-controlled firms in the United States. *Journal of International Business Studies, 22*(2), 209–224.
Mauro, P. (1995). Corruption and growth. *The Quarterly Journal of Economics, 110*(3), 681–712.
Mayer, T, & Zignago, S. (2005). *Market access in global and regional trade*. CEPII working paper 2.
McSweeney, B. (2002). Hofstede's model of national cultural differences and their consequences: A triumph of faith—A failure of analysis. *Human Relations, 55*(1), 89–118.
Mengistu, A. A., & Adhikary, B. K. (2011). Does good governance matter for FDI inflows? *Evidence from Asian Economies, Asia Pacific Business Review, 17*(3), 281–299.
Nordstrom, K. A., & Vahlne, J. E. (1994). Is the world shrinking? Psychic distance and the establishment of Swedish sales subsidiaries during the last 100 years. In Landeck, M. (Eds.), *International Trade: Regional and Global Issues* (pp. 41–56). New York: St Martin's Press.
North, D. C. (1990). *Institutions, institutional change and economic performance*. New York: Cambridge University Press.
Ozawa, T. (1979). International investment and industrial structure: New theoretical implications from the Japanese experience. *Oxford Economic Papers, 31*(1), 72–92.

Park, S. H., & Ungson, G. R. (1997). The effect of national culture, organizational complementarity, and economic motivation on joint venture dissolution. *Academy of Management Journal, 40*(2), 279–307.
Peng, M. W. (2003). Institutional transitions and strategic choices. *Academy of Management Review, 28*(2), 275–296.
Porter, M., Takeuchi, E., & Sakakibara, H. M. (2000). *Can Japan compete?*. London: Macmillan Press.
Quazi, R. (2007). Economic freedom and foreign direct investment in East Asia. *Journal of the Asia Pacific Economy, 12*(3), 329–344.
Rose-Ackerman, S. (1975). The economics of corruption. *Journal of Public Economics, 4*(2), 187–203.
Schwartz, S. H. (1994). Beyond individualism/collectivism: New cultural dimensions of values. In U. Kim, H. C. Triandis, C. Kagitcibasi, S. C. Choi, & G. Yoon (Eds.), *Individualism and collectivism: Theory, methods, and applications* (pp. 85–119). Thousand Oaks: Sage Publications.
Schwartz, H. S. (2008). *Cultural value orientations: Nature & implications of national differences*. Moscow: Publishing House of SU HSE.
Scott, W. R. (1995). *Institutions and organizations*. Thousand Oaks, CA: Sage Publications Inc.
Shenkar, O. (2001). Cultural distance revisited: Towards a more rigorous conceptualization and measurement of cultural differences. *Journal of International Business Studies, 32*(3), 519–535.
Shleifer, A., & Vishny, R. W. (1993). Corruption. *The Quarterly Journal of Economics, 108*(3), 599–617.
Solocha, A., & Soskin, M. D. (1994). Canadian direct investment, mode of entry, and border location. *MIR: Management International Review, 34*(1), 79–95.
Steenkamp, J. B. E. M. (2001). The role of national culture in international marketing research. *International Marketing Review, 18*(1), 30–44.
The Vienna Institute for International Economic Studies (WIIW). (2016). Available https://data.wiiw.ac.at/. Accessed December 5, 2016.
Tihanyi, L., Griffith, D. A., & Russell, C. J. (2005). The effect of cultural distance on entry mode choice, international diversification, and MNE performance: A meta-analysis. *Journal of International Business Studies, 36*(3), 270–283.
Trevino, L. J., & Mixon, F. G. (2004). Strategic factors affecting foreign direct investment decisions by multi- national enterprises in Latin America. *Journal of World Business, 39*(2), 233–243.
Trompenaars, F. (1993). *Riding the waves of culture: Understanding cultural diversity in business*. London: Nicholas Brealey.
Tsang, E., & Yip, P. (2007). Economic distance and the survival of foreign direct investments. *Academy of Management Journal, 50*(5), 1156–1168.
Tuman, J. P., & Emmert, C. E. (1999). Explaining Japanese foreign direct investment in Latin America, 1979–1992. *Social Science Quarterly, 80*(3), 539–555.
Voyer, P. A., & Beamish, P. W. (2004). The effect of corruption on Japanese foreign direct investment. *Journal of Business Ethics, 50*(30), 211–224.
Wei, S. J. (2000). How taxing is corruption on internal investors? *The Review of Economics and Statistics, 82*(1), 1–11.
Wheeler, D., & Mody, A. (1992). International investment location decisions: The case of U.S. firms. *Journal of International Economics, 33*(1–2), 57–76.
World Bank. (2005). Available http://www.worldbank.org/. Accessed April 20, 2017.
Xu, D. (2001). *The effect of institutional distance on multinational enterprise strategy*. York University, Toronto: PhD Dissertation.
Xu, D., Pan, Y., & Beamish, P. W. (2004). The effect of regulative and normative distances on MNE ownership and expatriate strategies. *Management International Review, 44*(3), 285–307.
Xu, D., & Shenkar, O. (2002). Institutional distance and multinational enterprise. *Academy of Management Review, 27*(4), 608–618.
Yeung, H. W. C. (1997). Business networks and transnational corporations: A study of Hong-Kong firms in the ASEAN region. *Economic Geography, 73*(1), 1–25.

Yiu, D., & Makino, S. (2002). The choice between joint venture and wholly owned subsidiary: An institutional perspective. *Organization Science, 13*(6), 667–683.

Yoshino, M. Y. (1976). *Japan's multinational enterprises*. Cambridge, MA: Harvard University Press.

Zaheer, S., & Zaheer, A. (1997). Country effects on information seeking in global electronic networks. *Journal of International Business Studies, 28*(1), 77–100.

The Financial Services Exports of China and the Role of RMB

Spyros Roukanas and Emmanouil Karakostas

Abstract The ascent of China as an economic power in recent years has given a rise to lots of consideration its role in the global economic system. China is the largest manufacturer in the world, and because of its huge population and relatively low wages, it has earned a competitive place in the global economy. Concerning services exports, their structure has changed dramatically over the period 2000–2017. Moreover, the establishment of the China (Shanghai) Pilot Free Trade Zone and the further deregulation of the financial sector have facilitated the provision of financial services. Despite the status of its currency, China is driving it towards a path of internationalisation. China's two primary aims are to promote the use of the Renminbi in foreign trade by increasing its appeal and availability, and to encourage its use as a store of value in international finance. The purpose of this paper is to show whether China has a Revealed Comparative Advantage in financial services exports. Furthermore, we will try to show the correlation between Chinese financial services exports and the exchange rate of Renminbi. The methodology adopted is the theory of comparative advantage.

Keywords Revealed comparative advantage · Competitiveness · Economy of China · Exchange rates

1 Introduction

China's economy is a major global growth driver. The IMF (2018a) predicts that although global growth for 2018 and 2019 had been revised upwards by 0.2% point to 3.9%, the growth is expected to moderate gradually in China. According to Bagaria and Ismail (2017), China is not only a powerful player in the world market for low-

S. Roukanas · E. Karakostas (✉)
Department of International and European Studies, University of Piraeus, 126 Gr. Lampraki Str., 18534 Piraeus, Greece
e-mail: ekarakwstas@unipi.gr

S. Roukanas
e-mail: sroukana@unipi.gr

M. Janowicz-Lomott et al. (eds.), *Economic and Financial Challenges for Balkan and Eastern European Countries*, Springer Proceedings in Business and Economics,
https://doi.org/10.1007/978-3-030-39927-6_5

and medium-technology-based exports, but its high-technology exports have also increased over time. But, what is the cause of China's growth? Rodrik (2006) suggests that China has benefited from two factors, the first one being its good fundamentals (such as low labour and material costs, and large market size) and the second being the government's effort to create a modern industrial-based economy. Nowadays, China is one of the most important services exporters (fifth in the world in 2014), as well as one of the largest services importers (Loungani et al. 2017).

As regards financial services in China, firstly, it is important to point out that China has got by far the biggest potential financial market for global financial firms, and as Carpenter et al. (2018, p. 4) mention:

> China's stock market not only offers high average monthly returns compared with stock markets in other large economies, but also exhibits low correlation with these markets.

China's stock market seems to poise for a greater role in domestic and international capital allocation. China's accession to the World Trade Organization has reduced antidumping investigations from other countries, and China is considered as a market economy country, although there are still some members of WTO that are treating China as a non-market economy (Urdinez and Masiero 2015).

The aim of this paper is to demonstrate whether China has a Revealed Comparative Advantage (RCA) in financial services exports, in order to assume that China is passing from labour cost and low-technology exports to financial services exports. Johansson (2010) argues that China's financial market integration with the rest of the world increases at a slow pace and from very low levels, for three main reasons: trade, foreign direct investment (FDI) and the internationalisation of Chinese firms. What is the role of the Renminbi? Cohen (2017) suggests that the internationalisation of China's currency has been pursued along two ways. The first focuses on the use of the currency in foreign trade; namely, China has arranged swap agreements with an increasing number of foreign central banks, facilitating the expanded use of the Renminbi as a means of payment. The other track focuses on the Renminbi's use as a store of value in international finance has emphasised the development of active markets for Renminbi deposits and Renminbi-denominated bonds, mainly in the Hong Kong "offshore" market. This paper will try to prove whether China has an RCA in financial services exports and whether there is a correlation with the Chinese currency. The present study is structured as follows: firstly, we present China's macroeconomic indicators for the period between 2007 and 2017, and a theoretical overview of China's comparative advantage and its definition, and finally, the correlation between China's exports of services and China's real exchange rate between 2007 and 2017. This research was based on the theory of Revealed Comparative Advantage and the finding of Pearson correlation. Finally, it was based on the analysis of the results to answer the research question.

2 The Economy of China

This chapter analyses China's macroeconomic data for the period between 2007 and 2017. The macroeconomic data under review are: GDP, the growth rate, government debt, fiscal deficit, inflation, unemployment and, finally, the current account balance. Table 1 shows China's main macroeconomic fundamentals from 2007 to 2017.

The data from the period 2007–2017 show that, first, the GDP has been continuously increasing during the period under review, reaching its highest value of 12.01 billion $ in 2017, from a 3.57 billion $ low in 2007. In contrast, the real GDP growth rate fell from 2007 to 2017, registering its highest value in 2007 at 14.2% and its lowest in 2016 at 6.7%. Government debt as a percentage of Chinese GDP has increased for the period under review, reaching its highest value of 47.8% in 2017. The general government net lending/borrowing ratio followed a downward path and in 2017 stood at −4%. Inflation has decreased in the period under review, but there were fluctuations from 2007 to 2011. The unemployment rate has been extremely steady, at approximately 4.0%. The current account balance has decreased significantly for the period under review, starting from its highest value of 9.9% in 2007 and reaching its lowest value of 1.4% in 2017.

According to Morrison (2017, p. 9): "'China's share of global GDP on a PPP basis rose from 2.3% in 1980 to 17.8% in 2016, while the U.S. share of global GDP on a PPP basis fell from 24.3% to 15.5%. Moreover, the PPP measurement also raises China's 2016 nominal per capita GDP (from $8113) to $15,399, which was

Table 1 Macroeconomic indicators of China for the period 2007–2017

Year	GDP, current prices (billions of US dollars)	Real GDP growth (annual % change)	Government debt (% of GDP)	General government net lending/borrowing (% of GDP)	Inflation rate, average consumer prices (annual % change)	Unemployment rate (%)	Current account balance (% of GDP)
2007	3.57	14.2	29.0	0.1	4.8	4.0	9.9
2008	4.6	9.6	27.0	0	5.9	4.2	9.1
2009	5.12	9.2	34.3	−1.7	−0.7	4.3	4.7
2010	6.07	10.6	33.7	−0.4	3.3	4.1	3.9
2011	7.52	9.5	33.6	−0.1	5.4	4.1	1.8
2012	8.57	7.9	34,3	−0.3	2.6	4.1	2.5
2013	9.64	7.8	37.0	−0.8	2.6	4.1	1.5
2014	10.53	7.3	39.9	−0.9	2.0	4.1	2.2
2015	11.23	6.9	41.1	−2.8	1.4	4.1	2.7
2016	11.22	6.7	44.3	−3.7	2.0	4.0	1.8
2017	12.01	6.9	47.8	−4	1.6	3.9	1.4

Source International Monetary Fund (2018b)

26.8% of the U.S. level and China currently has free trade agreements (FTAs) with 23 partners".

China has formed a financial services network, which includes institutional arrangements such as the Qualified Domestic Institutional Investor and Qualified Foreign Institutional Investor Schemes, as well as the Shanghai-Hong Kong Stock Connect, the Shenzhen-Hong Kong Stock Connect and the Bond Connect that generate significant advantages; for example, the financial services network has broadened the investment and financing channels, has promoted interconnectivity between the domestic and foreign capital markets and has increased the efficiency of financial resource allocation (Zhu et al. 2018). The next step of this paper is the study and review of the Revealed Comparative Advantage for the financial services exports of China.

3 The Revealed Comparative Advantage Approach

In this section, we will study China's comparative advantage *vis-a-vis* the financial services exports of the USA and Hong Kong, in order to determine both the competitiveness of China's financial services and the development of its Revealed Comparative Advantage over the period under review (2007–2017).

Comparative advantage provides the theoretical background for studying the benefits of international trade. The Revealed Comparative Advantage (RCA) method is the traditional method for revealing comparative advantage. Balassa gives the definition of the comparative advantage in his article (1965) "Trade Liberalization and Revealed Comparative Advantage".

According to the World Trade Organization (2012, p. 26), Revealed Comparative Advantage is the ratio of the share of product *k* in the exports of country *i* to its share in international trade.

In the formula form:

$$\mathrm{RCAi} = \left(\mathrm{X}_{\mathrm{i,j}} / \sum \mathrm{X}_{\mathrm{j}}\right) / \left(\mathrm{X}_{\mathrm{i,World}} / \sum \mathrm{X}_{\mathrm{World}}\right)$$

where

RCAi = Revealed Comparative Advantage for good i.
$\mathrm{X}_{\mathrm{i,j}}$ = exports of good i by country j.
$\sum \mathrm{X}_{\mathrm{j}}$ = total exports by country j.
$X_{\mathrm{i,World}}$ = world exports of good i.
$\sum \mathrm{X}_{\mathrm{World}}$ = total world exports.

Any value of the Revealed Comparative Advantage that is greater than the unit (RCA > 1) for the country (or sector) *k* of country *i* means that country *i* has a comparative advantage in this field. Table 2 shows the major exporters and importers of financial services of 2015 and 2016.

Table 2 Major exporters and importers of financial services, 2015 and 2016 (million dollars and share)

	Value		Share in 10 economies
	2015	2016	2015
Exporters			
European Union (28)	221,944	212,183	53.6
USA	102,461	96,752	24.7
Singapore	21,061	18,872	5.1
Switzerland	20,698	19,924	5.0
Hong Kong, China	19,179	18,121	4.6
Japan	10,288	11,646	2.5
Canada	8034	8084	1.9
India	5344	5083	1.3
Australia	2829	2731	0.7
Chinese Taipei	2422	2608	0.6
Importers			
European Union (28)	115,441	116,369	66.2
USA	25,162	25,232	14.4
Canada	7019	7634	4.0
Japan	5994	6200	3.4
Hong Kong, China	4811	4687	2.8
Singapore	4406	4530	2.5
Switzerland	3719	3782	2.1
India	3117	5021	1.8
China	2640	2035	1.5
Russian Federation	2001	2030	1.1

Source WTO (2017)

Table 3 shows the course of the financial services exports and the exports of goods and services of China, the USA, Hong Kong and the world for the period between 2007 and 2016.

Table 3 indicates that financial services exports increased between 2007 and 2016, but there was a slight reduction between 2014 and 2016 for the USA, Mainland China and the world, albeit not for Hong Kong. As regards the exports of goods and services, the table shows an increase from 2007 to 2016, but with slight reduction between 2014 and 2016 for Mainland China, the world and Hong Kong, albeit not for the USA. Table 4 shows the results of the calculation of the Revealed Comparative Advantage for the period 2007–2016.

Table 3 Financial services exports and the exports of goods and services of China, the USA, the world and Hong Kong, for the period 2007–2016

Year	Mainland China		USA		World		Hong Kong—China	
	Financial services exports[a], US dollars at current prices (million $)	Exports of services, US dollars at current prices (billion $)	Financial services exports[a], US dollars at current prices (billion $)	Exports of services, US dollars at current prices (billion $)	Financial services exports[a], US dollars at current prices (billion $)	Exports of services, US dollars at current prices (trillion $)	Financial services exports[a], US dollars at current prices (billion $)	Exports of services, US dollars at current prices (billion $)
2007	230$	125,447$	61,376$	488,394$	346,950$	3634$	12,440$	64,454$
2008	315$	145,343$	63,027$	532,819$	353,370$	4080$	11,998$	69,906$
2009	356$	122,563$	64,437$	512,721$	315,190$	3641$	11,286$	64,670$
2010	1331$	117,532$	72,348$	563,330$	338,000$	3923$	13,082$	80,541$
2011	849$	201,047$	78,271$	627,779$	385,670$	4474$	14,377$	91,304$
2012	1886$	201,576$	76,692$	656,411$	378,760$	4590$	15,559$	98,504$
2013	3185$	207,006$	95,131$	701,451$	419,530$	4884$	16,513$	104,777$
2014	4530$	219,141$	107,712$	741,917$	455,380$	5192$	17,668$	106,922$
2015	2339$	217,399$	102,461$	753,150$	437,450$	4920$	19,179$	104,356$
2016	3180$	208,404$	96,752$	752,365$	420,270$	4958$	18,121$	98,533$

Source World Bank Data (2018), [a]WTO (2018)

Table 4 Financial services exports—Revealed Comparative Advantage for the period 2007–2016

Revealed Comparative Advantage for the period 2007–2016			
RCA—value			
Years	Mainland China	USA	Hong Kong—China
2007	0.01	1.31	2.03
2008	0.02	1.37	1.98
2009	0.02	1.45	2.02
2010	0.12	1.48	1.88
2011	0.04	1.44	1.82
2012	0.10	1.41	1.91
2013	0.17	1.58	1.84
2014	0.22	1.67	1.89
2015	0.11	1.54	2.07
2016	0.17	1.52	2.17

Source Authors' calculations

The analysis of the data indicates that *for the period under review (2007–2016)* China *does not have a Revealed Comparative Advantage in comparison with the USA*. The USA has a Revealed Comparative Advantage, and the same stands for Hong Kong, in contrast to Mainland China. Hong Kong has the highest RCA values, the highest value being 2.17, and the USA has a stable value, with an average RCA of 1.47 during the period under review. Even though China has increased its total exports of goods and services compared to the USA, it is far behind in terms of financial services. China has a long road ahead to succeed in the financial field. It would be useful to refer to examine the role of China's currency in the global economic system. This will be done in the next session.

4 Overview of the Chinese Renminbi

It is important to refer to the currency of China. What is the path that China's exchange rate regime has followed until today? Prior to 1994, China maintained a dual exchange rate system; more specifically, China had two exchange rate systems, an official fixed exchange rate system (which was used by the government) and a relatively market-based exchange rate system that was used by importers and exporters in "swap markets". China's dual exchange rate system was criticised by the USA because of the restrictions that it placed on foreign imports. In 1994, the Chinese government unified the two exchange rate systems at an initial rate of 8.70 yuan to the dollar, and this was maintained until July 2005 (Morrison and Labonte 2011). As Yip et al. (2017, p. 3) point out:

> on 21 July 2005, China announced its exchange rate system reform with some key features, such as Renminbi was revalued against the USD with 2.1% revaluation, the Renminbi-USD exchange rate would be allowed to fluctuate within a very narrow band of ±0.3% and Renminbi would be monitored against an undisclosed basket of currencies instead of against the USD only.

China's exchange rate system reform since July 2005 has represented a shift away exit from a fixed exchange rate system.

According to Mertens and Shultz (2017, p. 1):

> China has changed its foreign exchange policy repeatedly over the past decades. Particularly, the People's Bank of China (PBOC), was classified as a conventional peg to the U.S. dollar from 2003 to 2005, from 2006 to 2008, the Renminbi was allowed to gradually appreciate under a policy classified as a crawling peg to the U.S. dollar, between 2008 and 2010, it was stabilized relative to the dollar, in 2010, the policy changed to a 'crawl-like arrangement' relative to the U.S. dollar, in 2015, published an exchange rate index of 13 currencies in an effort to shift markets away from interpreting Renminbi exchange rate movements as being driven only by its connection to the U.S. dollar and in 2016 the flexibility of the Renminbi is relative to a group or 'basket' of currencies.

China's current exchange rate regime is not conducive to the internationalisation of the Renminbi, because of the fact that the Renminbi is always facing unilateral appreciation or depreciation, and a relaxation of capital controls, which leads to large-scale

Table 5 Top 15 offshore Renminbi economies by weight

	Countries	Percentage
1	Hong Kong	75.03
2	UK	5.85
3	Singapore	5.07
4	Korea	2.86
5	USA	2.54
6	Taiwan	2.28
7	France	1.44
8	Australia	0.83
9	Germany	0.79
10	Japan	0.76
11	Luxembourg	0.40
12	Netherlands	0.33
13	Canada	0.23
14	Macau	0.23
15	Sweden	0.22

Source SWIFT(2018b)

capital inflows or outflows, and as a result could seriously threaten macroeconomic stability. Therefore, a floating exchange rate regime should be implemented (Zhang 2018).

Furthermore, Hong Kong remains (Table 5) the largest Renminbi clearing centre with a 76% share of activity, but a "marked decline" in Renminbi deposits occurred in Hong Kong, owing to factors including the capital controls imposed by the Chinese government and the emergence of new opportunities for direct investment into Mainland China (SWIFT 2018a).

Is the Chinese currency in the process of internationalisation? Zhang and Zhang (2017) indicate that the Chinese government has had five main motivations in order to promote Renminbi internationalisation since 2009: firstly, to match the Renminbi's global status with the Chinese economy's global status; secondly, to reduce reliance on the US dollar (USD) in cross-border trade and investment; thirdly, to facilitate the Chinese enterprises' international operations, such as outward direct investment or obtaining funds on international financial markets; fourthly, to stimulate the development of both Renminbi onshore and offshore financial markets; and, finally, to push forward domestic structural reforms, by using Renminbi's internationalisation.

According to McDowell and Steinberg (2017), the Renminbi has enormous potential as a major international reserve currency, because of various factors. We shall refer to two major factors. The first is China's economic size and share in world trade. For example, in 2015 about a quarter of its trade was settled in its own currency, which, in 2013, became the second most used currency in international trade finance. The other factor is the country's economic ties; that is, China represents

Table 6 Renminbi as a domestic and international payment currency

February 2016			February 2018		
1	USD	41.40%	1	USD	38.00%
2	EUR	31.47%	2	EUR	34.29%
3	GBP	8.78%	3	GBP	7.34%
4	JPY	3.16%	4	JPY	3.29%
5	**CNY**	1.76%	5	CHF	1.64%
6	CAD	1.73%	6	CAD	1.57%
7	CHF	1.52%	7	**CNY**	1.56%
8	AUD	1.52%	8	AUD	1.48%
9	SEK	1.02%	9	HKD	1.31%
10	HKD	1.00%	10	THB	1.06%

Source SWIFT (2018c)
Bold indicates in order to emphasize the Chinese currency among the other currencies

an important strategic partner, a key export market and a major source of development financing in the global economic system. Despite its advantages, China also has certain weaknesses, such as a lack of capital account openness, financial market development and monetary stability, while its banking sector has also been resistant to financial reform. Does the rise of Renminbi pose a challenge for the dollar? Haihong (2017) argues that the dollar is still the most important currency in the world and it has the most liquid, deep and broad market in the world. However, the Renminbi has gained in international influence (Table 6), which is now significant, particularly among BRICS countries, while the international monetary system passes from a bipolar bloc (consisting of the US dollar and the European or "euro" bloc) to a tri-polar currency bloc (including the Renminbi bloc) (Tovar and Nor 2018).

One of the strategies that the International Monetary Institute (2017) proposes for building the Renminbi credit market is trade. The IMI also suggests that trade should be the main path to Renminbi credit expansion, and funds should be directed "from virtual to real" so that the international competitiveness of enterprises can be enhanced. Since trade could be the way to achieve the internationalisation of a currency, it would be appropriate to examine the correlation between real exchange rates and financial services exports.

5 Calculation of the Pearson Correlation

This section attempts to study whether there is a correlation between the percentage change of China's financial services exports and the percentage change of the Real Broad Effective Exchange Rate for China and Hong Kong. The Pearson correlation coefficient is a statistical measure of the strength of a linear relationship between the paired data. The Pearson correlation calculation formula is:

$$r_{xy} = \frac{\sum_{i=1}^{n}(x_i - \bar{x})(y_i - \bar{y})}{\sqrt{\sum_{i=1}^{n}(x_i - \bar{x})^2 \sum_{i=1}^{n}(y_i - \bar{y})^2}}$$

where X is the percentage change of China's financial services exports and Y is the percentage change of the Real Broad Effective Exchange Rate for China. Positive values indicate positive linear correlation. Negative values indicate negative linear correlation. A value of 0 does not indicate a linear correlation. The closer the value is to 1 or −1, the stronger the linear correlation is. Table 7 shows the course of the percentage change of China's financial services exports and the percentage change of the Real Broad Effective Exchange Rate for China. Table 7 shows the percentage change of China's financial services exports and the percentage change of the Real Broad Effective Exchange Rate for China.

Table 7 shows that the percentage change of China's financial services exports has shown great fluctuations between 2007 and 2016, as well as the percentage change of the Real Broad Effective Exchange Rate for China. Table 8 shows the Pearson correlation coefficient between the percentage change of China's financial services exports and the percentage change of the Real Broad Effective Exchange Rate for China.

The value of the Pearson correlation coefficient between the percentage change of China's financial services exports and the percentage change of the Real Broad Effective Exchange Rate for China is 0.03. Table 9 shows the percentage change of

Table 7 Percentage change of China's financial services exports and percentage change of the Real Broad Effective Exchange Rate for China

Years	Percentage change of China's financial services exports (%)	Percentage change of the Real Broad Effective Exchange Rate for China[a] (%)
2007	58.49	4.24
2008	36.55	13.98
2009	13.25	−5.50
2010	273.46	4.44
2011	−36.19	6.47
2012	122.05	1.74
2013	68.88	7.61
2014	42.23	6.12
2015	−48.36	3.81
2016	35.92	−5.74

Source Knoema (2018a), [a]Bank for International Settlements (2018a)

Table 8 Pearson correlation coefficient between the percentage change of China's financial services exports and percentage change of the Real Broad Effective Exchange Rate for China

Year	Percentage change of China's financial services exports X_i	Percentage change of the Real Broad Effective Exchange Rate for China Y_i	$X_i * Y_i$	X_i^2	Y_i^2
2007	1.87	0.53	0.99	3.49	0.28
2008	−20.07	10.27	−206.11	402.80	105.47
2009	−43.37	−9.21	399.43	1880.95	84.82
2010	216.84	0.73	158.29	47,019.58	0.53
2011	−92.81	2.76	−256.15	8613.69	7.61
2012	65.43	−1.97	−128.89	4281.08	3.88
2013	12.26	3.9	47.81	150.30	15.21
2014	−14.39	2.41	−34.67	207.07	5.80
2015	−104.98	0.1	−10.4	11,020.80	0.01
2016	−20.7	−9.45	195.61	428.49	89.30
	Sum		*165.91*	*74,008.25*	*312.91*

r = 0.03

Source Authors' calculations

Table 9 Percentage change of Hong Kong's financial services exports and percentage change of the Real Broad Effective Exchange Rate for Hong Kong

Year	Percentage change of Hong Kong's financial services exports (%)	Percentage change of the Real Broad Effective Exchange Rate for Hong Kong[a] (%)
2007	34.22	−5.96
2008	−3.55	4.18
2009	−5.94	−5.01
2010	15.92	−3.21
2011	9.9	1.61
2012	8.22	0.59
2013	6.13	4.63
2014	7	9.48
2015	8.55	7.33
2016	−5.52	2.18

Source Knoema (2018b), [a]Bank for International Settlements (2018b)

Table 10 Pearson correlation coefficient between the percentage change of Hong Kong's financial services exports and the percentage change of the real broad effective exchange rate for Hong Kong

Year	Percentage change of Hong Kong's financial services exports X_i	Percentage change of the Real Broad Effective Exchange Rate for Hong Kong Y_i	$X_i * Y_i$	X_i^2	Y_i^2
2007	26.73	−7.54	−201.54	714.49	56.85
2008	−11.04	2.6	−28.7	121.88	6.76
2009	−13.43	−6.59	88.5	180.36	43.42
2010	8.43	−4.79	−40.37	71.03	22.94
2011	2.41	0.03	0.07	5.8	0
2012	0.73	−0.99	−0.72	0.53	0.98
2013	−1.36	3.05	−4.14	1.84	9.3
2014	−0.49	7.9	−3.87	0.24	62.41
2015	1.06	5.75	6.09	1.12	33.06
2016	−13.01	0.6	−7.8	169.26	0.36
	Sum		*−192.48*	*1266.55*	*236.08*
$r = -0.3$					

Source Authors' calculations

Hong Kong's financial services exports and the percentage change of the Real Broad Effective Exchange Rate for Hong Kong.

Table 9 shows that the percentage change of Hong Kong's financial services exports did not fluctuate significantly from 2007 to 2016, in contrast to the percentage change of the Real Broad Effective Exchange Rate for Hong Kong. Table 10 shows the Pearson correlation coefficient between the percentage change of Hong Kong's financial services exports and the percentage change of the Real Broad Effective Exchange Rate for Hong Kong.

The value of the Pearson correlation coefficient between the percentage change of Hong Kong's financial services exports and the percentage change of the Real Broad Effective Exchange Rate for Hong Kong is −0.3.

The analysis of the data shows that there is no significant correlation between the percentage change of China's financial services exports and the percentage change of the Real Broad Effective Exchange Rate for China, and there is a negative correlation of minor significance between the percentage change of Hong Kong's financial services exports and the percentage change of the Real Broad Effective Exchange Rate for Hong Kong. In the case of China, there is neither positive nor negative correlation between the aforementioned values because of the lack of Revealed Comparative Advantage, but in the case of Hong Kong there is a slightly negative correlation because of the role of Hong Kong as a financial centre.

6 Conclusion

In conclusion, summarising the results we can say, firstly, China does not have a Revealed Comparative Advantage in financial services *vis-à-vis* the USA and Hong Kong, which means that China has to make a lot of effort to become competitive in this area and, second, no significant correlation has been observed between the percentage change of China's financial services exports and the percentage change of the Real Broad Effective Exchange Rate for China.

The economic size of a country in terms of output or trade is one of the determinants for internationalising a currency, but the depth of financial markets in terms of the foreign exchange market is another one, and China has a long way to go, because of the role of Hong Kong as the largest capital source of Mainland China's overseas direct investment, the centre for cross-border Renminbi trade settlement and offshore Renminbi business, as well as a major overseas capital market for Mainland Chinese enterprises (Chrisman et al. 2016). Hong Kong has been the most important source of international capital for Mainland China, and Hong Kong's economy is increasingly correlated with the Mainland's external sector (Wong 2002). Finally, Hong Kong serves as the wealth management centre for Mainland China residents and, as Renminbi is increasingly used outside Mainland China, Hong Kong retains its role as the Mainland's testing ground for financial reforms (FSTB 2013). This is the main reason why Mainland China does not have a Revealed Comparative Advantage (RCA) in financial services exports, but Hong Kong has a Revealed Comparative Advantage (RCA) in financial services exports.

Acknowledgements This work has been partly supported by the University of Piraeus Research Centre.

References

Bagaria, N., & Ismail, S. (2017). An analysis of composition and structural transformation of exports of China. *International Journal of Applied Research, 3*(7), 1101–1106.

Balassa, B. (1965). Trade liberalization and "revealed" comparative advantage. *The Manchester School, 33*, 99–123.

Bank for International Settlements. (2018a). *Real broad effective exchange rate for China* [*RBCNBIS*]. Available via: https://fred.stlouisfed.org/series/RBCNBIS. Accessed February 21, 2018.

Bank for International Settlements. (2018b). *Real broad effective exchange rate for Hong Kong SAR [RBHKBIS]*. Available via: https://fred.stlouisfed.org/series/RBHKBIS. Accessed February 22, 2018.

Carpenter, J. N., Lu, F., & Whitelaw, R. F. (2018). *The real value of China's stock market*. Bank of Finland Institute for Economies in Transition. Available via: https://papers.ssrn.com/sol3/papers.cfm?abstract_id=3106656. Accessed April 23, 2018.

Chrisman, J., Richardson, D., & Lee, A. (2016). *Hong Kong's role in China's financial reform—The era of the "New Normal"*. Available via: https://www.dorsey.com/~/media/files/newsresources/

publications/2015/11/hk_role_china_financial_reform_lexis_112515.pdf. Accessed February 22, 2018.

Cohen, B. J. (2017). *Renminbi internationalization: A conflict of statecrafts*. Available via: https://www.chathamhouse.org/publication/renminbi-internationalization-conflict-statecrafts. Accessed February 20, 2018.

Financial Services and the Treasury Bureau. (2013). *Hong Kong: China's global financial centre*. The Government of Hong Kong, Special Administrative Region. Available via: https://www.fstb.gov.hk/fsb/topical/doc/pitchbook_brochure(Nov%202013)_e.pdf. Accessed February 20, 2018.

Haihong, Gao. (2017). The RMB Internationalization and the reform of the international monetary system. *Glob Econ Obs, 5*(1), 113–117.

International Monetary Fund. (2018a). Brighter prospects, optimistic markets, challenges ahead. World Economic Outlook. Available via: https://www.imf.org/en/Publications/WEO/Issues/2018/01/11/world-economic-outlook-update-january-2018. Accessed April 23, 2018.

International Monetary Fund. (2018b). World economic outlook (October 2017). Available via: http://www.imf.org/external/datamapper/datasets/WEO. Accessed April 22, 2018.

International Monetary Institute. (2017). RMB internationalization report 2017. Press release, International Monetary Institute, Renmin University of China. Available via: http://www.imi.org.cn/en/wp-content/uploads/2017/07/%E3%80%90IMI-Research-Report-No.-1702-EN%E3%80%91RMB-Internationalization-Report-2017-Press-Release.pdf. Accessed February 21, 2018.

Johansson, A. C. (2010). China's financial market integration with the world. *Journal of Chinese Economic and Business Studies, 8*(3), 293–314.

Knoema. (2018a). *China—Financial services exports in current prices*. Available via: https://knoema.com/atlas/China/topics/Foreign-Trade/Service-exports/Financial-services-exports. Accessed April 22, 2018.

Knoema. (2018b). *Hong Kong—Financial services exports in current prices*. Available via: https://knoema.com/atlas/Hong-Kong/topics/Foreign-Trade/Service-exports/Financial-services-exports. Accessed April 22, 2018.

Loungani, P., Mishra, S., Papageorgiou, C., & Wang, K. (2017). World trade in services: Evidence from a new dataset. International Monetary Fund. Available via: https://www.imf.org/en/Publications/WP/Issues/2017/03/29/World-Trade-in-Services-Evidence-from-A-New-Dataset-44776. Accessed April 15, 2018.

Mertens, M. T., & Shultz, P. (2017) *China's exchange rate policies and U.S. financial markets*. Federal Reserve Bank of San Francisco. Available via: https://www.frbsf.org/economic-research/publications/economic-letter/2017/october/china-exchange-rate-policies-and-us-financial-markets/. Accessed February 9, 2018.

McDowell, D., & Steinberg, D. A. (2017). Systemic strengths, domestic deficiencies: The Renminbi's future as a reserve currency. *Journal of Contemporary China, 26*(108), 801–819. https://doi.org/10.1080/10670564.2017.1337292.

Morrison, W. M. (2017). *China's economic rise: History, trends, challenges, and implications for the United States*. Congressional Research Service. Available via: https://www.hsdl.org/?abstract&did=803891. Accessed February 18, 2018.

Morrison, W. M. & Labonte, M. (2011). *China's currency: An analysis of the economic issues*. Congressional Research Service. Available via: http://www.au.af.mil/au/awc/awcgate/crs/rs21625.pdf. Accessed February 21, 2018.

Rodrik, Dani. (2006). What's so special about China's Exports? *China and World Economy, 14*(5), 1–19.

SWIFT. (2018a). *RMB internationalization: Where we are and what we can expect in 2018*. SWIFT Press releases. Available via: https://www.swift.com/resource/rmb-tracker-january-2018-special-report. Accessed February 27, 2018.

SWIFT. (2018b). *Monthly reporting and statistics on Renminbi (RMB) progress towards becoming an international currency*. RMB Tracker, February 2018. Available via: https://www.swift.

com/our-solutions/compliance-and-shared-services/business-intelligence/renminbi/rmb-tracker/document-centre?tl=en#topic-tabs-menu. Accessed March 3, 2018.

SWIFT. (2018c). *Monthly reporting and statistics on Renminbi (RMB) progress towards becoming an international currency.* RMB Tracker, March 2018. Available via: https://www.swift.com/our-solutions/compliance-and-shared-services/business-intelligence/renminbi/rmb-tracker/document-centre?tl=en#topic-tabs-menu. Accessed April 4, 2018.

Tovar, C. E., & Nor, T. M. (2018). Reserve currency blocs: A changing international monetary system? International Monetary Fund. Available via: https://www.imf.org/en/Publications/WP/Issues/2018/01/25/Reserve-Currency-Blocs-A-Changing-International-Monetary-System-45586. Accessed February 25, 2018.

Urdinez, F., & Masiero, G. (2015). China and the WTO: Will the market economy status make any difference after 2016? *The Chinese Economy, 48*(2), 155–172.

Wong, Y.-C. R. (2002). *The role of Hong Kong in China's economic development.* Paper presented as a part of ICSEAD's Public Lectures on Asia Series (Ajia Kouza), The University of Hong Kong, November 12, 2002.

World Bank. (2018). Exports of goods and services (current US$). Available via https://data.worldbank.org/indicator/NE.EXP.GNFS.CD?locations=CN-US. Accessed February 25, 2018.

World Trade Organization. (2018). *Trade in commercial services, 2005-onwards (BPM6).* Available via http://stat.wto.org/StatisticalProgram/WSDBViewData.aspx?Language=E. Accessed February 25, 2018.

World Trade Organization. (2017). *World trade statistical review 2017.* Switzerland: WTO.

World Trade Organization. (2012). *A practical guide to trade policy analysis.* Switzerland: WTO.

Yip, P. S. L., Tse, Y.-K., & Dong, Y. (2017). The exchange rate system reform in China: US pressure, implicit gradual appreciation and explicit exchange rate bands. EGC School of Humanities and Social Sciences, EGC Report No:2017/10. Available via: http://www3.ntu.edu.sg/hss2/egc/wp/2017/2017-10.pdf. Accessed February 10, 2018.

Zhang, B. (2018). Towards a floating RMB exchange rate regime. *China Economic Journal, 11,* 53–60. https://doi.org/10.1080/17538963.2018.1411070.

Zhang, M., & Zhang, B. (2017). The boom and bust of the RMB's internationalization: A perspective from cross border arbitrage. *Asian Economic Policy Review, 12,* 237–253. https://doi.org/10.1111/aepr.12179.

Zhu, J., Guo, K., Ai, M., Zhao, Y., & Bai, X. (2018). The further opening up of China's financial sector. *China Economic Journal, 11,* 44–52. https://doi.org/10.1080/17538963.2018.1416770.

The Succession in SMEs

Lambros Tsourgiannis, Giannoula Florou, Michael Nikolaidis, and Athanasios Mandilas

Abstract This paper aims to explore the business decisions undertaken by the successors of small and medium family enterprises (SMEs) and to identify the factors affecting the succession process. A primary survey was conducted in Autumn of 2017 to 450 SMEs operated in Greece. The main business decisions in which successors of SMEs are involved identified through PCA whilst cluster analysis performed to classify the successors of those enterprises into strategic groups according to the business decisions they make. Discriminant analysis conducted to check cluster predictability. Nonparametric tests performed to investigate the factors affecting the succession in those enterprises as well as to profile each strategic group of successors according to their demographic characteristics and their enterprises' characteristics. Successors found to be involved in two types of business decisions (a) long-term strategic planning decisions and (b) operational business decisions. Cluster analysis identified two strategic groups of successors: (i) long-term strategic planners and (ii) operational managers. Successor's designation and type, the age predecessor and successor, are associated with the successor's business decision. Furthermore, the size of the enterprise, the age of the predecessor, and the age of the successor are some factors that affect the succession of SMEs.

Keywords Business decisions · Succession in small and medium enterprises strategies

L. Tsourgiannis (✉)
Public Health and Social Care of Regional District of Xanthi, Region of Eastern Macedonia and Thrace, Xanthi, Greece
e-mail: ltsourgiannis@gmail.com

G. Florou · M. Nikolaidis · A. Mandilas
Accounting and Finance Department, School of Business and Economics, Eastern Macedonia and Thrace Institute of Technology, Kavala, Greece

M. Janowicz-Lomott et al. (eds.), *Economic and Financial Challenges for Balkan and Eastern European Countries*, Springer Proceedings in Business and Economics,
https://doi.org/10.1007/978-3-030-39927-6_6

1 Introduction

Small family business differs from non-family businesses in that their operation is not independent from the life cycle of the owner (Kimhi 1997). Therefore, succession process within family is crucial managerial decision that involves first of all the choice of a successor. That choice is affected by many factors including the birth order, age differential, and qualifications of the potential successors (Kimhi 1997). On the other hand, succession is typically a problematic issue as only 30% of the family firms survive the transition to the second generation and only 10% make it to the third generation (Beckhard and Dyer 1983a, b).

Stavrou (2003) proposed that family-owned businesses demonstrate an extraverted attitude during succession. Therefore, in those small businesses the difficulty of succession decisions is compounded by the complexities of family dynamics that are not present in non-family-owned businesses (Kuratko et al. 1993). The problem of finding a successor is not limited to the person with the most suitable track record and abilities, for example, but has the added complications of family membership and expectations (Brown and Coverley 1999). The predecessor plays four successive roles—sole operator, king, supervisor and consultant—and the successor three (assistant, manager and leader) according to Handler (1989). During the joint-reign phase, predecessors are often involved in the process of training the successor or introducing the successor into their business networks (Cabera-Suarez 2005; Cadieux et al. 2002; Fiegener et al. 1996; Goldberg 1996). Even though the successor has been appointed, many predecessors appear to remain in contact with their firms. In many cases, the predecessors even though they are officially retired, retain a right to oversee strategic decisions (Cabera-Suarez 2005; Chung and Yuen 2003; Feltham et al. 2005). Then, in addition to advising and supporting the firm's new manager (Handler 1989; Hunt and Handler 1999), some predecessors appear to maintain contact with the organization either by accepting an honorary position as president or by joining the board of directors (Handler 1989; Hunt and Handler 1999; St-Cyr and Richer 2003), acting as the firm's ombudsman or representative, or accepting a new position within the firm(Chung and Yuen 2003; Hunt and Handler 1999).

Generally, according to Handler (1994) the succession process includes seven stages: (1) the *pre-business* stage, where the successor may be only passively aware of some facets of the organization; (2) the *introductory* stage, where the successor may be exposed by family members to jargon and organization members although he or she has not worked even on a part-time basis in the business; (3) the *introductory–functional* stage, where the successor works as a part-time employee; (4) *the functional* stage, where the successor enters the organization as a full-time member; (5) the *advanced functional* stage, where the successor assumes managerial responsibilities; (6) the *early succession* stage, where the successor assumes the presidency; and (7) the *mature succession,* where the successor becomes the "de facto leader" of the organization. The succession process is only complete when the successor has gained legitimacy and is widely accepted by the stakeholders (Tatoglou et al.

2008). Completion of the process is contingent on the successor's ability to exercise appropriate leadership in the business (Fox et al. 1996).

According to Miller et al. (2006) and Poutziouris et al. (2006), there are three models of succession: conservative, wavering and rebellious. In the *conservative model*, the successor remains faithful to past and conservative successions, even after the retirement of the predecessor. Thus, the shadow of the predecessor—founder remains. Hence, the period of strong leadership is followed by a conservatism in which the strategies are committed to the past. Regarding the strategy against competitors, companies led by some conservative successors are subject to minor changes in their goals, their scope, product ranges or markets. The successors of the wavering *model* are characterized by a lack of determination as they want to give a touch of change and to put their touch, but they do not know how to do it. This is because they have to face a dilemma: to adopt new ideas and escape from the influence of the old or to follow the previous policies, respecting in that way the traditions of the founders or previous owners. In terms of strategy, the new owners are proposing and promoting new ideas such as entering in new markets or producing innovative products. The successor to the *rebellious model* rejects any perception and policy of previous generations. Usually, the successors of this model do not want to work within the family business but when they do, they follow a completely different pattern than the previous generation. Extensive changes in the field of purchases, products and operations are a key element of the strategy being pursued. The new successors undertake acquisitions, divestments, significant changes in products and processes as the successors want to leave their mark.

Decision criteria are affected by family considerations built into the firm's goals and the choice of alternatives to consider. Family involvement in implementation creates its own dynamics, politics and possibilities.

The SMEs consist of the vast majority of the enterprises operated within EU (99.9%) and Greece (99.8%). This figure had not been changed during the economic crisis in Greece. In particular, the Greek market remains highly fragmented consisted of a large number of small-scale enterprises and too many micro-enterprises (about 96.9%). SMEs generate added value and have a significant contribution to GDP (about 19.3% of GDP in terms of 2014). Moreover, the contribution of SMEs to total employment represents 87% of the workforce in enterprises (Hellenic Federation of Enterprises 2017).

As according to the knowledge of the researchers there are not any studies that explored the business decisions in which successors of small and medium family enterprises (that consist of a very important pillar of the Greek economy) are involved; this study aim to identify the business decisions in which successors of small and medium enterprises (SMEs) in Greece are involved as well as to identify the factors that affect the succession process in those enterprises.

In particular, it aims:

(a) to identify the factors that affect the business strategic decisions that successors of SMEs undertake,

(b) to classify them into strategic groups according to the strategic decisions they make,
(c) to profile each strategic group of according to their demographic characteristics,
(d) to identify the factors that affect the succession process in those enterprises.

2 Methodology

The null research hypotheses in this study that aims to reject are:

- **Ho1**: Successors of SMEs in Greece cannot be classified into strategic groups according to the factors that affect their business strategic decisions.
- **Ho2**: The demographic characteristics of successors are not significantly related to particular strategic business behaviour.
- **Ho3**: The succession process of SMEs is not significantly related to any particular factor.

An interview survey is based on a structured questionnaire throughout Greece conducted by the researchers in November of 2017 to gather the necessary information.

Cluster sampling method used to form the sample. In particular, the general population is stratified into two levels: regions and prefectures.

Initially the researchers based on the methodology presented by Oppenheim (2000), chose at random 10 regions from the 13 regions exist in Greece in order to have a more representative sample from the geographical point of view. In the second stage 1 prefecture from each chosen region selected at random. Finally, a random systematic sampling was used to form the sample of 50 SMEs in each prefecture. The sampling framework used for choosing the 50 SMEs in each prefecture is the list with the SMEs operated in each prefecture from the respective chamber of commerce. As Errington (1985) argued the only way in which this can be achieved is to ensure that the units for survey are selected at random from the larger population about which generalizations are to be made. The productive sample consists of 447 SMEs whilst in the 189 of them there are successors that have undertaken the business.

Multivariate analysis techniques were applied in three stages to the responses of the 189 SMEs in which there are successors that run the enterprise to reveal the key information as these contained. Principal component analysis (PCA) was used to identify the variables that accounted for the maximum amount of variance within the data in terms of the smallest number of uncorrelated variables (components). The anti-image correlation matrix, as well as Bartlett's test of sphericity and the measure of sampling adequacy (MSA), was used, in order to check the appropriateness of the data for subsequent factor analysis. The variables with a high proportion of large absolute values of anti-image correlations and MSA less than 0.5 were removed before analysis. An orthogonal rotation (varimax method) was conducted, and the standard criteria of eigenvalue = 1, scree test and percentage of variance were used in order to determine the factors in the first rotation (Hair et al. 1998). Different trial rotations followed where factor interpretability was used to compare the reduced through PCA 13 variables related factors affecting successors' business strategic decisions to a smaller set of underlying factors. These PCA scores were then subjected to both hierarchical and k-means cluster analyses to group successors with similar patterns of scores into similar clusters regarding their strategic business behaviour (Hair et al. 1998). Quadratic discriminant analysis was performed to assess how accurately the key factors identified through factor analysis could predict and discriminate cluster membership. Furthermore, chi-square analysis was conducted in order to profile each strategic group according to their demographic characteristics. Moreover, the same technique employed and to the total of the productive sample (447 SMEs) in order to identify the factors that affect the succession process in those enterprises.

3 Results and Discussion

The variables and the factors affecting successors' business strategic decisions along with their eigenvalues, the scree plot test and the percentage of variance results from PCA and factor analysis are shown in Tables 1 and 2.

Hierarchical and non-hierarchical clustering methods (Hair et al. 1998) were used to classify the successors regarding their strategic business behaviour. Cluster analysis was conducted on all 189 observations, as there were no outliers.

Successors appeared to fall into two groups according to their strategic business behaviour (Table 3): (a) the strategic planners and (b) operational managers.

Table 1 Variables affecting successors' business strategic decisions

Component	Eigenvalues	% of variance	Cumulative % of variance
1	8.246	63.430	63.430
2	1.183	9.101	72.531
3	0.725	5.578	78.109
4	0.609	4.667	82.796
5	0.528	4.064	86.860
6	0.436	3.350	90.210
7	0.355	2.734	92.944
8	**0.262**	**2.014**	**94.958**
9	**0.224**	**1.720**	**96.678**
10	**0.183**	**1.411**	**98.090**
11	**0.118**	**0.904**	**98.994**
12	**0.078**	**0.600**	**99.594**
13	**0.053**	**0.406**	**100.00**

Table 2 Main factors affecting successors' business strategic decisions

Main factors	Factor loading
Operational business decisions	
Negotiations regarding the purchasing of materials and merchandises	0.865
Decisions regarding the utilization of machinery equipment	0.838
Decisions regarding marketing	0.823
Decisions regarding payments	0.797
Decisions regarding sales of products	0.793
Decision regarding the work planning	0.715
Decisions regarding funding	0.692
Negotiations regarding sales of products	0.665
Decisions regarding the daily routine of the enterprise	0.651
Long term strategic planning decisions	
Decisions regarding the conduction of feasibility studies for applying for grants from Development EU programs	0.791
Decisions regarding the kind of products the enterprise will produce	−0.767
Decisions regarding the procurement of machinery equipment	0.717
Decisions regarding the long term planning of the enterprise	0.633

KMO MSA = 0.851 Bartlett test of sphericity = 2419.182 $P < 0.001$

Table 3 Classification of successors regarding their strategic business behaviour

Key strategic dimensions	Strategic planners	Operational managers	P
Operational decisions	−0.34345	0.42932	0.001
Long-term strategic decisions	0.50611	−0.63264	0.001
Number of consumers ($n = 189$)	105	84	

The strategic planners comprise 56% of the sample. They are involved mainly in long-term strategic decisions including the conduction of feasibility studies for applying for grants from the Development of EU Programs, and the kind of products/commodities they plan to produce/trade, the procurement of machinery equipment as well as long-term strategic planning.

The operational managers on the other hand, it comprises 44% of the sample. They are involved mainly in short-term operational decisions including:

(a) Negotiations regarding the purchasing of materials and merchandises
(b) Decisions regarding the utilization of machinery equipment
(c) Decisions regarding marketing
(d) Decisions regarding payments
(e) Decisions regarding sales of products
(f) Decision regarding the work planning
(g) Decisions regarding funding

Table 4 Summary of classification with cross-validation

Actual classification	Predicted classification	
	Strategic planners	Operational managers
Strategic planners	100	3
Operational managers	5	81
Total *N*	105	84
N correct	100	81
Proportion (%)	95.2	96.4
N = 189	*N* correct = 181	Proportion correct = 97.3%

(h) Negotiations regarding sales of products
(i) Decisions regarding the daily routine of the enterprise.

Discriminant analysis was performed to evaluate the prediction performance of group membership with the predictors derived from the factor analysis. Initially, the normality of the key strategic dimensions was checked. A summary of the cross-validation classification derived through quadratic discriminant analysis is shown in Table 4.

It is evident that, the two strategic dimensions could accurately predict and discriminate strategic group membership.

Therefore, the hypothesis ***Ho1***, *successors of SMEs in Greece cannot be classified into strategic groups according to the factors that affect their business strategic decisions,* can be rejected.

Furthermore, chi-square analysis conducted to profile each strategic group according to their demographic characteristics (Table 5) and to identify the factors that affect the succession process in those enterprises (Table 6).

Therefore, most of the successors of both strategic groups have a similar profile regarding their demographic characteristics. In particular, most of them are less than 31 years old and are the children of the predecessor whilst the predecessors are quite young (less than 51 years old) and are involved full time in the enterprise's activities.

Hence, ***Ho2***: "*The demographic characteristics of successors are not significantly related to particular strategic business behaviour*" can be rejected.

As the results of the chi-square analysis indicate (Table 6), there is a significant association among the following factors: (a) size of the enterprise, (b) predecessor' age, (c) successor's age, (d) kind of successor's involvement within the enterprise, and the succession process of the business. In particular, the enterprises in which there is a succession are a little bigger (48.9% of them have more than 5 people personnel) than those in which there is no succession (45.2% of the enterprises that there is no succession because they will be sold in the third party have more than 5 people personnel whilst 46.3% of the business in which there is no succession because they will be closed have more than 5 people workforce). Half of the predecessors in the cases there is a succession is less than 51 years old. On the other hand, the vast

Table 5 Profiling of successors regarding their demographic characteristics

Factors/characteristics	Strategic planners	Operational managers (%)	
Predecessor's age	<51 years old	45.7	57.1%
$x^2 = 114.702$	51–60 years old	22.9	32.1%
$df = 2$	>61 years old	31.4	10.7%
$P < 0.05$			
Successor's age	<31 years old	37.1	64.3%
$x^2 = 15.275$	31–40 years old	34.3	14.3%
$df = 2$	>41 years old	28.6	21.4%
$P < 0.001$			
Kind of involvement of predecessor in enterprises activities	Full time	62.8	82.1%
$x^2 = 10.695$	Part time	37.2	17.9%
$df = 1$			
$P < 0.05$			
Who is the successor?	Children	51.4	57.1%
$x^2 = 11.230$	Nephew/niece	8.6	17.9%
$df = 3$	Husband/wife	22.9	21.4%
$P < 0.05$	Other	17.1	3.6%

majority of the predecessors in the business in which there is no succession are less than 51 years old which might mean that either they sell the enterprise in order to do something else or they close it because their profitability is negative. In cases, there is succession, only 53% of them are more than 31 years old and 25.8% more than 41 years old, whilst the 64.3% of the possible successors of the enterprises in which there is succession because they will be sold are more than 31 years old and the 33.3% more than 41 years. In the cases that there is no succession because the enterprises will be closed, about 56.1 of the successors are more than 31 years old and 36.6% more than 41 years old. It could be supposed that many of the possible successors in the cases that there is not succession have another job. Furthermore, in the cases in which there is a succession, the 57.8% of the successors are involved full time and actively in the enterprises activities whilst the vast majority of the successors of the businesses that there is no succession (92.3% in cases that the enterprise will be sold to a third party and 75% in cases that the enterprise will be closed) work part time in the enterprise possible because the possible successors have their own jobs.

Hence, ***Ho3***, "*the succession process of SMEs is not significantly related to any particular factor*", can be rejected.

Table 6 Factors that affect the succession process in SMEs

Factors	There is a succession	No succession because the enterprise will be sold to third party (%)	No succession because the enterprise will be closed (%)	
Size of enterprise	<5 employees	51.6	54.8	53.7%
$x^2 = 39.275$	5–10 employees	13.6	33.3	31.7%
$df = 2$	>10 employees	34.8	11.9	14.6%
$P < 0.001$				
Predecessor's age	<51 years old	50.0	73.8	65.9%
$x^2 = 28.836$	51–60 years old	25.8	14.3	26.8%
$df = 2$	>61 years old	24.2	11.9	7.3%
$P < 0.001$				
Successor's age	<31 years old	47.0	35.7	43.9%
$x^2 = 17.636$	31–40 years old	27.3	31.0	19.5%
$df=2$	>41 years old	25.8	33.3	36.6%
$P < 0.001$				
Kind of involvement of successors in enterprises activities	Full time	57.8	7.7	25.0%
$x^2 = 212.500$	Part time	42.2	92.3	75.0%
$df = 1$				
$P < 0.001$				

4 Conclusions

According to the current study, the successors in SMEs in Greece can be classified into two groups; according to the way, they are involved in strategic decision making:

(a) Strategic planners who are involved mainly in long-term strategic decisions and
(b) Operational managers who are involved mainly in short-term operational decisions including.

The vast majority of both groups of successors are quite young, and they are the kids of predecessors whilst the predecessors are also young (less than 51 years old) and are full time involved in the activities of the enterprise.

Furthermore, there is succession in SMEs in Greece when the successor is quite young and plan to involved in the activities of the enterprise full time; whilst in cases there is no succession in SMEs, the successors are middle-aged and would be involved in the activities of the enterprise in a part-time base.

This study supports the arguments of other studies presenting that after the successor has been appointed, many predecessors appear to remain in contact with their firms and that in many cases the predecessors, even though they are officially retired, retain a right to oversee strategic decisions (Cabera-Suarez 2005; Chung and Yuen 2003; Feltham et al. 2005) This mostly happens in the SMEs Greece in the cases of operational managers. Furthermore, most of the operational managers appear to be in the *advanced functional* stage according to Handler (1994) theory, where the successor assumes managerial responsibilities; whilst the majority of the strategic planners seem to match with the *mature succession,* where the successor becomes the "de facto leader" of the organization.

Nevertheless, the current study is of the incontestable value, since according to the knowledge of the authors; this is the first attempt to explore the factors that affect the business strategic decisions that successors of SMEs undertake and classify them into strategic groups according to the strategic decisions they make and identify the factors that affect the succession process in those enterprises. Furthermore as only in the 44% of the surveyed enterprises, there is a succession process and 27% of them will be closed which means loss of productivity, working place, contribution to the GDP, the Greek State and local and regional authorities, and the relevant stakeholders (Chamber of Commerce, etc) should make efforts in order to be attractive and profitable for the successors to undertake their family business.

References

Beckhard, R., & Dyer, W. (1983a). Managing change in the family firm—Issues and strategies. *Sloan Management Review, 24*, 59–65.

Beckhard, R., & Dyer, W. (1983b). Managing continuity in the family-owned business. *Organizational Dynamics, 12*(5–1), 2.

Brown, R. B., & Coverley, R. (1999). Succession planning in family businesses: A study from East Anglia, UK. *Journal of Small Business Management, 37*(1), 93–97.

Cabera-Suarez, K. (2005). Leadership transfer and the successor's development in the family firm. *Leadership Quarterly, 16,* 71–96.

Cadieux, L., Lorrain, J., & Hugron, P. (2002). Succession in women-owned family businesses: A case study. *Family Business Review, 15*(1), 17–30.

Chung, W., & Yuen, K. (2003). Management succession: A case study for Chinese family-owned business. *Management Decision, 41*(7), 643–655.

Errington, A. (1985). *Delegation on farms: An examination of organisation structure and managerial control on farms in the vale of the white horse*. Ph.D. thesis University of Reading.

Feltham, T. S., Feltham, G., & Barnett, J. J. (2005). The dependence of family business on a single decisionmaker. *Journal of Small Business Management, 43*(1), 1–15.

Fiegener, M. K., Brown, B. M., Prince, R. A., & File, K. M. (1996). Passing on strategic vision. *Journal of Small Business Management, 34*(3), 15–26.

Fox, M., Nilakant, V., & Hamilton, R. T. (1996). Managing succession in family-owned businesses. *International Small Business Journal, 15*(1), 15–25.

Goldberg, S. D. (1996). Effective successors in family owned business: Significant elements. *Family Business Review, 11*(2), 185–197.

Hair, J. F., Anderson, R. E., Tatham, R. L., & Black, W. C. (1998). *Multivariate data analysis*. New Jersey: Prentice Hall Inc.

Handler, W. C. (1989). *Managing the family firm succession process: The next-generation family member's experience*. Ph.D. thesis, Boston University, UMI Dissertation Services.
Handler, W. C. (1994). Succession in family business: A review of the research. *Family Business Review, 7*(2), 133–157.
Hellenic Federation of Enterprises. (2017). *Medium and small enterprises in Greece—Part A: Contribution to the economy, developments and challenges*. Athens.
Hunt, J. M., & Handler, W. C. (1999). The practices of effective family firm leaders. *Journal of Developmental Entrepreneurship, 4*(2), 135–151.
Kimhi, A. (1997). Intergenerational succession in small family businesses: Borrowing constraints and optimal timing of succession. *Small Business Economics, 9*(4), 309–318.
Kuratko, D. F., Hornsby, J. S., & Montagno, R. V. (1993). Family business succession in Korean and US firms. *Journal of Small Business Management, 31*(2), 132–136.
Miller, D., Steier, L., & Le Breton-Miller, I. (2006). Lost in time: Intergenerational succession, change and failure in family business. In *Handbook of Research on Family Business* (pp. 371–387). UK. Northampton, MA, USA: Edward Elgar Cheltenham.
Oppenheim, A. N. (2000). *Questionnaire design, interviewing and attitude measurement*. New York: Continuum.
Poutziouris, P. Z., Smyrnios, K. X., & Klein, S. B. (2006). *Handbook of research on family business in association with IFERA*. Chetenham, UK, Northampton MA, USA: Edward Elgar.
Stavrou, E. T. (2003). Leadership succession in owner-managed firms through the lens of extraversion. *International Small Business Journal, 21*(3), 331–347.
St-Cyr, L., & Richer, F. (2003). *Stratégies de transmission réussie des PME québécoises*. Working Paper No. 03-01. HEC Montréal, Chaire de développement et de relève de la PME.
Tatoglu, E., Kula, V., & Glaister, K. W. (2008). Succession planning in family-owned businesses: Evidence from Turkey. *International Small Business Journal, 26*, 155.

Innovativeness of Serbian Enterprises as a Factor of Competitiveness Improvement at the International Market

Milica Jovanovic and Milica Djokic

Abstract In today's knowledge-driven economy, financial and capital assets no longer play the leading roles. Innovations are the main drivers of competitiveness and development of enterprises, as well as of the countries and societies as a whole. Only those who are capable and flexible enough to adapt to the given circumstances and continuously search for new solutions can survive at such dynamic world market. For that reason, investment in science, creation of new knowledge, research and development (R&D), and new technologies are crucial for the prosperity of the national economy. On the international market, with intense competition and sophisticated consumers, innovativeness becomes an imperative. The main goal of this paper is to explain the significance of knowledge and innovations in today's business and to identify the main challenges that small and medium enterprises in Serbia are faced with in increasing their innovativeness and ways of overcoming them in order to improve their competitiveness at the international market. The emphasis will be on considering the impact of investment in R&D on strengthening the position of domestic companies in the world market and on the indicators that represent the main weaknesses in domestic innovativeness.

Keywords Innovativeness · Research and development · Competitiveness · International business

1 Introduction

Globalization process during the last few decades of the twentieth century has resulted in political, economic, and social integrations around the world and has turned different national markets into the world market which exceeded the national borders. In such circumstances, the competitive power of the country has become one of the

M. Jovanovic (✉) · M. Djokic
Innovation Center, University of Nis, Nis, Serbia
e-mail: jovanovicmilicaa90@gmail.com

M. Djokic
e-mail: milica91nis@hotmail.com

M. Janowicz-Lomott et al. (eds.), *Economic and Financial Challenges for Balkan and Eastern European Countries*, Springer Proceedings in Business and Economics,
https://doi.org/10.1007/978-3-030-39927-6_7

main factors of economic progress. Rapid technology development, new business models, and increased competition have forced companies to continuously search for innovative ways to improve their performances and apply new technologies in order to retain their market positions. Good quality or low prices are no longer enough to remain leadership. Today, it is all about the knowledge, creativity, ideas, uniqueness, and innovativeness. To enhance competitiveness at the national, and especially at the global market, constant innovation is necessary. Therefore, it is not surprising that the investment in R&D activities and innovation capacity is getting more important than ever. This particularly refers to the small- and medium-sized enterprises sector which is the driving force of both developed and developing economies and significantly contributes to the country's competitiveness.

Within this context, the aim of this paper is to indicate the importance of knowledge and innovation in today's business from the perspective of small and medium enterprises and to explain the relationship between the innovativeness and competitiveness in the global level. Besides that, authors will analyze the existing business environment in Serbia in terms of innovation capability and its impact on national economy competitiveness. Innovation potential of Serbia is still far from desired, and especially far behind innovativeness of developed countries, mainly because the entrepreneurial culture and innovation climate are not supported in the right way. For that reason, some of the major issues will be discussed, as well as necessary measures for overcoming these obstacles.

2 Key Determinants of Innovativeness as a Competitiveness Factor

In a modern society, creation, distribution, use and integration of information and knowledge has never been more intensive. That has led to the knowledge-based economy, in which intellectual resources and innovations are crucial for business. Knowledge is now recognized as the driver of productivity and economic growth, leading to a new focus on the role of information, technology, and learning in economic performance (OECD 1996). The term "knowledge-based economy" results from a fuller recognition of the role of knowledge and technology in economic growth (OECD 1996). "The knowledge economy is the one in which knowledge in the form of intellectual capital is the primary factor of production" (Bedford 2013). Creation of new knowledge and its application through innovations are the primary sources of companies' productivity, further progress and market success, as well as the base for development and growth of whole economies.

Innovations are becoming central to creating and sustaining competitive advantage (Houghton and Sheehan 2000). In order to succeed and keep ahead of the competitors in today's unpredictable and fast-changing world, continuous improvement is essential. Better, more efficient education and training of the workforce, higher investment in R&D programs and institutional support for innovation are necessary to encourage new ideas and create an innovative environment. Many authors have conducted various studies to examine the impact of innovativeness on competitive advantage and have proved that being innovative is an imperative for success in dynamic and competitive business environment (Grossman and Helpman 1991; Cainelli et al. 2004; Cantwell 2005; Wang et al. 2007; Karo and Kattel 2011).

The significance of new ideas, knowledge, and technology in modern business is recognized by the European Commission as well, which emphasized that creation, use, and commercialization of new knowledge and technologies have become essential in the global battle for the realization of competitiveness, and that high-tech sectors have become the most important driving force of economic growth, productivity, environmental sustainability as well as the major source of high value-added and well-paid jobs (European Commission 2010).

Innovations may be introduced in various ways and are not associated only to the high-tech enterprises. Besides radically new products and services, they can also refer to unique methods and procedures, distinctive business models, different marketing approaches, innovative technology solutions, etc. Innovation capability of an organization depends closely on its intellectual and/or organizational knowledge assets and on its ability to employ these assets (Martín-de Castro et al. 2013). Innovativeness founded on knowledge and the ability to respond to a turbulent environment is perceived as a source of profitability and success of organizations in the present competitive environment Urbancová (2013). Knowledge-based activities provide the foundation for innovations development, while cooperative innovation projects and collaborations are being more common and closer than ever. An increasing need for innovations has led to knowledge and ideas exchange between enterprises, institutes, universities, and R&D centers and joint development.

There are various indicators used to measure different aspects of innovativeness at local, regional, and global level. One of the most known is the Global Innovation Index[1] (GII). Its complex structure gives an opportunity to continually track many different innovation variables and provides a significant database for future innovation strategies, indicating the areas which are adequately developed and those that need to be improved. The 2017 GII report included 127 countries, with Switzerland, Sweden, and the Netherlands leading at the top of the list. Serbia, with a score of 35.3 was ranked 62nd, which meant improvement since previous year, when it was at the 65th position (out of 128). The data implied that main weaknesses of the country's innovation inputs are low market and business sophistication, especially when it comes to domestic market competition, the state of cluster development and joint ventures/strategic alliance deals, along with unsustainable energy use, insufficient government expenditure on education per pupil and the absence of global R&D

[1]GII relies on two subindices—the Innovation Input Sub-Index and the Innovation Output Sub-Index, and each of these is built around certain pillars. The Innovation Input Sub-Index includes elements of the national economy that enable innovative activities—Institutions, Human capital and research, Infrastructure, Market sophistication and Business sophistication. The Innovation Output Sub-Index shows the results of innovative activities within the economy through two categories—Knowledge and Technology outputs and Creative outputs. The overall GII is expressed in the 0–100 score ranking and represents an average of the Input and Output Sub-Indices (GII report 2017).

companies. Innovation output analysis showed that total computer software spending is quite low, as well as the role of ICTs in business and organizational model creation. On the other hand, some of the innovation input categories which proved to be the biggest strengths are cost of redundancy dismissal, and number of ISO 14001 environmental certificates issued, pupil/teacher ratio, government's online service, and online e-participation. Number of scientific and technical journal articles, ISO 9001 quality certificates, Wikipedia yearly edits and value of ICT services exports in total trade appeared to be the most significant elements of innovation output according to the data presented.

3 Influence of the Innovation Factors on Enterprise Competitiveness

In knowledge economy, only countries in which the innovative enterprises are dominant can achieve a high rate of employment, a high standard of living, and a sustainable economic growth (Despotović et al. 2014). The ability of converting knowledge into innovation is a key characteristic of such enterprises. Besides that, innovative enterprises allocate significant resources for R&D and are dedicated to patenting and cooperation with scientific research organizations. Porter points out that innovations are the most important source of national competitiveness (Porter 1990). An innovation has a key role in achieving the long-term success of the enterprise and is representing an instrument of survival in conditions of uncertainty and acquiring competitive advantages (Santos-Vijande and Alvarez-Gonzalez 2007). The competitiveness of the national economy first and foremost depends on innovative activities of small- and medium-sized enterprises (SMEs) which can significantly contribute to the increase of productivity at the national economy level. SMEs represent a driving force of contemporary economies, taking their contribution into consideration from the aspect of technological innovations, employment, export Jovović (2017). In contemporary business conditions, each enterprise needs innovations, regardless of its size. However, SMEs are characterized by a larger innovational capability, flexibility, agility, and entrepreneurial spirit in comparison with larger systems, due to the fact that SMEs are more ready to quickly apply innovations (raw materials, products, services, processes, organization, production), new technologies, professional staff employment (Bošković et al. 2016; Tidd and Bessant 2009).

3.1 Innovation as a Pillar of Competitiveness—Position of Serbia

Innovation represents openness to new ideas as one of the aspects of enterprise culture (Hurley and Hult 1998). It refers to the capability of economy, enterprise, or an individual to be able to convert new business ideas into new products, services, technologies, and markets. The goal is for the process of acquiring new products and services to be more efficient (Dess et al. 2007). The key indicators of innovation can be observed via the twelfth pillar of the Global Competitiveness Index[2] (GCI) of the World Economic Forum (WEF). In the first stage of development, competitiveness of the national economy depends on the way public and private institutions are performing (1st pillar), infrastructure (2nd pillar), stable macroeconomic environment (3rd pillar), health and primary education (4th pillar), which represent the basic requirements. When a country becomes more competitive, with a higher degree of productivity, then it is located in the development phase which is led by efficiency. Competitiveness of such country will depend on higher education and training (5th pillar), goods and labor market efficiency (6th and 7th pillars), financial market development (8th pillar), technological readiness ability (9th pillar), large domestic and foreign markets (10th pillar), which are marked as the factors of efficiency increase. On the highest level of development, when the country shifts from the development phase into innovation-driven phase, companies compete by producing new and diverse products, using the sophisticated production processes (11th pillar) and innovation (12th pillar), i.e., based on the factors of innovation and sophistication. It can be concluded that innovation has a key role in strengthening and preserving the competitiveness in the most-developed countries (Perez-Moreno et al. 2016).

In the latest Report of the WEF, Serbia is, according to GDP per capita, listed into countries with middle level of development, where efficiency increase factors involvement ranged 50% from the total GCI value, while the lowest influence of innovation and sophistication factors involvement ranged 10% (World Economic Forum 2017). Also, according to most recent data, having in mind the last pillar of competitiveness—innovation, Serbia is ranked on 95th place from a total of 137 countries that were included in this report in the year of 2017. This position is the best rank Serbia has had in the last 7 years, as well as the best score so far, and the ranking was even 11 places higher than the average rank Serbia has had over the analyzed period of seven years. The worst position from the innovation aspect, Serbia had in the year of 2015, when she held 113th place among the 140 countries that were analyzed, which is given in Table 1.

In order to discover the causes of the unfavorable position of Serbia from the aspect of innovation, it is necessary to include all indicators into the analysis based on which the final mark is acquired within the 12th pillar of competitiveness. Those indicators have influence on the innovation activity of a certain country and its innovation as an ability of implementing innovations, and they determine the score and rank of that country within the 12th pillar of GCI (Krstić et al. 2016).

[2]Global Competitiveness Index is measuring the quality and competitiveness of the business environment in more than 140 countries worldwide. CGI is acquired via the analysis of more than 110 indicators, based on the research of leading managers' attitudes in countries which are included in research and reports of other international organizations. The factors of competitiveness included in this index are divided into 12 categories, otherwise known as the 12 pillars of competitiveness, in order to be able to perform the aggregation of factors to a certain degree.

Table 1 Showcase of Serbia's innovation index for 2011–2017 period

Year	2011/2012		2012/2013		2013/2014		2014/2015		2015/2016		2016/2017		2017/2018		The average scores and ranks of the analyzed period	
Number of analyzed countries	142		144		148		144		140		138		137			
	SC	R	SC	R	SC	R	SC	R	SC	R	SC	R	SC	R	SC	R
Serbia	2.9	97	2.8	111	2.9	112	2.8	108	2.9	113	3.0	108	3.1	95	2.9	106

WEF (2011, 2012, 2013, 2014, 2015, 2016, 2017)

Low innovation within the countries of Western Balkans, along with already-existent political, economic, and legal challenges, represents the factor of slowing down the process of accession to the European Union. The research shows that in those countries the increase of efficiency of national innovation systems influenced the general level increase in innovation (Cvetanović et al. 2015). All actions that are based on a goal of increasing innovation and advancement of competitiveness must be directed toward the improvement of the ability of shifting toward the knowledge economy. Primarily, the removal of basic restrictions for competitiveness and innovation is a must in those countries—as well as institutional and infrastructural restrictions and the problems of political stability.

3.2 Key Weaknesses of Domestic Innovation—Possibilities to Overcome

National innovation capacity refers to the ability of a certain country to produce and use newly found knowledge in the production of products and offering services. It is about a long-term potential of a certain country to produce and use new technologies. Some of the factors that determine the national system of innovations, as well as the national innovation capacity are the size of the country, availability of natural and human resources, development of the public institutions, dominant forms of entrepreneurial activity (Cvetanović et al. 2011). It is exactly capacity for innovation, as an indicator within the 12th pillar of competitiveness, the greatest weakness of Serbia's innovation, considering that Serbia is ranked 117th out of 137 possible countries included in the Report of WEF. This is the worst rank having in mind all of the indicators that are within innovation as a pillar of competitiveness. Besides that, Serbia had an unfavorable rank throughout all of the analyzed years when it comes to the indicator in question, since that the best rank achieved by Serbia was in the year of 2011–110th place out of 142 analyzed countries.

Along with capacity for innovation, as the biggest restriction of domestic competitiveness, Serbia lists the unfavorable rank in terms of company spending on R&D as well, despite considerably improving her position in the past seven years, which is given in Table 2. According to this indicator, Serbia is ranked 107th out of 137 analyzed countries. Besides the private sector, state sector allocations in this field are small as well. According to the most recent data, in the area of government procurement of advanced technology products, Serbia has improved her rank by 13 positions, but is still holding a very unfavorable position (105th out of 137 analyzed countries). For decades, the investments in R&D in Serbia are on a low level (less than 1% of GDP) compared with the investments in more developed parts of Europe (around 3% of GDP). As a consequence, the increase in number of SMEs in Serbia is not accompanied by the increased level of innovation (Bošković et al. 2016).

Table 2 Representation of the innovation factors within the 12th pillar of competitiveness for Serbia (2011–2017)

Year	2011/2012		2012/2013		2013/2014		2014/2015		2015/2016		2016/2017		2017/2018	
	SC	R	SC	R	SC	R	SC	R	SC	R	SC	R	SC	R
1. Capacity for innovation	2.5	110	2.5	120	2.8	133	30	130	3.1	132	3.2	130	3.5	117
2. Quality of scientific research institutions	3.8	61	3.6	67	3.7	66	3.7	69	3.8	67	4.0	60	4.2	47
3. Company spending on R&D	2.4	130	2.3	132	2.5	127	2.5	125	2.4	129	2.7	121	2.9	107
4. University-industry collaboration in R&D	3.4	81	3.2	99	3.2	104	3.2	95	3.2	95	3.2	96	3.2	95
5. Government procurement of advanced technology products	3.4	92	3.1	115	2.8	123	2.9	122	2.8	110	2.8	108	2.8	105
6. Availability of scientists and engineers	3.9	83	3.9	78	3.9	85	3.9	82	3.8	82	3.7	90	3.9	68
7. PCT patent applications/million pop	0.4	67	0.0	119	2.8	53	2.3	55	3.0	53	3.8	50	4.1	50

WEF (2011, 2012, 2013, 2014, 2015, 2016, 2017)

Weak cooperation of economy and universities in the area of R&D stands out as an important weakness of domestic innovativeness (95th place from 137 analyzed countries). For an efficient collaboration between scientific research organizations and SMEs, it is necessary to build an innovation infrastructure and develop new instruments—competence centers, technological institutes, vouchers for innovations—which will facilitate the transfer of knowledge and research results from science into economy. Introducing vouchers for innovations will advance the innovation capacity of SMEs through their better connection with external sources of knowledge, which is an important prerequisite for innovation development (Nikolić 2014). It is estimated that strengthening the connection between science and economy would be done by taking the following measures: (1) encouraging the usage of scientific research results; (2) strengthening the work of the Innovational Activity Fund; (3) further development of the Innovations Support Project; (4) establishing mutual innovation projects of the private sector and scientific research organizations; (5) improvement of transfer of knowledge and technology; (6) encouraging the foundation of companies based on the scientific research (spin-off); (7) establishment of public–private partnership; (8) scientific–technological parks; and (9) founding of scientific research clusters and competitiveness networks (Official Gazette 2016).

With a goal to strengthen the innovation capacity, enterprises enter into different forms of business networks, both internally and externally. Such networks mean connecting with key stakeholders, but primarily with enterprises with complementary resources. This way, it is much easier to get to innovations (by dividing high costs of R&D development and knowledge exchange) but primarily through organizational studying and technology transfer. Some authors (Child and Faulkner 1998) point out that networks are providing fast and effective information exchange between partners, which is a very important prerequisite for innovation development. Apart from connecting with other enterprises, an important role is given to the cooperation and connection with the scientific research organizations, especially via the mutual realization of projects.

Innovation activity of SMEs in Serbia is below the desired level, whereby innovation policy might have an important role directed toward:

- Strengthening of consciousness of managers about the importance of innovations for the competitiveness of the enterprises in contemporary business requirements;
- Creating an economic ambient that will encourage entrepreneurs to innovate;
- Providing financial support to SMEs through incentives for the development of domestic financial market;
- Providing systematical support to SMEs by changing legislative framework;
- Strengthening the cooperation of SMEs with large enterprises, universities and scientific research institutions, in order to accomplish synergetic effects and risk-sharing of the innovation process;
- Creating scientific research parks, business incubators, innovation clusters which will allow quick and efficient spreading of results of research and innovations (Ravić and Gavrić 2015).

Although SMEs could be financed via many sources—commercial bank loan, leasing, factoring, microcredits, angel investors, equity capital, securities and other, in Serbia SMEs are facing the restricted access to affordable sources of finance, mainly because of the insufficient development of the financial market. Therefore, the abilities of financing innovative SMEs in Serbia are reduced only to bank loans. It is necessary to develop other mechanisms of finance which are better suited to financing such enterprises, such as angel investors and equity capital funds—Venture Capital Funds, Development/Equity Capital Funds, Mezzanine Funds[3] (Nikolić 2014).

4 R&D Investment of Private and Public Sector in Serbia—Competitiveness Factor

The researches point out that economic growth which is based on traditional factors of production and low-cost strategy is short-lasting, while the economic efficiency that is long-lasting is based on science and innovations. Economic growth and improvement of the national competitiveness require investments in R&D. Such investments have a positive influence on economic efficiency, and return is at least equal or higher than traditional investment income on tangible assets. Also, R&D strengthens the efficiency of enterprises and branches, both on national and individual level (Pilinkiene 2015).

According to an OECD analysis from 2004, it was estimated that increasing investment in R&D in business sector by 1% leads to increase in productivity by 0.13%, while increasing those investments in public sector increases productivity by 0.17%. According to another research, increasing R&D expenditure by 1% in business sector (as a % of GDP) leads to an increase in export of middle-high technology products in the same year by 9% (as a percentage of total exports), also the same increase in expense in public sector leads to an increase in export of those products by 8%, with a two-year delay (Ciocanel and Pavelescu 2015). The state can encourage private sector investment in R&D through direct measures (loans, for instance) but also through indirect measures tax reliefs and warranties.

Following the Republic of Serbia's Strategy of scientific and technological development for the time period of 2016–2020, the following objectives stand out: "(1) inducing executive and relevant scientific research in the Republic of Serbia; (2) strengthening the connection of science, economy, and society in order to induce innovations; (3) establishing an efficient system of management for science and innovations in the Republic of Serbia; (4) ensuring availability of human resources for science and economy and social activities; (5) improvement of international cooperation in scientific and innovative domain; (6) increasing investments in R&D via public financing and inducing the investment of public sector in R&D" (Official Gazette 2016). When it comes to increasing investments in R&D, the strategical goal is for total investments in science, technological development and innovations

[3]Funds which invest into sources represent a combination of debt capital and equity capital.

to reach 3% of the GDP from all sources, but 1% from the state budget. It was estimated, that in order for further advancement of research and innovative system, material investments in science and research should be increased, with a goal that until 2020 that increase from the budget is at 0.6% GDP, but when it comes to total investments from all sources of financing, that increase should reach 1.5% GDP.

4.1 Small- and Medium-Sized Enterprises as a Driving Force of National Innovativeness

Small- and medium-sized enterprises are usually the core of the economy and its most flexible part. Flexibility, simple organizational structure, low risk level, and practicality of SMEs are essential characteristics that enable them to be innovative (Harrison and Watson 1998). Those have also appeared to be the main advantages in the current fast-changing environment, marked with high uncertainty and severe competition. In such circumstances, the major challenge for most business entities is to adapt to different conditions in the shortest period of time. That ability is one of the main features of the SMEs, which makes them capable to survive in modern times.

It has become clear that the capability to innovate has no longer been associated with the size of the company, as the significance of SMEs in innovation development has increased during the past few years. The fact that most of the major inventions in the last decades have come from individual inventors and small enterprises has only confirmed these findings. According to specialists' observations, 46 out of 58 leading inventions in America and Western Europe in the twentieth century belong to individuals and small firms, while the data of the National Science Fund of the USA indicate that firms with up to 500 employees, calculated for each dollar invested in scientific research activities, gave 24 times more new inventions than large corporations (with more than 10,000 employees) (WIPO 2008).

SMEs and entrepreneurs' sector in Serbia represents an extremely important segment of the economy: It includes 99.9% of active enterprises, employs almost two-third of total employees in non-financial sector and generates about 35% of Serbian

GDP (The Ministry of the Economy 2017). Although the country has gone through some difficult times over the past decades, along with world financial crisis, which led to very unfavorable economic circumstances, the number of SMEs has risen. All major economic indicators of the entrepreneurship sector have shown positive trends of recovery in recent years, which confirmed its huge potential. Despite that, it still lags behind SMEs in the EU and most of the countries in the neighborhood. According to the data provided by the Serbian Ministry of the Economy (2017), nearly half of the non-financial sector foreign trade in 2016 was created by SMEs (49.5%), which accounted for 40.8% of exports and 56.3% of imports. The main cause of concern is that in the exports of SMEs, products of low value and quality, as well as low-tech products take the dominant part (raw materials, labor-intensive, and resource-intensive goods). That is not surprising considering that most SMEs in Serbia have low innovation performance, mainly caused by very few technological innovations and weak collaboration with scientific research institutions. Researches show that process innovations are more frequent than product and service innovations in Serbian SMEs and that only 36.46% of all innovations are completely new for the market, while 63.54% of innovations are new just for the firm (Ivanović-Đukić and Lazić 2014). According to the same source, implemented innovations provided more flexible production systems and bigger capacities of production to the SMEs, while impact on the cost reduction was not significant.

This data demonstrate the strategic role of SMEs in the country's foreign trade and its competitiveness at the global market, making the further development of this sector one of the most important economic issues. In order to improve the export competitiveness, it is necessary to change its structure by increasing the share of high-tech and high-quality products and knowledge-intensive services. That requires investing in new technologies and enhancing the capability of SMEs to innovate. Even though creators of economic policy have realized the significance of innovative enterprises and business environment and have implemented some measures to promote innovation and encourage creative thinking, the results are not satisfactory yet.

5 Conclusion

Innovativeness of SMEs is an important determinant of Serbian national innovativeness. R&D expenditures of these companies determine the country's development potential, capacity for innovation, and national competitiveness. Therefore, Serbia has determined, in the Strategy of Scientific and Technological Development for the period from 2016 to 2020, incentive measures for these companies to increase spending in this area. In addition, the development of science technology parks, research, and development clusters and networks of competitiveness plays an important role, as well as the provision of better sources of financing. Undeveloped financial market in Serbia is a limiting factor of innovation for SMEs.

Serbia is ranked 95th in a list of 137 countries, according to the indicators of innovation, within the twelfth pillar of competitiveness. The main weaknesses of domestic innovation are insufficient innovative capacities, inadequate cooperation between the economy and universities and insufficient R&D allocations of public and private sector. On the other hand, according to the Global Innovation Index, Serbia is at the 62nd position of the 127 countries analyzed in 2017. According to these data, the key weaknesses of the country's innovation inputs are low market and business sophistication, the state of cluster development and joint ventures/strategic alliance deals, insufficient government expenditure on education and the absence of global R&D companies.

With a goal of improving innovativeness in Serbia, it is necessary to enhance cooperation between economy and science, strengthening consciousness about the importance of innovations from the aspect of competitiveness, both on micro- and macro-level, as well as the importance of networking and different forms of innovation networks which have a leading role in development and transfer of knowledge, which can lead to the increase of national innovation capacity. Besides that, the important factors of removing key weaknesses of domestic innovation are: The development of innovation infrastructure, creating conditions for larger investments in R&D, both in public and private sector, direct and indirect state measures as a support to the private sector and more efficient protection of the intellectual property.

References

Bedford, A. D. (2013). Expanding the Definition and measurement of knowledge economy: integrating triple bottom line factors into knowledge economy index models and methodologies. *Journal of Modern Accounting and Auditing, 9*(2), 278–286. https://doi.org/10.17265/1548-6583/2013.02.011.

Bošković, G., Savić, L., & Mićić, V. (2016). Innovation as a determinant of competitiveness and development of small and medium-sized enterprises in the Republic of Serbia. *Themes, 40*(1), 171–185. http://teme2.junis.ni.ac.rs/index.php/TEME/article/viewFile/110/103. Accessed 24 Jan 2018.

Cainelli, G., Evangelista, R., & Savona, M. (2004). The impact of innovation on economic performance in services. *The Service Industries Journal, 24*(1), 116–130. https://doi.org/10.1080/0264206041233130l162.

Cantwell, J. (2005). Innovation and Competitiveness. In J. Fagerberg, D. C. Mowery & R. R. Nelson (Eds.), *The oxford handbook of innovation*. Oxford University Press, Oxford. https://doi.org/10.1093/oxfordhb/9780199286805.003.0020.

Child, J., & Faulkner, D. (1998). *Strategies of co-operation*. New York: Oxford University Press.

Ciocanel, A. B., & Pavelescu, F. M. (2015). Innovation and competitiveness in European context. *Procedia Economics and Finance, 32*, 728–737. https://doi.org/10.1016/S2212-5671(15)01455-0.

Cornell University, INSEAD & WIPO. (2017). The global innovation index 2017: innovation feeding the World, Ithaca, Fontainebleau and Geneva. http://www.wipo.int/edocs/pubdocs/en/wipo_pub_gii_2017.pdf. Accessed 25 March 2018.

Cvetanović, S., Ilić, V., Despotović, D., & Nedić, V. (2015). Knowledge economy readiness, innovativeness and competitiveness of the Western Balkan countries. *Industrija, 43*(3), 27–53. https://doi.org/10.5937/industrija43-7908.

Cvetanović, S., Mladenović, I., & Nikolić, M. (2011). Theoretical basis of the concept of national innovation systems. *Ekonomika, 57*(4), 14–23. http://www.ekonomika.org.rs/en/PDF/ekonomika/2011/4-2011.pdf. Accessed 25 Jan 2018.

Despotovic, D. Z., Cvetanović, S. Ž., & Nedić, V. M. (2014). Innovativeness and competitiveness of the Western Balkan countries and selected EU member states. *Industrija, 42*(1), 27–45. https://doi.org/10.5937/industrija42-4602.

Dess, G., Lumpkin, T., & Eisner, A. (2007). *Strategic management*. Belgrade: Data Status.

European Commission (2010) *Science, technology and innovation in Europe*. Publications Office of the European Union, Luxembourg. http://ec.europa.eu/eurostat/documents/3930297/5969406/KS-GN-13-001-EN.PDF. Accessed 25 Jan 2018.

Grossman, G., & Helpman, E. (1991). *Innovation and growth in the global economy*. Cambridge MA: MIT Press.

Harrison, N. J., & Watson, T. (1998). The focus for innovation in small and medium service enterprises. In *Conference Proceedings of the 7th Annual Meeting of the Western Decision Sciences Institute* (pp. 7–11). Reno, NV, USA.

Houghton, J., & Sheehan, P. (2000). *A primer on the knowledge economy*. Working Paper. Melbourne, Victoria University.

Hurley, R., & Hult, G. (1998). Innovation, market orientation, and organizational learning: an integration and empirical examination. *Journal of Marketing, 62*(3), 42–54. https://doi.org/10.2307/1251742.

Ivanović-Đukić, M., & Lazić, M. (2014). Encouraging innovativeness of small and medium enterprises in Serbia to support competitiveness improvement in the post-crisis period. *Economic Themes, 52*(1), 49–62. https://doi.org/10.1515/ethemes-2014-0004.

Jovović, D. (2017). Model of open innovations and small and medium-sized enterprises development. *FACTA Universitatis-Economics and Organization, 14*(4), 345–357. https://doi.org/10.22190/FUEO1704345J.

Karo, E., & Kattel, R. (2011). Should "open innovation" change innovation policy thinking in catching-up economies? Considerations for policy analyses. *Innovation: The European Journal of Social Science Research, 24*(1–2), 173–198. https://doi.org/10.1080/13511610.2011.586496.

Krstić, B., Stanišić, T., & Radivojević, V. (2016). The impact of innovativeness factors on the EU countries competitiveness. *Industrija, 44*(2), 101–115. https://doi.org/10.5937/industrija44-10674.

Martín-de Castro, G., Delgado-Verde, M., Navas-López, J. E., & Cruz-González, J. (2013). The moderating role of innovation culture in the relationship between knowledge assets and product innovation. *Technological Forecasting and Social Change, 80*(2), 351–363. https://doi.org/10.1016/j.techfore.2012.08.012.

Nikolić, M. (2014). *Innovativeness of small and medium-sized enterprises as a factor in economic development of Serbia*. Dissertation, University of Nish.

Official Gazette, R. S. (2016). Strategy of scientific and technological development of the Republic of Serbia for the period from 2016 to 2020—research for innovation. Official Gazette RS no. 25/2016. http://www.mpn.gov.rs/wp-content/uploads/2015/08/Strategija-nauka-za-inovacije-17-NOVO.pdf. Accessed 28 March 2018.

Organization for Economic Cooperation and Development. (1996). *The knowledge-based economy*. Paris. https://www.oecd.org/sti/sci-tech/1913021.pdf. Accessed 30 March 2018.

Perez-Moreno, S., Rodriguez, B., Luque, M. (2016). Assessing global competitiveness under multicriteria perspective. *Economic Modelling, 53*, 398–408.

Pilinkienė, V. (2015). R&D investment and competitiveness in the Baltic States. *Procedia-Social and Behavioral Sciences, 213*, 154–160. https://doi.org/10.1016/j.sbspro.2015.11.419.

Porter, M. E. (1990). The competitive advantage of nations. *Harvard Business Review*, (2), 73–93. https://doi.org/10.1002/cir.3880010112.

Ravić, N., & Gavrić, G. (2015). The role and importance of innovation for the development of small and medium-sized enterprises in the Republic of Serbia. *Ekonomija: teorija i praksa, 8*(4), 47–63. https://doi.org/10.5937/etp1504047R.

Santos-Vijande, M. L., & Alvarez-Gonzalez, L. I. (2007). Innovativeness and organizational innovation in total quality oriented firms: the moderating role of market turbulence. *Technovation, 27*(9), 514–532. https://doi.org/10.1016/j.technovation.2007.05.014.

The Ministry of the Economy. (2017). The report on small and medium enterprises and entrepreneurship 2016. The Ministry of the Economy, sector for the development of small and medium enterprises and entrepreneurship, Belgrade. http://privreda.gov.rs/wp-content/uploads/2017/11/MSPP_izvestaj_2016.pdf. Accessed 30 March 2018.

Tidd, J., & Bessant, J. (2009). *Managing innovation—integrating technological, marketing and organizational change* (4th ed.). Chichester: Wiley Ltd.

Urbancová, H. (2013). Competitive advantage achievement through innovation and knowledge. *Journal of Competitiveness, 5*(1), 82–96. https://doi.org/10.7441/joc.2013.01.06.

Wang, T. Y., Shih-Chien, C., & Kao, C. (2007). The role of technology development in national competitiveness-evidence from Southeast Asian countries. *Technological Forecasting and Social Change, 74,* 1357–1373. https://doi.org/10.1016/j.techfore.2007.01.001.
World Economic Forum. (2011). *The Global Competitiveness Report 2011–2012*. World Economic Forum, Geneva.
World Economic Forum. (2012). *The Global Competitiveness Report 2012–2013*. World Economic Forum, Geneva.
World Economic Forum. (2013). *The Global Competitiveness Report 2013–2014*. World Economic Forum, Geneva.
World Economic Forum. (2014). *The Global Competitiveness Report 2014–2015*. World Economic Forum, Geneva.
World Economic Forum. (2015). *The Global Competitiveness Report 2015–2016*. World Economic Forum, Geneva.
World Economic Forum. (2016). *The Global Competitiveness Report 2016–2017*. World Economic Forum, Geneva.
World Economic Forum. (2017). *The Global Competitiveness Report 2017–2018*. World Economic Forum, Geneva.

Electric Energy Sector in Turkey and Energy Trading Between Turkey and Balkan Countries

Turker Susmus and Ozgur Babacan

Abstract Energy is the most important factor that provided the economic and social development and facilitates human life. Electricity is not only a scarce resource but also a strategic issue for countries. There is electricity in every area of our life, from home to industrial. The importance of electricity is increasing day by day owing to a particularly rapid population growth and the development of the industry sector. In this study, sources of electricity production and consumption in Turkey will be explained in detail, and additionally, electricity import and export data will be analyzed. On the other hand, overall energy production and consumption issues will be discussed except the electricity in Turkey. Because, there is a relationship with energy cost, Turkey's inflation, and current account deficit because the raw materials of energy inputs are based on imports. In addition, in this paper, it will be analyzed all Balkan Countries as electricity generation, consumption, total electricity installed capacity, total electricity imports and total electricity exports.

Keywords Energy trading with Balkan countries · Electricity sector in Turkey · Electric energy in Balkan countries

1 Introduction

There are four indispensable elements for living: Air, Earth, Water and Fire. There is no need to tell too much about these four elements. We all know the importance of water in human life. Water constitutes the building block of human beings. Air and soil are indispensable elements. Fire has been used as an indispensable source for people's heating and other needs for many years. However, when considering technological developments in nowadays, the "Fire" element has been replaced by the "Energy" element.

Electricity is the most important resource consumed in all areas of our lives. Individuals, businesses and countries need 24 h of uninterrupted electricity. Electricity

T. Susmus (✉) · O. Babacan
Faculty of Economic and Business Administrative Sciences, Ege University, Bornova, Turkey
e-mail: turker.susmus@ege.edu.tr

M. Janowicz-Lomott et al. (eds.), *Economic and Financial Challenges for Balkan and Eastern European Countries*, Springer Proceedings in Business and Economics,
https://doi.org/10.1007/978-3-030-39927-6_8

is an indispensable requirement for all sectors. Because the world population and industrialization are constantly increasing, the need for energy is also increasing. For this reason, energy is the most important problem of the twenty-first century. Since the electricity is not ready for using in the country, it is scarce and must be produced. It requires effective and efficient planning of energy production because of increasing energy needs of countries. As a result, it requires that the countries should be investing for growth and development of the countries because realization of the investments depends on the energy. For this reason, energy for developing countries is of vital importance. Because Turkey is in the developing countries group, it needs energy more and more. In this study, electric energy will be briefly expressed as energy. In the study, after dealing with the electricity sector in Turkey, Turkey and the Balkan countries' energy production, consumption, export and import data will be analyzed. Turkey and the Balkan countries will also be discussed as energy trading.

2 Overview to Energy Sources

Energy sources are named in two different ways, primary and secondary energy. Primary energy sources are fossil fuels such as coal, oil, natural gas and resources such as nuclear energy, solar energy, wind energy. Secondary energy sources such as electricity are produced as a result of processing primary energy sources. In addition, primary energy sources are classified under two headings as renewable energy sources and non-renewable energy sources. Although oil, coal, natural gas and nuclear energy are the main renewable energy sources, wind energy, solar energy, biomass energy, hydrogen energy, geothermal energy and hydroelectric energy are considered as renewable energy sources (Uysal et al. 2015, pp. 64–65).

Non-renewable energy is referred to as a non-renewable energy source. A renewable energy source can regenerate itself more quickly than the exhaustion of the energy source. It does not matter how much this resource is used here (Uysal et al. 2015, pp. 64–65). The secondary energy type widely used in the world is electricity energy. In Turkey, electric energy is produced from thermal plants, power plants, wind power plants and geothermal power plants (Kaya and Koç 2015, p. 63).

However, about 2/3 of the energy currently used worldwide is covered by renewable energy sources. Increasing the adequate and reliable resources in the energy supply contributes to the growth and development process. As a result, the geopolitical position of that country is strengthened (Demir 2013, pp. 3–4).

Biomass, which is mostly used for heating, is the largest source of renewable energy resources. The share of renewable energies in the electricity generation is 18%, and the contribution in the primary energy demand for heating is 26%. 80% of the world's energy production is still from fossil fuels, and the remaining 7% comes from nuclear power plants (Greenpeace 2007, p. 17).

Electricity has a different place in other energies for the following reasons (Rumeli 2010, pp. 311–312):

1. It is friendly to the environment.
2. It is produced from different energy sources; nuclear, thermal, hydraulic, etc.
3. It is produced as easily and high efficiency in large quantities.
4. It can be fast transmitted and distributed to very high distances in large quantities.
5. It can be supplied to desired quality (constant voltage, frequency and waveform) and uninterrupted 24 h.
6. It is an energy type that is used easily and efficiently.
7. It can be easily and efficiently converted to different types of energy; heat, motion, light, etc. For these reasons, the words like "white energy," "super energy," "white gold," "golden energy," "energy producing gold" are used for electric energy.

Resources are very limited in the production process. Electricity is both a basic production factor of the industry and a development indicator of the country in terms of industrialization. For that reason, it is very important factor for companies and countries. Due to ease of use, cleanliness and non-waste, the share of electric energy consumption in general energy consumption is increasing rapidly, especially in industrialized countries as compared to other energy sources (Cengiz 2006, p. 130). As seen in Fig. 1, in 2015, 68.5% of world electricity production was from fossil fuel generating plants. Hydroelectric plants provided 16.0%, nuclear plants 10.6%, geothermal, solar, wind, tide and other sources 4.9%, and biofuels, waste, etc., made up the remaining 2.2% (International Energy Agency 2017, p. 3).

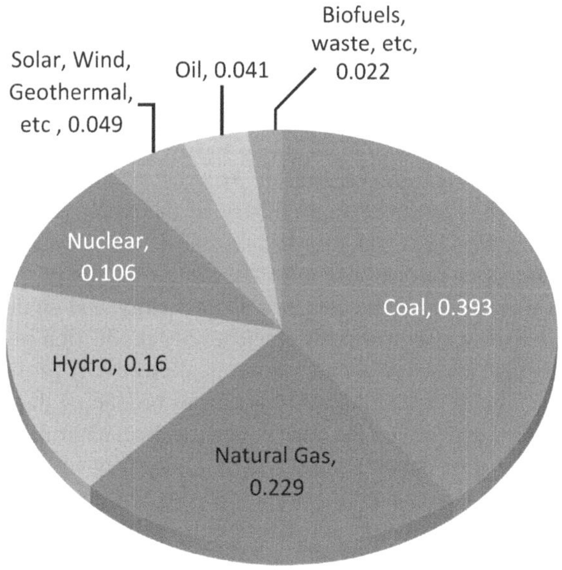

Fig. 1 Sources of world electricity production. *Source* International Energy Agency (2017, p. 3)

3 Relationship with Energy, Economic Growth and Current Account Deficit

The mechanization of the industrial revolution has led to the acceleration of the industrial sector. This has increased the use of energy. One country should make more production for its development. However, the increase in production requires more energy use. Energy is the most basic input in the production process for the realization of social and economic development. Energy consumption in Turkey increased rapidly after 1980 thanks to the acceleration of population and industrialization (Yanar and Kerimoğlu 2011, p. 193).

Energy affects the level of development of the countries and constitutes an important place in the determination of the international policies of the countries. Because there is a positive relationship with energy and level of development, the basis of hot and cold wars in the world lies in the struggle to have energy resources and control their energy resources. In this framework, as a result of increased production, the use of energy resources and energy demand will rise, leading to economic growth (Korkmaz and Develi 2012, p. 2).

Turkey, that has important targets for economic growth and development, provides approximately 3/4 of its energy needs from other countries. Turkey is in the top 15 of energy consumption in the world ranking. Although it is a very important potential for renewable energy sources, about 15% of renewable energy sources such as solar, wind and geothermal can be utilized. Because the energy deficit is the most important part of Turkey's current account deficit, it threatens many macroeconomic variables. Therefore, Turkey has to take important investments in renewable energy resources. Turkey is a bridge between the region demanding energy and region having the most intensive energy sources in the world. Turkey should be forcing multinational business associations on access to low-cost energy source, transfer and processing (Korkmaz and Develi 2012, p. 3).

Turkey is the second country in the world demand for electricity and natural gas after China. As it is known, most of the imported natural gas is used in the production of electric energy (Byzantine and Gurel 2016). On the one hand, Turkey is trying to meet the demands about energy, and on the other hand, Turkey is trying to diversify and to speed up electricity production investment. Turkey is getting to become attractive country in terms of electricity for investors (Bicen 2016, p. 2).

Table 1 shows the top 10 countries producing the most natural gas in the world. Turkey depends on the other countries about natural gas. According to the US Energy Information Administration, Turkey is the fifty-fifth in the world. There are no Balkan countries in the top 50 about oil production.

Table 2 shows the top 10 countries producing the most natural gas in the world. Turkey is dependent on foreign countries about natural gas. According to the US Energy Information Administration's data, Turkey is ranked 73 in the world in 2015. Romania is the 41st country in the Balkan countries. There are no Balkan countries in the first 40 for natural gas production.

Table 1 World proven oil reserves

	Countries	2015 (billions of barrels)	2016 (billions of barrels)
1	Venezuela	298.4	300.2
2	Saudi Arabia	268.3	267.2
3	Canada	172.5	171.1
4	Iran	157.8	158.1
5	Iraq	144.2	143.9
6	Kuwait	104.0	102.6
7	B. The Arab Emirates	97.8	98.6
8	Saudi Arabia	80	80.5
9	Libya	48.4	48.3
10	Nigeria	37.1	37.2
	Total	1655.3	1645.9

Electric Production Sector Report. http://www.enerji.gov.tr, p. 3. Access date: 20.04.2018

Table 2 World proven natural gas reserves

	Countries	2015 (billions of ft^3)	2016 (billions of ft^3)
1	Russia	1,688,240	1,688,250
2	Iran	1,201,170	1,201,170
3	Qatar	872,130	866,130
4	USA	369,500	308,400
5	Saudi Arabia	294,400	300,400
6	Turkmenistan	265,400	265,400
7	B. The Arab Emirates	215,300	215,300
8	Venezuela	197,300	198,300
9	Nigeria	180,300	180,300
10	China	164,200	175,300
	Total	6,938,623	6,895,740

Source Elektric Production Sector Report. http://www.enerji.gov.tr, p. 3. Access date: 20.04.2018

Renewable energy sources contribute significantly to the protection of the environment as well as reducing imports and external dependency in energy use. As a result, it is possible to say that renewable energy resources have a great importance in creating strategic energy policies such as energy resource diversity and energy security. The operating costs of renewable energy sources are generally low. However, the

Table 3 Relationship with current account deficit and imported energy in Turkey

Years	Current account deficit	Imported energy	Total imports
2008	−40,438,000	48,281,193	201,963,574
2009	−12,168,000	29,905,305	140,928,421
2010	−45,447,000	38,497,229	185,544,332
2011	−75,092,000	54,117,539	240,841,676
2012	−48,500,000	60,117,407	236,545,141
2013	−64,400,000	55,915,234	251,661,250
2014	−45,800,000	54,906,870	242,177,117
2015	−32,200,000	37,842,886	207,234,359

Source Erol and Güneş (2017, pp. 343–344)

initial investment costs of renewable energy sources are quite high compared to non-renewable energy sources. Renewable energy sources require high-tech support. In order to benefit from renewable energy resources, it is necessary to give importance to Research and Development studies (Demir 2013, p. 6).

It is possible to state the existence of a positive and strong correlation between economic growth, energy imports and the current account deficit in the most of the countries that meet by importing most of your energy needs. Real growth can only be achieved with increased production. The more countries which are dependent on the other countries for their energy needs desire to economic growth, the more their energy needs will increase. This energy requirement leads to an increase in external financing over time. As a result of the increase in the share of energy in imports, the developing countries' foreign exchange needs also increase, and then the exchange rates also increase (Erol and Güneş 2017, p. 342).

When Table 3 is examined, it can be said that when the imported energy increases, it increases in parallel with the current deficit. Considering this aspect, one of the important reasons in Turkey's current account deficit can be express energy imports.

Energy is a strategic issue for Turkey. When the energy policies in the country are examined recently, it is seen that energy supply and demand are considered as priority. Related institutions are working on energy demand projections for ever-increasing energy needs. Accordingly, energy consumption in the world is expected to increase at a rate of over 60% in 2030 as compared to 2017; it is projected to increase at a rate of over 100% for Turkey (Erdal Tanas Karagöl, Mehmet Rıda tür 2017, pp. 9–10). Therefore, because especially Turkey is to control current account deficit and to provide a sustainable growth, it produces energy itself without depending on the any other countries.

4 Electricity Production and Consumption as Sectors by Energy Sources in Turkey

Turkey is a country with a wide range of primary energy sources. There are fossil resource reserves such as coal, lignite, crude oil, natural gas, uranium and thorium in the country and renewable resource potentials such as hydraulic, geothermal, solar, wind, wave and biomass. Although it is generally used fossil fuels in the world, Turkey has not these reserves of resources sufficiently. However, there are coal, geothermal and hydroelectric energy reserves in Turkey, but these reserves constitute 1% of the world's resources assets (Erdal Tanas Karagöl and Mehmet Rıda tür 2017, p. 10).

According to Table 4, Turkey provided electricity generation from coal, hydropower plants and liquid fuel between 1970 and 1985. It has started to use natural gas in electric production; it has risen consumption of the natural gas in electric generation since 2000 years. As a result of the increase in the use of natural gas in electricity generation, the share of liquid fuels is extremely low. According to the data of 2016, Turkey's 33.7% of the electricity produced is coal, 32.5% of natural gas, 24.5% of hydroelectric power plants, 8.6% of renewable energy sources and 0.7% of liquid assets.

99% of natural gas, the most important source of electricity production, are imported by Turkey. In this case, unfortunately Turkey is dependent on other countries to produce electricity. 43% of the total natural gas reserves are in the Middle East, 29% in Russia and the Commonwealth of Independent States, and 16% in the African/Pacific countries. Natural gas produced in Turkey's meets only 0.8% of the total consumption (KPMG 2018, p. 9).

Table 5 shows the distribution of electricity consumption sector in Turkey. According to the table, while the consumption rate in residential and commercial sectors increased, consumption for illumination purposes decreased and consumption rates in industrial sector remained the same. In my opinion, the share of saving bulbs has been influential in the fall of lighting. When production and consumption data are analyzed, electricity production increased by 112% from 2002 to 2016, while consumption increased by 124%. Accordingly, Turkey can not be able to compensate the growing electricity demand adequately.

According to the result of the calculations, the electric energy need of Turkey in the year 2050 is approximately 1173 billion kWh. The economically usable hydroelectrical potential is known to be approximately 125 billion kWh, and the yearly thermal energy production is calculated as 688 billion kWh. So, Turkey requires 360 billion kWh energy produced by other energy resources. According to these values, renewable energy resources should be used until the year 2050 for this 360 billion kWh energy production. These resources are wind energy, sun energy, sea originated energy, biomass energy and hydrogen energy, which is the energy of future. The whole wind energy of Turkey is 200 billion kWh, and the sea originated energy potential by using one-fifth of seasides is 18.5 billion. The total potential of other energy resources is not known clearly (Yumurtaci and Asmaz 2004, p. 1163).

Table 4 Electricity generation and shares by energy resources in Turkey

Year	Total (GWh)	Coal (%)	Liquid fuels (%)	Natural gas (%)	Hydro (%)	Renewable energy and wastes (%)
1990	**57,543**	35.1	6.8	17.7	40.2	0.2
1991	**60,246**	35.8	5.6	20.8	37.6	0.2
1992	**67,342**	36.5	7.8	16.0	39.5	0.2
1993	**73,808**	32.1	7.0	14.6	46.1	0.2
1994	**78,322**	36.0	7.1	17.6	39.1	0.2
1995	**86,247**	32.5	6.7	19.2	41.2	0.4
1996	**94,862**	32.0	6.9	18.1	42.7	0.3
1997	**103,296**	32.8	6.9	21.4	38.5	0.4
1998	**111,022**	32.2	7.2	22.4	38.0	0.3
1999	**116,440**	31.8	6.9	31.2	29.8	0.3
2000	**124,922**	30.6	7.5	37.0	24.7	0.3
2001	**122,725**	31.3	8.4	40.4	19.6	0.3
2002	**129,400**	24.8	8.3	40.6	26.0	0.3
2003	**140,581**	22.9	6.6	45.2	25.1	0.2
2004	**150,698**	22.8	5.0	41.3	30.6	0.3
2005	**161,956**	26.6	3.4	45.3	24.4	0.3
2006	**176,300**	26.4	2.4	45.8	25.1	0.3
2007	**191,558**	27.9	3.4	49.6	18.7	0.4
2008	**198,418**	29.1	3.8	49.7	16.8	0.6
2009	**194,813**	28.6	2.5	49.3	18.5	1.2
2010	**211,208**	26.1	1.0	46.5	24.5	1.9
2011	**229,395**	28.8	0.4	45.4	22.8	2.6
2012	**239,497**	28.4	0.7	43.6	24.2	3.1
2013	**240,154**	26.6	0.7	43.8	24.7	4.2
2014	**251,963**	30.2	0.9	47.9	16.1	4.9
2015	**261,783**	29.1	0.9	37.9	25.6	6.5
2016	**274,408**	33.7	0.7	32.5	24.5	8.6

Source http://www.tuik.gov.tr. Access date: 10.03.2018

5 Generation, Consumption, Installed Capacity of Electricity in Balkan Countries

There are total of 199 countries producing electricity in the world. As can be seen from Table 6, in 2015, Turkey's electricity production in the world is the rank of 17, Romania 46, Greece 52, while Bulgaria is the rank of 56. Turkey produces 249 billion kWh of electricity although the total electricity generation of all the

Table 5 Distribution of electricity consumption to sectors

Year	Total (GWh)	Household (%)	Commercial (%)	Government (%)	Industrial (%)	Illumination (%)	Other (%)[a]
2000	**98,296**	24.3	9.5	4.2	49.7	4.6	7.7
2001	**97,070**	24.3	10.2	4.5	48.4	5.0	7.6
2002	**102,948**	22.9	10.6	4.4	49.0	5.0	8.1
2003	**111,766**	22.5	11.5	4.1	49.3	4.5	8.1
2004	**121,142**	22.8	12.9	3.7	49.2	3.7	7.7
2005	**130,263**	23.7	14.2	3.6	47.8	3.2	7.5
2006	**143,071**	24.1	14.2	4.2	47.5	2.8	7.2
2007	**155,135**	23.5	14 9	4.5	47.6	2.6	6.9
2008	**161,948**	24.4	14.8	4.5	46.2	2.5	7.6
2009	**156,894**	25.0	15.9	4.5	44.9	2.5	7.2
2010	**172,051**	24.1	16.1	4.1	46.1	2.2	7.4
2011	**186,100**	23.8	16.4	3.9	47.3	2.1	6.5
2012	**194,923**	23.3	16.3	4.5	47.4	2.0	6.5
2013	**198,045**	22.7	18.9	4.1	47.1	1.9	5.3
2014	**207,375**	22.3	19.2	3.9	47.2	1.9	5.5
2015	**217,312**	22.0	19.1	3.7	47.6	1.9	5.7
2016	**231,204**	22.2	18.8	3.9	46.9	1.8	6.4

Source http://www.tuik.gov.tr. Access date: 15.04.2018

Table 6 Total electricity net generation in Balkan countries, 2015

Balkan countries	Rank among the countries of the world	Billion (kWh)
Turkey	17	249
Romania	46	63
Greece	52	49
Bulgaria	56	46
Serbia	60	35
Bosnia and Herzegovina	85	15
Macedonia	113	6.1
Albania	116	5.9
Kosovo	119	5.8
Montenegro	132	2.9

Source https://www.eia.gov/beta/international/ (23.04.2018)

Table 7 Total electricity net consumption in Balkan countries, 2015

Balkan countries	Rank among the countries of the world	Billion (kWh)
Turkey	19	216
Greece	45	54
Romania	48	49
Bulgaria	60	32
Serbia	62	29
Bosnia and Herzegovina	87	11
Macedonia	106	7.6
Albania	118	5.1
Kosovo	121	4.9
Montenegro	136	2.8

Source https://www.eia.gov/beta/international/ (23.04.2018)

Balkan countries is 228.7 billion kWh. Accordingly, it is concluded that Turkey produces more electricity from all Balkan countries. In the future, if Turkey could give priority to renewable energy sources in electricity production by reducing dependence on foreign inputs, both Turkey can be able to reduce the current account deficit and increase electricity exports to Balkan countries.

As it can be seen from Table 7, in 2015, while Turkey is in the rank of 19 on electricity consumption in the world, Greece 45th, Romania 48th, Bulgaria 60th. Although the total power consumption of all the Balkan countries except Turkey is 195.4 billion kWh, Turkey consumes 216 billion kWh of electricity by itself. Accordingly, it is concluded that Turkey consumes more electricity from all Balkan countries.

When Table 8 is examined, in 2015, FYR Macedonia and Greece consumed more electricity than they produced. Greece's short of electric production was 10.2%, while FYR Macedonia's was 24.5%. Other Balkan countries produced more electricity than they consumed. Bulgaria's production surplus of electricity is 30.4%; Turkey is 13.2%. Turkey, Romania, Bulgaria and Bosnia and Herzegovina are countries that have potential for electricity export.

As it can be seen in Table 9, in 2015, while Turkey ranks 14th as the installed capacity of electricity in the world, Romania 36th, Greece 45th, Bulgaria is the rank of 57. Although the total electric installed capacity of all Balkan countries except Turkey has 71.6 million kW, Turkey has 73 million kW installed electricity capacity.

Table 8 Total electricity net generation and consumption in Balkan countries, 2015

Balkan countries	Generation billion (kWh)	Consumption billion (kWh)	Net difference
Turkey	249	216	33
Greece	49	54	−5
Romania	63	49	14
Bulgaria	46	32	14
Serbia	35	29	6
Bosnia and Herzegovina	15	11	4
FYR Macedonia	6.1	7.6	−1.5
Albania	5.9	5.1	0.8
Kosovo	5.8	4.9	0.9
Montenegro	2.9	2.8	0.1

Source https://www.eia.gov/beta/international/ (23.04.2018)

Table 9 Total electricity installed capacity in Balkan countries, 2015

Balkan countries	Rank among the countries of the world	Million (kW)
Turkey	14	73
Romania	36	24
Greece	45	19
Bulgaria	57	11
Serbia	71	7.3
Bosnia and Herzegovina	84	4.2
Albania	112	1.9
FYR Macedonia	116	1.7
Kosovo	119	1.6
Montenegro	130	0.9

Source https://www.eia.gov/beta/international/ (23.04.2018)

6 Electric Energy Trading Between Turkey and Balkan Countries

This section analyzes Balkan countries' electricity export and import data by comparing with the world. In addition, it will be discussed electricity trade with the Balkan countries and Turkey.

In 2015, the ranking of countries exporting electricity to the world is shown in Table 10. According to this, the top four exporting countries in the Balkan countries

Table 10 Total electricity exports, 2015

Balkan countries	Rank among the countries of the world	Million (kWh)	Rate in total (%)
Bulgaria	14	15	32.5
Romania	20	11	23.9
Serbia	26	7.2	15.6
Bosnia and Herzegovina	30	6	13
Turkey	41	3.2	6.9
Greece	48	1.5	3.3
Albania	58	1	2.2
Kosovo	65	0.6	1.3
Montenegro	68	0.5	1.1
FYR Macedonia	79	0.1	0.2
Total		46.1	100

Source https://www.eia.gov/beta/international/ (23.04.2018)

are Bulgaria, Romania, Serbia and Bosnia Herzegovina, respectively. These four countries constitute 85% of Balkan countries' total exports.

In 2015, the ranking of the countries that import electricity is shown in Table 11. Accordingly, the top 5 countries that import most in Balkan countries, respectively, are Greece, Turkey, Serbia, Romania and Bulgaria. These 5 countries constitute of 75.6% of the total exports of the Balkan countries.

As examined in Table 12, Bulgaria, Romania, Serbia and Bosnia and Herzegovina are the countries which have high foreign trade surplus of electricity in the Balkan

Table 11 Total electricity imports, 2015

Balkan countries	Rank among the countries of the world	Million (kWh)	Rate in total (%)
Greece	21	11	25.1
Turkey	34	7.1	16.2
Serbia	36	6.3	14.4
Romania	44	4.5	10.3
Bulgaria	45	4.3	9.8
Bosnia and Herzegovina	48	3.9	8.9
FYR Macedonia	50	2.7	6.2
Albania	53	2.4	5.5
Montenegro	68	1	2.3
Kosovo	74	0.7	1.6
Total		43.9	100

Source https://www.eia.gov/beta/international/ (23.04.2018)

Table 12 Total electricity export and import in Balkan countries, 2015

Balkan countries	Export million (kWh)	Import million (kWh)	Electricity foreign trading deficit or surplus
Bulgaria	15	4.3	**10.7**
Romania	11	4.5	**6.5**
Serbia	7.2	6.3	**0.9**
Bosnia - Herzegovina	6	3.9	**2.1**
Turkey	3.2	7.1	**−3.9**
Greece	1.5	11	**−9.5**
Albania	1	2.4	**−1.4**
Kosovo	0.6	0.7	**−0.1**
Montenegro	0.5	1	**−0.5**
FYR Macedonia	0.1	2.7	**−2.6**

Source https://www.eia.gov/beta/international/. Access date: 23.04.2018

countries. Turkey, Greece, Albania, Kosovo, Montenegro and FYR Macedonia have foreign trade deficit of electricity. But unfortunately, Turkey has the most foreign trade deficit of electricity in the Balkan Countries.

As can be seen in Tables 13 and 14, Turkey has a relationship with Bulgaria and Greece in about electricity trading. While Turkey imports electric energy from Bulgaria, it exports electric energy to Greece. However, these export and import figures are quite low.

Table 13 Distribution of *exported* electrical energy years (unit: Gwh)

Countries	2009	2010	2011	2012	2013	2014	2015	2016
Bulgaria			621.8	1.7	0.2	0.2	1.9	3.1
Greece	0.0	0.0	1790.3	1704.9	804.7	1909.4	2818.6	1444.3
Total	0.0	0.0	2412.1	1706.6	804.8	1909.6	2820.5	1447.4

Source https://www.teias.gov.tr/tr/turkiye-elektrik-uretim-iletim-2016-yili-istatistikleri. Access date: 15.03.2018

Table 14 Distribution of imported electrical energy by years (unit: Gwh)

Countries	2009	2010	2011	2012	2013	2014	2015	2016
Bulgaria	0.0	0.0	2094.1	3966.8	4571.2	5300.7	4.842.0	4587.0
Greece	0.0	0.0	838.7	3.7	173.2	4.0	8.4	68.3
Total	0.0	0.0	2932.8	3970.5	4744.4	5304.7	4850.4	4655.2

Source https://www.teias.gov.tr/tr/turkiye-elektrik-uretim-iletim-2016-yili-istatistikleri. Access date: 15.03.2018

7 Conclusion

Energy which has strategic issue for countries is a scarce resource, and it is the most important factor for economic development. Energy consists of Air, Earth, Water and Fire. And nowadays, in spite of the fact that fire is still important in our life, fire has left its place to the energy in economic life. Energy sources are named in two different ways, primary, secondary energy. In addition, primary energy sources are classified under two headings as renewable energy sources and non-renewable energy sources. Primary energy sources are coal, oil, natural gas, nuclear energy, solar energy, wind energy. Secondary energy sources are produced by primary energy sources such as electricity.

Turkey is the country which has the biggest demand for electricity in all Balkan Countries. Energy consumption in Turkey increased rapidly thanks to the acceleration of population and industrialization. Turkey is in the rank of 19 on electricity consumption in the world, Greece 45th, Romania 48th, Bulgaria 60th. Although Turkey has the highest electricity generation, consumption and production capacity in all Balkan countries, it has electricity deficit. Bulgaria, Romania, Serbia and Bosnia and Herzegovina have high foreign trade surplus of electricity in the Balkan countries. Turkey, Greece, Albania, Kosovo, Montenegro and FYR Macedonia have foreign trade deficit of electricity. Bulgaria, Romania, Serbia and Bosnia Herzegovina export electric energy and these 4 countries constitute 85% of Balkan countries' total exports. Turkey has a relationship with Bulgaria and Greece in about electricity trading. While Turkey imports electric energy from Bulgaria, it exports electric energy to Greece. However, these export and import figures are quite low. Because Turkey is dependent on foreign raw materials for electricity production, Turkey's current account deficit is going on increasing year by year. For that reason, Turkey has to give important investments of renewable energy resources.

References

Bicen, Y. (2016). Turkey electricity market development process: day-ahead and balancing power market features. *Karaelmas Fen ve Mühendislik Dergisi, 6*(2), 432–438.

Cengiz, S. (2006). Türkiye'nin Elektrik Enerjisi Piyasasında Yeniden Yapılanma. *Journal of Administrative Sciences, 4*(1), 125–147.

Demir, M. (2013). Enerji İthalatı Cari Açık İlişkisi, Var Analizi İle Türkiye Üzerine Bir İnceleme. *Journal of Academic Researches and Studies, 5*(9), 2–27.

Elektric Production Sector Report. http://www.enerji.gov.tr (20.04.2018).

Erol, E. D., & Güneş, İ. (2017). Türkiye'de Enerji İthalatı, Ekonomik Büyüme ve Cari Açık İlişkisi. *ASOS The Journal of Akademic Social Sciences, 5*(45), 340–352, Mayıs 2017.

International Energy Agency. (2017). *Electricity information: Overview*. https://www.iea.org/publications/freepublications/publication/ElectricityInformation2017Overview.pdf. Access date: 14.02.2018.

Kaya, K., & Koç, E. (2015). Enerji Üretim Santralleri Maliyet Analizi. *Mühendis ve Makine, 56*(660), 61–68.

Korkmaz, Ö., & Develi, A. (2012). Türkiye'de Birincil Enerji Kullanımı, Üretimi ve Gayri Safi Yurt İçi Hasıla (GSYİH) Arasındaki İlişki. *Dokuz Eylül Üniversitesi İktisadi ve İdari Bilimler Fakültesi Dergisi,* Cilt: 27, Sayı: 2, 1–25.
KPMG, Enerji Sektörel Bakış. (2018). http://www.kpmg.com.tr (19.04.2018).
Rumeli, A. (2010). Elektrik Enerjisi ve Türkiye. *Perşembe Konferansları*, 311–333.
Uysal, D., Yilmaz, K. Ç., & Tas, T. (2015). Enerji İthalatı ve Cari Açık İlişkisi: Türkiye Örneği. *Anemon Muş Alparslan Üniversitesi Sosyal Bilimler Dergisi, 3*(1), 63–78, Haziran: 2015.
Yanar, R., & Kerimoğlu, G. (2011). Türkiye'de Enerji Tüketimi, Ekonomik Büyüme ve Cari Açık Ilişkisi. *Ekonomi Bilimleri Dergisi, 3*(2), 191–201.
Yumurtaci, Z., & Asmaz, E. (2004). Electric Energy Demand of Turkey for the Year 2050. *Energy Sources, 26*, 1157–1164.
http://www.tuik.gov.tr (10.03.2018).
https://www.eia.gov/beta/international/ (23.01.2018).
https://www.teias.gov.tr/tr/turkiye-elektrik-uretim-iletim-2016-yili-istatistikleri (15.03.2018).

Profitability Determinants of Insurance Companies in the Republic of Serbia

Ivana Marjanović and Žarko Popović

Abstract The performance of insurance companies should be profoundly analysed in order to determine the growth possibilities of the insurance sector and its contribution to the development of the national economy. The aim of this paper is to investigate the influence of the firm-specific factors and external factors on profitability of insurance companies in the Republic of Serbia. In order to achieve this objective, multiple regression analysis is applied on the panel data covering the period from 2006 to 2016. The analysed sample consists of fourteen insurance companies that operate in the Republic of Serbia. As a measure of profitability, the Return on Asset (ROA) indicator is used. The results of the regression analysis indicate that a number of years operating on the market, capital adequacy, investment performance, market share and GDP growth rate are determinants that have statistically a significant impact on the profitability. These results should provide important information on what should insurance companies that operate in the Republic of Serbia and relevant policymakers focus in order to improve profitability, bearing in mind the fact that insurance sector can be an important determinant of financial and overall economic development of a country.

Keywords Insurance companies · Profitability · Panel data · Multiple regression analysis

1 Introduction

Insurance in the broadest sense represents the protection of property in the situation of risk realization, that is, occurrence of insured cases. The protection is based on the insured funds formed by collecting premiums. Through various types of protection, the insurance activity is present in everyday life. Legal entities and individuals are exposed to the continuing possibility of emergencies that can cause harm. Insurance is one of the most important forms of security against such events and represents an

I. Marjanović (✉) · Ž. Popović
Faculty of Economics, University of Niš, Trg Kralja Aleksandra Ujedinitelja 11, Niš, Serbia
e-mail: ivana.veselinovic@eknfak.ni.ac.rs

M. Janowicz-Lomott et al. (eds.), *Economic and Financial Challenges for Balkan and Eastern European Countries*, Springer Proceedings in Business and Economics,
https://doi.org/10.1007/978-3-030-39927-6_9

economic need for everyone who takes care of safety in business and everyday life. From the perspective of an individual, the role of insurance is twofold: the protection of the insured—his physical integrity and his property through compensation for damage caused by the realization of the insured case, while protecting the material position of the insured and protecting the third parties. From the perspective of the economy, it is reflected in the compensation of damages that could endanger the functioning of the economy of a country. Insurers are important players in innovation and the advancement of many fields: medicine, industry and new technologies, because they represent risk-takers and thus enable new ventures. Business operations in a modern market economy cannot be imagined without relying on insurance funds. The reimbursement of damages incurred during the business process ensures the renewal of the working capacity of the economic entities, enabling it to overcome the economic consequences of harmful events. Regarding individuals, the payment of insurance also addresses the issues of their well-being.

Today, insurance is an economic institution that compensates for damage caused by the devastating natural forces, accidents and many other events. It provides economic protection to insurers, from harmful acts and disorders that arise from the occurrence of the insured event or the occurrence of the insured danger. Insurance companies are also very important investors in the world market. The aim of insurance companies as institutional investors is to provide additional liquidity in the financial market, maximize profits with an acceptable level of investment risk and collect free capital and put it in the function of economic growth and development (Marović and Njegomir 2015). It is the known fact that financial system reflects the economic performance of a country, considering that a healthy economy requires an efficient financial system in order to direct funds to economically justified investments. Therefore, the existence of an efficient financial system is of particular interest to the national authorities.

Bearing in mind stated the role of insurance in economy its financial performance is a prominent parameter for determining the economic growth. Reliable and efficient operation of insurance companies enriches prosperity in society and further strengthened the economy of the country (Rahman et al. 2012). However, the business of any entity is affected by a large number of factors, both those related to the entity itself (firm-specific factors) and factors from the external environment. Regarding insurance companies, external factors are related to some features of macroeconomic environment, while firm-specific factors can refer to some particular characteristics of company such as age, financial structure or size of a company.

Taking into account the importance of aforesaid, the aim of this paper is to investigate and determine the main profitability factors of insurance companies in the Republic of Serbia. The main hypothesis of the paper is that there is a strong coherence between profitability of insurance companies measured by Return on Asset indicator and selected firm-specific and external factors. This paper contributes to the existing literature on profitability determinants of insurance companies by providing empirical data regarding profitability determinants of insurance companies in the Republic of Serbia.

In order to achieve the stated aim, the paper will be structured as follows: after introductory notes, a brief literature review on profitability determinants will be presented. Next part is dedicated to characteristics of the insurance sector in the Republic of Serbia. Afterwards, the presentation of the data and methodology are given, followed by the results of the analysis and discussion. Finally, concluding remarks will be offered.

2 Literature Review

Performance of financial institutions has become one of the important research areas in the last decades bearing in mind the fact that in contemporary conditions, financial institutions have a significant role in overall economic development. However, the trends of market liberalization and globalization led to increased market competition and the need to determine the main factors of the performance of financial institutions. There has been a lot of research in the area of banks' profitability determinants, while the area of determinants of insurance profitability gained attention in recent years (Table 1).

When it comes to research of the insurance sector in the Republic of Serbia, this area has become interesting in the last couple of years. Ikonić et al. (2011) investigated growth potential and profitability of insurance companies in the Republic of Serbia using CAMEL method. Kočović et al. (2014) assessed the performance of companies engaged in non-life insurance business in Serbia. Empirical research was conducted on the basis of financial statements of non-life and composite insurers during the period from 2006 to 2013 by using CAMEL indicators and multiple regression analysis. Their finding indicates the existence of significant and negative influence of the combined ratio, financial leverage and retention rate on the profitability of non-life insurers, measured by the Return on Asset (ROA), while the influence of the written premium growth rate, return on investment and company size is significant and positive. Mandić et al. (2017) use Fuzzy Analytic Hierarchy Process, and Technique for Order Performance by Similarity to Ideal Solution includes on the sample of all companies operating within the insurance sector in Serbia in the period from 2007 to 2014 and gives their assessment and rating.

Significance of the insurance sector as well as the fact that so far in the Republic of Serbia an analysis of the performance of both, life and non-life insurers, has not been performed, was authors' main motivation to conduct an analysis of the profitability determinants of insurers in the Republic of Serbia in order to determine the main drivers of its financial performance.

Table 1 Summary of literature review table

Author	Topic	Sample	Method	Findings
Chidambaran et al. (1997)	An empirical analysis of the economic performance of the US property–liability insurance industry	18 lines of insurance for the period 1984–1993	Two-step generalized least squares	Concentration ratio for the line and the share of direct writers in the line are both significant factors of performance
Francalanci and Galal (1998)	The impact of IT investment and worker composition on the productivity of life insurance companies	52 US life insurance companies for the period 1986–1995	The generalized estimating extension (GEE) of the GLM random estimator	Investments in IT along with changes in worker compensation have an overall positive effect on productivity
Beck and Webb (2003)	Investigation of demographic, economic and institutional determinants of life insurance companies	Panel data for 68 economies in the period 1961–2000	Fixed and random-effect panel data regression analysis	Significant factors: economic indicators, institutional and religious indicators Insignificant factors: education, the young dependency ratio, life expectancy and the size of the social security system
Shiu (2004)	Investigation of main performance determinant, UK general insurers	Panel data set over the period 1986–1999	OLS regression analysis and panel data analysis	Liquidity, unexpected inflation, interest rate level and underwriting profits are statistically significant determinants of the insurers' performance

(continued)

Table 1 (continued)

Author	Topic	Sample	Method	Findings
Chen and Wong (2004)	Investigation of the solvency of general (property–liability) and life insurance companies in Asia	The data from 1994 to 1999 for selected Asian countries	The data from 1994 to 1999 for selected Asian countries	Firm size, liquidity ratio, combined ratio, investment performance, surplus growth and operating margin significantly affect general insurers' financial health, while firm size, investment performance, change in asset mix and change in product mix significantly affect life insurers' financial health
Pervan et al. (2012)	Investigation of the factors that influenced insurance companies' profitability in the Bosnia and Herzegovina	All non-life and composite insurance companies that operated in B&H during the period 2005–2010	Generalized methods of moments (GMM) panel estimator	Negative and noteworthy impact of claim ratio on profitability Noteworthy positive impact of market share, age and past performance on profitability Foreign-owned firms had healthier performance than domestically owned The impact of level of the insurers' diversification was not significant

(continued)

Table 1 (continued)

Author	Topic	Sample	Method	Findings
Almajali et al. (2012)	Analysis of the main financial performance factors of Jordanian insurance companies	25 insurance companies during the period 2002–2007	Multiple regression analysis	Size, liquidity, leverage and management competence index have a statistically significant positive influence on the financial performance
Charumathi (2012)	Investigation of main Indian life insurers' profitability determinants	23 Indian life insurers during the period of 3 financial years	Multiple regression analysis	Company's size and liquidity have positive and significant impact on profitability of life insurers Premium growth, leverage and equity capital have negative and significant influence on insurers' profitability Relationship between underwriting risk and profitability has not been proven
Mehari and Aemiro (2013)	Evaluation of the impact of firm-specific characteristics on performance of insurance companies in Ethiopia	Nine insurance companies over the period from 2005 to 2010	Random-effect panel data regression analysis	Tangibility, insurers' size and leverage have statistically significant positive influence on ROA

(continued)

Table 1 (continued)

Author	Topic	Sample	Method	Findings
				Loss ratio has statistically significant negative influence on ROA Insurers' age, growth in writing premium and liquidity have statistically insignificant association with ROA
Sambasivam and Ayele (2013)	Examination of performance of insurance companies in Ethiopia	Nine insurance companies during the period 2003–2011	Multiple regression analysis	Leverage, growth, size, volume of capital and liquidity are identified as most important determinants of profitability Age and tangibility of assets are not significantly related to profitability
Olaosebikan (2013)	Analysis of the profitability of micro-life insurers in Nigeria	Unbalanced panel data set of 149 observations	Generalized methods of moments (GMM) dynamic panel data estimation	No significant influence of leverage, the ownership structure and firms' size Negative influence of the level of reinsurance on profitability Positive influence of the level of interest rates in the economy

(continued)

Table 1 (continued)

Author	Topic	Sample	Method	Findings
Bawa and Chattha (2013)	Examination of the financial performance of Indian life insurers	18 life insurers during a period of five years	Multiple regression analysis	Liquidity and size of life insurers have positive effect on profitability No influence of solvency and insurance leverage
Oscar et al. (2013)	Determination of financial performance of life insurers in Ghana	Ten life insurance companies for the period 2000–2010	Panel data regression analysis	Gross written premiums have positive relationship with insurers' profitability
Burca and Batrinca (2014)	Analysis of the financial performance determinants in the Romanian insurance market	21 insurance companies during the period 2008–2012	Fixed and random-effect panel data regression analysis	Financial leverage in insurance, company size, growth of gross written premiums, underwriting risk, risk retention ratio and solvency margin have significant influence on financial performance
Jan et al. (2014)	Analysis of insurance industry profitability in Pakistan	Six insurance companies for the period 2010–2013	Multivariate regression analysis	NPL ratio, gearing ratio and asset management have noteworthy impact on the profitability of insurance industry

(continued)

Table 1 (continued)

Author	Topic	Sample	Method	Findings
Lee (2014)	Examination of firm-specific and macroeconomic determinants of profitability of Taiwanese property–liability insurers	Panel data from 1999 to 2009 for 15 insurance companies	Panel data regression analysis	Reinsurance usage, underwriting risk, return on investment (ROI), input cost and financial holding group have significant influence on profitability in both models Economic growth rate has significant influence in operating ratio model but insignificant influence in ROA model
Mwangi and Murigu (2015)	Investigation of the factors that affect the profitability of general insurers in Kenya	23 general insurance firms during the period 2009–2012	Multiple regression analysis	Leverage, equity capital, management competence index have positive influence on profitability; Size and ownership structure have negative influence on profitability No significant influence of retention ratio, liquidity, underwriting risk and age
Öner Kaya (2015)	Analysis of firm-specific factors which influence profitability of non-life insurance companies in Turkey	24 non-life insurance companies during the period from 2006 to 2013	Panel data regression analysis	Age of the company, size of the company, current ratio, loss ratio and premium growth rate represent the main determinants of the profitability

3 Characteristics of the Insurance Sector in the Republic of Serbia

Condition and perspectives of insurance are strongly tied to characteristics of the macroeconomic environment in which insurance companies operate. The last decades of the previous century were characterized with major problems in the macroeconomic environment with a fall in the physical volume of industrial production and the decline of the gross domestic product. Hyperinflation, war, poorly guided macroeconomic policy and corruption and crime culminated in a deep socio-economic crisis. There are two factors that characterized macroeconomic environment of the Republic of Serbia (Kašćelan and Radulović 2008): the scarcity of financial instruments which hinders further development of insurance, i.e. underdeveloped financial market as well as low level of investment activities due to lack of financial resources. By 1990, the insurance sector was characterized with the presence of a small number of mostly state-owned insurance companies leading to the lack of motivation for innovation and development of insurance sector. Most of the companies in the insurance sector were involved only in non-life insurance. Unemployment and low wages have affected the level of life insurance development, as well as property insurance of citizens. Citizens, depending on their purchasing power, could afford only some obligatory non-life types of insurance, primarily insurance from autoliability. Also, hyperinflation which has completely devalued deposits led to distrust in any form of saving even in life insurance as one of the best forms of savings.

Changes in political and economic environment have greatly influenced the development of insurance in the Republic of Serbia in the last decade. The transition to the market economy slowly led to the change in insurance sector. Legislation is being harmonized with the European Union, most of the state insurance companies are privatized with the entrance of the foreign capital in the insurance sector and this consequently increases numbers of insurance companies that operate on market.

At the end of the third quarter of 2017, 21 insurance companies operated in Serbia, when there are two companies fewer than in the same period of the previous year. Among them, seventeen companies are involved only in insurance, while other four companies are involved in reinsurance activities. Regarding the insurance companies, four of insurance companies deal exclusively with life insurance, seven companies exclusively with non-life insurance and six companies are involved in life and non-life insurance (Insurance sector in Serbia—Report for the third quarter of 2017). If the ownership structure is observed, out of 21 insurance companies, 15 are in majority foreign ownership. The total premium in the third quarter of 2017 amounted to 70.9 billion dinars (594 million euros), which is 6.3% more than in the same period last year. In the structure of the premium, the share of non-life insurance was 77.5%, and a participation of life insurance 22.5%. The value of total premium and the share of each insurance company in the total premium is shown in Table 2.

Compared to the end of the third quarter of the previous year, the balance sheet total of insurance companies and reinsurance companies increased at the end of the third quarter of 2017 by 9.9% and amounted to 233.4 billion dinars (1.955 million

Table 2 Total premium and market share of insurance companies in Q3 2017 (National Bank of Serbia)

Company	Total premium (in thousands of RSD)	Market share (in %)
AMS	2,301,681.00	3.25
DDOR	8,606,590.00	12.14
Dunav	19,641,892.00	27.70
Generali Insurance	14,949,117.00	21.08
Energoprojekt	108,554.00	0.15
Globos	238,531.00	0.34
Grawe	2,586,946.00	3.65
Merkur Insurance	624,554.00	0.88
Milenijum	2,329,512.00	3.28
Sava non-life	1,522,818.00	2.15
Sava life	149,481.00	0.21
Societe Generale	1,323,240.00	1.87
Sogaz	564,091.00	0.80
Triglav	4,102,662.00	5.79
Uniqa non-life	2,803,127.00	3.95
Uniqa life	1,261,800.00	1.78
Wiener	7,801,768.00	11.00
Total	70,916,304.00	100.00

euros). Regarding the volume of capital, the increase of 6.8% was recorded compared to the same period of the previous year.

The solvency of an insurance company depends on the adequacy of technical reserves for the undertaken liabilities, as well as the fulfilment of the requirements relating to adequacy capital, and is determined as the ratio of the required and available margin solvency. At the level of all insurance companies in Serbia that are predominantly dealing with non-life insurance, a basic indicator of capital adequacy (ratio of available and required solvency margin) amounted to 206.2%, and for life insurers 241.5%.

The Serbian insurance market is underdeveloped compared not only with the average of the European Union countries and the OECD countries average, but also in comparison with the Central and Eastern European countries and Western Balkans countries (for which the data were available) according to the basic indicators that measure the level of insurance sector development: insurance density and insurance penetration rate (Fig. 1).

Insurance density quantifies the level of development of insurance within a country and is measured as the ratio of insurance premiums to the entire population of a specified country. Insurance penetration rate specifies the level of development of insurance sector in a country, and it is calculated as the ratio of gross written premium

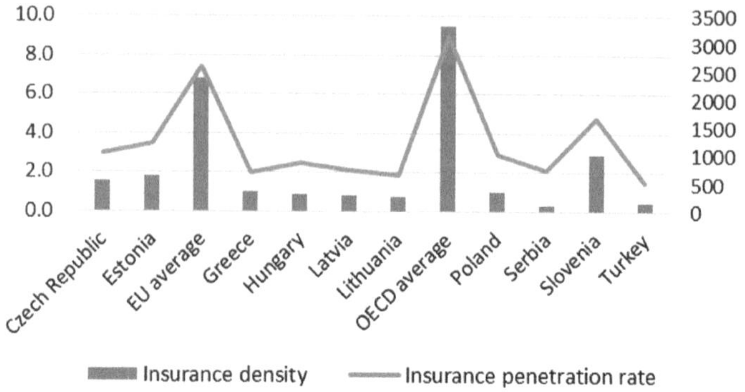

Fig. 1 Insurance density (in USD) and insurance penetration (in %) in 2016 (OECD (2018) and insurance sector in Serbia—Report for the fourth quarter of 2017)

in a particular year to the gross domestic product. It indicates the level of insurance activity in the economy.

Regarding these indicators and compared to the stated countries, Serbia has recorded the lowest insurance density with only USD 108, far below the average of European Union (USD 2383) or the OECD average (USD 3316). However, insurance penetration rate is higher in Serbia (2.1%) then in Turkey (1.5%), Lithuania (1.8%) or Greece (2.0%) but still below the average of European Union (7.4%) indicating that Serbian insurance sector is below level of development of most of the European Union countries.

The adoption of the regulations governing the insurance sector in the Republic of Serbia at the end of 2014 and in the first half of 2015 normative preconditions was created for a significant step towards the convergence of the state of the insurance sector in the Republic of Serbia to the level of development of this sector in the European Union, in order to secure the level of protection of insured persons that will correspond to the level in the European Union insurance (Insurance sector in Serbia—Report for the third quarter of 2017).

4 Data and Methodology

In order to examine profitability determinants of insurance companies in the Republic of Serbia, data for multiple sources were used. Firm-specific factors are obtained from financial data of insurance companies published by the National Bank of Serbia. Data on the macroeconomic conditions of the Serbian economy are gathered from Inflation Reports published by the National Bank of Serbia, and GDP growth data are attained from the World Bank. The research was based on the panel data for insurance companies operating in the Republic of Serbia in the period 2006–2016. Out of 17 insurance companies that currently operate in the Republic of Serbia, only

14 have operated constantly during the observed period and their performance is the subject of the analysis. Research was conducted by multiple regression analysis, and for computation, the STATA software (version 13.0) was used. As a measure of insurer's profitability, Return on Asset (ROA) indicator was used. The selection of explanatory variables is done according to the determinants identified by empirical studies in the relevant literature. Explanatory variables consist of firm-specific and external determinants. Firm-specific variables are internal variables, and they can be controlled by the insurers' management. On the other hand, external variables are related to the characteristics of macroeconomic environment, and they cannot be influenced by the insurers' management. Variables description is given in Table 3.

Variable AGE represents the number of years each of the analysed companies operates on the Serbian insurance market. When it comes to the expected influence of company's age on profitability, there is no unique answer. Loderer and Waelchli (2010) state several reasons for negative type of relationship mainly reflected in augmentation of organizational rigidities over time. Older companies have higher costs, slower growth rates and lower investment rates. Also, they find evidence of poorer governance and higher salaries of executives in older firms. Additionally, Sørensen and Stuart (2000) point out that older companies lose their flexibility and cannot adapt to the rapidly changing business environment. On the other hand, some authors have reported a positive relationship between age of company and company's performance (Table 4). This kind of relationship can be justified by the fact that older companies have higher profit rates, lower debt ratios, greater size, progressive

Table 3 Definition of variables

Variable	Description
ROA	Return on Asset is calculated as profit/loss before taxation divided by the value of total asset
AGE	Number of years the company operates in the Serbian insurance market
LIQ	Liquidity ratio is calculated as a ratio of current assets less inventories and current liabilities
LEV	Leverage ratio represents the ratio of total debt and the equity value of the company
LossR	Loss ratio represents the ratio of total losses incurred in claims and the total premiums earned
CapAdeq	Capital adequacy ratio is calculated as ratio of the equity value of the company and value of total asset
GROWTH	Written premiums growth rate
VoC	Volume of capital is calculated as natural logarithm of equity value of the company
InvInc	Natural logarithm of investment income
MarShare	Market share represents the ratio of an insurer's total asset to total asset of insurance sector
GDPgr	Growth rate of gross domestic product
INF	Inflation rate

Table 4 Review of profitability determinants influence

Variable	Influence on profitability in previous studies		Expected sign
	Positive	Negative	
AGE	Capasso et al. (2015), Osunsan et al. (2015)	Akben-Selcuk (2016), Loderer and Waelchli (2010), Chay et al. (2015), Pervan et al. (2017)	±
LIQ	Wolski and Bolek (2016), Lartey et al. (2013), Saleem and Rehman (2011), Zygmunt (2013), Ahmad (2016)	Olagunju et al. (2012), Siame (2012)	±
LEV	Abor (2005), Singapurwoko and El-Wahid (2011), Gill et al. (2011)	Velnampy and Niresh (2012), Chowdhury and Chowdhury (2010), Mwangi et al. (2014)	±
LossR		Doğan (2013b), Malik (2011), Öner Kaya (2015)	–
CapAdeq	Akhtar et al. (2011), Berhe and Kaur (2017), Abdul (2017), Olalekan and Adeyinka (2013)	Navapan and Tripe (2003), Mathuva 2009	±
GROWTH	Kočović et al. (2014), Öner Kaya (2015), Ullah et al. (2016)	Charumathi (2012), Burca and Batrinca (2014)	±
VoC	Gaur and Gupta (2011), Sritharan (2015), John and Adebayo (2013), Doğan (2013a)	Majumdar (1997)	±
InvInc	Chen and Wong (2004), Gatzlaff (2009), Lee and Lee (2012), Kočović et al. (2014), Lee (2014)		+
MarShare	Szymanski et al. (1993), Kurtz and Rhoades (1992), Genchev (2012), Aqil et al. (2014)		+
GDPgr	Beck and Webb (2003), Kozak (2011), Ward and Zurbruegg 2000), Berhe and Kaur (2017)		+
INF		Beck and Webb (2002), Shiu (2004), Ward and Zurbruegg (2002)	–

productivity levels and higher equity ratios (Coad et al. 2013). Consequently, the impact of the company's age on profitability can be twofold.

Variable LIQ refers to liquidity ratio and represents the ability of an insurer to meet its short-term liabilities when it is due. It is calculated as the ratio of current assets less inventory to current liabilities. Berhe and Kaur (2017) claim that lower level of liquidity ratio shows that an insurer has problems in meeting its short-term liabilities, and conversely, an exceptionally higher level of liquidity ratio could point to the fact that the insurer is keeping idle cash that could have been invested in some profitable way. There is evidence of strong and positive relationship between liquidity and profitability but also of an inverse relationship between liquidity and profitability (Table 4). Consequently, the expected influence of liquidity ratio on insurers' profitability remains equivocal.

Variable LEV represents the leverage ratio of an insurance company, and it is defined as the ratio of total debt and equity value of insurance company. Chowdhury and Chowdhury (2010) state the attitude of the traditional financial experts according to which an increase in a company's leverage will lead to increase in firm's value up to optimum point, and then, the value of the firm will decline if company's leverage is further increased beyond that optimum level. Based on extensive research, Harrington (2005) claims that there is an inverse relationship between leverage and profitability and that insurance companies with lower leverage have higher profitability. Consequently, the negative influence of insurance leverage on profitability may be expected as shown in several studies (Table 4). However, several empirical studies have reported positive influence of leverage on profitability. Therefore, the impact of leverage ratio on profitability is unclear.

Variable LossR refers to loss ratio, and it represents one of the most essential indicators of insurance companies' performance. It is also known as the underwriting risk and is calculated as the ratio of total losses incurred in claims and the total premiums earned. Higher value of loss ratio is a sign of financial problems in an insurance company because it indicates that insurance company is not gathering adequate amount of premiums to compensate the claims. Several studies have reported negative influence of loss ratio on profitability (Table 4). Thus, it is expected that loss ratio will have a negative influence on the profitability of insurance companies.

Variable CapAdeq refers to equity-to-asset ratio, and it represents one of the metrics of financial soundness, usually applied in the evaluation of financial institutions, especially banks. It is calculated as a ratio of the equity value of the company and value of total asset and represents a proxy for capital adequacy. Insurance companies with higher equity-to-asset ratio are considered to be financially stronger, and they are supposed to be safe in times of loss and bankruptcy (Berhe and Kaur 2017). Furthermore, companies with high level of equity-to-asset ratio have lower costs of funding primarily due to the fact that most of the assets are financed from own sources that are cheaper than debt. Some authors have reported positive association between capital adequacy and profitability, while others have found an inverse relationship (Table 4). Therefore, the impact of this indicator on profitability cannot be estimated in advance.

Variable GROWTH represents growth rate of gross written premium. Bearing the mind the fact that gross written premium represents the core source of income in insurance company it is expected that an increase in premium growth rate will cause an increase in insurer's profitability. However, if growth is not managed properly, it can lead to the occurrence of problems which can ultimately endanger the sustainability of insurers. Subsequently, the increase in premium growth rate can contribute to the increase in insurance companies' profitability only if it is followed by appropriate reinsurance policies, solid financial structure and a low loss ratio (Öner Kaya 2015). Positive association of premium growth rate and profitability has been shown in several studies (Table 4). However, some studies have shown that there is an inverse relation. Consequently, the impact of the premium growth on profitability can be dual.

Variable VoC represents a proxy of company's size. There are several firm size proxies in empirical corporate finance research. Dang et al. (2018) point out that the value of total assets, sales or market value of equity represents the most popular measures of firm size. Al-Khazali and Zoubi (2005) suggest that total assets, total sales revenue, book value of equity or market value of equity should be used as a proxy for size of the firm. Therefore, variable VoC is calculated as natural logarithm of company's equity value stated in the balance sheet. Regarding the influence of size on performance Thanh and Ha (2013) consider that firm size should have positive influence on performance due to the fact that small firms cannot operate efficiently mainly because of the high variable costs. They also claim that small firms have weak market power and that they are more exposed to short-term demand shocks and the market uncertainties. Additionally, Geroski et al. (2010) point out that small companies have lower level of diversification which can lower their chances of success on competitive market. Jónsson (2011) explains three categories of theories which should provide an answer for why managers strive to expand their firms. According to the principal–agent theory, the main reason for company's expanding is that the managers tend to increase their own benefits (prestige, higher salary, stock options). Other explanation for expending is offered by the strategic management theories and suggests that the managers strive for strategic positioning which can be obtained by expanding in order to attain scale economies. The institutional theory proposes that the managers tend to enlarge their firm as a response to institutional pressures. Halkos and Tzeremes (2007) claim that due to the usage of suitable inputs and enhanced coordination large firms could achieve better efficiency in production. However, they also underline that small firms could achieve higher efficiency due to their flexibility and because the so-called agency problem does not appear in small firms. Shiu (2004) advocates that big insurance companies can provide swift response to changing market conditions, achieve better diversification of the risks, hire more competent labour force and achieve economy of scale easier than small companies. On the other hand, major insurance companies often cannot create effective and efficient control of managers, and consequently, they encounter with agency problem. Therefore, the influence of firm size on performance remains unclear (Table 4).

Variable InvInc refers to an investment income, and it is a proxy of insurance companies' investment performance. Investment activity represents another aspect of insurance companies' performance. Houston (1964) states that during the assessment of insurer's performance, investment income should also be considered in conjunction with underwriting results. Gatzlaff (2009) concludes that for a long time, there is a consensus that investment results can impact overall performance of insurance companies and that insurance companies with better investment performance may well achieve a competitive advantage. Lee and Lee (2012) proclaim that extraordinary investment returns result in a superior financial performance for insurers. There has been evidence of negative association between insolvency and investment performance (Kim et al. 1995; Kramer 1996), meaning that investment performance is an important factor of financial soundness of an insurance company and that it contributes to its financial performance. Additionally, positive association of insurance companies' profitability and investment performance has been shown in several studies (Table 4). Hence, the positive influence of investment performance on profitability is expected.

Variable MarShare denotes market share, and it is quantified by the ratio of an insurer's total assets to the total assets of the whole insurance sector. Market share expresses the degree of a company's control over insurance industry, and it shows insurer's strength. The higher value of the market share is expected to contribute more to insurers' profitability. Pervan et al. (2012) state several reasons for such expectation: firstly, greater companies can achieve cost advantage due to economies of scale and scope; secondly, they have higher capital value and can invest more in research and development; thirdly, greater firms have higher negotiating power. Consequently, the positive influence of this variable on profitability is expected (Table 4).

Variable GDPgr represents the growth rate of gross domestic product, and it reflects a level of economic development and economic activity of a specific country over a year. Kjosevski (2012) summarizes several reasons in order to justify positive relation between GDP growth rate and profitability mainly reflected in the fact that the economic growth followed by the improvement of living standards and growth of individual incomes leads to an increase in consumption. Therefore, individuals are more willing to invest their income in different types of insurance, such as retirement and investment-related life insurance products. Bearing in mind the aforesaid, it is expected that GDP growth has positive influence on profitability (Table 4).

Variable INF refers to an inflation rate. Since some types of insurance products (such as life insurance) provide monetary reimbursements after a specified period of time, an increase in the inflation rate leads to a reduction people's desire to save, as monetary instability can endanger future benefits. Negative influence of inflation is expected as reported in several studies (Table 4). Hence, it is expected that inflation has negative influence on profitability.

The regression model for panel data has the following form:

$$\begin{aligned} ROA_{it} = {} & \beta_0 + \beta_1 AGE_{it} + \beta_2 LIQ_{it} + \beta_3 LEV_{it} + \beta_4 LossR_{it} + \beta_5 capAdeq_{it} \\ & + \beta_6 GROWTH_{it} + \beta_7 VoC_{it} + \beta_8 InvInc_{it} + \beta_9 MarShare_{it} \\ & + \beta_{10} GDPgr + \beta_{11} INF_{it} + \varepsilon_{it} \end{aligned} \tag{1}$$

where

- Y_{it}/X_{it} represent the value of specific indicator for company i in year t;
- $\beta_0, \beta_1, \ldots, \beta_{11}$—intercept and slope coefficients;
- ε_{it}—disturbance term, $i = 1, \ldots, 14$, $t = 1, \ldots, 11$.

Descriptive statistics of the stated variables are presented in Table 5. Regarding the ROA indicator, as the dependent variable, it can be observed that the variations

Table 5 Descriptive statistics of selected variables

	N	Minimum	Maximum	Mean	Std. deviation
ROA	152	−0.81	0.55	0.0035	0.10332
AGE	154	0.00	53.00	16.429	11.7043
LIQ	152	0.86	126.10	19.306	19.7563
LEV	152	0.08	20.53	4.4414	4.41194
LossR	151	0.27	263.52	36.335	24.6935
CapAdeq	152	0.02	1.23	0.3102	0.25907
GROWTH	147	−49.59	450.06	16.436	42.7303
VoC	152	12.42	16.19	13.738	0.78401
InvInc	152	11.40	17.62	14.585	1.38965
MarShare	154	0.00	33.28	6.3746	7.24228
GDPgr	154	−3.50	5.40	1.3220	2.54356
INF	154	0.92	11.86	6.4515	3.53299

between observed companies regarding this indicator are relatively high and that its ranges between −0.81 and 0.55. The average value of ROA indicator during the analysed period is 0.0035.

5 Empirical Results

Based on the available observations, the selection of the appropriate model is done. The choice of the adequate panel model is done according to the results of suitable statistical tests. After elimination of pooled OLS model (the results F-test and Breusch-Pagan Lagrange multiplier test reject pooled OLS assumption), the Hausman test was conducted in order to select between model with fixed or model with random effects. The Hausman test results shown in Table 6 suggest that the null hypothesis can be rejected at a significance level of 1% leading to the selection of model with fixed effects.

Table 7 shows the results of the estimated fixed-effect model. The value of F statistic is 3.29 at the significance level of 1%, meaning that the shown regression is statistically significant. Among observed explanatory variables, AGE, LossR, CapAdeq, VoC and MarShare have statistically significant impact on the dependent variable ROA at a significance level of 5%, while variables LEV and InvInc have

Table 6 Hausman's test results

	Chi-square statistic	Probability
Ho: difference in coefficients not systematic	44.25	0.0000

Table 7 Fixed-effect model results

ROA	Coefficient	Std. err.	t	$P > t$	(95% conf. interval)	
AGE	−0.0178897	0.0072853	−2.46	0.015	−0.0323141	−0.0034654
LIQ	−0.0003196	0.0005086	−0.63	0.531	−0.0013265	0.0006874
LEV	0.0086018	0.0051046	1.69	0.095	−0.001505	0.0187087
LossR	−0.0009018	0.0003845	−2.35	0.021	−0.001663	−0.0001405
CapAdeq	−0.3295448	0.0788493	−4.18	0	−0.4856609	−0.1734288
GROWTH	0.0001012	0.0002018	0.5	0.617	−0.0002984	0.0005007
VoC	0.1101036	0.0525298	2.1	0.038	0.0060982	0.214109
InvInc	0.0180566	0.0105524	1.71	0.09	−0.0028363	0.0389496
MarShare	−0.0076615	0.0037408	−2.05	0.043	−0.0150679	−0.000255
GDPgr	0.0040762	0.0032942	1.24	0.218	−0.002446	0.0105985
INF	0.0026498	0.015524	0.52	0.607	−0.0075187	0.0128182
_cons	−1.293058	0.6710775	−1.93	0.056	−2.621745	0.0356288

statistically significant influence on the dependent variable ROA at a significance level of 10%.

In order to test the multicollinearity of explanatory variables, the variance inflation factor (VIF) values are calculated. If the VIF value is less than 10, the model is free from multicollinearity, while greater VIF values indicate that the model suffers from multicollinearity. In our analysis, all VIF values are less than 10, and therefore, there is no multicollinearity of explanatory variables (Table 8).

The results of Pesaran's CD (cross-sectional dependence) test are shown in Table 9. The existence of cross-sectional dependence points to the fact that the occurrence of unexpected events in one company influences the operations in other company in the panel data set. Pesaran's CD is used to test whether the residuals are

Table 8 Variance inflation factor values

Variable	VIF
VoC	6.99
MarShare	6.95
InvInc	4.54
LEV	3.99
AGE	2.83
CapAdeq	2.37
INF	1.73
LIQ	1.35
GROWTH	1.25
LossR	1.23
GDPgr	1.18

Table 9 Pesaran's test of cross-sectional independence

Value	Probability
4.548	0.0000

correlated across entities, where the null hypothesis is no cross-sectional dependence and the results show there is no cross-sectional dependence, meaning that the results of the analysis will not be biased.

Furthermore, a model had to be tested for the existence of serial correlation in the idiosyncratic error term. For this purpose, we have used Wooldridge's test for autocorrelation in panel data (Table 10). Existence of serial correlation leads to results which are less efficient due to bias standard errors. The results show that the null hypothesis cannot be rejected at a significance level of 5%. Therefore, it can be concluded the data do not have first-order autocorrelation.

One of the basic assumptions of regression analysis is that the regression disturbances are homoscedastic with the equal variance across time and individuals (Baltagi 2008). However, with panel data this assumption is very restrictive and should be relaxed. Baltagi (2008) states that the assumption of homoscedastic disturbances in situations when heteroscedasticity is present will result in consistent estimates of the regression coefficients, but they will not be efficient. In the presence of heteroscedasticity, the standard errors of the estimates are biased, and the computation of robust standard errors is required. In order to test for the existence of heteroscedasticity, we have used the modified Wald test for group-wise heteroscedasticity in fixed-effect regression model, and the results show our model faces heteroscedasticity (Table 11).

Therefore, the existence of heteroscedasticity should be taken into consideration, and robust standard errors should be calculated. The results of the estimated model are shown in Table 12.

According to the obtained results, the number of years operating on the market, capital adequacy, investment performance, market share and GDP growth rate are determinants that have statistically significant influence on the profitability at a significance level of 5%, whereby investment performance and GDP growth rate have positive, while other determinants have negative impact on ROA. A significance level of 10% volume of capital can be claimed to be one of the determinants that affect profitability of insurance companies in the Republic of Serbia.

Table 10 Wooldridge test for autocorrelation in panel data

Value	Probability
0.221	0.6460

Table 11 Results of the modified Wald test

Chi square	Probability
5773.37	0.0000

Table 12 Fixed-effect model results with obtained robust standard errors

ROA	Coefficient	Robust Std. err.	*t*	*P* > *t*	(95% conf. interval)	
AGE	−0.0178897	0.0027666	−6.47	0	−0.0238666	−0.0119129
LIQ	−0.0003196	0.0005064	−0.63	0.539	−0.0014135	0.0007743
LEV	0.0086018	0.0049316	1.74	0.105	−0.0020523	0.0192559
LossR	−0.0009018	0.0005863	−1.53	0.149	−0.0021714	0.0003678
CapAdeq	−0.3295448	0.0484466	−6.8	0	−0.4342074	−0.2248823
GROWTH	0.0001012	0.0000964	1.05	0.313	−0.000107	0.0003094
VoC	0.1101036	0.0621112	1.77	0.1	−0.0240795	0.2442867
InvInc	0.0180566	0.006282	2.87	0.013	0.0044851	0.0316281
MarShare	−0.0076615	0.0026267	−2.92	0.012	−0.0133361	−0.0019869
GDPgr	0.0040762	0.0011857	3.14	0.008	0.0012748	0.0068777
Inflation	0.0026498	0.007291	0.36	0.722	−0.0131014	0.018401
_cons	−1.293058	0.8915047	−1.45	0.171	−3.219037	0.6329207

The obtained results have several implications. Firstly, regarding the age of the insurance company, the results show that older insurance companies in the Republic of Serbia are less profitable than younger companies. This result is in favour of the statement that older companies have problems with organizational rigidities that have enlarged over time. Therefore, the managers of insurance companies should try to accommodate to the new business conditions and create flexible organizational structure which should induce higher growth rates, higher investment, lower costs and consequently higher profitability. Secondly, capital adequacy has significant negative influence on profitability, meaning that companies which are financially sounder are less profitable compared to companies with a lower equity-to-asset ratio. The reason for this can be the fact that companies with lower level of this indicator use debt in order to obtain benefits of evolving business opportunities in term of investing in profitable projects which have higher return than the interest they have to pay on the debt. Additionally, a higher amount of equity means that the owners will have higher claims in terms of dividends, which will result in a reduction in retained earnings, which could be used for investments. Therefore, companies with lower value of equity-to-asset ratio achieve greater profitability than the companies with high value of this indicator which are lagging behind because they cannot provide competitive level of investment if they rely primarily on equity. Thirdly, investment performance has a significant positive influence on insurance companies' profitability, meaning that companies with higher investment income will have higher profitability. This result is in accordance with our expectations. Investment activity represents an important part of overall insurance company's activity, and superior investment performance leads to the creation of a competitive advantage and superior financial results. Hence, companies should strive to improve their profitability through carefully planned investment activities. Fourthly, market share has proven to be one of the determinants of insurance companies' profitability in the Republic of Serbia. However, the obtained results show that there is an inverse relation between market share and profitability, and consequently, companies with higher market share obtain lower profitability levels. This is in contrary to the expected influence of market share on profitability but in accordance with results obtained by Woo (1981) and Jumono et al. (2015). One of the possible explanations for attained result can be that an increase in market share generally involves higher level of investment which can cause reduction in the profitability in the short term. On the other hand, this inverse relation could mean that companies with higher market share do not realize cost advantage, that is, they do not use the benefits of economies of scale and scope. In order to obtain positive influence on profitability, companies should increase the differentiation of insurance products they offer. Also, they should focus on investing in research, so they could create competitive insurance products. Fifthly, the influence of GDP growth rate is significant and positive which is in line with expectations. The economic growth increases the possibility of insurance products selling and therefore insurers will obtain higher profit rates. Sixthly, the volume of capital could be considered as a significant determinant of profitability at a significance level of 10%, and hence, the managers of insurance companies should take into consideration this indicator during the decision-making process. Volume of capital has positive influence on profitability, meaning that companies with higher equity value obtain higher profitability rates, mainly due to economy of scale, better diversification of the risks and swift response to changing market conditions, as stated before.

6 Conclusion

The state of the insurance market in the Republic of Serbia has undergone significant changes in recent years. With the liberalization of the market and the entry of foreign capital, there was an increase in competition, and the issue of profitability of insurance companies became particularly important. Adequate identification of profitability determinants can help insurance companies and policymakers to focus their actions towards achieving better performance, which will ensure the endurance and progress of both insurance companies and the entire national economy.

The subject of this paper was a comprehensive analysis of the business performance of insurance companies in the Republic of Serbia. Through the appropriate empirical model, we have assessed the influence of the selected firm-specific and macroeconomic factors on the insurers' profitability. Our findings indicate that the number of years operating on the market, capital adequacy, investment performance, market share and GDP growth rate are determinants that have statistically significant impact on the profitability, wherein investment performance and GDP growth rate have statistically significant positive impact on the profitability. Conducted research has some significant implications for the insurance companies' management. Potential improvement of the profitability of insurance companies can occur if the management takes into account the impact of stated variables. Management of insurance companies that are longer on the insurance market should try to solve the problems with organizational rigidities which will lower the costs, increase investment and subsequently increase profitability. Profitability of insurance companies can be increased through investment activities which will be financed from external debt, taking into account maintenance of financial soundness.

The conducted research faces with usual limitations regarding the usage of data from financial statements. Besides being historical by nature, the accuracy of the data from financial statements depends on the respect of the principle of true and fair reporting.

The paper contributes to the empirical literature in the field of insurers' profitability determinants assessment by providing empirical data regarding the analysis of profitability determinants of insurance companies in the Republic of Serbia. Further research in this area can be directed towards examining the impact of market competition on the profitability and also other relevant factors that can affect the profitability of insurers which are not covered by this research.

Acknowledgements The paper is a part of the research done within the projects 179066 and 179013 funded by the Ministry of Education, Science and Technology of the Republic of Serbia. The authors also gratefully acknowledge the useful comments and suggestions of the anonymous reviewer.

References

Abdul, J. M. (2017). Impact of capital adequacy on the performance of Nigerian Banks using the Basel Accord Framework. *East Africa Research Papers in Business, Entrepreneurship and Management, 7*.

Abor, J. (2005). The effect of capital structure on profitability: An empirical analysis of listed firms in Ghana. *The Journal of Risk Finance, 6*(5), 438–445.

Ahmad, R. (2016). A study of relationship between liquidity and profitability of standard Charterd Bank Pakistan: Analysis of financial statement approach. *Global Journal of Management and Business Research*.

Akben-Selcuk, E. (2016). Does firm age affect profitability? Evidence from Turkey. *International Journal of Economic Sciences, 5*(3), 1–9.

Akhtar, M. F., Ali, K., & Sadaqat, S. (2011). Factors influencing the profitability of Islamic banks of Pakistan. *International Research Journal of Finance and Economics, 66*(66), 1–8.

Al-Khazali, O. M., & Zoubi, T. A. (2005). Empirical testing of different alternative proxy measures for firm size. *Journal of Applied Business Research, 21*(3), 79.

Almajali, A. Y., Alamro, S. A., & Al-Soub, Y. Z. (2012). Factors affecting the financial performance of Jordanian insurance companies listed at Amman Stock Exchange. *Journal of Management Research, 4*(2), 266.

Aqil, M., Aziz, S., Dilshad, M., & Qadeer, S. (2014). Impact of market share on profitability of heavy vehicles manufacturers—A case study of Hino Pak Ltd. *Journal of Economics and Finance, 3*, 16–20.

Baltagi, B. (2008). *Econometric analysis of panel data*. New York: Wiley.

Bawa, S. K., & Chattha, S. (2013). Financial performance of life insurers in Indian insurance industry. *Pacific Business Review International, 6*(5), 44–52.

Beck, T., & Webb, I. M. (2002). *Determinants of life insurance consumption across countries (No. 2792)*. Policy Research Working paper, World Bank and International Insurance Foundation. Retrieved from https://openknowledge.worldbank.org/handle/10986/15614.

Beck, T., & Webb, I. (2003). Economic, demographic, and institutional determinants of life insurance consumption across countries. *The World Bank Economic Review, 17*(1), 51–88.

Berhe, T. A., & Kaur, J. (2017). Determinants of insurance companies' profitability Analysis of insurance sector in Ethiopia. *International Journal of Research in Finance and Marketing (IJRFM), 7*(4), 124–137.

Burca, A. M., & Batrinca, G. (2014). The determinants of financial performance in the Romanian insurance market. *International Journal of Academic Research in Accounting, Finance and Management Sciences, 4*(1), 299–308.

Capasso, A., Gallucci, C., & Rossi, M. (2015). Standing the test of time. Does firm performance improve with age? An analysis of the wine industry. *Business History, 57*(7), 1037–1053.

Charumathi, B. (2012). On the determinants of profitability of Indian life insurers–An empirical study. In: *Proceedings of the World Congress on Engineering* (Vol. 1, No. 2, pp. 4–6), London.

Chay, J. B., Kim, H., & Suh, J. (2015). Firm age and valuation: Evidence from Korea. *Asia-Pacific Journal of Financial Studies, 44*(5), 721–761.

Chen, R., & Wong, K. A. (2004). The determinants of financial health of Asian insurance companies. *Journal of Risk and Insurance, 71*(3), 469–499.

Chidambaran, N. K., Pugel, T. A., & Saunders, A. (1997). An investigation of the performance of the US property-liability insurance industry. *Journal of Risk and Insurance*, 371–382.

Chowdhury, A., & Chowdhury, S. P. (2010). Impact of capital structure on firm's value: Evidence from Bangladesh. *Business & Economic Horizons, 3*(3).

Coad, A., Segarra, A., & Teruel, M. (2013). Like milk or wine: Does firm performance improve with age? *Structural Change and Economic Dynamics, 24,* 173–189.

Dang, C., Li, Z. F., & Yang, C. (2018). Measuring firm size in empirical corporate finance. *Journal of Banking & Finance, 86,* 159–176.

Doğan, M. (2013a). Does firm size affect the firm profitability? Evidence from Turkey. *Research Journal of Finance and Accounting, 4*(4), 53–59.

Doğan, M. (2013b). Relations between the profitability and capital structure of insurance companies: An analysis over Turkish capital market. *The Journal of Accounting and Finance, 57,* 121–136.

Francalanci, C., & Galal, H. (1998). Information technology and worker composition: Determinants of productivity in the life insurance industry. *MIS quarterly*, 227–241.

Gatzlaff, K. (2009). *Dimensions of property-liability insurer performance*. The Florida State University.

Gaur, J., & Gupta, R. (2011). Comparing firm performance on the basis of age, size, leverage, and group affiliation in Indian IT industry. *Romanian Journal of Marketing, 3,* 8.

Genchev, E. (2012). Effects of market share on the bank's profitability. *Review of Applied Socio-Economic Research, 3*(1), 87. Available at SSRN: https://ssrn.com/abstract=2184610 Accessed 21 Feb 2018.

Geroski, P. A., Mata, J., & Portugal, P. (2010). Founding conditions and the survival of new firms. *Strategic Management Journal, 31*(5), 510–529.

Gill, A., Biger, N., & Mathur, N. (2011). The effect of capital structure on profitability: Evidence from the United States. *International Journal of Management, 28*(4), 3.

Halkos, G. E., & Tzeremes, N. G. (2007). Productivity efficiency and firm size: An empirical analysis of foreign owned companies. *International Business Review, 16*(6), 713–731.

Harrington, C. (2005). *The effect of competitive structure on the relationship between leverage and profitability*. Working Paper, Central Connecticut State University, New Britain, ct.

Houston, D. B. (1964). Risk, insurance, and sampling. *The Journal of Risk and Insurance, 31*(4), 511–538.

Ikonic, D., Arsic, N., & Milosevic, S. (2011). Growth potential and profitability analysis of insurance companies in the Republic of Serbia. *Chinese Business Review, 10*(11).

Insurance sector in Serbia—Report for the fourth quarter of 2017, National Bank of Serbia. Retrieved from http://www.nbs.rs/internet/latinica/60/60_6/izvestaji/izv_IV_2017.pdf Accessed March 5, 2018.

Insurance sector in Serbia—Report for the third quarter of 2017, National Bank of Serbia. Retrieved from https://www.nbs.rs/internet/latinica/60/60_6/izvestaji/izv_III_2017.pdf. Accessed March 5, 2018.

Jan, S., Khurshed, I., & Sham, R. (2014). Determinants of profitability of Islamic and conventional insurance companies in Pakistan: An internal evaluation. *Abasyn University Journal of Social Sciences, 7,* 1.

John, A. O., & Adebayo, O. (2013). Effect of firm size on profitability: Evidence from Nigerian manufacturing sector. *Prime Journal of Business Administration and Management (BAM), 3*(9), 1171–1175.

Jónsson, B. (2011). Does the size matter? The relationship between size and profitability of Icelandic firms.

Jumono, S., Achsani, N. A., Hakim, D. B., & Fidaus, M. (2015). Market concentration, market share, and profitability (Study at Indonesian commercial banking in the period of 2001–2012). *Asian Social Science, 11*(27), 18.

Kašćelan, V., & Radulović, B. (2008). Osiguravajuće kompanije na finansijskom tržištu u regionu. *Montenegrin Journal of Economics, 7.* http://repec.mnje.com/mje/2008/v04-n07/mje_2008_v04-n07-a08.pdf. Accessed February 23, 2018.

Kim, Y. D., Anderson, D. R., Amburgey, T. L., & Hickman, J. C. (1995). The use of event history analysis to examine insurer insolvencies. *Journal of Risk and Insurance*, 94–110.

Kjosevski, J. (2012). The determinants of life insurance demand in central and southeastern Europe. *International Journal of Economics and Finance, 4*(3), 237.

Kočović, J., Paunović, B., & Jovović, M. (2014). Determinants of business performance of non-life insurance companies in Serbia. *Ekonomika preduzeća, 62*(7–8), 367–381.

Kozak, S. (2011). Determinants of profitability of non-life insurance companies in Poland during integration with the European financial system. *Electronic Journal of Polish Agricultural Universities, 14*(1), 01.

Kramer, B. (1996). An ordered logit model for the evaluation of Dutch non-life insurance companies. *De Economist, 144*(1), 79–91.

Kurtz, R. D., & Rhoades, S. A. (1992). A note on the market share-profitability relationship. *Review of Industrial Organization, 7*(1), 39–50.

Lartey, V. C., Antwi, S., & Boadi, E. K. (2013). The relationship between liquidity and profitability of listed banks in Ghana. *International Journal of Business and Social Science, 4*(3).

Lee, C. Y. (2014). The effects of firm specific factors and macroeconomics on profitability of property-liability insurance industry in Taiwan. *Asian Economic and Financial Review, 4*(5), 681.

Lee, H. H., & Lee, C. Y. (2012). An analysis of reinsurance and firm performance: Evidence from the Taiwan property-liability insurance industry. *The Geneva Papers on Risk and Insurance-Issues and Practice, 37*(3), 467–484.

Loderer, C., & Waelchli, U. (2010). Firm age and performance.

Majumdar, S. K. (1997). The impact of size and age on firm-level performance: some evidence from India. *Review of Industrial Organization, 12*(2), 231–241.

Malik, H. (2011). Determinants of insurance companies' profitability: An analysis of insurance sector of Pakistan. *Academic Research International, 1*(3), 315.

Mandić, K., Delibašić, B., Knežević, S., & Benković, S. (2017). Analysis of the efficiency of insurance companies in Serbia using the fuzzy AHP and TOPSIS methods. *Economic Research-Ekonomska istraživanja, 30*(1), 550–565.

Marović, B., & Njegomir, V. (2015). Insurance companies in the role of institutional investors (in Serbian). In: *The 26th meeting of insurers and reinsurers Sarajevo.*

Mathuva, D. M. (2009). Capital adequacy, cost income ratio and the performance of commercial banks: The Kenyan scenario. *The International Journal of Applied Economics and Finance, 3*(2), 35–47.
Mehari, D., & Aemiro, T. (2013). Firm specific factors that determine insurance companies' performance in Ethiopia. *European Scientific Journal, ESJ, 9*(10).
Mwangi, L. W., Muathe, S. M. A., & Kosimbei, G. K. (2014). Relationship between capital structure and performance of non-financial companies listed in the Nairobi Securities Exchange, Kenya. *Global Journal of Contemporary Research in Accounting, Auditing and Business Ethics (GJCRA)*, An Online International Research Journal (ISSN: 2311–3162), *1*(2), 72–90.
Mwangi, M., & Murigu, J. W. (2015). The determinants of financial performance in general insurance companies in Kenya. *European Scientific Journal, ESJ, 11*(1).
National bank of Serbia, Total premium. https://www.nbs.rs/export/download/osg-izv-3m/T1_III_2017.pdf. Accessed October 15, 2018.
Navapan, K., & Tripe, D. (2003). An exploration of the relationship between bank capital levels and return on equity. In *Proceeding of the 16th Australasian Finance and Banking Conference*, (AFBC'03), Palmerston North (pp. 1–15).
OECD (2018). Insurance activity indicators. *OECD insurance statistics* (database). https://doi.org/10.1787/data-00333-en. Accessed 02 Nov 2018.
Olagunju, A., David, A. O., & Samuel, O. O. (2012). Liquidity management and commercial banks' profitability in Nigeria. *Research Journal of Finance and Accounting, 2*(7–8), 24–38.
Olalekan, A., & Adeyinka, S. (2013). Capital adequacy and banks' profitability: An empirical evidence from Nigeria. *American International Journal of Contemporary Research, 3*(10), 87–93.
Olaosebikan, O. (2013). The determinants of the profitability of micro-life insurers in Nigeria. *The Geneva Papers on Risk and Insurance-Issues and Practice, 38*(1), 140–159.
Öner Kaya, E. (2015). The effects of firm-specific factors on the profitability of non-life insurance companies in Turkey. *International Journal of Financial Studies, 3*(4), 510–529.
Oscar Akotey, J., Sackey, F. G., Amoah, L., & Frimpong Manso, R. (2013). The financial performance of life insurance companies in Ghana. *The Journal of Risk Finance, 14*(3), 286–302.
Osunsan, O. K., Nowak, J., Mabonga, E., Pule, S., Kibirige, A. R., & Baliruno, J. B. (2015). Firm age and performance in Kampala, Uganda: A selection of small business enterprises. *International Journal of Academic Research in Business and Social Sciences, 1*(5), 412–422.
Pervan, M., Curak, M., & Marijanovic, I. (2012). Dynamic panel analysis of B&H insurance companies' profitability. *Recent Researches in Business and Economics*, 158–163.
Pervan, M., Pervan, I., & Ćurak, M. (2017). The influence of age on firm performance: Evidence from the croatian food industry. *Journal of Eastern Europe Research in Business and Economics, 2017.*
Rahman, S. U., Jan, F. A., Iqbal, K., & Ali, Z. (2012). Parameters of conventional and Islamic insurance companies' profitability: Evaluation of internal analysis. *Research Journal of Finance and Accounting, 3*(3), 11–18.
Saleem, Q., & Rehman, R. U. (2011). Impacts of liquidity ratios on profitability. *Interdisciplinary Journal of Research in Business, 1*(7), 95–98.
Sambasivam, Y., & Ayele, A. G. (2013). A study on the performance of insurance companies in Ethiopia. *International Journal of Marketing, Financial Services & Management Research, 2*(7), 138–150.
Shiu, Y. (2004). Determinants of United Kingdom general insurance company performance. *British Actuarial Journal, 10*(5), 1079–1110.
Siame, C. (2012). *The relationship between profitability and liquidity in South African listed firms.* Doctoral dissertation, University of Cape Town.
Singapurwoko, A., & El-Wahid, M. S. M. (2011). The impact of financial leverage to profitability study of non-financial companies listed in Indonesia stock exchange. *European Journal of Economics, Finance, and Administrative Sciences, 32,* 136–148.
Sørensen, J. B., & Stuart, T. E. (2000). Aging, obsolescence, and organizational innovation. *Administrative Science Quarterly, 45*(1), 81–112.

Sritharan, V. (2015). Does firm size influence on firm's profitability? Evidence from listed firms of Sri Lankan hotels and travels sector. *Research Journal of Finance and Accounting, 6*(6), 201–207.
Szymanski, D. M., Bharadwaj, S. G., & Varadarajan, P. R. (1993). An analysis of the market share-profitability relationship. *The Journal of Marketing*, 1–18.
Thanh, V. H., & Ha, N. M. (2013). The effect of banking relationship on firm performance in Vietnam. *International Journal of Economics and Finance, 5*(5), 148.
Ullah, G. W., Faisal, M. N., & Zuhra, S. T. (2016). Factors determining profitability of the insurance industry of Bangladesh. *International Finance and Banking, 3*(2), 138.
Velnampy, T., & Niresh, J. A. (2012). The relationship between capital structure and profitability. *Global Journal of Management and Business Research, 12*(13).
Ward, D., & Zurbruegg, R. (2000). Does insurance promote economic growth? Evidence from OECD countries. *Journal of Risk and Insurance*, 489–506.
Ward, D., & Zurbruegg, R. (2002). Law, politics and life insurance consumption in Asia. *The Geneva Papers on Risk and Insurance-Issues and Practice, 27*(3), 395–412.
Wolski, R., & Bolek, M. (2016). Liquidity–profitability relationship analysed once again. The case of Poland. *European Scientific Journal, ESJ, 12*(7).
Woo, C. Y. (1981). Market share leadership—Does it always pay off? In *Academy of Management Proceedings* (Vol. 1981, No. 1, pp. 7–11). Academy of Management, Briarcliff Manor, NY 10510.
Zygmunt, J. (2013). Does liquidity impact on profitability? In *Conference of informatics and management sciences, March*, 38–49.

Instruments for Financing Damage in Animal Production in Poland and the European Union

Marietta Janowicz-Lomott and Krzysztof Łyskawa

Abstract The main goal of the chapter is to propose solutions that increase the effectiveness/rationality of spending budgetary funds in the protection of livestock production. The Holistic concept of risk management in agriculture, according to the OECD, is one that recognizes all possible risks, their relationships and interactions, flows of information among the stakeholders and the various forms of public–private partnership. However, the current activities of the European Union and individual member states have focused primarily on crop production. Meanwhile, animal production in many regions and countries is the major part of farm income. EU regulations allow the use of subsidized animal insurance in the field of (a) natural disasters; (b) an adverse climatic event which can be assimilated to a natural disaster and other adverse climatic events; (c) animal diseases or plant pest; and (d) protected animals. However, from the point of view of insurance companies and farmers themselves, it is much more important to prepare solutions that will stabilize the income of farmers raising animals. The chapter discusses the possible insurance solutions and income stabilization tool in relation to animal production.

Keywords Insurance · Agriculture · Animal production · Agricultural risk management in EU · Mutual fund · Income stabilization

1 Introduction

One of the major issues in the contemporary world is the fact that in countries which are the least capable of handling population growth, this growth is the fastest. Highly developed countries have efficient agriculture which is able to feed their own population and create surplus of exports. Developing countries in Africa, Southeast Asia

M. Janowicz-Lomott (✉)
SGH Warsaw School of Economics, al. Niepodległości 162, 02-554 Warsaw, Poland
e-mail: mjanow@sgh.waw.pl

K. Łyskawa
Poznan University of Economics and Business, al. Niepodległości 10, 61-875 Poznan, Poland
e-mail: krzysztof.lyskawa@ue.poznan.pl

M. Janowicz-Lomott et al. (eds.), *Economic and Financial Challenges for Balkan and Eastern European Countries*, Springer Proceedings in Business and Economics,
https://doi.org/10.1007/978-3-030-39927-6_10

and South America suffer from food shortage, in many cases a very severe one. At the same time, it is paradoxical that countries with the highest percentage of population involved in agriculture cannot feed themselves. Therefore, it is so crucial to create proper instruments which secure the sustainability of farm household functioning in the case of realization of certain risk types. Experiences of highly developed countries and their scientific potential may form the background for creating solutions which secure sustainability of functioning also in developing countries. The role of animal production for the functioning of modern world is commented by Czyżewski et al. (2009, p. 33–34). They stress livestock production should be developed and supported in the CAP in order to achieve sustainable production (despite the difficulties of the environmental impact) (Czyżewski et al. 2018, p. 428–430). On the other hand, a number of publications on agriculture risk management and animal production (Casasús and Lombardi 2016; Janowicz-Lomott and Lyskawa 2014) point to the need to undertake a variety of activities to ensure the stabilization of farms. Defining proper instruments to eliminate the negative effects of catastrophic or operational events is particularly important.

Implementation of risk management concepts in agriculture is associated with expectations of agricultural producers towards the insurance market—they expect insurance offer which will help to finance elimination of effects of fortuitous events. The idea of livestock insurance dates back to the ancient times as its first records can be found in ancient Palestine and Babylon. In the Middle Ages, in order to cover fortuitous events in the livestock, farmers formed associations where they shared the meat of animals killed perforce, and funds collected in this way constituted compensation. These associations, acting as local unions of livestock insurance, started to collect these funds for compensation in the form of repartition (European Commission 2006, p. 6).

The aim of the present chapter is to outline possible, acceptable within the EU policy and present in the European countries solutions for supporting animal production in relation to preventing the effects of fortuitous events in EU states. The case study in the chapter concentrates on Poland, in particular on a dedicated solution for poultry insurance (with reference to actual loss as well as its indirect forms) and offering solution for income stabilization for the whole animal production.

2 The Role of Animal Production for the Functioning of Farm Households in the European Union

The 'polluter-pays' principle is, next to the principles of precaution and prevention European Community is the biggest food producer in the world. Rural areas constitute 92% of the area of EU-25 member states and are inhabited by 56% of its population. The value of agricultural production increases annually and in 2012–2014 it exceeded EUR 400 bn. Plant production has a slight value advantage over animal production (Fig. 1). Leading countries in animal production include (as per data of 2016): France

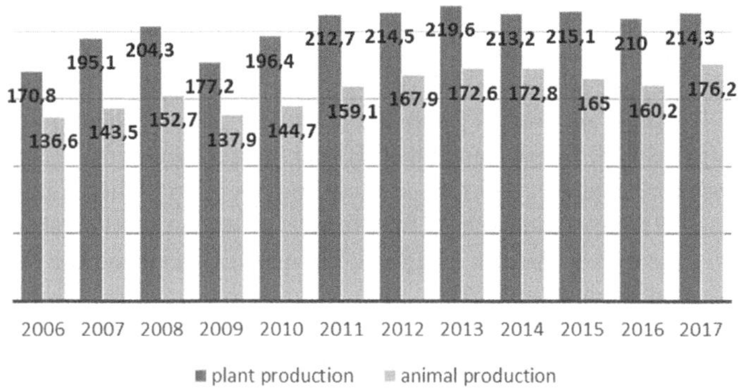

Fig. 1 Plant and animal production in EU states (EU-28) in 2006–2017 in bn EUR. *Source* Eurostat

(EUR 24.9 bn), Germany (EUR 23.9 bn), Spain (EUR 16.9 bn), Great Britain (EUR 15.2 bn), Italy (EUR 14.9 bn) and Poland (EUR 11.3 bn).

The structure of final animal production in EU-25 is dominated by milk (33.23%), cattle for slaughter (24.7%), pigs (18.91%), poultry (9.23%), sheep and goats (5.99%), eggs (4.91%), other animal products (0.79%) and horses (0.68%) (CAP Source: Eurostat).

3 Permissible and Used Risk Management Solutions in Animal Production in the European Union

A detailed effect analysis of particular risk realization associated with animal production necessitates a broader perspective than in other types of production activity. In particular, it concerns a different approach to actual and indirect (consequential) losses. The first aspect of loss for agricultural producer is direct loss, i.e. the loss of the livestock. The general principle assumes compensation of a significant part of direct loss due to death or disease, i.e. the value of animals affected by the disease. Major type of risk in animal production concerns sanitary risks. Epidemics of livestock may cause major loss for the economy as well as farmers and all participants of production chain. It needs to be stressed that in the face of such risks, EU member states are obliged to use control measures laid down in EU directives in case such diseases occur. For this aim financial resources were secured and are used by member states during realization of programmes aimed at controlling the quantity and severity of disease occurrence in order to protect animals and public health.

It also needs to be stressed that certain intensified weather factors may also have direct impact on animals. Additionally, climatic phenomena may affect pastures and availability of feed, i.e. the balance of a farm household (Lemairea et al. 2014).

Actions of governments and European institutions concentrate on the area of direct losses. The general principle assumes compensation of a significant part of direct losses due to death or disease, i.e. the value of animals affected by the disease. Some member states finance also losses not covered by EU funds by the means of public funds. Such solutions are used in Denmark, Finland, France, Ireland, Italy, Luxembourg, Portugal, Spain, Sweden and Great Britain. Other member states established certain forms of mandatory system of co-financing direct loss. These public–private solutions have the form of a mandatory fund formed by resources from farmers' taxes. Such system functions in Austria, Belgium, Germany, Greece and the Netherlands (European Commission 2006, p. 5).

Indirect losses, such as production decrease and consequent farm income loss, are usually covered by the farmers themselves. Some member states compensate them partially in the form of aid programmes launched ad hoc (e.g. Austria, Belgium, Ireland) or loss compensation with value higher than the actual value of animals consigned for emergency slaughter. In other member states, lack of support from the public sector led to introduction of commercial insurance products for certain types of animal production (Germany, the Netherlands, Sweden, Spain, Great Britain and Italy). There are also some forms of public–private partnership where the government functions as insurer or reinsurer of subsidized indirect loss insurance. A significant aspect is the fact that agricultural producers do not use these type of solutions frequently (Table 1).

4 Construction of Direct and Indirect Loss Insurance on the Example of Poultry Production Insurance in Poland

4.1 Characteristics of Poultry Production (Broilers) in Poland and Standard Scope of Insurance Coverage

Taking into account the role of Poland in poultry production worldwide and specific character of risk in this type of activity, further part of the chapter concentrates on this type of production. Poultry insurance is a great example of animal production insurance in EU countries (both indirect and indirect losses). Poultry breeding triggers all concerns of farmers connected with diseases, fortuitous events or fluctuation of prices of materials for agricultural production and finished goods. In the case of broilers, agricultural producer in a year may perform 5–8 production cycles, i.e.

Table 1 Livestock insurance in the EU states after 2014

Country	S	DL	IL	Country	S	DL	IL	Country	S	DL	SP
Belgium				France				Holland		X	X
Bulgaria	X	X		Great Britain		X	X	Austria		X	X
Czech	X	X		Italy	X	X		Poland	X	X	
Denmark		X	X	Cyprus				Portugal			
Germany				Latvia	X	X	X	Romania		X	X
Estonia	X	X		Lithuania	X	X	X	Slovenia			
Ireland				Luxemburg				Slovakia			
Greece		X		Hungarian		X	X	Finland		X	
Spain		X		Malta				Sweden		X	X

S premium subsidy; *DL* direct loss; *IL* indirect loss
Source Own elaboration based on GDV (2016) and Asseldonk (2017)

Table 2 Length of production cycle, conversion degree and nutrition level for layers and broilers

Species of poultry	Breeding cycle	The degree of feed conversion[a]	Level range feed (kg/bird/cycle)	Quantity (kg/place/year)
Laying hens	12–15 months	2.15–2.5	5.5–6.6 (depending on the production method)	34–47 (during laying of eggs)
Broilers	35–55 days (5–8 cycle/year)	1.73–2.1	3.3–4.5	22–29

[a]Feed conversion ratio in kg per kg of eggs
Source Michułka (2003)

placement, feeding and sales of animals. Conversion coefficients[1] clearly indicate a significant feed consumption among the animals (Table 2).

Current development of agriculture in Poland is to a great extent stimulated by a broad range of direct subsidies, but also other forms of support for agricultural sector from the European Union. This, in combination with satisfactory economic situation on the market of poultry meat, allowed realization of considerable financial outlays on investments in this sector. However, significant price changeability on the market and possibility of certain risk realization may cause decrease of margin below the limit resulting from, for instance, the value of incurred mortgage. The scale of this risk is illustrated in the following picture. The biggest price fluctuations in 2010–2016 were observed with reference to poultry production whereas the smallest concerned sheep and goats. Yet, in the second case one may observe lack of increasing livestock prices with simultaneous growth of production costs (Fig. 2).

Despite such significant price fluctuations over recent years, the scope of insurance has changed only slightly and covers loss which includes: death of animal, loss of its

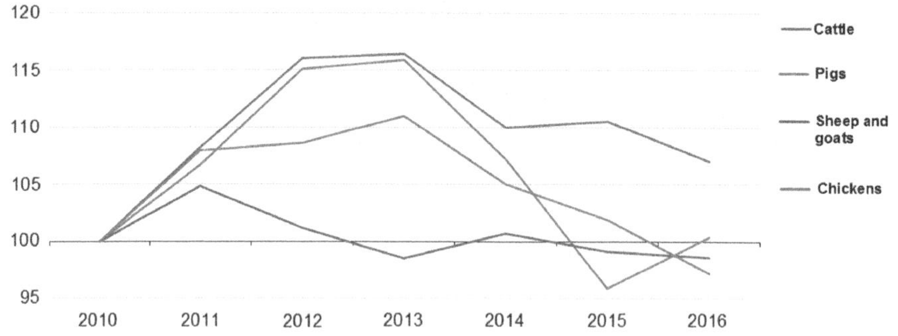

Fig. 2 Fluctuation of animal production prices. *Source* Eurostat

[1]Feed conversion ratio is a number of food units which an animal needs to consume in order to produce 1 unit of 'yield', i.e. meat, eggs, wool/fibre, milk or pulling power (currently in developed countries this factor is of low significance). In our case, it will be the kilogram of broiler livestock at procurement price.

fitness for use as a result of an accident, fire, thunder, flood, hurricane, disease or other fortuitous events. Protection may be expanded additionally by emergency slaughter resulting from the aforementioned situations. Some insurers add the possibility of optional coverage of veterinary costs, transport insurance or others. The sum of insurance in such products is equal to the market value of the animal, taking into account its age. As for insurance premium, it is strongly diversified and depends on the scope of coverage selected by the farmer and may range from one to a few or even a dozen per cent. This type of insurance has been so far the most common form of livestock insurance among farmers. Yet, it was and still is a relatively small part of insurance market in Poland and worldwide. Moreover, probably it will be the most preferred form of insurance in developing countries in the foreseeable future (Roberts 2007, p. 24).

Nonetheless, it needs to be observed that low interest in animal insurance requires a different approach to secure this type of production. Alternative approach occurs when the insured risk affects the insured profit of particular enterprises, i.e. protection encompasses not only direct, but also indirect loss. Payment of compensation may result from:

- animal mortality (caused by, for instance, disease),
- production loss caused by negative climatic factors,
- outbreak of contagious disease or environmental pollution (e.g. avian influenza for poultry),
- considerable increase of farm operation cost after loss event.

When the insurance contract between the breeder and insurer is concentrated on expected gross profit of the first one, every significant decrease of this profit is the basis for payout of compensation provided that the cause of this situation is realization of one of the events specified in the insurance contract.

4.2 *Example of Using Profit Loss Insurance in Case of Avian Influenza*

Alternative to traditional insurance solution is based on two crucial pillars. Its basic scope refers to financial consequences connected with the occurrence of one of the contagious diseases fought ex officio or accidents which took place in the insured livestock. Full scope encompasses responsibility of the insurer also for other types of diseases which may occur among the animals.

However, the basic requirement in this insurance is keeping accounting documents.

Insurance scope is established through detailed defining of loss:

(a) animal loss and/or lowered production efficiency of animals
(b) drop in the value of animal products
(c) disruption of production process, prohibition of supply and limitations of sales

However, when analysing the consequences of, for instance, facility lockdown after the occurrence of avian influenza in the neighbourhood, the farmer may incur additional costs:

- the cost of feed and animal maintenance on the same level
- herd density increases, partial slaughter is necessary
- the costs of decontamination and disinfection
- higher costs of manure removal
- loss caused by delayed herd repopulation, temporary breeding bans

Compensation does not include losses caused as a result of fire, thunder or explosion. The loss of animals only will be encompassed by different property insurance, and potential consequential costs may be covered only within the scope of additional claims which may be obtained after negotiations with the insurance company.

According to terms and conditions, income loss means lower contribution margin taking into account current costs in the production process subject to insurance. Contribution margin is the difference between proportionate market services and special costs of the insured production process. Lower contribution margin of production process takes place in the case of drop-in income from manufactured goods and/or increased production costs of market goods.

The insurer is responsible for income loss which, unless agreed otherwise, took place within 12 months since the moment the loss event occurred (liability period).

The sum of insurance, unless the Parties agree otherwise, is established on the basis of agreed calculation sheet which serves to specify sums for all insured production processes.

Below a sample loss scenario in the case of avian influenza occurrence in the closest neighbourhood of poultry farm is presented (Table 3).

Description of loss scenario

Sales ban imposed as a result of being located in the danger zone of H5N8 serotype avian influenza. The loss started in week 4 of breeding.

The consequences include: (1) increased costs of: feed, veterinary care, electricity caused by the lockdown and in effect longer breeding of broilers, (2) sale of broilers after obtaining a special permission, the goods sold on day 50 from placement are of lower quality and the quantity is smaller (part of animals is dead as a result of suffocation), (3) another placement on day 115 since the beginning of lockdown (two placement are out).

Indemnity period—refers to time when the insurer is held responsible for negative effects of the insured event.

Reference period—comparable in length (the number of production cycles) period before the loss occurred. There is the obligation of keeping documentation back for 3 years.

In the summary above key elements of economic calculation of broiler production are compared. Reference data were the results from 2017 whereas the loss would take place in 2018. Nonetheless, it needs to be stressed that in normal circumstances reference period is assumed as the data from the previous 3 years which is treated as the mean. As a result of outbreak of avian influenza in the neighbourhood, the

Table 3 Calculations of reference period and the loss in poultry insurance

			Avian influenza	Loss settlement
Specification of elements		2017	2018A	2018A
Number of coops	[items]	5	5	
Amount placed	[items/batch]	100,000	100,000	
Number of placements in a year	[items/year]	6	6	
Survivability	[%]	95.0%	92.0%	
Final bird weight	[kg/item]	2.64	2.68	
Number of fattened items in a year	[items/year]	2,850,000	2,560,000	–290,000
Weight of livestock annually	[kg/year]	7,524,000	6,860,800	–663,200
Price of feed	[PLN/t]	1,259	1,259	
Price of livestock	[PLN/kg]	3.57	3.57	
Price of a chick	[PLN/item]	1.30	1.30	
Annual income from sale	[PLN/year]	26,860,680	24,493,056	–2,367,624
Monthly income from sale	[PLN/month]	2,238,390	2,041,088	–197,302
Cost of feed				
FCR	[kg/kg]	1.66	1.65	1.66
Annual amount of feed	[kg/year]	12,489,840	12,602,700	–112,860
Monthly amount of feed	[PLN/month]	1,040,820	1,050,225	–9,405
Price of feed	[PLN/t]	1,259	1,260	
Annual cost of feed	[PLN/year]	15,724,709	15,879,402	–154,693
Monthly cost of feed	[PLN/month]	1,310,392	1,323,284	–12,891

(continued)

Table 3 (continued)

Other costs for the coop and placement: chicks, heating, litter, veterinary care, cleaning and disinfection, lab tests, catching chicks, removal of manure, electricity, workers, maintenance, renovation, insurance, depreciation on premises and equipment, waste utilisation, transport, tax, additional mortgage costs, other costs				
Total		**179,118**	**188,107**	–8,989
Other costs annually				
Total		**5,373,550**	**5,643,213**	–269,663
Income from sale of broilers	[PLN/year]	26,860,680	24,493,056	–2,367,624
Income from sale of manure	[PLN/year]	12,000	10,000	
Total		**26,872,680**	**24,503,056**	–2,369,624
Costs of feed consumption	[PLN/year]	15,724,709	15,879,402	–154,693
Other costs	[PLN/year]	5,373,550	5,643,213	–269,663
Total		**21,098,259**	**21,522,615**	–424,356
Margin on sales	[PLN/year]	5,774,421	2,980,441	–2,793,980
Margin on sales	[%]	21.5%	12.2%	–9.32%
Margin on item	[PLN/item]	2.03	1.16	– 0.86
Margin on kilogram	[PLN/kg]	0.77	0.43	– 0.33
Monthly margin	[PLN/month]	481,202	248,370	–232,831.66

Source Own elaboration

sales of animals decreased (though in the lockdown and sales ban period the income decreased only slightly—the sales decreased, but bigger animals were sold more often). The costs associated with cleaning and disinfection also increased, but only in the period of lockdown. In the face of no placement in two subsequent cycles, the farmer did not incur these costs (an important note: part of costs may be included in permanent contracts concluded with suppliers and in such case they can be found in a detailed claims settlement).

In effect, the compensation paid under insurance will cover:

(a) decrease in sales value by PLN 2,367,624
(b) sum of increased and saved costs—PLN 424,356
(c) direct surplus for two cycles where no production was conducted—PLN 248,370
(d) direct surplus from the cycle affected by the loss—PLN 35,700

As a result, the total value of compensation will amount to PLN 3,076,050.

It needs to be highlighted that in this insurance the sums obtained from the sales and compensation under other insurance contracts, but also payments from public funding and animal carcass disposal facilities will be credited towards the compensation. This rule is also in force when as a result of epizootic or disease the insuring party receives payment from public funding, but also animal carcass disposal facilities provided they do not resign from claims intentionally or the right to claims does not cease.

As we deal with insurance of profit loss and increased costs, in terms and conditions one may find a provision that insurance cannot lead to enrichment. Economic benefits, which after the cease of liability period occur as the effect of insured event, need to be taken into account. This means that, for instance, the scale of natural deaths from reference year will not be included while specifying the severity of damage.

5 Income Stabilization Fund for Animal Production

Insurance solutions used so far had been inefficient. In effect, a new instrument, income stabilization tool (IST), was introduced by the regulation on support for rural development (Regulation (EU) No 1305/2013, art. 35 and 39) as a part of the Common Agricultural Policy. IST is aimed at creating a certain level of security for farmers by protecting them with one contract against the negative effects (Liesivaara et al. 2012) of unfavourable tendencies in total income of farms from their source (Pigeon et al. 2012, p. 2).

Allowance from mutual fund[2] with regard to income stabilization may be granted only when income decrease of a farmer participating in the fund exceeds 30% of their mean annual income from the previous three years or the mean from three years calculated on the basis of five previous years, excluding the lowest and highest value. The income is determined as the sum of income gained by the farmer from

[2]For more see Janowicz-Lomott and Lyskawa (2009).

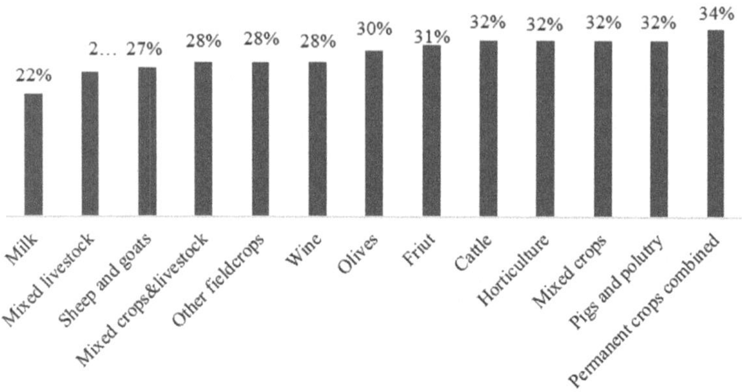

Fig. 3 Share of farm households with loss exceeding 30% according to selected farm types in EU in 2007–2013 (%). *Source* DG AGRI

the market, including all forms of public support, after deduction of production costs. Payments from the mutual fund for farmers compensate less than 70% of lost income in the year when the producer starts to qualify for this form of support. 65% of the paid allowance may be financed from the II pillar of CAP. This shows that despite introduction of income stabilization tools, farms will participate in loss compensation and will co-finance the difference between the historical mean and the actual income (on the level of 30%). Such formula for calculating the sum of allowance also stresses the aim of using income stabilization tools (IST)—to stabilize the functioning and possibly guarantee survival of a farm household, yet not fully compensate the incurred loss.

When analysing the changeability of income with respect to conditions which must be met to qualify for income compensation in accordance with IST, even over 1/3 of farms in the European Union (depending on production type) declare income loss over 30% of the mean from previous three years (Fig. 3). This indicates a necessity to prepare budgets for claims worth billions euro.

Assuming the situation maintaining the current functioning of farms specializing in animal production, we prepared a cost simulation of IST functioning for animal production (in accordance with the Regulation No 1305/2013) based on income data from the Polish FADN database.[3] Three groups of animal production resulting from FADN classification were analysed: TF 5—dairy cows, TF 6—herbivorous animals, and TF 7—granivorous animals (Table 4).

[3]The sample of Polish FADN is representative due to three criteria: localization, economic size and agricultural type. The number of farms in the sample, in accordance with the plan of choice, amounts to 12,100.

One of the criteria for grouping farms in the sample is the agricultural type of farm household determined with the share of Standard Output (SO) values from particular groups of agricultural activities in the total SO value of the farm.

Table 4 Simulation of animal production IST premium in Poland

Items	2010	2011	2012	2013	2014	2015
TF 5—dairy cows						
Number of farms from the FADN database	1750	1764	1909	1802	1811	1808
Calculated net premium (%)	4.62	4.11	6.79	6.43	7.41	14.83
Calculated net premium with RDP co-financing (%)	1.62	1.44	2.38	2.25	2.59	5.19
TF 6—herbivorous animals						
Number of farms from the FADN database	331	399	468	278	289	334
Calculated net premium (%)	8.20	10.05	14.21	17.09	20.28	18.18
Calculated net premium with RDP co-financing (%)	2.87	3.52	4.97	5.98	7.10	6.36
TF 7—granivorous animals						
Number of farms from the FADN database	1245	1178	1171	662	669	656
Calculated net premium (%)	8.25	8.35	9.18	13.46	26.16	24.62
Calculated net premium with RDP co-financing (%)	2.89	2.92	3.21	4.71	9.16	8.62

Source Own elaboration

These estimations indicate that without involvement of Rural Development Programme (RDP) funds it would be difficult for agricultural producers to accept insurance premium. The rate of premium (paid by the farmer), taking into account the share of EU funds on the level of 65% of expenditures, seems feasible to be paid by the farmer, yet it needs to be compared with the profitability of animal production. Additionally, it is only the level of payments to the fund resulting from the necessity to pay compensation claims which does not include all other fund costs (such as administration) (Kowalczyk et al. 2013, p. 158).

6 Conclusions

The European Union's environmental standards are one of the highest in the world.

In contrary to plants, animal production is based on live organisms of higher order. They move, react to various stimuli (not only food), require individual treatment, and people who specialize in breeding are expected to have special qualifications.

This high specialization of animal production makes it impossible to replace this type of activity in case of losing financial liquidity. Simultaneously, withdrawal or suspension of such activity is often connected with lack of possibility to launch it again (e.g. due to outflow of workers, sales of equipment or sudden need to adjust the buildings as a result of change in law provisions).

It needs to be stressed that insurance products offered currently to EU and Polish farmers may form the basis for risk management in farm households in the scope of animal production. However, their limitation regarding the types of covered events or reluctance of insurance companies by offering solutions connected with operation risk (associated with production only) make it necessary to implement instruments based on the idea of mutual fund, especially in the scope of income stabilization. Also, a broad scope of possible and practical solutions will constitute the basis for amendment of existing legal and administrative regulations. In effect, it will be possible to rationalize public expenditures incurred for ad hoc social welfare in the event of natural disasters, i.e. disaster loans and subsidies for retrieve agricultural production. Projected instruments will become a part of a bigger complex system of risk management in agriculture. This is one of the main guidelines of the European Commission with respect to shaping the rules of farm functioning. Moreover, it promotes competitiveness of domestic and EU farms with other strong global economies.

References

Asseldonk, M. (2017). *Study on risk management*. European Commission, Participatory Workshop, Brusselss, 6 July 2017, Brussels.

Casasús, I., & Lombardi, G. (2016). Mountain pastures and livestock farming facing uncertainty: environmental, technical and socio-economic challenges. *Cahiers Options Méditerranéennes*, 7–360.

Czyżewski, A., Poczta-Wajda, A., & Stępień, S. (2009). Future of the CAP in the new financial perspective 2014-2020. Challenges and Consequences for Poland. Prace Naukowe Uniwersytetu Ekonomicznego we Wrocławiu, (*59 Global Challenges and Policies of the European Union-Consequences for the "New Member States"*), 30–39.

Czyżewski, B., Matuszczak, A., & Muntean, A. (2018). Influence of agricultural policy on the environmental sustainability of European farming. *Journal of Environmental Protection and Ecology, 19*(1), 426–434.

European Commission. (2006). *Agricultural Insurance Schemes*. Joint Research Centre, Brussels.

GDV. (2016). *Landwirtschaftliche Mehrgefahrenversicherung für Deutschland*. Berlin: Gesamtverband der Deutschen Versicherungswirtschaft e. V.

Janowicz-Lomott, M., Lyskawa, K. (2009) Chosen alternative methods of financing some random events, on example of rural enterprise (Wybrane, alternatywne metody finansowania skutków zdarzen losowych na przykladzie przedsiebiorstwa rolnego). *Pieniądze i Więź, 1*(12), 104–116.

Janowicz-Lomott, M., Łyskawa, K. (2014) The new instruments of risk management in agriculture in the European Union. *Procedia—Economics and Finance, 9*.

Kowalczyk, P., Poprawska, E., & Ronka-Chmielowiec, W. (2013). *Metody aktuarialne*. Warszawa: Wydawnictwo Naukowe PWN.

Lemairea, G., Franzluebbersb, A., Carvalhoc, P., & Dedieu, B. (2014). Integrated crop–livestock systems: Strategies to achieve synergy between agricultural production and environmental quality. *Agriculture, Ecosystems & Environment, 190*, 4–8.

Liesivaara, P., Myyra, S., Jaakkola, A. (2012) *Feasibility of the income stabilisation tool in Finland*. Dublin.

Mihułka, M. (2003). *Charakterystyka technologiczna hodowli drobiu i świń w Unii Europejskiej*. Warszawa: Ministerstwo Środowiska.

Pigeon, M., de Frahan, B., & Denuit, M. (2012). *Actuarial evaluation of the EU proposed farm income stabilization tool*. EAAE: Dublin.
Roberts, R. (2007). *Livestock and aquaculture insurance in developing countries*. Rome: Food and Agriculture Organization of the United Nations.

Private Voluntary Health Insurance: Market in Poland and Determinants of Demand—Review of Literature

Adam Śliwiński and Iwona Borkowska

Abstract In the time of the demographic changes, which result in a direct burden on state care financing and influence on changes in the structure of expenditure on health, it is very important to know why people take into consideration the decision of buying private health insurance. This study is attempted to answer this question and is focused on the identification of factors determining the propensity to conclude PVHI by individuals, based on the research carried out by leading global researchers, as well as outlining the impact of identified factors on the demand for PVHI. The paragraph 1 of this paper describes the specifics of financing health care in Poland and the specifics of the private voluntary health insurance market. The next paragraph presents the analysis of factors of demand on private voluntary health insurance on the basis of the literature review. The study finishes the description of the obtained results: the demand factors for PVHI, their impact on the demand for PVHI and conclusions indicating further directions of the research. The study used a descriptive qualitative method of the collected material: selected by key words of scientific publications, documents and expert materials as well as legal acts.

Keywords Private voluntary health insurance · Determinants · Demand

1 Introduction

In the majority of healthcare systems, people are entitled to a wide range of services provided by the states. For example, in Poland the scope of services includes basic health care, outpatient specialist care, hospital treatment, rehabilitation, long-term care as well as palliative and hospice care, spa treatment, medical emergency services

---

A. Śliwiński · I. Borkowska (✉)
SGH Warsaw School of Economics, Al. Niepodległości 162, 02-554 Warsaw, Poland
e-mail: iwborkow@outlook.com

A. Śliwiński
e-mail: asliwin@sgh.waw.pl

M. Janowicz-Lomott et al. (eds.), *Economic and Financial Challenges for Balkan and Eastern European Countries*, Springer Proceedings in Business and Economics,
https://doi.org/10.1007/978-3-030-39927-6_11

and drug reimbursement for medications.[1] These are the benefits entirely covered or co-financed from public funds. However, despite such a wide range of medical services available under the public system, Poles incur additional expenses for treatment from their own pocket in order to ensure faster access or higher standards of necessary medical services. These are mainly direct payments, participation of private voluntary health insurance (PVHI) in financing medical services is marginal in Poland.

This situation results from historical conditions. Over the years, the priorities and directions of activities in the field of health care in Poland as well as the sources of its financing were changing. Until 1999, a centralized budgetary model for health care was in force in Poland. Main assumptions of this model were the lack of private sector in health care and broad free access to all services provided by healthcare providers financed from the state budget. Then, a reform took place, and the existing system was replaced by the decentralized system of mandatory health insurance, complemented with financing from state and territorial self-government budgets. In addition to the changes in financing, conversion of public healthcare units from budgetary ones into independent public healthcare institutions was also implemented. Nevertheless, this did not solve the problems with accessibility to medical services. Growing health needs resulting from such factors as demographic changes and technological development make the demand for medical services increase. This situation in correlation with limited public funds for its financing and broad statutory entitlements, which are the remnant of the previous system, causes the need for changes and new solutions—allowing the inflow of additional financial resources to the healthcare system. The answer to this problem may be the spread of private health insurances. These insurances are now available in Poland and observed the dynamic of collected gross written premium, despite the lack of special incentives for purchasers.

However, the PVHI market in Poland is still small, and it is necessary to stimulate its development on the basis of factors determining clients demand. An innovative insurance market should be aware of factors that influence the behavior of its clients. Polish Insurance Market is not so innovative (Śliwinski et al. 2013), and these factors in Poland have not been recognized so far and research described in this paper and as well as future steps are an attempt to fill this gap. It should be added that this paper is the first stage of the work aimed at determining the determinants of demand for PVHI and is focused on determining the range of factors used by researchers in PVHI demand research. The obtained results will determine the directions of empirical research in the subsequent stage of the work. Due to the fact that the demand factors on PVHI in Poland have not been well researched so far, the analysis process has been based on world literature research.

[1]The full catalog of guaranteed services is included in Art. 15 para. 2 of the Act of August 27, 2004, on Healthcare Services Financed from Public Funds, Dz.U. [Journal of Acts] 2004, No 210, item 2135, as amended.

Table 1 Structure of financing health care in Poland in 2015 (% of current healthcare expenditure)

	Government schemes	Compulsory contributory health insurance schemes	Voluntary health insurance schemes	Financing schemes of non-profit institutions serving households	Enterprise financing schemes	Household out-of-pocket payments
Poland	9.2	60.7	5.0	1.1	0.7	23.3

Source Eurostat; healthcare expenditure by financing scheme, 2018

1.1 Financing Health care in Poland

The main source of financing health care in Poland is contributions for mandatory health insurance, almost 60.7% (2015). Other public sources of financing health services in Poland are the state budget financing 5.2% (2015) of the total expenditure on health care and local government units financing 4.0% of total expenditure. Private sources of financing health care in Poland include direct expenditures of households (23.3% in 2015), private health insurances and other private expenses (see Table 1).

Current expenditure on health care in 2015 amounted to PLN 114,142.4 billion (EUR 26,542.9 billion) and was higher than in 2014 by approximately PLN 6.7 billion (EUR 1.6 billion).[2]

The share of expenditure on health in Poland in 2016 in GDP was 6.4% and was lower than in other European countries, including Lithuania (6.5%), Estonia (6.7%), Slovakia (6.9%), Czech Republic (7.3%) and Hungary (7.6%) The share of expenditure on health in GDP in 2016 in selected countries around the world is shown in Fig. 1.

Underfunding public health care and a simultaneous increase in health needs causes public dissatisfaction and an increase in private health spending, including the development of private voluntary health insurance (PVHI).

1.2 Market and the Role of Private Voluntary Health Insurance in Poland

In Poland, private voluntary health insurance contracts are concluded with insurance companies performing insurance activities [3] and are offered based on the provisions

---

[2]Publication of the Central Statistical Office Health and Health in 2016, 2017; 158–159.

[3]The insurance undertaking may perform insurance activities in the form of a joint stock company, mutual insurance company or an European company defined in the Council Regulation (EC) No. 2157/2001 of October 8, 2001, on the Statute for a European company (SE) (Official Journal EC L 294, 10.11.2001, p. 1, Journal of the EU, Polish Special Edition, Chapter 6, vol. 4, p. 251) https://www.knf.gov.pl/dla_rynku/procesy_licencyjne/ubezpieczeniowy/krajowy_zaklad_ubezpieczen_reasekuracji/forma_prawna, Accessed April 25, 2018.

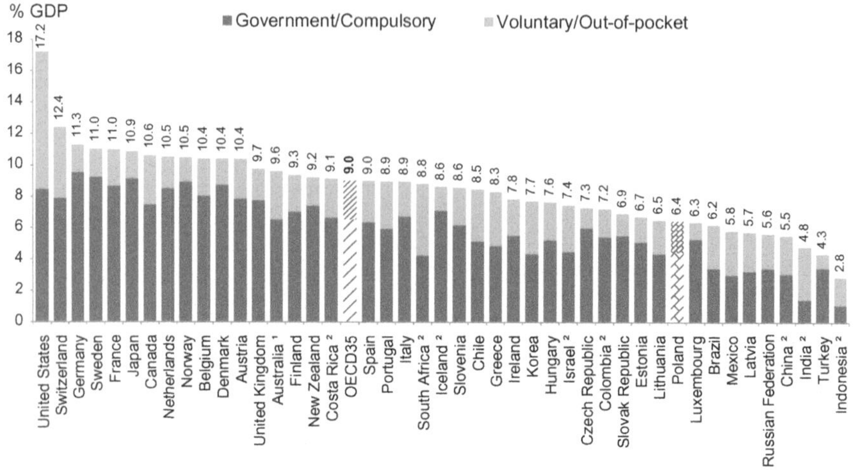

Fig. 1 Share of expenditure on health in GDP in 2016 (or in the nearest year), in selected OECD countries around the world. *Note* Expenditure excludes investments, unless otherwise stated. 1. Australian expenditure estimates exclude all expenditure for residential aged care facilities in welfare (social) services. 2. Includes investments. *Source* Health at a glance 2017, OECD indicators

of the Act on Insurance and Reinsurance Activities,[4] which specify the insurance division by sections, classes and types of risk. These may be concluded by insurers offering life insurance—Life Insurers (Section I—insurance from Class 5 "accident and sickness insurance, if supplementary to insurance listed in Class 1–4") and by insurance companies offering property and personal insurance—Non-Life Insurers (Section II—Class 1 insurance "accident insurance" and Class 2 "sickness insurance"). The division adopted in the legal regulation affects the scope of defining the participants of the private health insurance market as well as the level of collected premiums.

To calculate the value of the Polish health-related insurance market, the value of the gross written premium collected by both Life and Non-Life Insurers was assumed in this paper. The value of the Polish health-related insurance market is presented in Fig. 2 which shows the gross written premium collected from:

- accident insurance,
- sickness insurance understood as private voluntary health insurance—PVHI.[5]

Among health-related insurances, the highest dynamic of the gross written premium is observed in sickness insurance (PVHI). Gross written premium collected in

---

[4]Act of September 11, 2015, on Insurance and Reinsurance Activities, Dz.U. [Journal of Acts] 2015, position: 1844, as amended.

[5]In the financial reporting of Polish insurance companies, there is no separate category of health insurance. The publication includes data of all insurance classes. In the case of companies offering sickness insurance from Section II, the premium is given together with the premium collected from the travel insurance, which additionally causes the problem to be the definition of the actual size of the private health insurance market.

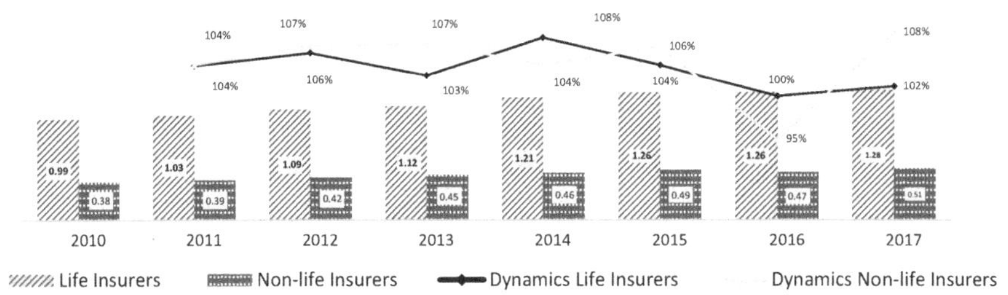

Fig. 2 Gross written premium collected in Poland from health-related insurances: accident insurance and sickness insurance in billion euros (years: 2010–2017). *Source* Own study; Polish Financial Supervision Authority

Poland separately from accident insurance and sickness insurance on the background of the Polish Insurance Market in year 2010 and 2017 is presented in Table 2.

PVHI products offered in Poland include benefits that can be divided into the following modules (Holly 2013): service module (medical), financial and annuity module (cash payments), logistics (e.g., setting treatment standards) and care module (e.g., assistance). According to the analyses carried out by the Polish Insurance Association, the value of the PVHI market which can be called the service module in 2017 amounted to EUR 159 million (PLN 684 million) and 2.2 million people was covered by this type of insurance.

In Poland, there is also other private voluntary health insurance (PVHI) available.[6] Persons who are not covered by public mandatory insurance may voluntarily insure themselves in the National Health Fund (NFZ)[7] if they reside on the territory of the Republic of Poland. For the payment of the premium, the insured is entitled to the same scope of benefits as persons under the public system; however, he/she is struggling with the same problems with access to benefits as other people insured by this institution.

Analyzing the PVHI market in Poland, it should also be paid attention to the medical services market in the country that are prepaid (medical subscriptions), which constitutes a "quasi-insurance" element of the healthcare system in Poland. The entities offering medical subscriptions in setting the price do not use actuarial risk estimation methods and do not create insurance provisions. These services provide benefits specifically defined in the contract and implemented in private medical facilities. These can be the benefits to which persons are entitled under the public system and benefits "over," e.g., dental benefits in the scope exceeding the scope of services guaranteed in the public system. Medical subscriptions usually concern outpatient

[6]Legal basis for the conclusion of the contract: art. 68 of the Act of August 27, 2004, on Healthcare Services Financed from Public Funds, Dz.U. [Journal of Acts] 2008, No. 164 item 1027, as amended.

[7]National Health Fund (NFZ)—a state organizational unit operating under the Act of August 27, 2004, on Healthcare Services Financed from Public Funds, Dz.U. [Journal of Acts] 2008 No. 164 item 1027, as amended and on the basis of the statute given. The fund performs the role of a payer in the Polish healthcare system: the funds from obligatory health insurance contributions from the National Health Fund finance health services provided to insured persons and reimburse medicines.

Table 2 Gross written premium collected in Poland from health-related insurances: accident insurance and sickness insurance in thousand euros (2010; 2017) on the background of the Polish Insurance Market

Type of insurance	Class	2017	2010	2017/2010 (%)
Life: total		5,706,242.57	7,290,359.34	78
Sickness insurance	5	282,803.38	124,914.72	226
Annuity insurance	4	31,480.38	19,410.28	162
Life insurance linked to insurance capital funds insurance	3	2,623,714.12	1,888,023.58	139
Accident insurance	5	998,930.13	867,037.19	115
Marriage insurance, birth insurance	2	26,039.57	27,882.76	93
Life insurance	1	1,743,274.99	4,363,090.81	40
Non-Life: total		8,788,376.05	5,171,064.84	170
Assistance insurance	18	229,189.53	80,483.02	285
Casco insurance of railway rolling stock insurance	4	9,145.12	3,818.17	240
Sickness insurance	2	160,129.64	79,929.06	200
Motor vehicle liability arising out of the possession of land vehicles insurance	10	3,443,966.02	1,750,595.15	197
Other damage and loss property insurance	9	707,220.25	409,683.28	173
General liability insurance	13	454,213.30	289,206.05	157
Casco insurance of land vehicles insurance	3	1,779,592.60	1,222,843.68	146
Suretyship insurance	15	104,433.73	73,940.78	141
Goods-in-transit insurance	7	30,424.64	22,254.71	137
Fire and natural forces insurance	8	739,503.31	557,866.96	133
Accident insurance	1	347,112.51	295,144.31	118
Liability for ships in sea and inland navigation insurance	12	4,676.97	4,449.91	105
Various financial risks insurance	16	177,641.60	183,219.37	97
Aircraft liability arising out of the possession of aircraft insurance	11	5,064.31	5,662.55	89
Credit insurance	14	90,613.88	108,165.52	84
Casco insurance of aircraft insurance	5	5,435.31	7,417.32	73
Vessels in sea and inland navigation insurance	6	13,778.19	20,610.19	67
Legal protection insurance	17	23,096.65	55,774.81	41

Source Own study; Polish Financial Supervision Authority

services. The value of this service market, estimated by experts, is over EUR 0.7 billion (PLN 3 billion).

2 Analysis of Factors of Demand on Private Health Insurance on the Basis of World Literature Review

2.1 Factors Used to Research Demand for Private Health Insurance—Analysis of World Literature

Private health insurance may play a different role[8] depending on the healthcare system in the particular country. It can therefore be expected that the demand for such a service may also be determined by many factors. This chapter contains an analysis of the research carried out by leading global researchers, to determine the most commonly used factors for the research determinants of demand for private health insurance as well as a review of the determinants identified by them for PVHI. The list of studies used for analysis is indicated in Table 3. Detailed information on the publication of the research in question is provided in the reference list at the end of this article.

The study showed that irrespectively of the role of PVHI in a given country in the analyzed research, sociodemographic factors and factors related to income and the source of its obtaining were most often used to determine the determinants of demand for PVHI. Table 4 indicates the number of times the analyzed factor occurred in the research selected for this study.

2.2 Determinants of Demand for Private Health Insurance—A Review of the Results of Research in World Literature

The determinants of demand for PVHI identified in world literature research can be divided into the following categories: (1) income and time value, (2) education, (3) age, gender and family size, (4) health status, (5) attitude in relation to risk and (6) other determinants of demand. This chapter provides an overview of the identified factors that have a significant impact on the demand for PVHI.

---

[8]More information on the role of PVHI in the country where research has been carried out in voluntary health insurance in Europe: Role and regulation; Sagan A, Thomson S; Copenhagen (Denmark): European Observatory on Health Systems and Policies; 2016 and at http://international.commonwealthfund.org.

Table 3 Summary of the analyzed research described in the world literature

No.	Country	Author/authors	Year of publication
1	USA	Phelps	1973
2	USA	Friedman	1974
3	USA	Auerbach and Ohri	2006
4	USA	Fang et al.	2008
5	Australia	Cameron et al.	1988
6	Australia	Cameron and McCallum	1995
7	UK	Propper	1987
8	UK	Propper	1999
9	UK	Propper et al.	1987
10	UK	Besley et al.	1999
11	UK	Emmerson et al.	2001
12	UK	King and Mossialos	2002
13	UK	Wallis	2003
14	Taiwan	Liu and Chen	2002
15	Ireland, Italy, Portugal and the UK	Jones et al.	2006
16	EU:15 countries	Paccagnella et al.	2013
17	Spain	Vera-Hernandez	1999
18	Netherlands	Van De Ven and Van Praag	1981
19	Ireland	Finn and Harmon	2006

Source Own study

2.2.1 Income and Value of Time

The literature on the subject (Cameron et al. 1988; Cameron and McCallum 1995) indicates that income is the main determinant of PVHI demand. It can be assumed, therefore, that higher income is significantly connected with the probability of concluding an insurance contract. However, according to a study conducted by researchers Emmerson et al. (2001), there is a decrease in demand for PVHI at the highest level of income obtained.

The research on the impact of income on the propensity to buy insurance was also investigated by other researchers: Phelps (1973), Propper (1987), Propper et al. (1999), Vera-Hernandez (1999), Liu and Chen (2002), King and Mossialos (2002), Wallis (2003), Finn and Harmon (2006), Jones et al. (2006), Auerbach and Ohri (2006). They also confirm that income has a significant impact on the decision to purchase health insurance. In a study conducted by researchers Paccagnella et al. (2013), who investigated the determinants of purchasing health insurance among people aged 50+ in 15 European countries, using data from the SHARE study (Survey of Health, Aging and Retirement in Europe) for examination, it was found that

Table 4 Range of factors studied in the analyzed research

No.	Analyzed factors	The incidence of a factor in the analyzed research
1	Age	17
2	Income	15
3	Gender	15
4	Employment status, together with industry and employment	14
5	Education	14
6	Health condition	10
7	Family size	9
8	Marital status	8
9	Region: city/country, but also world regions	6
10	Waiting time (waiting list)	6
11	Ownership of an apartment	5
12	Supporter of a specific political party	4
13	Smoking/non-smoking	4
14	Number of visits to the specialist	3
15	Race	3
16	The level of public spending on health	2
17	Number of visits to the general practitioner	2
18	Cognitive ability	2
19	Previous use of public health care	2
20	Previous use of private health care	2
21	Existence of private clinics	2
22	Number of beds in public hospitals	2
23	Buying/reading printed newspapers	2
24	Previous use of medical services	2
25	Receiving benefits from the employer	1
26	Receiving private pensions	1
27	Entitlement for future retirement	1
28	Daily activities for health	1
29	Other health activities	1
30	Number of beds in private hospitals	1
31	Expected status of health	1
32	Waiting time (regional waiting list)	1
33	Household savings	1
34	Social class	1
35	Prices of medical services	1

(continued)

Table 4 (continued)

No.	Analyzed factors	The incidence of a factor in the analyzed research
36	Being privately insured	1
37	Risk aversion	1
38	Suffering from risks associated with the labor market	1
39	Days of inpatient hospital care	1
40	Annual expenditure on health in the family (no expenses on treatment by a family doctor)	1
41	Number of medical consultants in public hospitals under a part-time employment contract	1

Source Own study

the economic and financial status of a household resulting from income positively influenced the probability of PVHI purchase in six out of 15 countries studied: Sweden, Denmark, Germany, Spain, Greece and Italy.

According to the researchers Propper (1987), Besley et al. (1999), Vera-Hernandez (1999), Emmerson et al. (2001), Liu and Chen (2002), Wallis (2003), Paccagnella et al. (2013), Auerbach and Ohri (2006), purchase health insurance depends not only on the income we have at our disposal, but also on the source of its obtaining (employment status, type of work performed). Propper (1987) notes that self-employed due to the fact that their future income may be less reliable than full-time employees are less likely to buy high-contribution premium insurances than full-time employees with the same income, place of residence and state of health. Propper (1987) found a negative relationship between self-employment and demand for PVHI. Emmerson et al. (2001) also note that full-time employees are more likely to buy PVHI than self-employed or non-working people.

Some researchers note that income should be considered together with the time value. They believe that the purchase of health insurance depends not only on the income we have at our disposal, the sources of obtaining it, but also on the value of time. For example, Besley et al. (1999), who focus on losing time related to waiting for medical services, show a positive relationship between the waiting time for public sector benefits and the demand for PVHI.

2.2.2 Education

Another factor, whose impact on the purchase of health insurance was examined by a wide range of researchers, (Vera-Hernandez 1999; Emmerson et al. 2001; Liu and Chen 2002; Paccagnella et al. 2013; Finn and Harmon 2006; Auerbach and Ohri 2006) is the impact of the level of education on the purchase of PVHI. The conducted research states that people with higher education are more likely to buy health insurance. In the literature, we will find the following explanation why education is important for the purchase of health insurance: education increases the efficiency of health production (Grossman 1972), and education is an important correlation of good health (Grossman 1999).

Researchers Van De Ven and Van Praag (1981) identify education as a variable affecting material well-being, through a positive correlation between education and the expected increase in income. Research results (Psacharopoulos and Patrinos 2004) also prove that education increases individual income. The obtained income significantly influences the decision to purchase insurance. However, for Czapiński (2008) the rate of return on investment in education at various levels and directions is not constant (depends on many factors both macroeconomic and determining the situation of individuals and the structure of demand on the labor market), but only exceptionally it is negative. Nevertheless, education is one of the important factors affecting the demand for PVHI.

2.2.3 Age, Gender and Family Size

According to research, the age, gender of the "head of the family" and family size have a significant impact on the purchase of PVHI. Age can act as an important determinant of the propensity for insurance because (1) it is a variable associated with increased expected medical consumption and (2) is associated with an increased supply of wealth (Van De Ven and Van Praag 1981). This variable may therefore have a positive effect as well as a negative one (Van De Ven and Van Praag (1981). According to these researchers "young families are generally relatively less well-off and rather healthy, although they may expect high medical costs because of births and childhood diseases; at middle age the financial status improves, while at the end of life the health status is expected to worsen". Van De Ven and Van Praag (1981), therefore, assumed that the age impact on PVHI demand at the beginning of life should be positive and then negative. Researchers Paccagnella et al. (2013) also confirm that specific family characteristics may affect the purchase of PVHI, and they showed a positive effect of the partner's presence in the household on demand for PVHI in the Netherlands, Belgium, France and Austria. According to research by Liu and Chen (2002) in Taiwan, the propensity to buy PVHI increases with age, but also with the size of the family.

Age was indicated as an important factor of demand for PVHI in research: Propper et al. (1999), King and Mossialos (2002), Wallis (2003), Auerbach and Ohri (2006). Emmerson et al. (2001), on the other hand, state that if age is an important determinant of demand, individuals aged 40–65 are most willing to buy PVHI, than those who are under 30 and over 70 years old.

Gender is indicated as a significant determinant of demand in research by Propper (1999), King and Mossialos (2002), Wallis (2003), Auerbach and Ohri (2006), Fang et al. (2008). Propper (1999) states that women are more likely to demand medical care than men based on the use of public health care and the assumption that demographic characteristics of people using public and private health care are the same. Auerbach and Ohri (2006) for Propper (1999) confirm women are more likely to buy PVHI than men.

The size of the family is indicated as a significant determinant of demand in Liu and Chen's (2002) research, Besley et al. (1999), Emmerson et al. (2001).

2.2.4 Health Status

According to Arrow (1963), the demand for health insurance is identified with the demand for medical services, in which source is not as regular as the source of demand, for example, for food or clothing. It is irregular and unpredictable. The use of medical services, except those of a preventive nature, brings satisfaction only in the event of illness. Therefore, it may be expected that private health insurance will be purchased by those who have a bad health or are able to increase the demand for medical services, e.g., older people (due to chronic diseases), people with children (due to higher expected demand for medical services) and women (due to the expected future consumption related to childbirth).

The research on the impact of the variable on the demand for PVHI insurance was also addressed by Cameron and McCallum (1995). The researchers mentioned that based on the research carried out, current health conditions significantly affect the purchase of private hospital insurance in Australia, due to the risk associated with high costs of co-payment for hospital services in this country.

Propper (1987) confirmed that health condition is a significant determinant of demand for PVHI, but she noticed that the health condition of the dependents is more important than the health of the buyer. Also, the health of women in the household is more important in deciding whether to buy insurance than men's health. Jones et al. (2006) confirm that the probability of buying PVHI insurance increases with better health. Paccagnella et al. (2013), however, state that poor health positively affects the purchase of PVHI in Denmark, the Netherlands, Switzerland and Austria.

2.2.5 Attitude in Relation to Risk

According to the literature on the subject, readiness to purchase health insurance results from an attitude in relation to risk. People with aversion (risk aversion) are willing to devote some of their resources to protect themselves against the possible consequences of the risk. Insurance is, however, a method of limiting uncertainty regarding possible financial losses (Nyman 1999), and the greater the risk aversion among society is, the more it is willing to sacrifice some of its resources to reduce this risk. It is more likely to conclude an insurance contract. Risk aversion shows how much someone does not like uncertainty and how much he/she wants to avoid it. The relationship to risk depends on the amount of income received and the composition of the household: People with higher incomes and families have less risk aversion (Friedman 1974). Phelps (1973) also confirms that people with higher incomes are characterized by lower risk aversion than people with lower incomes, and this attitude has an impact on the purchase of PVHI.

2.2.6 Other Determinants of Demand

World literature also describes research on other factors determining demand for PVHI, including sympathizing with a particular political party, e.g., Wallis (2003) said that sympathizing with political parties is a significant determinant of demand for PVHI in the UK. Besley et al. (1999), Emmerson et al. (2001) and King and Mossialos (2002) stated that in Great Britain supporters of the Conservative Party were more likely to conclude PVHI insurance contracts than supporters of the Labor Party.

The results of research carried out by Wallis (2003) confirm a significant impact on the demand for PVHI also factors such as being smokers, being the owner of an apartment (also confirmed by Emmerson et al. 2001), private retirement and reading printed newspapers.

Propper et al. (1999), however, indicate that the strong determinant of demand for PVHI is the quality side of supply, i.e., the availability of medical services within the private sector of medical services.

Other determinants identified by the researchers for PVHI are social class (Vera-Hernandez 1999) region of residence (Liu and Chen 2002—people living in cities are more likely to conclude a PVHI agreement, Auerbach and Ohri 2006), having savings (Emmerson et al. 2001).

3 Conclusion

A study of world literature showed that the demand factors for PVHI, which were most often studied in the world, include age, income, gender, employment status, education, health status, as well as family size and marital status.

Undeniably, the key determinant of the demand for PVHI according to the researchers is the income we receive and the source of its obtaining. The level of income obtained according to researchers is inseparably connected with the education. The analyzed research states that people with higher education are more likely to buy health insurance. The inclination to insurance is also influenced by age, which is a variable associated with increased expected medical consumption and is associated with an increased supply of wealth.

In conclusion, the results obtained in the study should be noted that regardless of the role of health insurance in a particular country the researchers analyzed the same categories of data. However, their results and directions of impact on demand should be interpreted in the context of the healthcare system in force in a particular country, the sources of its financing and benefits that are not available within the public healthcare system. Thus, in order to learn the factors determining the demand for PVHI in Poland, it cannot be based solely on international surveys, but it should be the direction of selection of factors for the empirical study.

This study was preceded by a description of financing health care in Poland and the description of the Polish private voluntary health insurance market. As shown by the prepared analysis, the share of expenditure on health in GDP in Poland (6.4% of GDP) is lower than in other European countries, which undoubtedly affects the availability of services and satisfaction of patients. At the same time, the Polish private voluntary health insurance market is developing. The presented data show that in year 2017 were collected twice more gross written premium from PVHI (sickness insurance), than in year 2010 (dynamic 2017/2010; +226% for Life and + 200% for Non-Life companies). For comparison, the gross written premium collected from accident insurance increased by only 115% for Life and 118% for Non-Life companies in the same period of time. It should also be emphasized that the dynamics of the gross written premium from PVHI in the discussed period was higher than the dynamics of the whole insurance market in Poland: gross written premium collected by Life insurance companies (dynamic 2017/2010; +78%), as well as Non-Life insurance companies (dynamic 2017/2010; +170%). Business lines, which in the analyzed period grew faster than health insurance that are the assistance insurance (dynamic 2017/2010; +285%) and casco insurance of railway rolling stock (dynamic 2017/2010; +240%).

Unfortunately, despite the observed high dynamics of the collected gross written premium in Poland from PVHI, the nominal value of this market is small. In 2017, the gross written premium collected from PVHI (sickness insurance) was EUR 0.44 billion (PLN 1.9 billion) and its share in the whole Life and Non-Life insurance market was just above 3%.

The growth of the market, without special legal regulations affecting customer demand, raises research interest. In Poland, there were made attempts to implement laws affecting the development of private health insurances but no specific solutions have been worked out or implemented. However, despite this situation, the demand for PVHI has been growing faster than for the other types of insurances. This is the demand which determinants have not been recognized yet. If such factors as income, age, gender and family size are significant determinants of the demand for private voluntary health insurance, as it results from the research, three hypotheses can be put forward on the basis of Poland:

(1) the higher the income, the higher the demand for PVHI is, because only people with higher income may be willing to voluntarily pay premiums for health insurance, which will cover the same benefits as in the public system. This does not include the group with the highest level of income, where a drop-in demand for PVHI is observed,
(2) demand for PVHI depends on age and sex, and the demand for medical services is related to these features, which are variable in lifetime. The positive impact of age on demand is expected among families with small children and women waiting for birth of a child, as well as people aged 45–65. On the other hand,

among people over 65 are expected to fall in demand due to the reduction of the product offer for this group as well as the decline in income,

(3) the larger the family, the lower the demand for PVHI is, because health expenditure decreases with the increase of the family size, which may affect the propensity to purchase private health insurance.

In further empirical studies, which are the second stage of the work, these hypotheses will be confirmed. However, it is expected that the strongest determinant of demand is after all is the income that the person who makes the decision to finance premiums for PVHI obtains.

References

Arrow, K. J. (1963). Uncertainty and the welfare economics of medical care. *American Economic Review, 53,* 941–973.

Auerbach, D., Ohri, S. (2006). Price and the demand for nongroup health insurance. *INQUIRY: The Journal of Health Care Organization, Provision, and Financing*, 122–134.

Annual Bulletin. Insurance market 2010, 2011, 2012, 2013, 2014, 2015, https://www.knf.gov.pl/?articleId=57191&p_id=18

Annual Bulletin. Insurance market 2016, 2017, https://www.knf.gov.pl/publikacje_i_opracowania?categories=/publikacje_i_opracowania/dane_statystyczne/ubepieczeniowy&pageNumber=0. Accessed April 25,2018

Besley, T., et al. (1999). The demand for private health insurance: do waiting lists matter? *Journal of Public Economics, 72,* 155–181.

Cameron, A. C., McCallum, J. (1995). Private health insurance choice in Australia: the role of long-term utilisation of health services. In *Economics and Health, Proceedings of the Seventeenth Australian Conference of Health Economists* (143–162).

Cameron, A., et al. (1988). A microeconometric model of the demand for health care and health insurance in Australia. *Review of Economic Studies, 55*(1), 85–106.

Central Statistical Office. (2017). Health and health care in 2016, Warsaw, 158–159.

Czapiński, J. (2008). Human capital and social capital versus material prosperity, Polish paradox. Zarządzanie Publiczne No. 4.

Emmerson, C., et al. (2001). Should private medical insurance be subsidised? *Health Care UK, 2001,* 49–65.

Fang, H., Keane, M., & Silverman, D. (2008). Sources of advantageous selection: evidence from the medigap insurance market. *Journal of Political Economy, 116*(2), 303–350.

Finn, C., Harmon, C. (2006). *A dynamic model of demand for private health insurance in Ireland.* Discussion Paper No. 2472, The Institute for the Study of Labour.

Friedman, B. (1974). Risk aversion and the consumer choice of health insurance option. *The Review of Economics and Statistics, 56*(2), 209–214.

Grossman, M. (1972). On the concept of health capital and the demand for health. *Journal of Political Economy, 80,* 223–225.

Grossman, M. (1999). *The human capital model of demand for health.* NBER Working Paper 7078.

Holly, R. (2013). *Insurance in organization of health care in Poland* (204–205). Warsaw: Krajowy Instytut Ubezpieczeń.

https://www.knf.gov.pl/dla_rynku/procesy_licencyjne/ubezpieczeniowy/krajowy_zaklad_ubezpieczen_reasekuracji/forma_prawna. Accessed April 25, 2018.

Jones, A. M., et al. (2006). The impact of having supplementary private health insurance on the use of specialists. *Annales d'Economie et Statistiques, 83*(84), 251–275.

King, D., & Mossialos, E. (2002). The determinants of private medical insurance prevalence in England, LSE Health and Social Care Discussion Paper, numer 3.

Liu, T. C., & Chen, C. S. (2002). An analysis of private health insurance purchasing decisions with national health insurance in Taiwan. *Social Science and Medicine, 55*(5), 755–774.

Nyman, J. A. (1999). The value of health insurance: the access motive. *Journal of Health Economics, 18,* 141–152.

OECD. (2017). *Health at a glance 2017: OECD indicators*. Paris: OECD Publishing.

Paccagnella, O., et al. (2013). Voluntary private health insurance among the over fifties in Europe. *Health Economics, 22*(3), 289–315.

Phelps, C. E. (1973). The demand for health insurance: a theoretical and empirical investigation, Santa Monica. The RAND Corporation Report R-1054-OEO.

Propper, C. (1987). An econometric estimation of the demand for private health insurance in the UK, Centre for Health Economics, University of York. Discussion Paper 24.

Propper, C. (1999a). The demand for private health care in the UK the arguments and the evidence. *Journal of Social Policy, 30*(4), 685–704.

Propper, C. et al. (1999). The demand for private medical insurance in the UK: a cohort analysis, CMPO Working Paper Series No. 99/013.

Psacharopoulos, G., & Patrinos, H. A. (2004). Returns to investment in education: a further update. *Education Economics, 12,* 111–134.

Śliwinski, A. et al. (2013). *Innovations in the context of the risk management*. Technology Innovation and Industrial Management, (TIIM): Phuket, Thailand.

Van De Ven, W., & Van Praag, B. (1981). The demand for deductibles in private health insurance. *Journal of Econometrics, 17,* 229–252.

Vera-Hernandez, A. (1999). Duplicate coverage and demand for health care: the case of Catalonia. *Health Economics, 8,* 579–598.

Wallis, G. (2003). The determinants of demand for private medical insurance: evidence from the British household panel survey. Presented at: The 2004 Royal Economic Society Annual Conference, University of Wales, Swansea, UK. https://discovery.ucl.ac.uk/id/eprint/18591/. Accessed April 25, 2018.

Healthcare Goods and Services—An Economic Perspective

Dan Sava

Abstract The purpose of this paper is to provide an insight into the health system from the point of view of economics. We consider health goods and services are true economic goods, because providers and patients, when supplying and demanding them, behave as economic agents. From this perspective, goods and services rendered within the health system were assigned to categories from economic perspective: public, private and common goods; capital and consumer goods; complementary and substitution goods; credence and experience goods; merit and demerit goods; tangible and intangible goods; superior, normal and inferior goods; necessity and luxury goods, etc. Because they are not homogenous, the specific demand for, and the elasticity of it is analyzed, as well as the relationship with access to care. The paper is limited to large categories of goods, but detailed examples are provided whenever possible. The paper attempts to enrich knowledge about health services, from economic perspective, providing a valuable input to policymaking, useful in creating effective targeted health policies rather than comprehensive large interventions. It is also useful for teaching, research, healthcare management, marketing and designing health insurance regulation and policies.

Keywords Health services · Economic goods

1 Introduction

In the common health economics literature, the description of health services is too vague to capture the complexity of the subject. The healthcare services are described as "treatment… or other services… related to illness, disability or injury" (Legal Glossary 2017). The WHO does not define health services but mentions various types of them (WHO 2018). Health services are complex services of various types and with little homogeneity. There is a say within the medical world: "there are no diseases, but patients," meaning that every treatment should be customized for the patient and not be conceived as a standard product.

D. Sava (✉)
Bucharest, Romania

M. Janowicz-Lomott et al. (eds.), *Economic and Financial Challenges for Balkan and Eastern European Countries*, Springer Proceedings in Business and Economics,
https://doi.org/10.1007/978-3-030-39927-6_12

Health services may be delivered for free in many countries, but they are not free goods, like air. On the contrary, they are economic goods. They cost money and are traded for money, because they are scarce and require an effort to produce (Business Dictionary 2018). The behavior of the suppliers and consumers of these services is similar to the behavior regarding any other economic good. So it is worth to look at the health services from the perspective of economics.

Since the beginnings of economic science, for the purpose of understanding the characteristics of economic goods, there has been a drive to categorize them. These categories were developed in correspondence to various perspectives: the effect of a delivery on the consumer or society, the character of the demand for these goods, the relationship between goods, characteristics of the goods who influence the demand for them, novelty of goods, price of goods, etc. It is time for using these economic categories for describing healthcare services, the purpose being a better understanding of these goods, informing the customers about them, providing an insight for policymakers. This is what this paper is trying to accomplish.

2 Types of Services

2.1 Health Services

The very health service is the treatment. This is the ultimate traded good. The supply is a doctor or a healthcare provider, for example, a hospital. On the demand side, there is a patient (customer). This is the primary health services market. However, in order to deliver the treatment, some precursory activities have to be made. In order to prescribe a treatment, a doctor needs to diagnose a patient. So in real life, there is a chain of activities (services) delivered to a patient. The health service is a package of services always delivered in the same sequence: examination, pre-diagnostic lab tests and/or image tests, diagnostic, pre-treatment tests, prescription of the treatment, delivering the treatment. The pre-diagnostic tests and pre-treatment tests are not always necessary. In all this sequence of services, the patient is the demand, but only in the first step, the patient exercises a direct demand. For all the other steps, the patient agrees to the demand which is created by the doctor on his/her behalf. There are cases when a patient does not agree with the demand created by a doctor or can not afford the service. In these cases, a market failure occurs as a result of price or income elasticity of demand. When all the steps in the sequence are observed, we consider this a consumed demand. If the package of services is short of certain mandatory steps and the treatment is not delivered, we consider this an unconsumed demand (failed demand).

Although the demand in this sequential package of services is a patient, the supply can be a single doctor or health service provider (hospital) or several suppliers each one in charge with producing only a single service of this package (labs, nurses, pharmacies). These suppliers in the primary health services market, in turn, constitute a demand in a subsequent, secondary market. The hospital buys equipment, medical supplies and pharmaceuticals from the respective producers. Although the hospital is a producer of health services on the primary market, it is a consumer of medical goods and labor in the secondary market.

2.2 *Public, Private and Mixed Goods*

From the point of view of rivalry and exclusion from consumption, goods can be defined as public or private.

2.2.1 Public Goods

Public goods are goods which consumed yield benefits to others who cannot be excluded from consuming them. This is because public goods are non-rival in consumption (the supply is available for everyone) and non-excludable in consumption (nobody can be excluded from consuming it). The provision of public goods may have limitations in space and in capacity.

Since everybody benefits from the same quantity of public goods, the aggregate demand curve for public goods is the total of individual demand curves summed up vertically. The economic reasoning behind this is that the marginal cost to produce a public good is zero ($MC = 0$). Because everybody benefits without demanding it, people are reluctant to pay for these goods but want to benefit from them, the case of *free-riders* (Hardwick et al. 1999). Public goods ought to be provided free of charge using public money. In this case, Pareto optimality is satisfied and social welfare is maximized (Hardwick et al. 1999). As these goods or services look "free" for the consumer, some people might want to abuse these goods or services. In these cases, governments might rationalize the use of services by introducing user fees, uniform provision, setting up waiting lists and allowing queuing (Vilma et al. 2007).

Public goods provision is accompanied by positive externalities. Some people want to benefit from the public good but do not want to pay for it. This is the *free-rider* phenomenon. Some people do not want to pay because they consider their payment is insignificant in regard to the budgets of healthcare systems; this is the *drop-in-the-bucket* issue (Hardwick et al. 1999). Furthermore, these people show no *willingness-to-pay* (Hardwick et al. 1999). To overcome these problems and curb these behaviors, the state might subsidize the provision of such goods or produce them itself, if the aim of the activity is public welfare (Hardwick et al. 1999). Very often, health services are delivered on local monopolistic markets, sometimes this situation leading to a *market failure* and consequently the supply of fewer services than necessary, at higher prices and low quality. This is another reason for governments to step in and impose quality standards, negotiate and contract better services, subsidize costs to keep prices low and increase access to care.

2.2.2 Private Goods

Private goods are defined as goods which consumed reduce the supply or availability to others. Therefore, private goods are rival and excludable in consumption. Virtually all goods and services available on the market are private goods with few exemptions, public goods like clean air or public order provision. In the case of private goods, the marginal cost for producing it is positive and increasing (MC > 0). Since people buy different quantities of private goods at the same price, the aggregate demand curve sums up individual demand curves horizontally (Hardwick et al. 1999). As virtually all goods and services in the market are private goods, people have a tendency to behave accordingly toward all goods, even toward public goods.

There is also a category of goods in between these two above mixed goods which display only one of the two characteristics (non-rivalness and non-exclusion). There are two kinds of mixed goods: club goods and common goods.

2.2.3 Club Goods

Some health services can be also seen as club goods (excludable but non-rival in consumption); it is the case of members who subscribe at an HMO or other private insurance scheme/health network. Their decision to purchase private health services reduces the demand for public health services. Thus, the latter becomes more available for non-members of the club.

2.2.4 Common (Public Pool) Goods

The other mixed goods, common or public pool goods, which are rival in consumption but non-excludable, include some healthcare services, like vaccination or treatment of infectious diseases. There might be queues to acquire these services (rivalry), but no one can prevent other people to benefit from them (non-excludable). In this case, when the demand for these services increases, the demand for private services decreases.

To illustrate the above with types of health services, we use the headings from the matrix (Economics Online 2018) in Table 2.1.

In conclusion, we may say that health services can be public, private or mixed goods. This is an empirical evidence of the non-homogeneity of health services.

2.2.5 Externalities

In the provision and consumption of goods, the actions of producers and consumers determine gains and losses for third parties, who are neither providers nor consumers, and no compensation is paid for these gains and losses (Case et al. 2009). These are named externalities and can be either positive or negative. Positive externalities are

Table 2.1 Health services as public, private and mixed goods

Characteristics	Excludable	Non-excludable
Rival	**Private goods** Consultations Surgical operations Lab and image tests Cosmetic surgery	**Common (public pool) goods** Vaccination Treatment of infectious diseases (TB, AIDS) Treatment of sexually transmitted diseases
Non-rival	**Club goods** Private health insurance schemes Departmental health networks HMO membership	**Public goods** Preventive sanitation services Chlorinating tap water Infection control surveillance

regarded as public goods, whereas negative externalities are regarded as public bads. There are private marginal costs in producing a good and social marginal cost in case of externalities. The difference between them is external marginal costs in case of negative externalities. The social marginal cost is equal to the sum of private marginal cost + externality marginal cost (SMC = PMC + EMC) (Case et al. 2009). In case of positive externalities, the marginal social benefit is greater than marginal private benefit, the marginal social cost being consistently greater. MSB > MPB and MSCSB > MSCPB (Hurley et al. 2006).

An interesting discussion can be made in regard to certain health services: gynecological, obstetrical and pediatric services. Although they are obviously private goods (they are rival and excludable at first glance) and have no direct positive externalities on other individuals than patients themselves or their close relatives, these services can be regarded as generating positive externalities from a "political" point of view. One who is interested in the welfare and future of a nation would notice that healthy and fertile women as well as healthy children are basic conditions for a future healthy and strong nation. From this perspective, governments may consider these services mixed goods (common goods) and subsidize them.

There are also activities outside the health system which have negative externalities on public health (pollution, junk food, drug and alcohol consumption, criminality and disobedience of traffic rules). Governments should address these negative health externalities (Vilma et al. 2007). There is a very simple way of tackling this issue, Pigou's tax/subsidy solution. According to this, a tax should be imposed on producers of bad externalities or an excise on public bads, money collected being used to subsidize public services with good externalities. However, this solution does not always work in markets of imperfect competition (Hardwick et al. 1999). Therefore, tackling the problem might involve regulatory measures too. It is the case of curbing the supply of addictive drugs (a public bad) by making them illegal.

As seen before, various health services fall into different categories, some are private goods, some are mixed goods (club and public pool goods) and some are pure public goods. The latter should be provided by the state, whereas for club goods the state should foster increased coverage and for common goods should subsidize and provide social marketing for tackling the rivalry in consumption. Without state intervention, public and mixed goods (with positive externalities) will be consumed in lower quantity than necessary, a case of welfare loss (Economics Online 2018). Therefore, in developing public health policies, an externality analysis of goods traded in the economy as well as of available health services might be necessary.

2.2.6 Elasticity

Elasticity is an economic notion which describes the variation of demand in relationship with a change of price, of income or of price of other related good (Hardwick et al. 1999). The demand for sanitation (public good) is elastic in regard to price, whereas the demand for hospital care is price inelastic, but the nature of the service is different (Perkins 1977). The demand for public goods is elastic in regard to income. This is an argument for variability and complexity of health services; they are not homogenous goods. Further, in the case of complementary goods and substitution goods, the cross elasticity of demand is analyzed, not only the elastic;ity of demand for the initial good (Hardwick et al. 1999). Analyzing the elasticity of demand for healthcare services is particularly important because it is closely related to access to care, a key feature of the healthcare goods and services markets.

2.3 *Merit and Demerit Goods*

Because of the positive externalities they yield and the social benefits of their provision, health services are regarded as merit goods. By definition, they are healthy, as opposed to alcoholic beverages, drugs and other harmful addictive substances which are considered demerit goods. This is obvious from the attitude of people toward suppliers of merit and demerit goods, respectively. However, there is a discussion to be made in regard to nosocomial infections which appear during the provision of medical services, transforming them in demerit goods. Merit goods yield positive externalities, a fact which is not obvious for many people, and cosumers tend to maximize their short time utility, neglecting the long-term and social effects; so merit goods are consumed in lower quantities than they could be consumed. Therefore, merit goods should benefit from social marketing by public entities. On the contrary, the demand for demerit goods should be hampered. Typical examples are anti-tobacco or anti-alcohol campaigns.

2.4 *Complementary and Substitution Goods*

Many goods are associated when consumed within the market. They are traded and consumed together, and often an increase in demand for one good leads to the increase in demand for the other goods. Complementary goods have negative cross elasticity of demand; when the price of one falls, the demand for it increases and the demand for the other one increases too. The same happens when the price of one increases, the demand for it falls and the demand for the complementary good falls too. Some health services are complementary goods. For example, the increased demand for health consultations leads to an increased demand for lab tests. Another example is medical consultations and prescriptions. The complementary goods display negative cross elasticity of demand: the number of prescriptions increases as the price of medical consultations decreases.

However, there are health services which are substitution goods, for which an increase in demand for one would lead to a decrease of demand for the other. It is the case of hospital and ambulatory services in a competitive market. They have positive cross elasticity of demand. In a non-competitive market (hospital integrated ambulatory) although both provide substitutable services, the rise in demand for ambulatory services induces the rise in demand for hospital services. This perverse effect leads to allocative inefficiencies within the health system. Another example of substitution goods is pharmaceuticals and alternative therapies. The number of alternative therapy sessions increases as the price of pharmaceuticals increases too. The demand shifts to alternative therapies. Within the health services market, there are many complementary and substitution goods. The variation of demand for these goods influences access to care. In this case, policymakers might increase access to care by fostering an increase of supply for substitution goods which are more cost-effective, for example, replacing hospital care with ambulatory care.

2.5 Superior Goods, Normal Goods, Inferior Goods

Superior goods are goods whose demand rises when the income rises. There are certain health services which can be considered superior goods such as sophisticated dental services (implants), surgical treatment of baldness, cosmetic surgery, newly introduced imaging techniques or surgical therapies. These can be considered as superior goods. Private health services which usually cost more than public health services can be considered superior goods, because people acquire those services when their income rises. It is very important, because routine provision of these services leads to higher increases in healthcare services costs. However, when these services are delivered more and more, they become less expensive, due to economies of scale in the supply chains, and they move from the category of superior goods to the category of normal goods. The demand for normal goods increases when income increases as for the superior goods, and the difference is that normal goods are so abundant they lose the "luxury" scent of superior goods. Most of the health services are normal goods, for example, medical consultations followed by prescriptions and subsequent pharmaceutical consumption. There are also health services which fall into inferior good category. The characteristic of inferior goods is that the demand increases when income decreases. It is the case of retired people whose income decreases with retirement and cannot afford to buy prescribed pharmaceuticals and switch to alternative therapies like herbal teas or traditional healing methods. These alternative therapies are cheaper; they are inferior goods. In these cases, there is always the issue of effectiveness of these alternative therapies. Usually, they cannot be compared to pharmaceuticals because they do not have recognized effectiveness studies. The case of inferior health goods, or inferior health services is particularly important in countries where large parts of population are fallen into poverty. Usually, the supply of these inferior health goods and services is not regulated making room for swindle and quackery.

2.6 Capital Goods and Consumer Goods

Goods that are durable and are used to produce other goods or services are considered capital goods. Obviously, medical equipment falls into this category. But, healthcare services like pediatric services can be regarded as capital goods too, because they are meant to restore health of children, an investment in future society. A good health status is an essential condition for the capability to work, a production factor. Therefore, whenever somebody wants to cure an illness will decide based on a trade-off between investment in healthcare services as capital goods and acquiring the opposite (a consumer good such as leisure). Personal and social perceptions about this trade-off influence the demand for health care. Individual perceptions and personality play a crucial role the decision to acquire a good or another. For people who are more self-conscious of their health, the demand for health services is more inelastic.

2.7 Composite Goods

A composite good is an abstraction of a bundle of goods acquirable within a given budget. Health services can be considered composite goods in case of patients who suffer a severe medical condition requiring a catastrophic expenditure; for example, selling a house in order to get surgery. When people think of acquiring (demand) health services, they make a choice taking into consideration other goods which are possible to be acquired with the same money. In other words, composite goods have opportunity costs. In our case, the opportunity costs do not match the life-saving catastrophic expenditure. From this point of view, health services are an example of composite goods.

2.8 Producer, Intermediate and Final Goods

Healthcare services are final goods when they are rendered to a patient (surgical operation, treatment). But these medical services (final goods) contain other medical services such as diagnostic services, medical consultations, medical supplies and materials or pharmaceuticals (intermediate or producer goods). The intermediate or producer goods are traded on a secondary market where the physician is the demand playing the agency role on behalf of the patient. As there is asymmetric information in the primary healthcare market, between the doctor and the patient, and it is very likely there might be an asymmetric information also in the secondary market, between producers of equipment or pharmaceuticals and the doctor in charge; this is due to the sophistication of equipment and the marketing technics used for selling pharmaceuticals. Thus, by pricing mechanisms of producer or intermediate goods, they influence the price of final goods, altering the demand for them.

2.9 Experience and Credence Goods

Experience goods are goods whose value can not be estimated in advance but after they are consumed (Nelson 1970). Information is the key issue, in this respect. Health services might be considered examples of experience goods because their value cannot be appreciated in advance, but after they are delivered, especially in cases when the treatment is obviously successful. In the same time, health services can be considered as credence goods, when it is difficult for a patient to assess the success of the treatment. It is the case of treatment of chronic hepatitis or anti-cholesterol or anticoagulation therapy. Depending on a patient, a full range of health services can be considered credence goods, because of asymmetric information, when the patient relies on the reputation of a doctor or the hospital and not his/her own assessment of the service to be acquired. This is one of the reasons why credentialing systems and accreditation of healthcare providers were developed. These features influence the demand for health services. The demand for reputed healthcare providers is higher than for unknown ones. However, there might be the opposite effect, when the patient associates the medical service with something bad, the demand for the service decreases. It is the case of people who do not want to go to hospital because all the people they know, and go to hospital, die.

2.10 Tangible and Intangible Goods

Some health services such as consultations or operations are intangible goods (they cannot be stored) as some other medical goods like prescriptions or pharmaceuticals are tangible. The services which are intangible lead to *consumer satisfaction dilemma*. When satisfaction is not guaranteed, customers hesitate to buy; the demand decreases. Thus, the demand for health services is influenced by satisfaction expectations (a typical social and psychological factor), whereas when consumers can pretend always to be dissatisfied, producers hesitate to deliver the service. In order to overcome this hurdle, within the healthcare realm, quality of care data was used to demonstrate in a "tangible" way the benefits of the services.

2.11 Durable, Non-durable Goods

Looking at the way, health services are produced and consumed (instantly) and the fact they are consumed on-the-spot makes them fall into the category of non-durable goods, as opposed to prostheses which are durable. Furthermore, health services might restore health condition but the improvement might be only temporary. Even "durable" health goods like lab tests results, prescriptions or pharmaceuticals are in fact not durable because they lose validity or expire. Their perception as being non-durable goods influences negatively the demand for healthcare services. However, the opposite is available too especially in cases of prostheses and teeth reconstruction. These are durable goods, with a solid demand.

2.12 Ordinary Goods and Necessity Goods

From the point of view of the elasticity of demand, in response to price changes, health services can be ordinary goods (increased price reduces demand and vice versa). The demand is elastic. For example, dental or ophthalmologic services. From the point of view of elasticity of demand in response to income changes, the health services are necessity goods—a kind of normal goods—for which the elasticity >0. Examples are pediatric services and emergencies. For these services, the elasticity of demand is rather low; demand is inelastic, because these services are perceived as having highest utility, either because they are necessary in life—threatening situations—or because they are necessary for a very loved member of the family.

On the other hand, people have the tendency to go to the doctor when they feel ill not when they get richer, although demanding health services is easier for affluent people. This illustrates that access is different for various strata of society, and there is no "typical" elasticity for health care, but various services have various elasticities depending on personal perception; but in general the elasticity of demand for care in response to income variation is different for poor and for rich people.

2.13 Positional and Luxury (Veblen) Goods

The above is a type of normal goods and are similar to superior goods. There are certain health services which can be considered positional, like some dermatological services or IVF. Others might be considered luxury or Veblen goods (for which demand increases when price increases). These services comprise cosmetic surgery, hair implants, cosmetic dermatology and such. The income elasticity of demand for these goods is >1. There is tendency to oversupply these goods, which are expensive by nature.

2.14 Household Goods

There is certain medical equipment which is used in home care situations. This equipment might comprise infusion pumps, ventilators, dialysis machines and monitors. These can be considered household goods. They are designed and mounted at patient's home for the purpose of improving the quality of life of these patients. Home care services fall into this category too.

2.15 The Demand for Healthcare Services and Access

The demand for health services is determined by personal perceptions about the disease, by price, opportunity costs, non-monetary costs and the income of the individual. The trust in the future benefit of the health service demanded is a typical psychological factor influencing the demand for care. Other psychological factors influencing the demand for health services are self-respect and social pressure. Access depends on the resource availability, geographical location, transport barriers, time availability, cost of care, providers' attitude, social acceptability, effective coverage. As health services are provided in special settings, patients have to cover the distance to the respective setting, but although their rights to receive care are equal, because of the various distances in regard to the provider location, some people find their access is hampered by this. Thus, inequalities in healthcare services provision appear. This is what is usually considered access from the point of view of healthcare managers and policymakers. But the individual factors influencing the demand for care can be also considered factors influencing access, from a public health perspective. This is because access is not determined only by the producers' characteristics but also by factors depending on the patient. Thus, the same factors influencing the demand for healthcare services are determining the variation in access to care.

2.16 Non-homogeneity of Health Services

Health services are not homogenous by their nature and also from the economic point of view. Some are associated and some are in competition (medical treatment versus surgical treatment). They have various economic characteristics, and these are translated in variation of the demand for health services and variation in the elasticity of demand for them. Table 2.2 illustrates that

Table 2.2 Economic characteristics of health services

Service	Social benefits	Demand variation with income	Position in production sequence	Patient assessment and understanding	Tangible (T) or intangible (IT)	Durable (D) or non-durable (ND)
Alternative therapies	Private	Inferior	Final	Experience	T	ND
Cosmetic surgery	Private	Superior	Final	Experience	IT	ND
Dental services	Private	Normal	Final	Experience	IT	D
Health insurance	Club	Normal	Final	Credence	IT	ND
Imaging tests	Private	Normal	Intermediate	Credence	IT	ND
In vitro fertilization	Private	Superior	Intermediate	Experience	IT	ND
Infection control surveillance	Public	Normal	Final	Credence	IT	ND
Interventional cardiology	Private	Superior	Intermediate	Experience	IT	ND
Lab tests	Private	Normal	Intermediate	Credence	IT	ND
Laparoscopic surgery	Private	Normal	Intermediate	Experience	IT	ND
Medical consultations	Private	Normal	Intermediate	Experience	IT	ND
Medical equipment	Private	Normal	Producer	Experience	T	ND
Obstetrical services	Private	Normal	Final	Experience	IT	ND
Pharmaceuticals	Private	Normal	Producer	Experience	T	D
Prescriptions	Private	Normal	Final	Experience	T	ND
Preventive sanitation services	Public	Normal	Final	Credence	IT	ND
Radiation therapy	Private	Normal	Intermediate	Credence	IT	ND
Screening	Private	Normal	Final	Credence	IT	ND

(continued)

3 Conclusion

The advantages of the economic analysis of health services rely on categorizing health services based on patient behavior toward them. It is obviously a more practical and sound approach than the theoretical, medical or managerial approach which usually

Table 2.2 (continued)

Service	Social benefits	Demand variation with income	Position in production sequence	Patient assessment and understanding	Tangible (T) or intangible (IT)	Durable (D) or non-durable (ND)
Surgical operations	Private	Normal	Final	Credence	IT	ND
Treatment of infectious diseases	Public	Normal	Final	Credence	IT	ND
Vaccination	Common	Normal	Final	Credence	IT	ND
Wheelchairs	Private	Normal	Producer	Experience	T	D

Economic categories of goods

disregards the relationship between medical services and patient behavior. This economic approach provides better support for managerial decisions and clarifies certain inherent dilemmas present in policymaking.

The economic perspective on health services is limited by the large variability and non-homogeneity of these services, and to some extent, its use is limited by its nature of multidisciplinary approach.

The main application of economic analysis of health services is policymaking. It provides a valuable insight in designing health policies aimed at improving access to care and financing health services. Recognizing the lack of homogeneity of health services, it provides evidence for designing focused interventions and policies, rather than adopting wide comprehensive policies. Another beneficiary might be public health. Public health interventions can be better designed using it. There might be an educational benefit, by improving schools curricula in order to provide information and introduce elements of rationality in developing health services consumer behavior. Health insurers might find this kind of analysis useful for designing better health insurance packages. Private health services providers can use it for marketing purposes.

References

Business Dictionary http://www.businessdictionary.com/definition/free-good.html. Accessed March 30, 2018.

Case, K. E. et al (2009). *Principles of economics*. Prentice Hall Pearson.

Economics Online https://www.economicsonline.co.uk/Market_failures/Positive_externalities.html. Accessed March 30, 2018.

Hardwick, P. et al. (1999). *An introduction to modern economics*. London, New York: Longman.

Hurley, J. et al (2006). *Introduction to the concepts and analytical tools of health sector reform and sustainable financing*. A Pre-Course Distance Learning Module, Center for Health Economics and Policy Analysis, McMaster University, in Basics of Health Economics– World Bank Institute.

Legal Glossary. (2017). https://www.oregonlaws.org/glossary/definition/health_care_services. Accessed March 29, 2018.

Nelson, P. (1970). Information and consumer behavior. *Journal of Political Economy, 78*(2), 311–329.

Perkins, G. M. (1977). The demand for local public goods: elasticities of demand for own price, cross prices, and income. *National Tax Journal, 30*(4), 411–422.

Vilma, G., et al. (2007). Public goods and externalities: a research agenda for public health economics. *Journal of Public Health Management and Practice, 13*(2), 227–232.

WHO http://www.who.int/topics/health_services/en/. Accessed March 29, 2018.

The Path for Introducing Diagnosis Related Groups (DRGs) in Albanian Health care

Niccolò Persiani, Alberto Romolini, Laura Yzeiraj, Edi Dragusha, and Emiljan Karma

Abstract Diagnosis Related Groups (DRGs) are the most used payment system in health care and the best way of introducing efficiency and effectiveness in its management. For this reason, they are particularly needed for transition countries which have to improve the quality and the quantity of the services delivered to customers. Albania especially is currently living in a period of deep innovation. The consolidation of its democracy, the increasing wealth of the population and the growth of the social needs require a new management approach for public administration and the construction of a more compliant model with the EU standards. This transformation also deeply involves the healthcare sector, which is actually redefining the financing, information system and accountability. For these reasons Albania could be a relevant case study in order to observe, starting from the first steps, the path for introducing a DRG payment system in modern health care. Using the case study method, this paper analyses the background, the governance and the financing of Albanian health care, focusing on the actual reform strategies. The results of the research have been the basis for defining the "National Guidelines of Quality Standards for Introduction of DRGs-based Payment", adopted by the Albanian Ministry of Health (in 2017 became Ministry of Health and Social Protection), which represents an early roadmap for the introduction of DRGs and its future implementation to the whole of Albanian health care.

N. Persiani (✉)
University of Florence, Largo Brambilla, 1, 50129 Florence, Italy
e-mail: niccolo.persiani@unifi.it

A. Romolini
International Telematic University Uninettuno, Corso Vittorio Emanuele II, 39, 00186 Rome, Italy
e-mail: a.romolini@uninettunouniversity.net

L. Yzeiraj · E. Dragusha · E. Karma
Catholic University Our Lady of Good Counsel, Rr. D. Hoxha, Tirana, Albania
e-mail: l.yzeiraj@unizkm.al

E. Dragusha
e-mail: e.dragusha@unizkm.al

E. Karma
e-mail: e.karma@unizkm.al

M. Janowicz-Lomott et al. (eds.), *Economic and Financial Challenges for Balkan and Eastern European Countries*, Springer Proceedings in Business and Economics,
https://doi.org/10.1007/978-3-030-39927-6_13

Keywords Albanian health care · Governance · Healthcare financing · Transition economies · DRG

1 Introduction

Albanian health care is actually rapidly evolving. After a long transition from the previous model of the Soviet period, the country has tried to enhance its economic growth period and its healthcare services. This growth is permitting the creation of a new welfare state-based not only on foreign donors but also on quality services provided by public and private entities (World Health Organisation 2014).

As described below, after the first reforms finalised introducing a public insurance as payor, a diffused contribution by the citizen and a public sector completely separated by the private one, the new national perspective is targeted on a financing model based on performance. In this approach, the Central Government must increasingly reach a central role, leaving to the market the selection of the different level of efficiency.

For these reasons, the introduction of modern instruments of payment for healthcare services is one of the main challenges and, perhaps, one of the main gaps for the entry process in the European Union.

The Health National Strategy, agreeing with the principal international Institutions (World Bank, World Health Organisation) and donors (Italian Agency for Development Cooperation, Swedish International Development Cooperation Agency, Swiss Agency for Development and Cooperation, etc.), identifies, among others, the introduction of a modern Diagnosis Related Groups (DRGs) payment system as a key instrument for developing quality and efficiency in healthcare services and strengthening controls on national healthcare expenses.

DRG, in fact, has become one of the most widely used systems for classification and payment of hospital services in developed countries (Buczak-Stec et al. 2017; Busse et al. 2011), and in all countries, it has been seen as the main solution to introducing higher levels of efficiency in health care and promoting cost containment in the hospital sector.

However, in these countries, the introduction of a national DRG has taken several years. In most European nations, as it can be observed in the experiences of Germany, Italy, England and Portugal, the introduction of DRG has needed the creation of several organisations and innovations in the information system. Instead, in many post-Soviet countries, like Poland or Kazakhstan, (Chanturidze et al. 2016), the introduction has been programmed in a shorter period of time, sometimes less than one year.

This work is related with the studies about the problems and perspectives of the healthcare systems of countries in transition, with particular attention paid to the European countries in the post-Soviet period (Lewis 2000; Mckee 1991). A large part of the studies and literature is focused on the countries belonging to the former Soviet Union or to the former Soviet Bloc (Cercone 2002; Chawla et al. 1998;

Gamkrelidze et al. 2002; Hovhannisyan et al. 2001; Kurkchiyan 1999; McKee et al. 2002; Rahminov et al. 2000); however, the literature has given less attention to the Albanian experience (Lastrucci et al. 2016a, b), especially concerning the healthcare system.

The study of Albanian health care and its introduction of DRG is instead an interesting example of DRG implementation for two reasons:

- The path is at an early stage and the country is on time to reflect about the future steps.
- The Albanian experience has been preceded and accompanied by a clear strategy of improving the National Healthcare Information System and modern rules of cost accounting.

The aim of this paper was, therefore, to delineate the path for the introduction of a DRG payment system in Albania. It analyses the transition from the current healthcare system towards a financing model based on performance rather than on the traditional historical expenditure.

The research has been conducted during the activities of an Institution Building programme, "Introducing health information system: a modern approach to transparency and accountability in Albanian Public Health", financed by the Italian Albanian Debt for Development Swap Agreement (IADSA) for the Albanian Government. The project analyses the main features of the Albanian healthcare service and the challenges that the country will face in future. The results have indeed permitted the definition of the National Guidelines of Quality Standards for Introduction of DRGs-based Payment adopted by the Ministry of Health. The guidelines will be the base of the future extension to the whole Albanian healthcare system.

Concerning the method, this research applies the case study method (Eisenhardt 1989; Yin 1994). The paper analyses the governance and the financing model of the Albanian health care starting from the central level to the local entities following an approach already used by Cepiku (2005).

The paper is organised as follows. After the overview of the background of Albanian health care, the paper analyses the current model of governance and the financing approach. The following pages are then dedicated to the definition of the path for the introduction of a DRG payment system in Albania, and at the end the conclusions, the limits and future steps for this research are discussed.

2 Background

During the long period of dictatorship, the Albanian government aimed to introduce a centralised healthcare model according to the classic Soviet approach to health care (the so-called Semashko Model) completely free for each service delivered to the population (Maciocco 2009). The effectiveness of this system was maintained for 50 years, surviving until the breaking off of diplomatic relations with the Soviet

Union. Indeed, the Soviet aid was decisive for the development of health care after the war, in terms of supply of drugs, technologies and training.

Particularly, the 1960s saw the development of the first national primary healthcare system through the creation of epidemiological centres in each of the 26 districts where the country was divided and through the midwifery network provision to every village, with the function and the responsibility for pre-natal care and vaccinations. Only in the 1970s did Albania start the construction of a basic hospital network with a hospital for every district, responsible for basic care and clinics for specialist treatments.

Moreover, in the 1980s, the Albanian Ministry of Health started a modest path of decentralisation through the identification of specific districts for hospital, management and administration (Cepiku 2005).

It must be highlighted how the quality of services was very low due to the obsolete medical technologies, the low level of training and the absence of a qualified scientific research (Nuri and Tragakes 2002; Tomini et al. 2013).

As in almost all the countries of the former Soviet Bloc, Albanian health care, starting in the 1990s, showed a significant decrease in health public expenditure as a result of the significant financial difficulties in the years after the end of the Soviet Era (Albanian Council of Ministers 2001; Bonilla-Chacin 2003; Bonilla-Chacin et al. 2005; Kornai and Eggleston 2001). This lack generated an increased difficulty to access healthcare services for the poorest part of the population (Falkingham 2004) and the diffusion of "informal" payments, which still have a strong presence in the country (Albanian Ministry of Health 2000; Balabanova and McKee 2002; Belli and Shahriari 2002; Ensor and Savelyeva 1998; Tomini et al. 2013; Tomini and Groot 2013).

Most of the demand was filled in by private entities (Goldstein et al. 1996) and the public health care soon collapsed.

In order to face the crisis, starting from the early 1990s, several initiatives were undertaken to reform the regulatory framework of health care. This process involved the main intergovernmental organisations (the World Bank and the WHO) in the role of main donors and promoters of policy documents processed during these years (Akin et al. 1987; The World Bank 1987, 1993).

A new governance of the public health care was thus processed in order to facilitate the access to public services and to improve the quality, ensuring at the same time the financial self-sufficiency of the system.

To achieve these goals, the Ministry of Health published the first Strategic Plan (Ministry of Health of the Republic of Albania 1993) identifying three fundamental actions:

- Decentralisation so that the Ministry of Health could become gradually a regulatory entity.
- Creation of a public insurance fund in order to reach a significant increase in health expenditure.
- Introduction of an accreditation system for quality in healthcare entities.

These goals have been reconfirmed in the following "Long-term Strategy for the Development of the Albanian Health System (LTSDAHS) 2004" (Ministry of Health of the Republic of Albania 2004) and within the "National Strategy for Development and Integration 2007–2013" and the "National Strategy for Health 2007–2013".

In accordance with these plans, the former healthcare model was abolished (Laws n. 7718 and n. 7738/1993) and replaced with a public insurance system (Laws n.7850/1994, and n.7870/1994) accompanied with the privatisation of some complementary sectors (pharmaceutical and dentistry).

The results are a combined model (Bismark and Beveridge), characterised by sophisticated governance and based on compulsory and voluntary contributions as well as on state budget funding.

3 Healthcare Governance

Many reforms in the last decade have created governance composed of a plurality of actors with specific functions. The most important actors actually are:

- The Ministry of Health. It assumes a central role as the main planner and decision-maker of health care. It is responsible for, planning, policy formulation and allocation of resources and the administration for health as well as for the definition of the essential services provided. Many healthcare institutions, especially on the tertiary level (hospitals), work under its direct supervision.
- The Institute of Public Health. It depends on the Ministry of Health and is responsible for the protection of public health (with particular reference to the prevention and control of infectious diseases and to the National Programme of vaccinations), the environmental health, the control over the quality of food, drinking water and air quality. The institute organises and conducts research and surveys, collects statistic data (health indicators), monitors the quality of services and provides technical support as a national research and training centre.
- The Compulsory Health Insurance Fund (CHIF). As former National Health Insurance Institute (since 1994) and regulated by law n.10383/2011 (on force in 2013), it is an autonomous institution accountable to the parliament. It provides and manages the compulsory health insurance scheme in accordance with national healthcare policies set by the Ministry of Health. CHIF operates through Regional Directorates, branches and local agencies distributed throughout the country.

The service supplying mode is more complex and articulated. It is organised on a territorial basis with reference to the 12 regional prefectures (counties), 61 districts (municipalities) and 373 administrative units (Law n.115/2014 on the territorial and administrative division of local government units in the Republic of Albania).

At a district level, there are three Directorates (Primary Health care, Hospital care and Public Health) depending on the Ministry of Health and the CHIF.

Services of first, secondary and tertiary levels within the territory are supplied by a network of public entities.

Table 1 Primary health care—Year 2016

Classification	Number	Visits
Health centre	414	3,141,755
Clinics	2062	1,627,521
Policlinics	46	3,350,847

Source National Institute of Statistics (INSTAT 2016)

In urban areas, the first level of services is administered by the Ministry of Health, while in the rural areas the services are under the management of the local government. A specific organisation (Tirana Regional Health Authority) was designed in 2000 as pilot project in order to integrate the programs of first and second level.

In rural areas, there are clinics that offer minimum services, while health care centres in the larger cities guarantee the other activities. A trained nurse or a midwife directs a clinic; they provide the care for the mother, the child and provide vaccinations.

The 414 health centres and 46 policlinics, located in the urban centres, are composed of a number of physicians and nurses variable with respect to the territory served. The centres ensure, as said above, the primary healthcare services, such as basic health care for adults, paediatric assistance, care of women, postnatal care and prevention services care for emergencies (initial management and stabilisation of urgent problems). They, therefore, offer outpatient specialised visits using the medical staff of the hospitals.

Primary healthcare works with about 1730 family physicians and paediatricians and about 7000 nurses and midwives (QKEV—National Continuing Education Centre 2018). Of a total of over eight million (Table 1) visits per year on the national territory, the Region of Tirana, which has a greater part of the population, has the largest number, covering about the 32% of total.

Secondary and tertiary level health care are instead provided by a network of 40 hospitals (District, Regional and University).

The district hospitals are structured with at least four specialised departments (internal medicine, paediatrics, general surgery and obstetrics/gynaecology), through which they offer inpatient care in the territory. Some of them are also entrusted by emergency services, anaesthesia and intensive care, radiology, biochemical laboratories and service pharmacies.

The regional hospitals offer instead 10–12 specialist departments and must ensure services with greater specialisation.

Moreover, university hospitals are mainly located in Tirana and Durres. They offer also third-level services and high-level specialisations. They are of course teaching and research hospitals in accordance with the university institutions.

Hospitals are the prevailing response for the needs of the population with a set of 8.357 beds and 11.331, employees (Table 2):

Albanian health care sees also the strong presence of private hospitals and polyclinics which integrates the public offer.

Table 2 Hospitals in Albania—Year 2016

Classification	Number of hospitals	Number of beds	Number of employees
District hospitals	24	2015	2916
Regional hospitals	11	3571	4948
University hospitals	5	2215	3467
Private hospitals	7	556	n/a
Total	47	8357	11331

Source Compulsory Health Insurance Fund (CHIF) and for private hospitals as in their websites

Their services are not financed by the public sector and their activity is excluded from the CHIF, although recently the government has developed some limited packages of health services provided directly from private entities and offered to the population. They include mainly the needs not covered by public hospitals (such as dialysis) or are undersized (cardiologic surgery, etc.).

4 Healthcare Financing

The characteristics of the actual financing system depend on the described diffusion of healthcare entities and the central role of the Compulsory Health Insurance Fund (CHIF).

CHIF is actually financed from:

- State budget through the Ministry of Finance;
- Health compulsory insurance of the active resident population (3.4% of gross salary for employees and of self-employed);
- State contribution for inactive population;
- Voluntary contributions as integration for services not completely covered by the fund;
- Ministry of Health for other services different from the ones budgeted and contracted with CHIF;
- Transfers from Ministry of Health for the subvention of direct payments for different categories in need;
- Donations and grants from other national and international sources;
- Disbursement of funds approved in the state budget for balancing the CHIF budget, etc.

The composition of revenue and the expenditure of CHIF have remained essentially unchanged over the last few years and it is represented in Table 3.

Hospital financing covers more than 50% of CHIF's expenditure increasing, while primary care has only around only 20% of the budget. But if the latter is financed by a mix of cost refunding, activity-based budget and quality standard prizes the

Table 3 Revenues and expenditure of the Compulsory Health Insurance Fund (CHIF)—(values in millions of Lekë[a])

	2015			2016			2017		
	Plan	Fact	%	Plan	Fact	%	Plan	Fact	%
Revenues	*34,814*	*34,050*	*100*	*35,794*	*35,922*	*100*	*39,405*	*38,228*	*100*
From which									
State budget	8859	8859	26.00	8020	8020	22.30	8549	6782	17.70
Health insurance	9040	8702	26.00	10,452	10,699	29.80	11,154	12,268	32.10
Other revenues	161	156	0.50	178	254	0.70	178	92	0.20
State budget for hospital services	16,754	16,334	48.10	17,144	16,949	47.20	19,524	19,087	49.90
Expenditures	*34,814*	*32,529*	*113*	*35,794*	*34,796*	*100*	*39,405*	*39,090*	*100*
From which									
Drugs' reimbursements	8707	7703	26.70	8776	8671	24.90	10,100	10,088	25.80
Primary health care	7441	6778	23.50	8010	7636	21.90	8061	8021	20.50
Administrative expenditures	820	718	2.50	844	787	2.30	879	866	2.20
Investments	266	174	0.60	250	71	0.20	6	1	0.00
Durres hospital	826	826	2.90	770	770	2.20	834	834	2.10
Other hospitals from 2009	16,754	16,330	56.60	17,144	16,860	48.50	19,524	19,279	49.30

[a]Exchange rate of 1 Lek = 0.0071 €
Source Compulsory Health Insurance Fund (CHIF)

Table 4 Efficiency ratios

Indicator	Albania	FYROM	Montenegro	Serbia	EU28
Total expenditure on health (% GDP)	5.9	6.5	6.4	10.4	9.9
Bed occupancy rate	49.5	55	70	70	76
Average length of stay	5.9	7.9	8.5	10	8.0
Bed rotation rate	31.0	25.6	30.3	25.3	34.7
Bed turnover rate	5.9	6.4	3.6	4.5	2.5

Source WHO, INSTAT, EUROSTAT (2014)

financing of district and regional hospitals are carried out by CHIF substantially on historical base (Persiani 2014).

The fund, in this case, only provides a fixed budget, established by the ministerial decree, without any particular relation to production, quality or quantity. University hospitals moreover receive special additional funding for teaching activities, research and high specialisation over-costs.

As in all historical-based financing experiences, in Albania, the attention of the entities to efficiency and effectiveness has become very low and the introduction of the modern managerial approach has been slowed down. The results are low expenditure on health per GDP, scarce services to the population and low rates of performance.

Relating to the recent data published by World Health Organisation (WHO 2014) which compares Albania with the more similar countries and with the EU, (Table 4) can be observed all the difficulties of its National Services.

The average total expenditure is 40% lower than the EU and one point less than the countries of the area. The bed occupancy rate is instead 34% less than the EU rate and its length of stay is 25%. These indicators describe a situation which needs an evolution and relevant organisational changes.

This data is the background of the actual strategic plan for the introduction DRG, viewed as a solution to those kinds of inefficiencies.

5 The Introduction of DRG in Albanian Health care

The strategic decision of introducing DRGs in Albanian health care is updated and contained in all the recent politic and strategic documents, although the definitive choice has been activated by the actual government only recently in accordance with all the principal international institutions operating in the country.

We have to particularly mention the World Bank, which considers the introduction of DRG as part of its actual financing strategy for Albania and Italian cooperation which decided to dedicate in 2014–2016 part of the resources of Italian Albanian

Debt for Development Swap Agreement (IADSA) in financing a research and institution building project with the specific goal of defining the strategic document for introducing DRG in the country.

This project, named "*Introducing Health Information System: A Modern Approach to Transparency and Accountability in Albanian Public Health*" clearly identifies all the expected benefits of a new modern health financing system and particularly the introduction of the use of Diagnosis Related Groups (DRGs).

The aims of the project were:

- Improving the efficiency of resource allocation across hospitals and between the hospital sector and other levels of care
- Driving the restructuring of the health delivery system (re-profile or close inefficient hospitals and departments)
- Creating incentives for hospitals to supply higher-quality services using fewer or lower-cost inputs and allowing the hospitals to enhance the quality of the health services provided (allocating the fair amount for each service provided)
- Increasing provider management autonomy (in effect, decentralisation of hospital management)
- Introducing (public to public and public to private) competition for providers, allowing payment by government health purchasers to private health facilities
- Generating information for better management of the health sector.

For this reason, first of all, the scheduled activities have been oriented to face the principal weaknesses of the actual organisation and particularly:

1. *The difficulty of collecting cost and activity data from the hospitals.* At the beginning of the project only a few hospitals had a complete electronic patient file, and some of them (the most important university hospital included) did not send readable data to CHIF. In this direction, the project tried to define the standards of a modern patient file and a strong programme of healthcare informing has been started for the country. Inside the project, specific software was moreover bought to grant a correct transmission to CHIF.
2. *The lack of modern cost accounting in health entities.* A cost-accounting system for health care was regulated by "cost guidance for calculating the costs and economical and technical indicators" (Year 2011) elaborated by CHIF. However, the cost-accounting method was really basic and not completely used in the country. A long experiment of introduction of a more complex accounting system in the previous years in the hospital in Durres as a national pilot experience had substantially failed.
3. *The need of widespread training to the operators.* The innovation of DRGs introduction and the managerial approach required for its useful use has drove the project to the implementation of several training activities dedicated to administration staff and physicians.

Keeping in mind these prerequisites, the project has produced as an output in the document titled "*National Guidelines of Quality Standards for the Introduction of DRGs-based Payments*", which consists of actually the more detailed project for DRG introduction in Albania.

The programme developed in "twenty-four months" is divided into seven specific steps which should permit the transition to DRGs.

The steps identified and their specific levels of implementation are the following.

Step 1: Implement a standardised system for medical coding

In Albanian hospitals, the International Classification of Diseases ninth revision (ICD-9) translated in Albanian is currently in use for coding only the principal diagnosis of a hospitalisation. This classification of hospitalisation is used only for statistical purposes, mainly for reporting hospital activities to the Ministry of Health and to the Compulsory Health Insurance Fund (CHIF). Furthermore, Albanian hospitals currently do not code procedures performed during the in-hospital stay.

For this reason, the first step is dedicated to the adoption of a more efficient disease classification (ICD 9 CM or ICD 10) and implementing a medical coding protocol in all hospital reporting systems with the related training activities. This step is actually carried forward.

Step 2. Implement a standardised hospital discharge form

The main data entry form for the grouper software is normally the hospital discharge form (HDF) that is filled out at the time of a patient's discharge. In this form, information from both real clinical care as well as medical records is used to produce a complete and accurate summary that reflects the real complexity of patient conditions and clinical interventions.

For these reasons, the second step (also actually running) of the path is focused on the adoption of common hospital discharge forms and the review of all hospital protocols for the management of the patient data.

Step 3. Implement the standardised cost-accounting methodology for hospitals

The creation of case groups for hospital payment requires that cases grouped into each category be both clinically coherent and of similar cost or resource intensity. A cost-accounting process is used to determine the unit cost per case, which, together with expert clinical opinion, is then used to assign each diagnosis code to a case group.

The project has produced specific cost-accounting national guidelines that will be useful for creating the country-specific grouper, the DRG relative weights and to determine hospital case mixes.

Step 4. Set up the hospital data reporting system

Albanian hospitals are now required to report a lot of data to the CHIF and to the Ministry of Health. However, this data is currently used only for statistical purposes and not for the allocation of resources among hospitals or within the hospital services; consequently, they are subjected to a lack of quality, accuracy and completeness.

Furthermore, all the hospitals do not have the necessary IT infrastructures or health management information systems, including specialised software for hospitals allowing for the collection and transmission of the minimum basic data set for DRGs. The project has identified specific software for collecting data and an ambitious programme of the informing of healthcare entities is actually running in order to make possible the new use of data for managerial purposes.

Step 5. Grouping hospital cases with similar clinical characteristics and similar resource requirements
Once fully operative, the new Healthcare Information System will provide detailed data on hospital activity and costs, and it will be possible to conduct analyses that will allow for the calculation of the cost per department bed-day and the cost of each individual case treated in each department. These analyses of hospitals' data will help in orienting the choice of which of the various versions of DRG classification systems and grouper software is more suitable to adopt for the Albanian context.

It will permit the selection of an adequate grouper to be adapted to the Albanian context through a pilot test.

Step 6. Select a transition strategy for moving to DRG-based payment system and develop a contracting system
Mainly due to actual financing system, the deployment of hospital services over the territory is not concordant to the population's health needs and hospitals in Albania present large differences in hospital efficiency indicators, as well as in the average cost per case treated. In this context, the shift to DRG prices in the hospital payment system is likely to create large changes in newly contracted budgets for some Albanian hospitals and potentially a have large implication on resource allocation between hospitals relative to their historical patterns. Therefore, there will be the need to assess the financial impact of this transition. These risks have to be mitigated and minimised through the use of DRG adjustments and through the selection of an appropriate payment system transition strategy.

At first, a safe "paper system" without any real change in the flow of funding is prescribed to avoid any financial risk or interruption in service flow.

Only after this will the definition of a transition strategy and a hospital contracting framework be defined.

Step 7. Create a quality monitoring and auditing system
Normally, DRG-based hospital payment system incentivises hospitals to increase efficiency by reducing excess inputs used to treat each case. As hospitals adjust to the system, however, they will adapt their behaviour to further their own self-interests under the new system, which may also lead to some potentially unintended consequences (adverse incentives), such as:

- Hospitals reduce inputs excessively to the point of premature discharging of patients, undertreating patients or reducing the quality of care;
- Increasing the number of discharges, which can be both a positive incentive and adverse incentives in the case of repeated admissions after discharge;
- Avoidance of high resource intensity (severe) cases or cases with low payment rates

- "Gaming" of the system through upcoding or assigning cases to a case group that is reimbursed at a higher rate than the case group to which the case actually belongs. Upcoding does not affect the quality of patient care directly, but it is an important source of excessive costs and inefficiency in the system
- Shifting some services to before hospital admission and after hospital discharge.

In the last step, the necessary auditing and monitoring functions to support and promote the incentives created by the DRG system are therefore described.

All these steps have been scheduled in three years, and most of them have been activated. The Ministry of Health is actually coordinating all the operators and is interfacing with financial institutions and donors to support the costs.

6 Conclusions

Albania is a typical transition country of the post-Soviet era. At the beginning of 1990s, its health care experienced an enormous crisis, with low-quality services offered to citizens and with a very poor level of quality and updating performances. Since this period, Albania has tried to reform the overall healthcare model, introducing an expenditure model based more on the performance rather than on the historic expenditure. This process is still underway and the country needs to conclude it and increase the level of healthcare services. In order to complete this process, the government has decided to establish a roadmap for introducing a DRGs payment approach. The overall goal of this strategy is to improve efficiency, effectiveness and quality in the management of healthcare services. We have to underline that the DRG introduction in Albania is going forward in accordance with the EU integration.

The healthcare Albanian system is now organised into three levels of activities, and hospital supply represents currently the main response to the healthcare services demand. The healthcare financing is, however, based mainly on the historical expenditure and the resources allocated with a performance approach are again scarce. The overall picture of Albanian hospitals presents a relevant number of critical points. First, we can observe large regional disparities in hospital health service distribution: the largest volume of resources is provided to university and private hospitals instead of the large part of the country, which are without adequate structures.

Second, the hospital performance and efficiency are too low in comparison with similar countries. The levels of efficiency and quality between the public and private sector are really disadvantageous for the first and patient mobility is really strong towards the second. Consequently, the public hospital has a low level of autonomy and the market is quite absent.

The third point is low management culture: we can observe a traditional idea of hospital managers and physicians which is kept in the Albanian mentality. The past scarce training and low level of motivation have been individuated as the prior causes.

In this context, the project named "Introducing Health Information System: A Modern Approach to Transparency and Accountability in Albanian Public Health" starts in order to analyse the expected benefits of a new modern health financing system and to design a road map for the introduction of the use of Diagnostics Related Groups (DRGs).

The output document "National Guidelines of Quality Standards for Introduction of DRGs-based Payment" offers a clear roadmap to introduce a modern payment system, accompanied with a wide revolution of the National Information System, a strong assimilation of managerial culture and a substantial investment in training activities.

The plan built over three years and started in 2017 is seen really as the greatest opportunity for healthcare growth and for modernising its actual situation.

The more evident limit of this research is that the application of the roadmap is strongly connected, as in all transition countries, with the political situation of the country and to the governmental attitude in finding the resources for its implementation. Moreover, its success depends on the deep diffusion of a new modern managerial culture in all healthcare levels.

Regarding the future steps, after the complete implementation of the path, we have to mention the need for creating a modern performance evaluation system of public and private entities for supporting national planning.

References

Akin, J., et al. (1987). *Financing health services in developing countries: An agenda for reform*. Washington.

Albanian Council of Ministers. (2001). *National strategy for socio-economic development*. Tirana.

Albanian Ministry of Health. (2000). *Albanian Public's perceptions of the health care system*. Tirana: Albanian Health System Recovery and Development Project.

Balabanova, D., & McKee, M. (2002). Understanding informal payments for health care: The example of Bulgaria. *Health Policy, 62*, 243–273.

Belli, P., Shahriari, H., & Curtio Medical Group. (2002). *Qualitative study on informal payments for health services in Georgia*. Washington: The World Bank.

Bonilla-Chacin, M. E. (2003). *Health and poverty in Albania: Background paper for the Albania. Poverty assessment. Europe and Central Asia sector for human development*. Washington: The World Bank.

Bonilla-Chacin, et al. (2005). Health care during transition and health systems reform: evidence from the poorest CIS countries. *Social Policy & Administration, 39*(4), pp. 381–408.

Buczak-Stec, E., et al. (2017). The impact of introducing a new hospital financing system (DRGs) in Poland and hospitalisations for atherosclerosis: An interrupted time series analysis (2004–2012). *Health Policy, 121*(11), 1186–1193. https://doi.org/10.1016/j.healthpol.2017.09.009. Epub 2017 Sep 20.

Busse, R., et al. (2011). *Diagnosis-related groups in Europe: Moving towards transparency, efficiency and quality in hospitals*. UK: Open University Press.

Cepiku, D. (2005). Healthcare management and governance in transition countries: The Albanian experience. In: *CEIS Health Report 2005: Seven Keywords of NHS* (pp. 312–324). Roma: Italpromo Esis Publishing srl. (first published in Managerialità e governance nei sistemi sanitari dei Paesi in transizione: il caso dell'Albania. In: Rapporto CEIS Sanità: Sette parole chiave del SSN).

Cercone, J. (2002). *Moldova: The health sector in transition. Policy note*. Washington: The World Bank.
Chanturidze, T., et al. (2016). Introducing diagnosis-related groups in Kazakhstan: Evolution, achievements, and challenges. *Health Policy, 120*(9), 987–991. https://doi.org/10.1016/j.healthpol.2016.07.007. Epub 2016 Aug 3.
Chawla, M., et al. (1998). Financing health services in Poland: New evidence on private expenditures. *Health Economics, 7*(4), 337–346.
Eisenhardt, K. M. (1989). Building theories from case study research. *Academy of Management Review, 14*(4), 532–550.
Ensor, T., & Savelyeva, L. (1998). Informal payments for health care in the former Soviet Union: Some evidence from Kazakhstan. *Health Policy and Planning, 13*(1), 41–49.
Falkingham, J. (2004). Poverty, out-of-pocket payments, and access to health care: Evidence from Tajikistan. *Social Science and Medicine, 58*(2), 247–258.
Gamkrelidze, A., et al. (2002). *Health care systems in transition: Georgia*. Copenhagen: European Observatory on Health Care Systems.
Goldstein, E., et al. (1996). *Trends in health status, services and finance: The transition in Central and Eastern Europe* (Vol. I). World Bank Technical Paper, No. 341. Washington: The World Bank.
Hovhannisyan, et al. (2001). *Health care systems in transition: Armenia*. Copenhagen: European Observatory on Health Care Systems.
Kornai, J., & Eggleston, K. (2001). Choice and solidarity: The health sector in Eastern Europe and proposals for reform. *International Journal of Health Care Finance and Economics, 1*, 59–84.
Kurkchiyan, M. (1999). *Report on health care in Armenia*. Mimco, Washington: The World Bank.
Lastrucci, V., et al. (2016a). The Barber-Johnson technique for assessing hospitals efficiency: The case of the Republic of Albania. *European Journal of Public Health, 26*(1), 102.
Lastrucci, V., et al. (2016b). The measurement of hospitals cost efficiency: A model for countries in transition. *European Journal of Public Health, 26*(1), 332.
Lewis, M. (2000). *Who is paying for health care in Eastern Europe and central Asia. Human development sector Unit Europe and Central Asia Region*. Washington: The World Bank.
Maciocco, G. (2009). *Politica, salute e sistemi sanitari*. Roma: Il pensiero scientifico editore.
McKee, M. (1991). Health services in Central and Eastern Europe: Past problems and future prospects. *Journal of Epidemiology and Community Health, 45*, 260–265.
McKee, M., et al. (2002). *Health care in Central Asia*. Milton Keynes: Open University Press.
Ministry of Health of the Republic of Albania. (1993). *A new policy for the health care sector in Albania*. Tirana.
Ministry of Health of the Republic of Albania. (2004). *The long term strategy for the development of the Albanian Health System*. Tirana.
Nuri, B., & Tragakes, E. (2002). *Health care systems in transition: Albania*. Copenhagen: European Observatory on Health Care Systems 4(6).
Persiani, N., et al. (2014). *Reforming the financial health care system: The case of the Republic of Albania*. China-USA Business Review.
Rahminov, R., et al. (2000). *Health care systems in transition: Tajikistan*. Copenhagen: European Observatory on Health Care Systems.
The World Bank. (1987). *Financing health services in developing countries*. Washington, DC: An Agenda for Reform.
The World Bank. (1993). *World development report 1993. Investing in health*. New York NY: Oxford University Press.
Tomini, S. M., & Groot, W. (2013). Paying informally for public health care in Albania: Scarce resources or governance failure? *Applied Economics, 45*(36), 5119–5130.
Tomini, S. M., et al. (2013). Catastrophic and impoverishing effects of out-of-pocket payments for health care in Albania: Evidence from Albania living standards measurement surveys 2002, 2005 and 2008. *Health Policy and Planning, 28*(4), 419–428.

World Health Organisation. (2014). *European health for all database*. Regional Office for Europe. www.who.int.

Yin, R. (1994). *Case study research: Design and methods* (2nd ed.). Thousand Oaks: Sage Publishing.

On a Bertrand Dynamic Game with Differentiated Goods, Heterogeneous Expectations and Asymmetric Cost Functions

Georges Sarafopoulos and Kosmas Papadopoulos

Abstract The aim of this paper is to study the dynamics of a nonlinear Bertrand-type duopoly game with differentiated goods, linear demand and asymmetric cost functions. The game is modeled with a system of two difference equations. Existence and stability of equilibrium of this system are studied. We show that the model gives more complex, chaotic and unpredictable trajectories as a consequence of change in the parameter of speed of adjustment, which is followed by the bounded rational player, and in the parameter of product differentiation. A higher (lower) degree of player's adjustment destabilizes (stabilize) the economy. Also, a higher or lower degree of product differentiation destabilizes the economy. The chaotic features are justified numerically via computing Lyapunov numbers, sensitive dependence on initial conditions, bifurcation diagrams and strange attractors.

Keywords Bertrand duopoly game · Discrete dynamical system · Heterogeneous expectations · Asymmetric costs · Stability · Chaotic behavior

1 Introduction

Cournot, in 1838, has introduced the first formal theory of oligopoly. In 1883, another French mathematician Joseph Louis Francois Bertrand modified Cournot game suggesting that firms actually choose prices rather than quantities. Originally Cournot and Bertrand models were based on the premise that all players follow naïve expectations, so that in every step, each player (firm) assumes the last values that were taken by the competitors without estimation of their future reactions. However, in real market conditions, such an assumption is very unlikely since not all players share naive beliefs. Therefore, different approaches to firm behavior were proposed. Some authors considered duopolies with homogeneous expectations and found a variety of

G. Sarafopoulos (✉) · K. Papadopoulos
Department of Economics, Democritus University of Thrace, 69100 Komotini, Greece
e-mail: gsarafop@econ.duth.gr

K. Papadopoulos
e-mail: hurdlerofthrace@yahoo.gr

M. Janowicz-Lomott et al. (eds.), *Economic and Financial Challenges for Balkan and Eastern European Countries*, Springer Proceedings in Business and Economics,
https://doi.org/10.1007/978-3-030-39927-6_14

complex dynamics in their games, such as appearance of strange attractors (Agiza 1999; Agiza et al. 2002; Agliari et al. 2005, 2006; Bischi and Kopel 2001; Kopel 1996; Puu 1998; Wu et al. 2010; Sarafopoulos 2015b; Zhang et al. 2009). Also, models with heterogeneous agents were studied (Agiza and Elsadany 2003, 2004; Agiza et al. 2002; Den Haan 2001; Hommes 2006; Fanti and Gori 2012; Tramontana 2010; Zhang et al. 2007; Sarafopoulos 2015a).

In the real market, producers do not know the entire demand function, though it is possible that they have a perfect knowledge of technology, represented by the cost function. Hence, it is more likely that firms employ some local estimate of the demand. This issue has been previously analyzed by Baumol and Quandt (1964), Puu (1995, 2005), Naimzada and Ricchiuti (2008), Askar (2013, 2014). Bounded rational players (firms) update their strategies based on discrete time periods and by using a local estimate of the marginal profit. With such local adjustment mechanism, the players are not requested to have a complete knowledge of the demand and the cost functions (Agiza and Elsadany 2004; Naimzada and Sbragia 2006; Zhang et al. 2007; Askar 2014).

In this paper, we study the dynamics of a Bertrand-type duopoly with differentiated goods where each firm behaves with heterogeneous expectations strategies. We show that the model gives more complex chaotic and unpredictable trajectories as a consequence of change in two parameters, the speed of players' adjustment and the parameter of horizontal product differentiation. The paper is organized as follows: In Sect. 2, the dynamics of the duopoly game with heterogeneous expectations, linear demand also a linear cost function for one player and a quadratic cost function for the other are analyzed. In Sect. 3, we set the first player as bounded rational and the second as a naïve player. The existence and local stability of the equilibrium points are also analyzed. In Sect. 4, we change the strategies between two players setting the second player as bounded rational. In each case of Sects. 3 and 4, numerical simulations are used to show complex dynamics via computing Lyapunov numbers, and sensitive dependence on initial conditions.

2 The Game

In this study, we consider heterogeneous players and more specifically, we consider that the Firm 1 (Firm 2) chooses the price of its product in a rational way, following an adjustment mechanism (bounded rational player), while the Firm 2 (Firm 1) decides by naïve way, selecting a price that maximizes its output (naïve player). We consider a simple Bertrand-type duopoly market where firms (players) produce differentiated goods and offer them at discrete time periods on a common market. Price decisions are taken at discrete time periods $t = 0, 1, 2, \ldots$ At each period t, every firm must form an expectation of the rival's strategy in the next time period in order to determine the corresponding profit-maximizing prices for period $t + 1$. We suppose that q_1, q_2 are the production quantities of each firm. Also, we consider that the preferences of consumers represented by the equation:

$$U(q_1, q_2) = a(q_1 + q_2) - \frac{1}{2}\left(q_1^2 + q_2^2 + 2dq_1q_2\right) \tag{1}$$

where α is a positive parameter (α > 0), which expresses the market size and $d \in (-1, 1)$ is the parameter that reveals the differentiation degree between two products. For example, if $d = 0$, then both products are independent and each firm participates in a monopoly. But, if $d = 1$, then one product is a substitute for the other, since the products are homogeneous. It is understood that for positive values of the parameter d the larger the value, the less diversification we have between two products. On the other hand, negative values of the parameter d are described that the two products are complementary. The inverse demand functions (as functions of quantities) coming from the maximizing of (1) subject to the budget constraint, and are given by the following equations:

$$p_1(q_1, q_2) = a - q_1 - dq_2 \quad \text{and} \quad p_2(q_1, q_2) = a - q_2 - dq_1 \tag{2}$$

The direct demand functions (as functions of prices):

$$q_1(p_1, p_2) = \frac{a(1-d) - p_1 + dp_2}{1-d^2} \quad \text{and} \quad q_2(p_1, p_2) = \frac{a(1-d) - p_2 + dp_1}{1-d^2} \tag{3}$$

where p_1, p_2 are the products' prices for two players.

In this work, we suppose that two players follow different cost functions:

$$C_1(q_1) = c \cdot q_1 \tag{4}$$

and

$$C_2(q_2) = c \cdot q_2^2 \tag{5}$$

and $c > 0$ is the marginal cost for player 1. With these assumptions, the profits of the firms are given by:

$$\mathrm{P}_1(p_1, p_2) = p_1q_1 - C_1(q_1) = (p_1 - c) \cdot \frac{a(1-d) - p_1 + dp_2}{1-d^2} \tag{6}$$

and

$$\begin{aligned}\mathrm{P}_2(p_1, p_2) &= p_2q_2 - C_2(q_2) \\ &= \frac{a(1-d) + c - p_1 + dp_2}{1-d^2} \cdot \left[p_2 - c \cdot \frac{a(1-d) + c - p_1 + dp_2}{1-d^2}\right]\end{aligned} \tag{7}$$

Then, the marginal profits at the point of the strategy space are given by:

$$\frac{\partial \mathrm{P}_1}{\partial p_1} = \frac{a(1-d) + c - 2p_1 + dp_2}{1-d^2} \tag{8}$$

and

$$\frac{\partial \mathrm{P}_2}{\partial p_2} = \frac{\left[\left(1-d^2\right) + 2c\right] \cdot [a(1-d) + dp_1] - 2p_2\left[\left(1-d^2\right) + c\right]}{\left(1-d^2\right)^2} \tag{9}$$

3 First Case: (First Player: Bounded Rational, Second Player: Naïve)

We suppose that the first firm decides to increase its level of adaptation if it has a positive marginal profit, or decreases its level if the marginal profit is negative (bounded rational player). If k > 0 the dynamical equation of the first player is:

$$\frac{p_1(t+1) - p_1(t)}{p_1(t)} = k \cdot \frac{\partial \mathrm{P}_1}{\partial p_1} \tag{10}$$

where $k \in (0, 1)$ expresses the speed of adjustment of player 1, it is a positive parameter which gives the extent of production variation of the firm following a given profit signal. Moreover, it captures the fact that relative effort variations are proportional to the marginal profit.

The second firm decides with naïve way by selecting a production that maximizes its profits (naïve player):

$$p_2(t+1) = \arg\max_{p_2} \mathrm{P}_2(p_1(t), p_2(t)) \tag{11}$$

The dynamical system of the players is described by:

$$\begin{cases} p_1(t+1) = p_1(t) + k \cdot p_1(t) \cdot \frac{\partial P_1}{\partial p_1} \\ p_2(t+1) = \frac{\left[\left(1-d^2\right)+2c\right] \cdot [a(1-d)+dp_1(t)]}{2\left[\left(1-d^2\right)+c\right]} \end{cases} \tag{12}$$

We will focus on the dynamics of this system to the parameter k.

3.1 Dynamical Analysis

3.1.1 The Equilibriums of the Game

The equilibriums of the dynamical system (12) are the nonnegative solutions of the algebraic system:

$$\begin{cases} k \cdot p_1^* \cdot \frac{\partial P_1}{\partial p_1} = 0 \\ p_2^* = \frac{\left[\left(1-d^2\right)+2c\right]\cdot\left[a(1-d)+dp_1^*\right]}{2\left[\left(1-d^2\right)+c\right]} \end{cases} \tag{13}$$

which obtained by setting $p_1(t+1) = p_1(t) = p_1^*$ and $p_2(t+1) = p_2(t) = p_2^*$ in Eq. (12).

- If $p_1^* = 0$, then $p_2^* = \frac{a(1-d)\cdot\left[\left(1-d^2\right)+2c\right]}{2\left[\left(1-d^2\right)+c\right]}$ and we have the boundary equilibrium:

$$E_0 = \left(0\,,\ \frac{a(1-d)\cdot\left[\left(1-d^2\right)+2c\right]}{2\left[\left(1-d^2\right)+c\right]}\right) \tag{14}$$

- If $\frac{\partial P_1}{\partial p_1} = \frac{\partial P_2}{\partial p_2} = 0$, then we form the system:

$$\begin{cases} p_1^* = \frac{a(1-d)+c+dp_2^*}{2} \\ p_2^* = \frac{\left[\left(1-d^2\right)+2c\right]\cdot\left[a(1-d)+dp_1^*\right]}{2\left[\left(1-d^2\right)+c\right]} \end{cases} \tag{15}$$

The solutions are

$$p_1^* = \frac{a(1-d)+c}{2-d} + \frac{d}{2}\cdot\frac{a(1-d)(2+d)+dc}{\frac{4\cdot\left[\left(1-d^2\right)+c\right]}{\left[\left(1-d^2\right)+2c\right]} - d^2} \tag{16}$$

and

$$p_2^* = \frac{a(1-d)(2+d)+dc}{\frac{4\cdot\left[\left(1-d^2\right)+c\right]}{\left[\left(1-d^2\right)+2c\right]} - d^2} \tag{17}$$

giving the Nash equilibrium:

$$E_* = \left(p_1^*, p_2^*\right) \tag{18}$$

3.1.2 Stability of Equilibriums

The study of the local stability of the equilibrium is based on the localization on the complex plane of the eigenvalues of the Jacobian matrix of the dimensional map (Eq. 12). In order to study the local stability of equilibrium points of the model (12), we consider the Jacobian matrix $J(p_1, p_2)$ along the variable strategy (p_1, p_2) (Gandolfo 1997; Medio and Lines 2005; Sedaghat 2003; Elaydi 2005):

$$J(p_1, p_2) = \begin{bmatrix} f_{p_1} & f_{p_2} \\ g_{p_1} & g_{p_2} \end{bmatrix} \tag{19}$$

where

$$\begin{aligned} f(p_1, p_2) &= p_1 + k \cdot p_1 \cdot \frac{\partial \mathrm{P}_1}{\partial p_1} \\ g(p_1, p_2) &= \frac{\left[\left(1-d^2\right)+2c\right] \cdot [a(1-d)+dp_1]}{2\left[\left(1-d^2\right)+c\right]} \end{aligned} \tag{20}$$

The Jacobian matrix is:

$$J(p_1, p_2) = \begin{bmatrix} 1 + k \cdot \left(\frac{\partial P_1}{\partial p_1} + p_1 \cdot \frac{\partial^2 P_1}{\partial p_1^2}\right) & \frac{kdp_1}{1-d^2} \\ \frac{d\left[\left(1-d^2\right)+2c\right]}{2\left[\left(1-d^2\right)+c\right]} & 0 \end{bmatrix} \tag{21}$$

At the equilibrium E_0:

$$J(E_0) = \begin{bmatrix} 1 + k \cdot \frac{a(1-d)+c+dp_2}{1-d^2} & 0 \\ \frac{d\left[\left(1-d^2\right)+2c\right]}{2\left[\left(1-d^2\right)+c\right]} & 0 \end{bmatrix} \tag{22}$$

with

$$Tr = 1 + k \cdot \frac{a(1-d)+c+dp_2}{1-d^2} \quad \text{and } Det = 0.$$

The characteristic equation of $J(E_0)$ is:

$$l^2 - Tr \cdot l + Det = 0 \tag{23}$$

with solutions

$$l_1 = 0 \quad \text{and } l_2 = Tr = 1 + k \cdot \frac{a(1-d)+c+dp_2}{1-d^2} \tag{24}$$

Since $|l_2| > 1$, the equilibrium E_0 is unstable.
At the Nash equilibrium point E_* the Jacobian matrix is:

$$J(E_*) = \begin{bmatrix} 1 - \frac{2kp_1^*}{1-d^2} & \frac{kdp_1^*}{1-d^2} \\ \frac{d[(1-d^2)+2c]}{2[(1-d^2)+c]} & 0 \end{bmatrix} \tag{25}$$

with

$$Tr = 1 - \frac{2kp_1^*}{1-d^2} \text{ and } Det = -kd^2 p_1^* \frac{[(1-d^2)+2c]}{2(1-d^2)[(1-d^2)+c]}$$

The Nash equilibrium is locally asymptotically stable if the following conditions become true simultaneously:

$$\begin{aligned} &\text{(i) } 1 - Det > 0 \\ &\text{(ii) } 1 - Tr + Det > 0 \\ &\text{(iii) } 1 + Tr + Det > 0 \end{aligned} \tag{26}$$

Since

$$1 - Det = 1 + kd^2 p_1^* \frac{[(1-d^2)+2c]}{2(1-d^2)[(1-d^2)+c]} > 0 \tag{27}$$

And

$$1 - Tr + Det = \frac{kp_1^*}{2(1-d^2)} \cdot \frac{(1-d^2)(4-d)+2c(2-d^2)}{(1-d^2)+c} > 0 \tag{28}$$

the conditions (i) and (ii) are always satisfied. The third condition becomes:

$$1 + Tr + Det > 0 \Leftrightarrow k < \frac{4(1-d^2)[(1-d^2)+c]}{p_1^*[(1-d^2)(4+d^2)+2c(2+d^2)]} \tag{29}$$

with

$$p_1^* = \frac{a(1-d)+c}{2-d} + \frac{d}{2} \cdot \frac{a(1-d)(2+d)+dc}{\frac{4\cdot[(1-d^2)+c]}{[(1-d^2)+2c]} - d^2}$$

If we focus on the parameter d, the stability condition becomes:

$$k < \frac{4(1-d^2)\left[(1-d^2)+c\right]}{p_1^*\left[(1-d^2)(4+d^2)+2c(2+d^2)\right]}$$

$$\Leftrightarrow -(4+kp_1^*)\cdot d^4 + \left[4(2+c)+kp_1^*(2c-3)\right]\cdot d^2 + 4(kp_1^*-1)\cdot(1+c) < 0 \tag{30}$$

Proposition *The Nash equilibrium $E_*(p_1^*, p_2^*)$ of the dynamical system Eq. (12) is locally asymptotically stable if:*

$$0 < k < \frac{4(1-d^2)\left[(1-d^2)+c\right]}{p_1^*\left[(1-d^2)(4+d^2)+2c(2+d^2)\right]} \tag{31}$$

3.1.3 Numerical Simulations

To provide some numerical evidence for the chaotic behavior of the system Eq. (12), as a consequence of change in the parameter k of the speed of player's adjustment, we present various numerical results here to show the chaoticity, including its bifurcations diagrams, strange attractor, Lyapunov numbers and sensitive dependence on initial conditions (Kulenovic and Merino 2002). In order to study the local stability properties of the equilibrium points, it is convenient to set some specific values to the parameters, for example: $a = 5,\ c = 0.5,\ d = 0.2$. For the stability condition, it means that:

$$0 < k < 0.371$$

Numerical experiments are computed to show the bifurcation diagram with respect to k, strange attractor of the system Eq. (12) in the phase plane (p_1, p_2), and Lyapunov numbers. Figure 1 shows the bifurcation diagrams with respect to the parameter k against variable p_1(left) and p_2(right). In these figures, the Nash equilibrium E^* is locally asymptotically stable for k < 0.371. For k > 0.371, the Nash equilibrium E^*

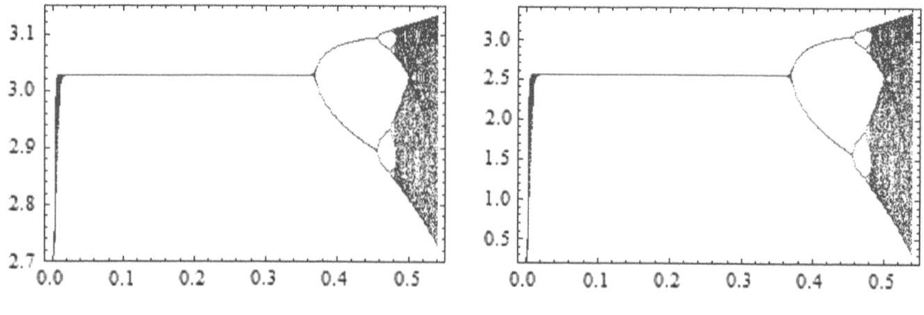

Fig. 1 Bifurcation diagrams with respect to the parameter k against variable p_1(left) and p_2(right), with 400 iterations of the map Eq. (12) for $a = 5,\ c = 0.5,\ d = 0.2$

becomes unstable and one observes complex dynamics behavior such as cycles of higher order and chaos. Figure 2 shows the graphs of the orbit of the point (0.1, 0.1) (strange attractor) and the Lyapunov numbers' diagram of the same orbit for $a = 5$, $c = 0.5$, $d = 0.2$, $k = 0.54$. If the Lyapunov number is greater of 1, one has evidence for chaos. From these results, when all parameters are fixed and only k is varied the structure of the game becomes complicated through period-doubling bifurcations, more complex bounded attractors are created which are aperiodic cycles of higher order or chaotic attractors. To demonstrate the sensitivity to initial conditions of the system Eq. (12), we compute two orbits with initial points (0.1, 0.1) and (0.101, 0.1), respectively. Figure 3 shows sensitive dependence on initial conditions for x-coordinate of the two orbits, for the system Eq. (12), plotted against the time with the parameter values $a = 5$, $c = 0.5$, $d = 0.2$, $k = 0.54$. At the beginning, the time series are indistinguishable, but after a number of iterations, the difference between them builds up rapidly. From Fig. 3, we show that the time series of the system Eq. (12) is sensitive dependence on initial conditions, i.e., complex dynamics behavior occur in this model.

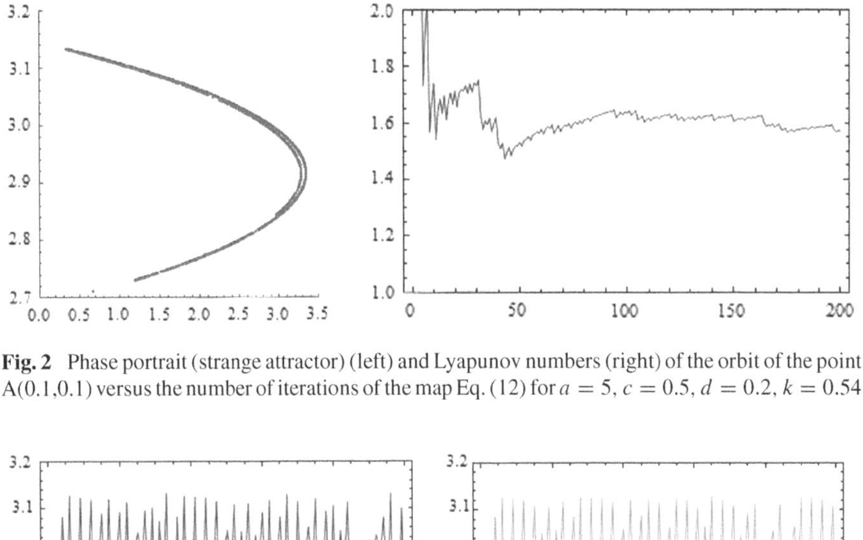

Fig. 2 Phase portrait (strange attractor) (left) and Lyapunov numbers (right) of the orbit of the point A(0.1,0.1) versus the number of iterations of the map Eq. (12) for $a = 5$, $c = 0.5$, $d = 0.2$, $k = 0.54$

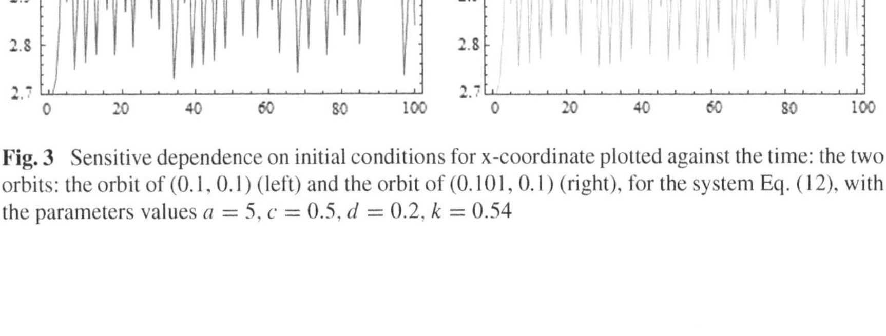

Fig. 3 Sensitive dependence on initial conditions for x-coordinate plotted against the time: the two orbits: the orbit of (0.1, 0.1) (left) and the orbit of (0.101, 0.1) (right), for the system Eq. (12), with the parameters values $a = 5$, $c = 0.5$, $d = 0.2$, $k = 0.54$

4 Second Case: (First Player: Naïve, Second Player: Bounded Rational)

The first firm decides by naïve way, selecting a production that maximizes its profits (naïve player):

$$p_1(t+1) = \arg\max_{p_1} \mathrm{P}_1(p_1(t), p_2(t)) \tag{32}$$

We suppose that the second firm decides to increase its level of adaptation if it has a positive marginal profit, or decreases its level if the marginal profit is negative (bounded rational player). If k > 0 the dynamical equation of the first player is:

$$\frac{p_2(t+1) - p_2(t)}{p_2(t)} = k \cdot \frac{\partial \mathrm{P}_2}{\partial p_2} \tag{33}$$

where $k \in (0, 1)$ as at the previous case, it expresses the speed of adjustment of player 2. The dynamical system of the players is described by:

$$\begin{cases} p_1(t+1) = \dfrac{a(1-d) + c + dp_2(t)}{2} \\ p_2(t+1) = p_2(t) + k \cdot p_2(t) \cdot \dfrac{\partial P_2}{\partial p_2} \end{cases} \tag{34}$$

We will focus on the dynamics of this system to the parameter k.

4.1 Dynamical Analysis

4.1.1 The Equilibrium of the Game

The equilibriums of the dynamical system (34) are the nonnegative solutions of the algebraic system:

$$\begin{cases} p_1^* = \frac{a(1-d)+c+dp_2^*}{2} \\ k \cdot p_2^* \cdot \frac{\partial P_2}{\partial p_2} = 0 \end{cases} \tag{35}$$

which obtained by setting $p_1(t+1) = p_1(t) = p_1^*$ and $p_2(t+1) = p_2(t) = p_2^*$ in Eq. (34).

- If $p_2^* = 0$, then $p_1^* = \frac{a(1-d)+c}{2}$ and we have the boundary equilibrium:

$$E_0 = \left(\frac{a(1-d)+c}{2}, 0\right) \tag{36}$$

- If $\frac{\partial \mathrm{P}_1}{\partial p_1} = \frac{\partial \mathrm{P}_2}{\partial p_2} = 0$, then we form the system:

$$\begin{cases} p_1^* = \frac{a(1-d)+c+dp_2^*}{2} \\ p_2^* = \frac{\left[(1-d^2)+2c\right]\cdot\left[a(1-d)+dp_1^*\right]}{2\left[(1-d^2)+c\right]} \end{cases} \tag{37}$$

giving the same Nash equilibrium as at the first case:

$$E_* = \left(p_1^*, p_2^*\right) \tag{38}$$

4.1.2 Stability of Equilibriums

The study of the local stability of the equilibrium is based on the localization on the complex plane of the eigenvalues of the Jacobian matrix of the dimensional map (Eq. 34). In order to study the local stability of equilibrium points of the model (9), we consider the Jacobian matrix $J(p_1, p_2)$ along the variable strategy (p_1, p_2):

$$J(p_1, p_2) = \begin{bmatrix} f_{p_1} & f_{p_2} \\ g_{p_1} & g_{p_2} \end{bmatrix} \tag{39}$$

where

$$\begin{aligned} f(p_1, p_2) &= \frac{a(1-d)+c+dp_2}{2} \\ g(p_1, p_2) &= p_2 + k \cdot p_2 \cdot \frac{\partial \mathrm{P}_2}{\partial p_2} \end{aligned} \tag{40}$$

The Jacobian matrix is:

$$J(p_1, p_2) = \begin{bmatrix} 0 & \frac{d}{2} \\ kp_2 \cdot \frac{d\left[(1-d^2)+2c\right]}{(1-d^2)^2} & 1 + k \cdot \left(\frac{\partial P_2}{\partial p_2} + p_2 \cdot \frac{\partial^2 P_2}{\partial p_2^2}\right) \end{bmatrix} \tag{41}$$

At the equilibrium E_0:

$$J(E_0) = \begin{bmatrix} 0 & \frac{d}{2} \\ 0 & 1 + k \cdot \frac{\partial P_2}{\partial p_2} \end{bmatrix} \tag{42}$$

with

$$Tr = 1 + k \cdot \frac{\partial P_2}{\partial p_2}(p_2 = 0) \quad \text{and } Det = 0.$$

The characteristic equation of $J(E_0)$ is:

$$l^2 - Tr \cdot l + Det = 0 \tag{43}$$

with solutions

$$l_1 = 0 \quad \text{and } l_2 = Tr = 1 + k \cdot \frac{\left[\left(1-d^2\right)+2c\right] \cdot \left[a(1-d)+dp_1\right]}{\left(1-d^2\right)^2} \tag{44}$$

Since $|l_2| > 1$, the equilibrium E_0 is unstable. At the Nash equilibrium point E_* the Jacobian matrix is:

$$J(E_*) = \begin{bmatrix} 0 & \frac{d}{2} \\ kp_2 \cdot \frac{d\left[\left(1-d^2\right)+2c\right]}{\left(1-d^2\right)^2} & 1 + k \cdot p_2 \cdot \frac{\partial^2 P_2}{\partial p_2^2} \end{bmatrix} \tag{45}$$

with

$$Tr = 1 + k \cdot p_2 \cdot \frac{\partial^2 P_2}{\partial p_2^2} \quad \text{and } Det = -kd^2 p_2^* \cdot \frac{\left[\left(1-d^2\right)+2c\right]}{2\left(1-d^2\right)^2}.$$

The Nash equilibrium is locally asymptotically stable if the following conditions become true simultaneously:

$$\begin{aligned} &\text{(i) } 1 - Det > 0 \\ &\text{(ii) } 1 - Tr + Det > 0 \\ &\text{(iii) } 1 + Tr + Det > 0 \end{aligned} \tag{46}$$

Since

$$1 - Det = 1 + kd^2 p_2^* \cdot \frac{\left[\left(1-d^2\right)+2c\right]}{2\left(1-d^2\right)^2} > 0 \tag{47}$$

and

$$1 - Tr + Det = \frac{kp_2^*}{2} \cdot \frac{\left(1-d^2\right)(4-d)+2c(2-d)}{\left(1-d^2\right)^2} > 0 \tag{48}$$

the conditions (i) and (ii) are always satisfied. The third condition becomes:

$$1 + Tr + Det > 0 \Leftrightarrow k < \frac{4(1-d^2)^2}{p_2^*[(1-d^2)(4+d^2)+2c(2+d^2)]} \tag{49}$$

with

$$p_2^* = \frac{a(1-d)(2+d)+dc}{\frac{4\cdot[(1-d^2)+c]}{[(1-d^2)+2c]} - d^2}$$

If we focus on the parameter d, the stability condition becomes:

$$k < \frac{4(1-d^2)^2}{p_2^*[(1-d^2)(4+d^2)+2c(2+d^2)]}$$

$$\Leftrightarrow -(4+kp_2^*)\cdot d^4 + [8+kp_2^*(2c-3)]\cdot d^2 + 4[kp_2^*(1+c)-1] < 0 \tag{50}$$

Proposition *The Nash equilibrium $E_*(p_1^*, p_2^*)$ of the dynamical system Eq. (34) is locally asymptotically stable if:*

$$0 < k < \frac{4(1-d^2)^2}{p_2^*[(1-d^2)(4+d^2)+2c(2+d^2)]} \tag{51}$$

4.1.3 Numerical Simulations Focusing on k

As at the first case, numerical experiments are computed to show the bifurcation diagram with respect to k, strange attractor of the system Eq. (34) in the phase plane (p_1, p_2), and Lyapunov numbers. In order to study the local stability properties of the equilibrium points, it is convenient to take the parameters values as follows: $a = 5,\ c = 0.5,\ d = 0.2$. For the stability condition, it means that:

$$0 < k < 0.205$$

Figure 4 shows the bifurcation diagrams with respect to the parameter k against variable p_1(left) and p_2(right). In these figures, the Nash equilibrium E^* is locally asymptotically stable for k < 0.205. For k > 0.205, the Nash equilibrium E^* becomes unstable, and one observes complex dynamics behavior such as cycles of higher order and chaos. Figure 5 shows the graphs of the orbit of the point (0.1, 0.1) (strange attractor) and the Lyapunov numbers' diagram of the same orbit for $a = 5,\ c = 0.5,\ d = 0.2,\ k = 0.3$. If the Lyapunov number is greater of 1, one has evidence for chaos. From these results, when all parameters are fixed and only k is varied the structure of the game becomes complicated through period-doubling bifurcations, more complex bounded attractors are created which are aperiodic cycles of higher

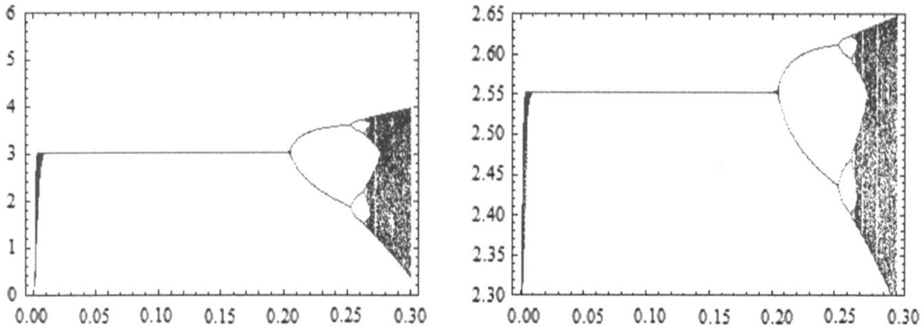

Fig. 4 Bifurcation diagrams with respect to the parameter k against variable p_1(left) and p_2(right), with 400 iterations of the map Eq. (34) for $a = 5,\ c = 0.5,\ d = 0.2$

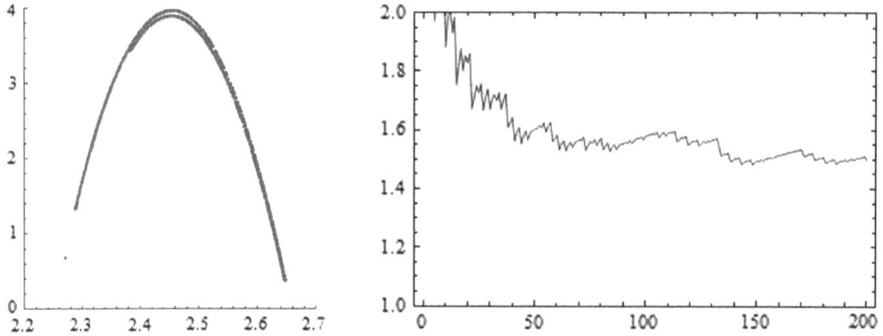

Fig. 5 Phase portrait (strange attractor) (left) and Lyapunov numbers (right) of the orbit of the point A(0.1, 0.1) versus the number of iterations of the map Eq. (34) for $a = 5,\ c = 0.5,\ d = 0.2,\ k = 0.3$

order or chaotic attractors. To demonstrate the sensitivity to initial conditions of the system Eq. (34), we compute two orbits with initial points (0.1, 0.1) and (0.101, 0.1), respectively. Figure 6 shows sensitive dependence on initial conditions for x-

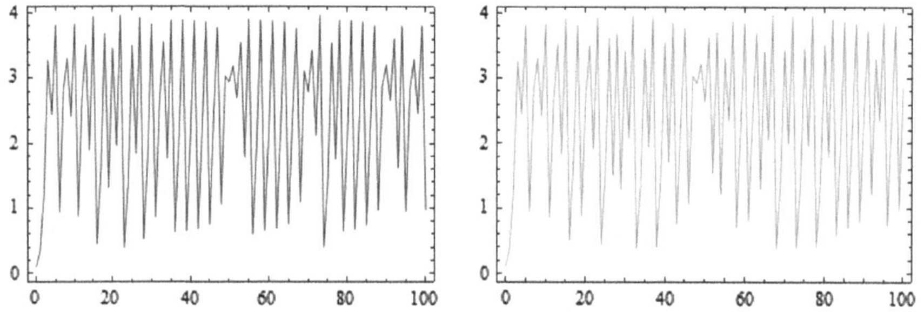

Fig. 6 Sensitive dependence on initial conditions for x-coordinate plotted against the time: the two orbits: the orbit of (0.1, 0.1) (left) and the orbit of (0.101, 0.1) (right), for the system Eq. (34), with the parameters values $a = 5,\ c = 0.5,\ d = 0.2,\ k = 0.3$

coordinate of the two orbits, for the system Eq. (34), plotted against the time with the parameter values $a = 5$, $c = 0.5$, $d = 0.2$, $k = 0.3$. At the beginning the time series are indistinguishable, but after a number of iterations, the difference between them builds up rapidly. Also, from Fig. 6, we show that the time series of the system Eq. (34) is sensitive dependence on initial conditions, i.e., complex dynamics behavior occur in this model.

4.1.4 Numerical Simulations Focusing on d

To provide some numerical evidence for the chaotic behavior of the system Eq. (34), as a consequence of change in the parameter d of the product differentiation degree, we present various numerical results here to show the chaoticity, including its bifurcations diagrams, strange attractor, Lyapunov numbers and sensitive dependence on initial conditions. In order to study the local stability properties of the equilibrium points, it is convenient to take the parameters values as follows $a = 5$, $c = 0.5$, $k = 0.2$. Figure 7 shows the stability space between parameters k (horizontal axis) and d (vertical axis) in which we can see that for $k = 0.2$ there is a small stability "window" on the parameter d. The Nash Eq. becomes stable for values of parameter d from about 0 until 0.3. This means that when d is between these values the Nash equilibrium of the system Eq. (34) is stable.

Numerical experiments are computed to show the bifurcation diagram with respect to d, strange attractor of the system Eq. (34) in the phase plane (p_1, p_2), and Lyapunov numbers. Figure 8 shows the bifurcation diagrams with respect to the parameter d against variable p_1(left) and p_2(right). Also, in these diagrams, the Nash equilibrium E^* is locally asymptotically stable for $0 < d < 0.3$. For $d > 0.3$ or $d < 0$ the Nash

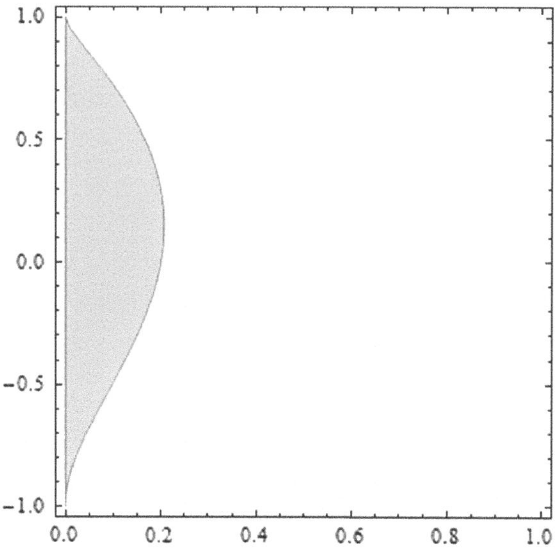

Fig. 7 Stability space between k (horizontal axis) and d (vertical axis) of Eq. (51) for $a = 5$, $c = 0.5$, $k = 0.2$

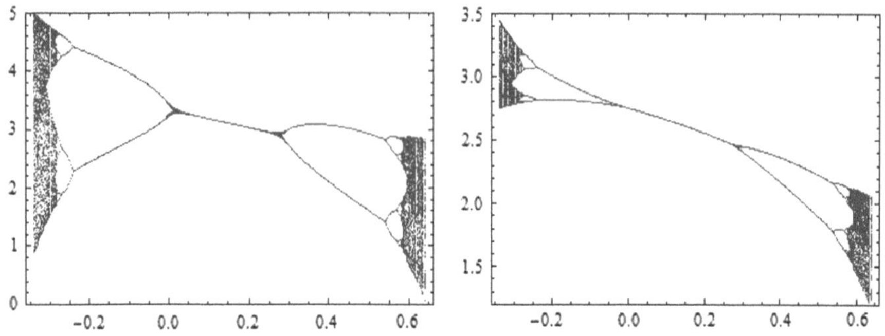

Fig. 8 Bifurcation diagrams with respect to the parameter d against variable p_1(left) and p_2(right), with 400 iterations of the map Eq. (34) for $a = 5,\ c = 0.5,\ k = 0.2$

equilibrium E* becomes unstable, and one observes complex dynamics behavior such as cycles of higher order and chaos. Figure 9 shows the graphs of the orbit of the point (0.1, 0.1) (strange attractors) for $a = 5,\ c = 0.5,\ k = 0.2,\ d = 0.61$ (left) and for $d = -0.34$ (right). Figure 10 shows the Lyapunov numbers' diagram of the same orbit for $a = 5,\ c = 0.5,\ k = 0.2,\ d = 0.61$. If the Lyapunov number is greater of 1, one has evidence for chaos. From these results, when all parameters are fixed and only d is varied the structure of the game becomes complicated through period-doubling bifurcations, more complex bounded attractors are created which are aperiodic cycles of higher order or chaotic attractors. To demonstrate the sensitivity to initial conditions of the system Eq. (34), we compute two orbits with initial points (0.1, 0.1) and (0.101, 0.1), respectively. Figure 11 shows sensitive dependence on initial conditions for x-coordinate of the two orbits, for the system Eq. (34), plotted

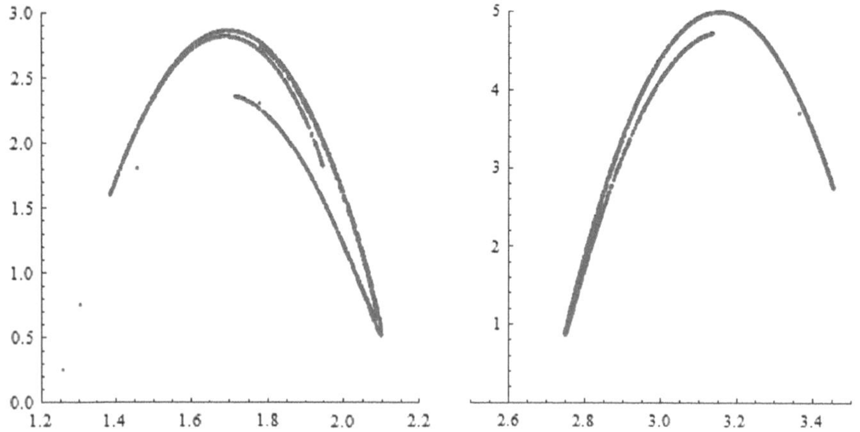

Fig. 9 Phase portrait (strange attractor) (left) of the orbit of the point A(0.1, 0.1) versus the number of iterations of the map Eq. (34) for $a = 5,\ c = 0.5,\ k = 0.2,\ d = 0.61$ (left) and for $d = -0.34$ (right)

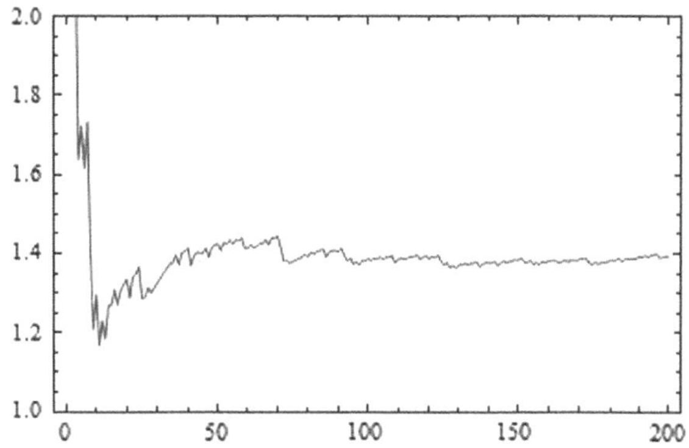

Fig. 10 Lyapunov numbers of the orbit of the point A(0.1, 0.1) versus the number of iterations of the map Eq. (34) for $a = 5$, $c = 0.5$, $k = 0.2$, $d = 0.61$

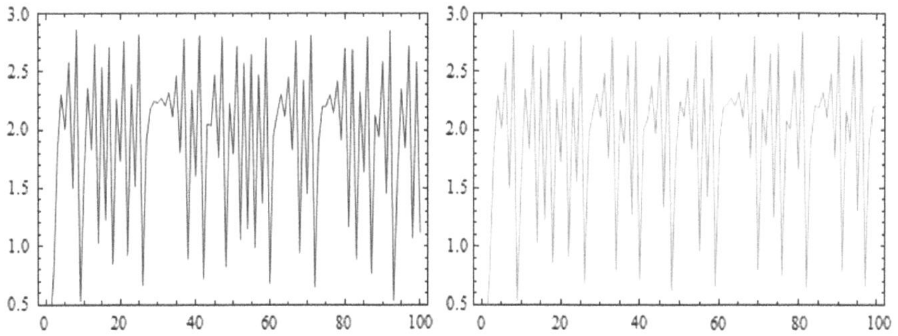

Fig. 11 Sensitive dependence on initial conditions for x-coordinate plotted against the time: the two orbits: the orbit of (0.1, 0.1) (left) and the orbit of (0.101, 0.1) (right), for the system Eq. (34), with the parameters values $a = 5$, $c = 0.5$, $k = 0.2$, $d = 0.61$

against the time with the parameter values $a = 5$, $c = 0.5$, $k = 0.2$, $d = 0.61$. At the beginning, the time series are indistinguishable, but after a number of iterations, the difference between them builds up rapidly. So it is clearly shown that the time series of the system Eq. (34) are sensitive dependence on initial conditions, i.e., complex dynamics behavior occur in this model.

5 Conclusion

In this study, we analyzed through a discrete dynamical system based on the marginal profits of the players, the dynamics of a nonlinear discrete time Bertrand-type duopoly game, where the players have heterogeneous expectations with different cost functions. The stability of equilibrium, bifurcation and chaotic behavior are investigated. We proved that the parameters of speed of players' adjustment and the product differentiation degree may change the stability of Nash equilibrium and cause a structure to behave chaotically, through period-doubling bifurcation. The chaotic features are justified numerically via computing Lyapunov numbers, sensitive dependence on initial conditions, bifurcations diagrams and strange attractors. Also, we have shown that in the case of asymmetric costs the speed of adjustment of the bounded rational player with quadratic cost leads the system more easily to instability.

References

Agiza, H. N. (1999). On the analysis of stability, bifurcation, chaos and chaos control of Kopel map. *Chaos, Solitons & Fractals, 10,* 1909–1916.

Agiza, H. N., & Elsadany, A. A. (2003). Nonlinear dynamics in the Cournot duopoly game with heterogeneous players. *Physica A, 320,* 512–524.

Agiza, H. N., & Elsadany, A. A. (2004). Chaotic dynamics in nonlinear duopoly game with heterogeneous players. *Applied Mathematics and Computation, 149,* 843–860.

Agiza, H. N., Hegazi, A. S., & Elsadany, A. A. (2002). Complex dynamics and synchronization of duopoly game with bounded rationality. *Mathematics and Computers in Simulation, 58,* 133–146.

Agliari, A., Gardini, L., & Puu, T. (2005). Some global bifurcations related to the appearance of closed invariant curves. *Mathematics and Computers in Simulation, 68,* 201–219.

Agliari, A., Gardini, L., & Puu, T. (2006). Global bifurcations in duopoly when the Cournot point is destabilized via a subcritical Neimark bifurcation. *International Game Theory Review, 8,* 1–20.

Askar, S. S. (2013). On complex dynamics of monopoly market. *Economic Modelling, 31,* 586–589.

Askar, S. S. (2014). Complex dynamic properties of Cournot duopoly games with convex and log concave demand function. *Operations Research Letters, 42,* 85–90.

Baumol, W. J., & Quandt, R. E. (1964). Rules of thumb and optimally imperfect decisions. *American Economic Review, 54*(2), 23–46.

Bischi, G. I., & Kopel, M. (2001). Equilibrium selection in a nonlinear duopoly game with adaptive expectations. *Journal of Economic Behavior & Organization*, 46, 73–100.

Bischi, G. I., Naimzada, A. K., & Sbragia, L. (2001). Oligopoly games with local monopolistic approximation. *Journal of Economic Behavior & Organization, 46,* 73–100.

Den Haan, W. J. (2001). The importance of the number of different agents in a heterogeneous asset—Pricing model. *Journal of Economic Dynamics and Control, 25,* 721–746.

Elaydi, S. (2005). *An introduction to difference equations* (3rd ed.) New York: Springer.

Fanti, L., & Gori, L. (2012). The dynamics of a differentiated duopoly with quantity competition. *Economic Modelling, 29,* 421–427.

Gandolfo, G. (1997). *Economic dynamics*. Berlin: Springer.

Hommes, C. H. (2006). Heterogeneous agent models in economics and finance, In L. Tesfatsion, & K. L. Judd (Eds.), *Handbook of computational economics. Agent—Based computational economics* (Vol. 2, pp. 1109–1186). Elsevier Science B. V.

Kopel, M. (1996). Simple and complex adjustment dynamics in Cournot duopoly models. *Chaos, Solitons & Fractals, 12,* 2031–2048.

Kulenovic, M., & Merino, O. (2002). *Discrete dynamical systems and difference equations with mathematica*. Chapman & Hall/Crc.

Medio, A., & Lines, M. (2005). Introductory notes on the dynamics of linear and linearized systems. In M. Lines (Ed.), *Nonlinear dynamical systems in economics* (pp. 1–26). Wien, New York: Springer, CISM.

Naimzada, A. K., & Ricchiuti, G. (2008). Complex dynamics in a monopoly with a rule of thumb. *Applied Mathematics and Computation, 203,* 921–925.

Naimzada, A. K., & Sbragia, L. (2006). Oligopoly games with nonlinear demand and cost functions: Two bounded rational adjustment processes. *Chaos, Solitons & Fractals, 29,* 707–722.

Puu, T. (1995). The chaotic monopolist. *Chaos, Solitons & Fractals, 5*(1), 35–44.

Puu, T. (1998). The chaotic duopolists revisited. *Journal of Economic Behavior and Organization, 37,* 385–394.

Puu, T. (2005). Complex oligopoly dynamics. In M. Lines (Ed.), *Nonlinear dynamical systems in economics* (pp. 165–186). Wien, New York: Springer, CISM.

Sarafopoulos, G. (2015a). On the dynamics of a duopoly game with differentiated goods. *Procedia Economics and Finance, 19,* 146–153.

Sarafopoulos, G. (2015b). Complexity in a duopoly game with homogeneous players, convex, log linear demand and quadratic cost functions. *Procedia Economics and Finance, 33,* 358–366.

Sedaghat, H., (2003). *Nonlinear difference equations: Theory with applications to social science models*. Kluwer Academic Publishers (now Springer).

Tramontana, F. (2010). Heterogeneous duopoly with isoelastic demand function. *Economic Modelling, 27,* 350–357.

Wu, W., Chen, Z., & Ip, W. H. (2010). Complex nonlinear dynamics and controlling chaos in a Cournot duopoly economic model. *Nonlinear Analysis: Real World Applications, 11,* 4363–4377.

Zhang, J., Da, Q., & Wang, Y. (2007). Analysis of nonlinear duopoly game with heterogeneous players. *Economic Modelling, 24,* 138–148.

Zhang, J., Da, Q., & Wang, Y. (2009). The dynamics of Bertrand model with bounded rationality. *Chaos, Solitons & Fractals, 39,* 2048–2055.

Forecasting Meal Requirements Using Time Series Methods in Organization

Mustafa Yurtsever and Vahap Tecim

Abstract After the Industrial Revolution, organizations are mostly obliged to provide catering services to their employees. The aim of the managers in the organization is customers' satisfaction on the highest level and no unnecessary loss of food. Forecasting is defined as the prediction of future events based on known past values of relevant variable. The ability to accurately predict expected meal counts allows managers to plan the right amount of food to buy and produce food and to plan appropriate staff levels so that food can be prepared and served efficiently. The purpose of this study is to determine which forecasting model will predict the number of meal counts at university dining facilities in the most accurate way. Forecasting techniques including ARIMA, artificial neural network and Facebook Prophet algorithm are applied to data gathering from dining halls over twelve months. The result of this study is that artificial neural network is the most accurate forecasting method. Facebook Prophet API is another appropriate forecasting method because of its simple use and high-level accuracy. Enriched, accurate and impressive reports are always welcomed by managers. This work will also provide the ability to report forecasts to managers in an understandable, comparable and manageable way.

Keywords Time series · Forecasting · ARIMA · Artificial neural network · Meal requirement

1 Introduction

Businesses or institutions may have to make different decisions in their daily lives. The decisions to be taken in the future are of great importance for businesses or institutions to make more profits or to be able to efficiently operate production and

---

M. Yurtsever (✉)
IT Department Smart Card Unit, Dokuz Eylül University, Buca-Izmir, Turkey
e-mail: mustafa.yurtsever@deu.edu.tr

V. Tecim
Department of Management Information Systems, Dokuz Eylul University, Buca-Izmir, Turkey
e-mail: vahap.tecim@deu.edu.tr

M. Janowicz-Lomott et al. (eds.), *Economic and Financial Challenges for Balkan and Eastern European Countries*, Springer Proceedings in Business and Economics,
https://doi.org/10.1007/978-3-030-39927-6_15

service activities. Failure to take corrective actions for the future will lead to results that institutions will not want. In conditions of uncertainty, businesses and institutions need to be able to plan ahead of their future rather than leaving it alone. Forecasting studies are important for future decisions.

Planning can be described as a process that shows the way in which a given goal can be achieved in light of present values and possible future developments. So, planning is an important part of production management. Forward uncertainties make it difficult to plan. Every effort to reduce uncertainty makes a significant contribution to make a correct decision. The most important factors that play a role in the decision making of the enterprises in the production process are the future sales amount of the goods or service to be produced. Determining the amount of demand for a product or service is one of the most important in terms of businesses.

The higher the difference between the actual data and estimated data, negative consequences such as overproduction or insufficient production arise. Conversely, incomplete service provision creates customer dissatisfaction. Therefore, accurate estimation is an important prerequisite for decisions regarding the design, planning and operation of production systems. At this stage, the collection of information, the determination of the forecast period, the selection of the forecasting method and finally the evaluation of the forecast validity ensure that this process is executed correctly.

Every organization uses forecasting techniques to plan large or small events. The forecast is defined as an estimate of future events based on known past values of the relevant variables (Makridakis et al. 1998). Products and services may be unacceptable to the customers when managers cannot effectively manage their planning activities. In order for managers to make effective decisions, accurate forecasting is necessary. Incorrect estimates can lead to poor decisions that could lead to ineffective management in general operations.

Miller and Shanklin (1988) noted that forecasting is particularly critical in food service operations due to the deteriorating nature of the product. In addition, most food products are prepared immediately before serving. Incorrect estimates result in overproduction or underproduction. Overproduction leads to more food that is left over or wasted, and unused food leads to increased food costs. Even when some foods can be integrated into another day's menu, the quality of the food can be reduced. Overestimation also increases the cost of labor, because additional food processing requires additional labor. A low estimate leads to a food problem that occurs before a customer's request is met, which leads to problems that need to be solved more urgently. In addition, a low estimate will result in reduced employee morale and managerial trust. Estimated food production in the food service sector affects customers' satisfaction, employee morale, managerial trust, stock, personnel and financial status (Messersmith and Miller 1992).

Lasek et al. (2016) stated that the restaurant sales forecast is affected by many factors such as time, weather conditions and economic factors. This is a situation that cannot be left to the intuition of the managers.

It is important to accurately estimate customers' counts in university residential catering establishments. While the high number of students aiming to eat for a particular meal can lead to increased costs, low predictors may leave fewer menu choices for students and may not be as satisfying as dining experiences (Blecher and Yeh 2008).

In the institutions, it is possible to arrange the number of meals that staff and students have already reserved in advance. Therefore, it is easy to organize meals and cafeteria services. They do not allow food to be eaten outside the organization and organize food expenses according to groups of people served. Smart card systems have been produced to do these tasks quickly and accurately without using human power. The information of the people passing through the entrance of the dining hall is recorded in the database by means of smart card readers, fingerprint readers, facial recognition systems. Reports relating to the recorded data can be taken, and the reports received can be used to make the decision-making processes of the managers effective. Although the primary goal is to provide control of smart card systems, estimates can be generated using the obtained data.

Generally, managers in the university catering organizations are responsible for forecasting decisions. They use data such as past production information and past food counts to estimate customer demand. The forecast is also influenced by many variables such as population changes, weather, menu items, special student activities, holidays, food trends, day of the week and the budget of student.

2 Methodology

In this study, data from the dining facilities of Dokuz Eylül University were evaluated with different prediction models. The data obtained in the period of 2016 were collected and used to estimate the food numbers of 2017 period. Later, the actual data for the 2017 period were used to determine the accuracy level. Forecasting models used in the analyses are ARIMA, artificial neural network and Facebook Prophet algorithm. At these dining facilities, the most appropriate forecasting method was based on accuracy and ease of use. In this study, several common accuracy methods were used: mean squared error (MSE) and mean absolute percentage error (MAPE). Each estimation method is given a ranking.

As shown in Fig. 1, the data in this study were collected and recorded on a daily basis during the period of 2016 in Dokuz Eylül University dining facilities. The study includes Monday to Friday numbers, and the weekend was not included in the survey. The data are the sum of the numbers of lunch and dinner on a daily basis. All the data were saved in an Excel spreadsheet.

To assess the forecasting performance of different models, each dataset is divided into two samples of training and testing. The training data are used for model development. The test data are used to evaluate the established model.

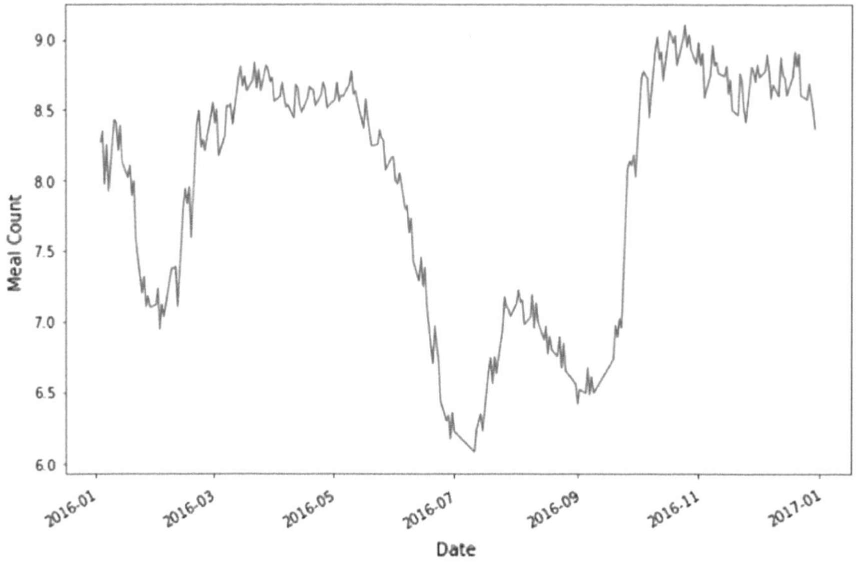

Fig. 1 2016 year meal counts

2.1 *Artificial Neural Networks*

Initially, it consists of interconnected simple processing elements called artificial neural networks (ANNs), neurons or nodes that are developed to mimic basic biological nervous systems, especially the human brain. ANNs are powerful computing devices and can learn from examples and generalize to examples that have never been seen before (Zhang et al. 1998).

In a simple way, ANNs that imitate the way the human brain works can learn from the verb, generalize, work with an unlimited number of variables and so on. It has many important features. The smallest units that form the basis for the work of ANN are called artificial nerve cells or processing elements. As shown in Fig. 2, the simplest artificial nerve cell consists of four main components: inputs, weights, activation function and output.

Fig. 2 Artificial neural network model

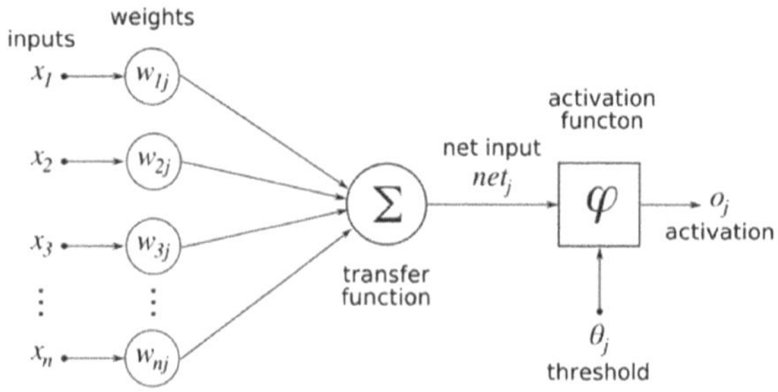

Inputs (x_1, x_2, …, x_n) are in the form of information that enters the cell from other cells or from the external environment. These are determined by the samples for which the learning of the network is desired. The weights (w_1, w_2, …, w_n) are the values that represent the effect of the input set or any other operation element on the preceding set on that operation element. Each input is multiplied by the weight value that connects it to the input process element, and combined through the sum function. "*b*" denotes a bias on the *X* unit; n is the total number of units. *X* is defined as:

$$X = \sum_{i-1}^{n} w_i x_i + b \tag{1}$$

Several artificial neural network models (perceptron, Adaline, MLP, LVQ, Hopfield, recurrent, SOM, ART, etc.) have been developed for use in artificial neural networks for specific purposes and in various fields. It is a multilayer perceptron artificial neural network that finds the most common usage area in our network structures and is also used in our work. An MLP typically consists of several node layers. The first or lowest layer is an entry layer from which external information is retrieved. The last or highest layer is an output layer from which problem resolution is obtained. The input layer and output layer are separated by one or more intermediate layers called hidden layers (Zhang et al. 1998). Figure 3 shows the structure of the feedforward neural network. The biggest advantage of neural networks is the ability to model flexible nonlinear models. With ANNs, there is no need to specify a specific model form. It is modeled adaptively based on features presented from the data. This data-based approach is suitable for many empirical datasets where there is no theoretical guideline to suggest an appropriate data generation process (Zhang 2003). A neural network can be trained by the past data of a time series to capture the properties of the series. The model parameters (link weights and node bias) are set repeatedly with the least reduction of prediction errors. For each training cycle,

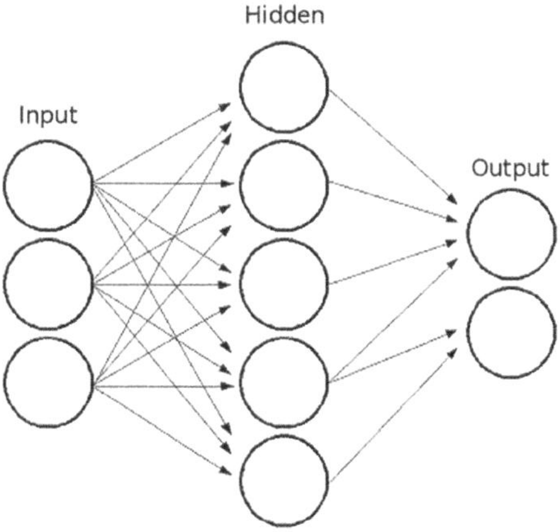

Fig. 3 Multilayer perceptron artificial neural network model

an input vector is randomly selected from the training set, the trained network entry layer (Tseng et al. 2002).

2.2 Box–Jenkins Methodology and ARIMA Models

Time series models are different from multiple and Poisson regression models in that they do not contain cause–effect relationship. They use mathematical equation(s) to find time patterns in series of historical data. These equations are then used to project into the future the historical time patterns in the data. An ARMA (p, q) model is a combination of AR(p) and MA(q) models and is suitable for univariate time series modeling. The autoregressive model specifies that the output variable depends linearly on its own previous values (Lasek 2016). The autoregressive model of order p AR (p) for time series X_t is defined as:

$$X_t = c + \sum_{i=1}^{p} \varphi_i X_{t-i} + \varepsilon_t \tag{2}$$

where $\varphi_1, \ldots, \varphi_p$ are the parameters of the model, c is a constant and εt is white noise. The other common approach in time series analysis is a moving average model. The notation MA(q) indicates the moving average model of order q:

$$X_t = \mu + \varepsilon_t + \theta_{1\varepsilon_t - 1} + \ldots + \theta_{q\varepsilon_t - q} \tag{3}$$

where μ is the mean of the series, the $\theta_1,\cdots,\theta_q$ are the parameters of the model and the $\varepsilon_t, \cdots, \varepsilon_{t-q}$ are white noise error terms (Lasek et al. 2016). Fitting an MA model to a time series is more complicated than fitting an AR model because in the former one the random error terms are not foreseeable. Autoregressive (AR) and moving average (MA) models can be effectively combined together to form a general and useful class of time series models, known as the ARMA models. Mathematically, an ARMA (p, q) model is represented as:

$$X_t = c + \varepsilon_t + \sum_{i=1}^{p} \varphi_i X_{t-i} + \sum_{i=1}^{q} \theta_i \varepsilon_{t-i} \tag{4}$$

Here, the model orders p, q refer to p autoregressive and q moving average terms. An autoregressive integrated moving average ARIMA model is a generalization of an autoregressive moving average ARMA model. ARIMA models (Box–Jenkins models) are applied in some cases where data show evidence of non-stationarity. Time series, which contain trend and seasonal patterns, are also non-stationary in nature. Thus, from application viewpoint ARMA models are inadequate to properly describe non-stationary time series. In ARIMA models, a non-stationary time series is made stationary by applying finite differencing of the data points. The mathematical formulation of the ARIMA (p, d, q) model using lag polynomials is given below:

$$\varphi(L)(1 - L)^d y_t = \theta(L)\varepsilon_t$$
$$(1 - \sum_{k=1}^{p} \alpha_k L^k)(1 - L)^d X_t = \left(1 + \sum_{k=1}^{q} \beta_k L^k\right)\varepsilon_t \quad (5)$$

The integer d controls the level of differencing. The Box–Jenkins method refers to the iterative application of the following four steps:

Identification: Using plots of the data, autocorrelations, partial autocorrelations and other information, a class of simple ARIMA models is selected. This amounts to estimating appropriate values for p, d and q. To determine a proper model for a given time series data, it is necessary to carry out the autocorrelation and partial autocorrelation analysis. These statistical measures reflect how the observations in a time series are related to each other. For modeling and forecasting purpose, it is often useful to plot the ACF and PACF against consecutive time lags. These plots help in determining the order of AR and MA terms.

Estimating the model's parameters: This part of the Box–Jenkins methodology is the most straightforward one. Once a model has been identified, its parameters have to be efficiently estimated, and the resulting fit assessed. If the model is found to be poor, the cycle is repeated.

Model checking: Once, an appropriate model had been chosen and its parameters estimated. Box–Jenkins methodology required examining the residuals of the actual values minus those estimated through the model. If such residuals are random, it is assumed that the model is appropriate (Makridakis and Hibon 1997).

Correction of the model: If not another model is considered, its parameters estimated and its residuals check for randomness.

One of the most important and widely used time series models is the autoregressive integrated moving average (ARIMA) model. The popularity of the ARIMA model stems from the well-known Box–Jenkins methodology as well as its statistical properties in the modeling process. A linear correlation between time series values is assumed, and therefore a nonlinear model cannot be captured by the ARIMA model. The approach of the linear models to the complex real-world problem is not always satisfactory (Zhang 2003).

2.3 *Facebook Prophet Algorithm*

Prophet model is developed by Facebook's Core Data Science team for analyzing and forecasting time series. Prophet model forecast time series dataset based on additive and nonlinear model fit with seasonal and trending data. The Prophet has a number of intuitive and easily interpretable features that allow the gradual development of the quality of the prediction model. The prophet algorithm predicts y_t by computing growth, seasonality and holidays. In the formula, $g(t)$ is a trend function that models non-periodic variations in the value of time series, $s(t)$ represents periodic changes (e.g., weekly and annual seasonality) and $h(t)$ represents the effects of the holidays (Taylor and Letham 2017). The mathematical formulation of the Prophet algorithm is represented as:

$$y(t) = g(t) + s(t) + h(t) + e_t \tag{6}$$

The error term e_t represents information that was not reflected in the model. Trend is modeled by fitting a piecewise linear curve over the trend or the non-periodic part of the time series. To fit and forecast the effects of seasonality, Prophet relies on Fourier series to provide a flexible model. Holidays and events cause predictable shocks to a time series. The Prophet allows the analyst to provide a special list of past and future events. Unlike ARIMA models, measurements do not have to be done at regular intervals (Taylor and Letham 2017).

The prediction model has easy interpretable parameters that can be changed by the analyst to apply assumptions on estimates. Moreover, analysts typically have experience with regression and may expand the model to include new components. Using time as a regressor, Prophet is trying to fit several linear and nonlinear functions of time as components.

Simple, adjustable versions and scalable performance monitoring in combination allow many and many analysts to estimate the various time series.

2.4 Forecast Evaluation Methods

There are many ways to measure forecast accuracy. The mean error measures are computed only for the last half of the data. The first part is used to fit the forecasting model. The second part of data is used to test the model. It is called the forecasting sample. The choice of an error measure can affect the ranking of methods. Two criteria will be used to make comparisons between the forecasting ability of the ARIMA time series models, the neural network models and Facebook Prophet algorithm. The first is mean squared error, MSE, which measures the overall performance of a model. The formula for MSE is:

$$MSE = \frac{1}{n}\sum_{t=!}^{n}(Y_t - F_t)^2 \tag{7}$$

where Y_t is the predicted value for time t, F_t is the actual value at time t and n is the number of predictions. This measure defines error as the sum of squares of the forecast errors when divided by the number of periods of data.

The second evaluation method is MAPE, which means average of the sum of all of the percentage errors for a given dataset is taken without regard to sign. MAPE is widely used as a measure of prediction accuracy because it expresses error as a percentage and thus can be used in model evaluations on different datasets. The formula MAPE is:

$$MAPE = \frac{1}{n}\sum_{t=1}^{n}\frac{|Y_t - F_t|}{Y_t} \tag{8}$$

2.5 Comparison of Forecasting Techniques

In this section, three forecasting techniques (ARIMA, artificial neural network and Facebook Prophet algorithm) for forecast meal counts at university dining halls were compared. In this study, the Python programming language was used to construct prediction models. Two hundred and forty-eight learning samples and 101 test samples were used.

The MLP model created in the study has a three-layered architecture consisting of an entrance layer, an output layer and a hidden layer. The data are made suitable for the structure of the network before entering the networks created with MLP; required input and output vectors were created. The training data were presented to the neural network model. Figure 4 shows the actual and estimated values of artificial neural networks.

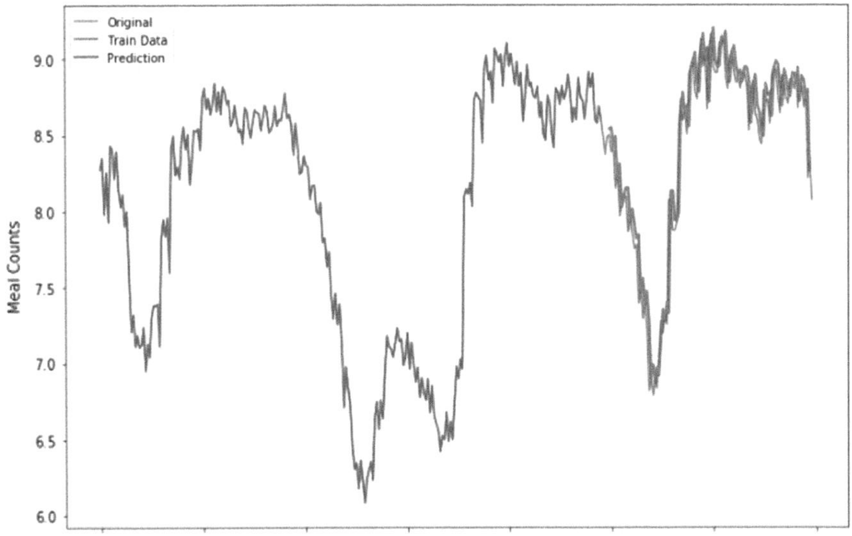

Fig. 4 Graph of real and estimated values with artificial neural network

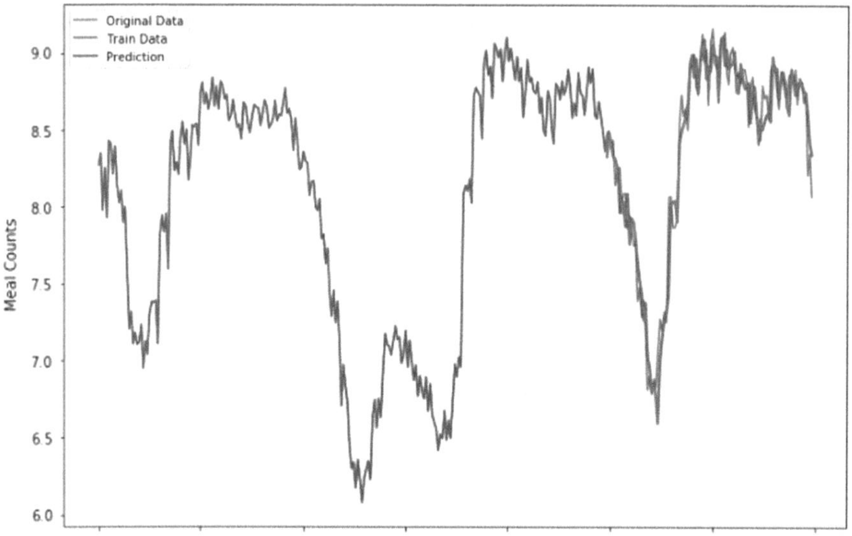

Fig. 5 Graph of real and estimated values with ARIMA

The Box–Jenkins methodology suggests short and seasonal (long) differencing to achieve stationarity in the mean, and logarithmic or power transformation to achieve stationarity in the variance. Box and Jenkins suggest logarithmic or power transformations to achieve stationarity in the variance (Makridakis and Hibon 1997). Logarithmic transformations are applied to the data. By comparing the MSE and MAPE criteria, the most suitable model for the dataset was determined from the models generated for both daily and monthly data. As a result, the use of the ARIMA (6, 0, 1) model, which does not have a fixed term for daily data, was deemed suitable from these models. Figure 5 shows the actual and estimated values of ARIMA.

Prophet follows the sklearn API. We create an instance of the Prophet class and then call its fit and predict methods. The input to Prophet is always a data frame with two columns. The datestamp (ds) column must contain a date, and y column must be numeric. Predictions are then made on a data frame with a column ds containing the dates for which a prediction is to be made. The forecast object here is a new data frame that includes a column with the forecast, as well as columns for components and uncertainty intervals. Figure 6 shows the actual and estimated values of Facebook Prophet algorithm.

The results obtained for datasets in the study result are given in Table 1. When Table 1 is examined, MSE and MAPE values of ARIMA, MLP and Facebook Prophet models for daily data are found as (0.0250456–1.46), (0.0021–1.405) and (0.0014617–0.39), respectively. The results show that the MLP model has lower MSE and MAPE values, while Facebook Prophet algorithm has similar results to the MLP model. Conceptually, the ARIMA and artificial neural network approach

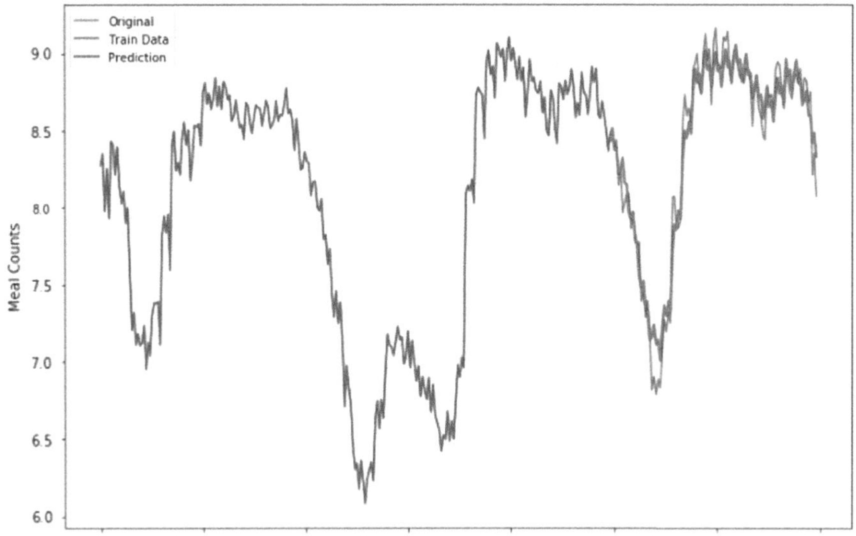

Fig. 6 Graph of real and estimated values with Facebook Prophet algorithm

Table 1 Forecasting technique results

Forecasting technique	MSE	MAPE
ARIMA	0.025	1.46
Artificial neural network	0.014	0.39
Facebook Prophet algorithm	0.021	1.40

are also nonparametric techniques and very similar, because they are trying to discover appropriate internal representations of time series data (Ho et al. 2002). As a result, artificial neural networks can be used as an alternative to statistical methods in predicting meal data when adequate network structure and sufficient data are used.

3 Conclusion

This work provides useful information for food service managers in relation to the use of forecasting methods to predict attendance at university-based catering establishments. The ability to use forecasting techniques effectively can help provide valuable information to maintain customer satisfaction, reduce errors and control food and labor costs.

Many real-life forecast situations are more complicated and difficult due to variables such as weather, food menu items, special student events and holidays. For this reason, it is also recommended that food service managers apply appropriate quantitative methods to obtain better predictive accuracy. As the analysis is done for a particular catering center, the results of this study are not directly applied to other locations and situations. However, the design of the work can be applied to other institutional operations and even to the food service sector. Finally, further research may be able to investigate which simple estimation technique would be most useful and feasible for other residential establishments in different universities and colleges.

References

Blecher, L., & Yeh, R. J. (2008). Forecasting meal participation in university residential dining facilities. *Journal of Foodservice Business Research, 11*(4), 352–362.

Lasek, A., Cercone, N., & Saunders, J. (2016). Restaurant sales and customer demand forecasting: Literature survey and categorization of methods. In *Smart city 360°* (pp. 479–491).

Ho, S. L., Xie, M., & Goh, T. N. (2002). A comparative study of neural network and Box-Jenkins ARIMA modeling in time series prediction. *Computers & Industrial Engineering, 42*(2–4), 371–375.

Makridakis, S., & Hibon, M. (1997). ARMA models and the Box-Jenkins methodology. *Journal of Forecasting, 16*(3), 147–163.

Makridakis, S., et al. (1998). *Forecasting methods and applications* (3rd ed.). New York: Wiley.

Messersmith, A. M., & Miller, J. L. (1992). *Forecasting in foodservice*. New York: Wiley.

Miller, J. L., & Shanklin, C. W. (1988). Forecasting menu-item demand in foodservice operations. *Journal of the American Dietetic Association, 88*(4), 44–49.

Taylor, S. J., & Letham, B. (2017). Forecasting at scale. *The American Statistician*, (just-accepted).

Tseng, F. M., Yu, H. C., & Tzeng, G. H. (2002). Combining neural network model with seasonal time series ARIMA model. *Technological Forecasting and Social Change, 69*(1), 71–87.

Zhang, G., Patuwo, B. E., & Hu, M. Y. (1998). Forecasting with artificial neural networks: The state of the art. *International Journal of Forecasting, 14*(1), 35–62.

Zhang, G. P. (2003). Time series forecasting using a hybrid ARIMA and neural network model. *Neurocomputing, 50,* 159–175.

The Upcoming Role of the Enterprise Architect—From Overseeing Visualization and Documentation to Becoming the Enabler for Change and Innovation

Daniel Marth, Christian Ploder, and Thomas Dilger

Abstract Organizations are facing the challenge of transforming their business models into digital firms, as companies are becoming part of the platform economy. The orchestration of the IT application landscape and strategic business–IT alignment is essential to gain transparency in surviving the digitalization. The important issues of IT and business alignment, cost reduction, organizational change, transformation, and fulfillment of legal requirements are becoming more important. The necessity of the "enterprise architect" rises importance. Enterprise architects do not, in general, consider themselves as active drivers for change. The research project answers the question of how are enterprise architects fostering business and IT alignment. The study focuses on an exploration in the evolution and changing role of the enterprise architect in the context of digital transformation. The research methodology consists of a systematic literature and applies a qualitative, explorative, and summative content analysis in the DACH region. Results indicate that fostering business and IT alignment require more than ever the role of an active intra-organizational networker and communicator in our complex digital organizational ecosystem. The profession of enterprise architects therefore has great opportunities but needs to transform the role from overseeing visualization to becoming the enabler for digitalization.

Keywords Enterprise architecture management · Enterprise architect · Role of the enterprise architect · Profession of the enterprise architect

D. Marth (✉) · C. Ploder · T. Dilger
MCI Management Center Innsbruck, Universitätsstraße 15, 6020 Innsbruck, Austria
e-mail: Daniel.Marth@web.de

C. Ploder
e-mail: Christian.Ploder@mci.edu

T. Dilger
e-mail: Thomas.Dilger@mci.edu

M. Janowicz-Lomott et al. (eds.), *Economic and Financial Challenges for Balkan and Eastern European Countries*, Springer Proceedings in Business and Economics,
https://doi.org/10.1007/978-3-030-39927-6_16

1 Introduction

Digitization is the process of changing to a digital firm, where key drivers are the demand by customers, new occurring technologies, and the prospect of greater economic benefits. (Friedrich et al. 2011) As the complexity of corporate information technology has increased exponentially, enterprises are confronted to quickly adapt to changing market situations. These unpredictable changing and volatile market environments force enterprises to realize major transformations if they want to survive. Because of these disruptive characteristics and impacts of digitalization, all enterprises no matter in which industry or part of the world they are operating have to follow the motto—digitalize or drown (Dreischmeier et al. 2015).

Charles Darwin's evolution theory (1858) argues, that "it is not the strongest of the species that survives, nor the most intelligent, but rather the one most responsive to change". This concept often described as a kind of digital Darwinism makes today's globalized ecosystem an even more competitive world as enterprises which want to stay in the game quickly must understand technology as an enabler if they want to stay competitive (Kreutzer and Land 2015). Therefore, organizations that manage flexibility in reorganizing their business capabilities will achieve an integrated holistic management perspective to oversee complexity and stay in the market. In this context, Enterprise Architecture "provides a meaningful foundation for high-performing organizations, as there are simply too many moving pieces" (McClure 2007). Henderson and Venkatraman (1993) already underlined this with his strategic alignment model that "companies must manage the increasing technological complexities accrued while they generate added value to business processes through the strategic alignment between business and IS/IT."

The problem, which many organizations face, is the lack of an integrated view on the entire organization. This is a result of decades of one-by-one implementations of specific IT solutions. As changes in the corporate strategy or business goals have a direct influence on the organizational structure, business processes, software systems, data management, or technical infrastructure, there is a need for business–IT alignment to ensure that changes are adjusted to the enterprise ecosystem. (Jonkers et al. 2006).

2 The Role of the Enterprise Architect

The enterprise architect is responsible for building a holistic view "by encompassing the scope of business and IT in an organization, while domain architects center on one specific portion of the enterprise" (Nsubuga et al. 2014). It is crucial to understand the business capabilities connect them with the business strategy (Strano and Rehmani 2007).

The role is perceived in various ways in the literature. Bredemeyer and Malan (2004) argue that architects are engaged in the process of creating great enterprises.

According to Strano and Rehmani (2007), scholars have argued that the enterprise architect needs to have a broad knowledge of various management disciplines. As on the other hand, the role is dealing with business strategy, change management, and organizational dynamics, and therefore, it is crucial to have excellent technical skills to understand information technology not only on the surface. Often the enterprise architect is compared to the job of a city planner (Bolles 2004).

Research by a group of Swedish scholars (Nsubuga et al. 2014) has examined how the role is perceived in the context of organizational development. In their study, they adopted based on their literature review the changing role of the enterprise architect to the proactive enterprise development model. They argue that like the model, the perception and role of the enterprise architect change. Following their argumentation, the enterprise architects act in five different roles. During the first strategic situational analysis phase, he acts as a change agent as the enterprise architect is aware of internal or external information regarding strategy, new technologies, and changing market circumstances. During the architectural design of the enterprise, the enterprise architect is necessary as a design expert. In the pre-evaluation, execution of the architectural implementation of the architectural changes, the enterprise architect acts as facilitator, consultant, and conflict resolver (Nsubuga et al. 2014).

Although the role of the enterprise architect is continuously changing and not yet clearly defined (Bredemeyer and Malan 2004), the profession is becoming more important (Gøtze 2013) as it is perceived in various ways. Gray (2014) points out that it can be helpful when the enterprise architect has charisma as he is the person who must be able to wear different hats to understand situational, social, political, human resource, and structural aspects of the organization. Nevertheless, the job profile depends on the organizational size and the EAM maturity of the organization (Roeleven 2010). Enterprise architects have to adopt and implement the right concepts and need to apply the right frameworks (Levine 2014). A concluded overview is given in Table 1, where the authors compared the different perceptions of the enterprise architect in literature.

According to Levine (2014), enterprise architects need to "analyze, organize, and synthesize technical, organizational, and process information to plan and guide development, adoption, and operations over a long arc of time."

The skillset of an enterprise architect following (Gøtze 2013)"requires extensive personal and professional skills." Among academic literature publications, the description of responsibilities and core competencies varies. According to Steghuis and Proper (2008), a standardized setting of task and responsibilities for the role of the enterprise architect does not exist yet.

Research identified analytical skills, communication skills, negotiation, abstraction capacity, sensitivity, and empathy as the five most important intermediary competences (Strano and Rehmani 2007). Walker points out the necessity of well-established people and communication skills as the job requires permanent interaction with different stakeholder group (Walker 2007).

Enterprise architects have to be well-educated as someone in the role of an enterprise architect should be skillful in systems and strategic thinking, project management, and IT governance operations (Florentine 2017). On the other hand, being

Table 1 Comparison in literature about role perception (own illustration)

Bredemeyer, Dana	Strano, Carolyn; Rehmani, Qamar	Steghuis, Claudia; Proper, Erik	TOGAF	Gotze	Nsubuga, William Michael; Magoulas, Thanos; Pessi, Kalevi	Evernden
2004	2007	2008	2011	2013	2014	2015
Creditable expert	Change agent	Change agent	Visionar	Boundary-focused architect	Change agent (strategic situation analysis)	Starting architect without specific domain expertise
Strategist	Communicator	Communicator	Coach	Dialogic architect	Facilitator (formulation of vision, mission, strategy)	Domain expert-specific knowledge
Politician	Leader	Leader	Team leader	Enterprising architect	Consultant and conflict resolver	Domain-specific architect
	Manager	Manager	Business-to-technical		Design expert	Enterprise architect/what important capabilities and skills are required?
	Modeler	Modeler	Computer scientist		Coordinator of change	
			Industry expert			

rational when analyzing and producing architectural descriptions is another important skill (Evernden 2015).

The functional role of an enterprise architect can be described as "filling a niche in organizations between IT and more business centric roles" (Florentine 2017). They need to ensure the long- and short-term strategic alignment between the operating organization and the business model by integrating people, process, and technology (CAEAP 2012). Rich Pearson describes the function of an enterprise architect as somebody who can translate a business strategy of an organization into IT solutions and manage and IT system architecture to support this business strategy (Florentine 2017). The Open Group describes enterprise architect as visionaries, coaches, team leaders, business-to-technical liaisons, computer scientists, and industry experts (The Open Group 2011). Therefore, one of the most important tasks of the enterprise architect is being the communicator and translator to the different stakeholder groups especial on the executive level by articulating and executing the technical vision of the organization (The Open Group 2011).

Levine (2014) argues that an enterprise architect needs to follow four steps (love, sell, close, deliver) to achieve deep impact via the implementation of EA concepts and frameworks, which is like the job of a salesman. In the role as a visionary leader, the enterprise architect acts in different roles by being on the one hand a technologist and on the other hand by being able to speak the language of Return on Investment to business people (Gray 2014). Walker (2007) points out that the job involves "governance committees, architecture review boards, technology life cycles, portfolio management, architecture strategy and strategic project support. As this profession is multidimensional this job includes various different roles (Strano and Rehmani 2007).

The role of the enterprise architect can be characterized as a shared service. Firstly, the role provides a holistic vision of the enterprise solution and development initiatives to drive and ensure technological implementation across value streams, secondly, providing expertise and knowledge to the different domain architects, and thirdly, transmitting strategic themes and key business aspects in the appropriate language to the different stakeholder groups. Fourthly, orchestration of domain architects and change project initiatives to ensure that individual product and project strategies align with the objectives of the corporate strategy. (Uludag et al. 2017) The responsibilities can be summarized in creation, application, and maintenance of EA (Steghuis and Proper 2008).

The future role of enterprise architects is constantly facing obstacles, barriers, and political power plays within the organization as their level of impact is often limited in being an executive department with no formal power and budget for fulfilling their job (Walker 2007). According to Strano and Rehmani (2007), the "impact of not having the role filled might increase the potential for chaos and confusion, inadequate information to support key decisions, increased complexity, local versus enterprise optimization, reduced efficiency and effectiveness, and increased risk of finding the wrong solution." In handling the digital transformation of the organization, enterprise architects are also confronted with the challenge of overseeing and implementing new legacy systems in combination with new technologies or business models to stay competitive in their respective industry (Manwani and Bossert 2016). Research by Forrester outlines that enterprise architects are confronted with non-technical-related challenges such as project guidance, gap of skilled architects, no budget, no mandate, and need for new technologies.

Another challenge is the gap of personal skills of the individual enterprise architect which can be described as the "inability to enforce architecture compliance [...], sell enterprise architecture value, being pulled inappropriate into projects operationally, [...], develop the interpersonal skills to communicate effectively with both business and IT" (Gray 2014). When it comes to stakeholder management, the enterprise architect is also confronted with the challenge of forming and applying such an EA instrument in a qualitative manner so that all concerns are respected (Opt' Land et al. 2009). Another challenge in the life of an enterprise architect is the constant battle for additional resources to get the job done as EA initiatives usually involve various business units across the organization (Walker 2007). However, enterprise architects have to carefully select their "battlefields" in the organization due to the lack of limited resources (Bontinck et al. 2016) and already existing overload of work.

Enterprise architects need to take on a proactive approach to ensure EA involvement and innovation taking place (Bontinck et al. 2016). Therefore, the role of an enterprise architect will become more important and relevant for many organizations (Gøtze 2013). However, *no regulatory standard exists of how the role regarding qualifications and tasks should be defined, as this strongly depends on the individual organization* (CAEAP 2012). EA being an evolving and maturing management discipline, the role of the enterprise architect is developing further and changing (Bredemeyer and Malan 2004).

No empirical study yet has been realized until the present days, which investigates the evolving role of the enterprise architect in the DACH region and how the role of the enterprise architect fosters business and IT alignment. Bredemeyer and Malan (2004) already indicated that this new role has to decide on a path of either being present as an inactive player in the organization only documenting or by actively involving themselves in the change process to make an excellence contribution to the enterprise (Bredemeyer and Malan 2004). As theory still had defined the role not precisely, Strano and Rehmani (2007) "*raised questions about whether the role of enterprise architect is an extension of the systems architect role or a unique discipline, if the role is mostly technical or managerial, and what competencies are required to perform the daily tasks of practicing architects.*" Further, it is surprising that no research studies are available to this moment on the type of people who practice enterprise architecture (Evernden 2015) as education, training, and how to become an enterprise architect becomes an important issue in practice as companies are highly searching for these people.

Gøtze (2013) confirms this tendency that the enterprise architects shall focus more on problem identification rather than problem solving and not get involved actively in operational projects. Practice lacks a clear role definition and role delimitation to other architectural roles . Bontinck et al. (2016) argue that enterprise architects have reached a crossroad, where they have the chance to step up in shaping and leading the transformation toward a digital enterprise, but they must decide whether they are able to transforming their role in the organization or not. However, enterprise architects do not, in general, consider themselves as active drivers for change. This leads to the **research question**: Tour guide for the digital transformation—**"How does an enterprise architect foster business and IT alignment?"**.

3 Research Method

A systematic literature review (Levy and Ellis 2006; Webster and Watson 2002) in the domain was executed to identify research gaps. Next, semi-structured interviews (Flick et al. 2017) with domain experts in the form of problem-centered expert interviews (Witzel 2000) were conducted. Surveys were carried out with three different groups: (1) enterprise architects (EAr); (2) EAM consultants, and (3) business architects (BAr). Collecting these heterogeneous perceptions of the role is aimed at questioning if a common understanding of the role of the enterprise exists in non-academic communities exists. Experts for interview conduction were approached directly in person by the authors at EAM conventions (LEAN EAM,[1] Nov 2016 in Munich; EAMKON,[2] May 2017 in Stuttgart) or through online expert groups in business communities (Xing Group "Enterprise Architecture Management" or LinkedIn "Enterprise Architecture Forum").

Overall, 30 experts were approached either directly in person at different EAM symposia or through online business networks. In total, fifteen interviews were conducted during the period of the June 22 and July 24, 2017. Participating experts in this research study came from Germany, Austria, and Switzerland. All interview partners were male and had profound knowledge, expertise, and work experience in the field of enterprise architecture management. Interviews were designed for a duration of 30–45 min and were realized either in person via a face-to-face interview (1) or via telephone interview (14).

Witzel (2000) characterizes this type of interview in three ways: problem centering (focus and objective of the research), object orientation (issues that are developed in regard to the specific problem), and process orientation (increasing the knowledge base concerning the problem) (Witzel 2000). Problem-centered interviews consist of guiding questions in combination with narrative stimuli to collect the information from the interviewee (Witzel 2000). This type of interviewing is like a natural conversation where the participant feels comfortable enough to talk about a certain topic brought up by a question from the interviewer. On the other hand, does the interviewer moderate the conversation with the help of a beforehand designed inter-

[1]Lean EAM (2016) https://lean-konferenz.de/lean-eam-konferenz-2016.

[2]EAMKON (2017) https://www.eamkon.de/image/inhalte/file/EAMKON_Fachkongress_2017.pdf.

view guideline. To ensure that the interview aligns with the research objective, the design of the interview guideline followed the procedure and requirements according to (Helfferich 2011).

Questions were designed based on three from literature derived main deductive categories "Enterprise Architecture Management"; "Business–IT alignment," and "Enterprise Architect." With the purpose of an adequate qualitative content data analysis (IT supported by MAXQDA), a suitable transcription of the interviews was done (Mayring 2014) by the use of Kuckartz simplified transcription rules (Kuckartz 2014). The researcher team used the mixed summative content-based approach, where material is reduced only to its most essential parts. The categories were defined beforehand based on the theoretical background of the thesis by rules to sort statements or segments within a respective category (Mayring 2014).

4 Discussion

The authors indicate and compare the relevant aspects derived from the conducted interviews for this reflection and discussion of outcomes. Authors will refer to the expert statements according to their anonymized identification letters (Exp. A, Exp. B, etc.) and statement numbers (e.g., [S12]) in the transcribed interviews.

This present research mentions a heterogeneous variety of existing role perceptions of the enterprise architect. Strano and Rehmani (2007) questioned the role of the enterprise architect whether it is an extension of the systems architect role or an exclusive discipline. According to Saint-Louis and Lapalme (2016) findings, the role can be categorized, firstly, in the role of a problem-solving specialist for the organization, secondly, as an investigator who is aware of the best practice tools, methods, and techniques, and thirdly, as an integrator to bring together all stakeholders and decision makers to find a consent for an effective solution. Fourthly, as a facilitator who can explain in detail the organizations' problems to propose solutions (Saint-Louis and Lapalme 2016).

Experts were asked about how the role is currently perceived within their organization and if role descriptions exist. Participant K [S36] indicates that the enterprise architects need to be the chief of the EAM system but is aware of the fact [S30] that perceptions vary. Nevertheless, F [S19] highlights that the perception depends on the individual person and how this person sells the role to others within the organization to make an impact. But not always are the right individuals in this position (F[S45]) to make this necessary impact happen. From his experience about the interpretation of the role of the enterprise architect Expert B [S13] reports that a great variety of understandings in organizations exists as the differentiation between the architectural domains, and therefore, responsible roles also exist.

Expert P [S17] points out that currently the role is not noticed at all within the organization. However, the desired job to be done profile of the role would be the

Table 2 Role perceptions of the enterprise architect (own illustration)

Coach, consultant, and sparing partner	13
Knowledge and information expert and distributor	8
Perception depends on professional or academic background	7
No awareness/no impact	7
Executive position	5
Networker/business–IT relationship manager	4
Moderator, mediator, and communicator	4
Administrator and documenter	4

shared business partner which connects the different departments for improving decision making and bringing the big puzzle together. Expert O [S15] reports that enterprise architects are not perceived from the business site as usually only the business architects are in contact with the stakeholders. However, from O's point of view [S25], it is a problem that enterprise architects might not have understood that the job goes beyond design as also organizational development and entrepreneurial thinking are included in this profession.

Expert G [S40] mentioned that a clear perception and impact within the organization of the enterprise architect only can be achieved in companies with a service-orientated architecture. M [S33] mentions the alternative of establishing a supporting role of a business relationship manager, as usually the expectation of the role profile of the enterprise architect is often overloaded.

The results show that the role is perceived generally in a coaching or consulting role as the architect is a valuable knowledge and information distributor within the organization. However, it seems that in practice no widely accepted understanding of the role has been defined yet. On the one hand, this is because of the continuing and evolving changing role of the enterprise architect (Bredemeyer and Malan 2004). On the other hand, this also confirms the results of the nonexistence of a regulatory criteria catalog for the qualifications of the enterprise architect (CAEAP 2012). Table 2 summarizes stated interpretations of the role.

4.1 Skillset of the Enterprise Architect

Experts in the present research identified EAM as the enabler for the digital transformation. In other words, this means that being the enabler for the digital transformation requires for the role of the enterprise architect also to become the change agent for the digital transformation. Levin compared the role of the enterprise architect to a salesman in the organization, who has to love, sell, close, and deliver the product (Levine 2014).

Table 3 Skills and capabilities of the enterprise architect (own illustration)

Communication, moderation, conflict solving, and persuasiveness	25
General knowledge about organization, business, and IT	21
Analytical, structured, and abstract thinking capabilities	12
IT and technology skills	9
Open minded, unselfconsciousness, and no fear of contact to new people	4
Social skills	4
Extensive professional experience	3
Used to train yourself in a process of continuous learning in new topics	3

Participants in the present research were questioned about the required skillset of an enterprise architect. The researcher wanted to investigate if compared to the findings in the literature additional new skills are required, when becoming the change agent for the digital transformation. Table 3 illustrates the results of the most important skills and capabilities mentioned by the experts. Participants overall pointed out the need of being a highly communicative personality to actively being involved as communicator, moderator, and problem solver with the different stakeholder groups. Expert J [S47] describes this as the architectural elevator by being able to move up and down on the different organizational levels in the organization. The general overall knowledge about the organization, business, and IT therefore helps the enterprise architect on the other hand to communicate in the right kind of language to the stakeholder groups.

Expert F [S45] underlines the willingness of being in a generalist role, because through this superficial general knowledge about the organization, business, and IT, the person can provide support and assistance everywhere in the organization. Because of his expertise and insights into ongoing current projects and activities, the enterprise architect can provide transparency of organizational and foster communication (Exp. [S21]) across existing intra-organizational borders to prevent silo thinking. Results clearly indicate a shift in the skillset in being in the position of an active business–IT relationship manager.

4.2 *Tasks and Responsibilities*

Research claims that no universal set of tasks and responsibilities for the role of an enterprise architect exists, but describes it as creation, application, and maintenance of EA (Steghuis and Proper 2008). To gain further understanding about the main tasks and responsibilities, the expert participants were questioned what the main tasks and responsibilities of somebody in this role are. Expert C [S21] pointed out that the field of task and responsibilities is very heterogenous as this strongly depends, where in the organization this role is affiliated.

Table 4 Tasks and responsibilities of the enterprise architect (own illustration)

Documentation and visualization of as is system landscape and elaboration of as to be landscape	9
Strategic development of EA standards and principles	7
Reduction of IT complexity	3
Project portfolio management and support	3
Research and testing of innovations and trends	1
Field of tasks depends on where the role is integrated in the organizational chart	1

Results of this question are shown in Table 4. Experts identified the main task of the enterprise architect as being in charge for documentation and visualization of the as is system landscape and the elaboration of the future as to be landscape. In addition, experts pointed out that the role oversees the continuous strategic development of EA standards and principles. The findings in this study relate and confirm the task description by Bernard (2005) for the chief architect who summarizes the tasks as "managing the EA program and documentation process, selecting and implementing the framework and documentation methodology, identifying the EA standards and managing EA configuration management sub-process" (Bernard 2005).

4.3 Career Path

The literature review in this present study has shown no empirical evidence has been published yet regarding education for a systematic career path of an enterprise architect. M [S23], F[S35] and C[S39] also raised the question during the interviews, what is required to be or to become an enterprise architect.

Expert K [S46] and A [S31] agree that somebody who wishes to fulfill the position needs to have a technical IT background. Ideally, it would be a business computer science degree (Exp. L [S33]; Exp. [S25]; Exp. M [S25]). Despite the increasing demand by the industry for this position (The Open Group 2011), only few universities (St. Gallen, Munich, Osnabruck, Duisburg, Essen) in the DACH region include teaching modules about EAM in their curricula as Expert M [S25] points out. Lecturing and teaching the complexity of enterprise architecture in organizations on a theoretical basis seem impossible without having seen examples in real organizations in practice to develop a first understanding why EA matters for organizations (Exp. B [S29]. It is not a surprise that many experts agreed that it is difficult to start working as an enterprise architect right after university. Many years of work experience in different organizations, projects, and areas are needed to acquire a well-established standing within the organization and reach a certain level of seniority and acceptance by the different stakeholder groups (Exp. N [S29]; Exp. D [S35]; Exp. J [S41]; Exp. J [S25]).

Table 5 Career path of the enterprise architect (own illustration)

IT background (computer science degree, IT consultant, architect)	10
No clear career path defined	9
Professional experiences in change management projects	4
Raw university education in the field of EAM	3
Junior enterprise architect	2

Furthermore, professional experience in many change managements projects (both from an organization and technical perspective) is required before stepping in this role, where suggestions have an enterprise wide impact. (Exp. K [S46]). Expert L [S33] describes the classical career path of an enterprise architect by starting out working as an IT consultant to get experience from the business, process, and organizational perspective. On the other hand, Expert F [S35] describes the career path through the following steps: software engineer; senior developer, solution architect, and enterprise architect. Then the novice turn into the domain expert with specific knowledge becomes in the next step a domain-specific architect before than being able to work as an enterprise architect. This approach is mostly similar to the approach described by (Evernden 2015), who describes the starting architect as a novice without specific domain expertise but general know-how about EA. M [S23] points out the idea of establishing the role of a junior enterprise architect for somebody, who understands the basic concepts of EAM as a management discipline to get started. In a survey done by McKinsey in 2016, the results showed that every second chief of enterprise architect wishes to establish a structured career path for this profession (Pütter 2016). Table 5 provides an overview of potential career paths. It can be summarized as although various external certification and training possibilities for enterprise architects like TOGAF, COBIT or ITIL exist, no clear career development path has yet been established.

4.4 Future Evolving Role

Research results by Chuang and Loggerenberg (2010) show that often enterprise architects with a technical background expect the business to provide the required information in their engineerable mindset expectation as these persons are often not interested in the business model of the organization.

Scheibenreif (2016) underlines that enterprise architects must understand the impacts of the main ongoing business and sociocultural macro trends (demographic change, urbanization of big cities, individualization of society, digital business models, human enterprise, economic shift from the west to Asia/Pacific), as the old mindset of enterprise architects did not include this entrepreneurial thinking and therefore siloed in his ivory tower (Exp. O [S21]).

Participants in this research were asked by the investigator for their opinion if the role of the enterprise architect is changing from overseeing visualization and documentation to becoming the enabler for change and innovation. The question followed a similar assumption by Bontinck et al. (2016), who pointed out that enterprise architect must decide if they want to become opportunity architect by being an active enabler in the process of the digital transformation or if not. Relevant results in Table 6 illustrate that the majority (15) of the experts agree that enterprise architects will become the tour guide for the digital transformation as enabler and driver for innovation. Although this description would be an ideal profile of the profession, experts (A[S29]; N[S23]) still are skeptical as they point out that they will not see it happen in practice.

Table 7 provides a summarized overview of the given answers in the category of the future evolving role.

4.5 Fostering Business–IT Alignment

Stakeholder management and understanding their problems, needs, and requirements are one of the most important aspects (Exp. L [S17]; Exp. D [S57] how the enterprise architect can foster business and IT alignment. However, the level of communication differs depending on the different target groups (Exp. O [S33]; Exp. E [S37]), which the enterprise architect addresses, and therefore, the language must be adopted.

Expert L [S17] underlines the importance and necessity of elaborating a stakeholder analysis for the organization in preparation for setting up an EAM to understand various questions, which differ depending on the point of view to develop possible suggestions or solutions and to identify the right stakeholders. In addition, integration and explanation to the different stakeholder groups, what is EAM about and how it can help in practice is crucial to promote the adding value and benefits (Exp. L [S19]; Exp. J [S45]). Because of the vast knowledge and expertise about people, processes, and systems in the organization, enterprise architects are usually able to identify the right stakeholders which help in supporting EA initiatives (Exp. M [S37]). One important point which is often underestimated in stakeholder management according to Expert A [S25] is the aspect of personal networking to establish trust and beliefs. Table 8 summarizes the fostering of business–IT alignment.

5 Conclusion

EAM is becoming the fundamental enabler for the digital transformation. The management practice offers business and IT the ability to establish an intra-organizational vocabulary for a better understanding but still lacks the problem of organizational silo thinking. Fostering business and IT alignment requires a proactive intra-organizational enterprise architect acting as a change manager and innovation driver

Table 6 Statements confirming the evolving role (own illustration)

Exp.	Statements
A (neutral)	"I would like to have it perceived in that way, but now I do not see this aspect in practice. [...] **This role has not specified deliverables** [...] but has a tremendous knowledge over the entire organization, processes, departments **and therefore would be in an interesting position to push innovations forward**". [S29]
B (yes)	"[...] over the last years, **the Enterprise Architect has become the driver for information** [...] and I could definitely see that they make an impact on pushing innovation forward". [S17]
C (yes)	"Yes, the role is slowly evolving as IT is included everywhere". [S26–27]
D (yes)	"I think **this description fits. He is the tour guide**, administrator but not necessary has to be the impeller to ensure that everyone moves in the same direction as he organizes the general condition and the environment". [S37]
E (yes)	"**I agree, that Enterprise Architects have to consider themselves as tour guides as they have to form the target as to-be architecture**". [S27] "Many Enterprise Architects [...] are **limited in their competences** to enable change and this **might be the reason why they do not consider themselves as change agents**". [S33]
F (yes)	"**Being the tour guide fits the description of the role as this would be the targeting ideal perception of the profession.** However, the role is steering, but not necessary has to be the one taking the lead but has to be the moderator and coordinator [...] so that the transformation is ensured and controlled from a holistic perspective so that strategic consistency fits [...]". [S31]
G (yes)	"**It has to be the person in charge of the entire architecture and this cannot be a passive job**". [S49]
I (no)	"I do not see the change takin place. [...] I do not believe that an Enterprise Architect in the future will have different competences as the role would then be considered part of the management and then would have less time for current architecture or the identification of further states". [S27]
J (yes)	"**I believe tour guide fits the description. Architecture is collaboration [...] but the digitalization is realized through the projects, where the architects provide guidance** [...]". [S25]
K (yes)	"Yes, I would see it similar. Digitalization as the current main ongoing challenge and being the enabler that the digital transformation can take place". [S37–38] "**In my opinion, this role will become more and more important in organizations as he provides the necessary holistic perspective of all information of the entire organization**". [S52]
L (yes)	"The EA designer, which would be the next maturity level is the person who is able not only to provide transparency, as this role is also able to develop a strategy and visualize a future as to be target architecture". [S25]
M (yes)	"I believe that this is the exact direction as the person has the holistic perspective and is able to communicate with the different stakeholder groups to explain complex issues or situations and this help the people in understanding the organization better". [S27] "The Enterprise Architect has to be involved in strategic decision making". [S35]

(continued)

Table 6 (continued)

Exp.	Statements
N (neutral)	"This would be the perfect case. However, in practice I would question this […] as from my experience usually EA initiatives start in the business department based on the market demand […] but I would see it as a possibility". [S23] "[…] if Enterprise Architects could focus on innovations topics in the context of the organization than is could be seen, how technology and methods […] are being used value adding for the enterprise". [S43]
O (yes)	"**I do absolutely agree** […] part of the task is to explain the different business departments, how the world is changing, which velocity we need to be successful and that we have to start thinking from sketch at certain points". [S18–19]
P (yes)	"Definitely. […] role will be more of an enabler […] and organizational designer". [S18/19/21]

Table 7 Future evolving role (own illustration)

Digital tour guide, change manager, innovator, and integrator	56
Bridging people, processes, and systems as support function	7
Executive position close to management	5
Entrepreneurial designer of an organization	3
More tasks relating to security issues (e.g., GDPR)	2
Empowerment of the enterprise architect	2
Impact of the enterprise architect depends on the organization	1

Table 8 Fostering business–IT alignment (own illustration)

Managing stakeholder and understanding their needs	28
Providing transparency	12
Fostering communication, collaboration, and committees	11
Being the information manager (distributor)	10
Providing basis for decision making	4
Business capability map	2

by being involved in the strategic development of the organization. Enterprise architect is perceived generally in a coaching or consulting role as a valuable knowledge and information distributor within the organization. However, it seems that in practice no widely accepted understanding of the role has been defined yet as a clear understanding of what the job to be done lacks.

Most experts agreed that the future evolving role of the enterprise architect is becoming the tour guide and enabler for change and innovation in organizations. However, this is not yet everywhere in practice the understanding as this depends on the level of EAM maturity of the organization. As stakeholder management is tremendously important, establishing a mutual communication strategy for EAM needs to be on the top agenda of every enterprise architect.

Although various external certification and training possibilities for enterprise architects like TOGAF, COBIT, or ITIL exist, no clear career development path has yet been established. Providing transparency and understanding why EAM matters are important besides having an EA roadmap in place of how the transition can be executed.

Research results contribute with a further investigation in the changing role of the enterprise architect. What it takes to start a career as an enterprise architect still occurs mysterious. The results of the study prove the need for the change in the understanding of the enterprise architect in becoming the change agent for the organization. However, from the perspective of the authors, a clarification in the practitioner's community needs to be compelled with respect to separate architectural roles. Where does the job of the enterprise architect start and what are the domain architects responsible for? It seems that these boarders occur still to be blurry although the literature argues in a different way. Within the practitioner's community, a rather wide and heterogeneous understanding of the role still exists with no common understanding whether the enterprise architect is a domain architect or in charge as the enterprise architect with the overall holistic perspective of the organization. The authors would like to suggest that a standardized industry-specific pattern catalog for the role compared to existing architectural reference models (e.g., BEAN) would help the practitioners' community to clarify and establish a common understanding of what the role of the enterprise architect is about.

Limitations were the broad scope of the formulated research question which with respect to the results leaves room for interpretation. Further, this research is limited to experts in the DACH region. Experts from the three countries are not distributed evenly (12 experts from Germany, two experts from Austria, one expert from Switzerland). Further involvement of other relevant key stakeholder (CIOs, domain architects, etc.) surrounding the enterprise architect could enhance further insights. As the provided results rely on the explorative perceptions of the authors, a certain bias should be taken into consideration.

References

Bernard, S. A. (2005). *An introduction to enterprise architecture, Internat* (2nd. ed.) Bloomington, Indiana: AuthorHouse.

Bolles, G. (2004). This old infrastructure: Enterprise architecture. http://www.cioinsight.com/c/a/Past-News/This-Old-Infrastructure-Enterprise-Architecture. Accessed August 4, 2017.

Bontinck, G., Cumps, B., Viaene, S., Bille, W., & Vanden Brande, J. (2016) From enterprise architect to opportunity architect. https://doi.org/10.13140/rg.2.1.1293.0967.

Bredemeyer, D., & Malan, R. (2004). *What it takes to be a great enterprise architect.* Cutter Consortium Enterprise Architecture Report, 1–21.

CAEAP. (2012). *Enterprise architecture: A professional practice guide*. Center for the Advancement of the Enterprise Architecture Profession.

Chuang, C. H., & van Loggerenberg, J. (eds) (2010) *Challenges facing enterprise architects: A south African perspective*. IEEE. https://doi.org/10.1109/hicss.2010.449.
Dreischmeier, R., Close, K., & Trichet, P. (2015) *The digital imperative*. https://www.bcgperspectives.com/content/articles/digital_economy_technology_strategy_digital_imperative/. Accessed August 14, 2017.
Evernden, R. (2015). The architect role—what kind of architect are you? *Journal of Enterprise Architecture, 11*, 28–30. https://doi.org/10.1386/jsca.5.3.217_1.
Flick, U., Evv, Kardorff, & Steinke, I. (Eds.). (2017). *Qualitative forschung: Ein Handbuch* (12th ed.). Reinbek bei Hamburg: Rowohlt Taschenbuch Verlag.
Florentine, S. (2017). *Why you need an enterprise architect*. http://www.cio.com/article/3197390/enterprise-architecture/why-you-need-an-enterprise-architect.html. Accessed July 9, 2017.
Friedrich, R., Le Merle, M., Peterson, M., & Koster, A. (2011) *The next wave of digitization—Setting your direction, building your capabilities*. https://www.strategyand.pwc.com/media/uploads/Strategyand-Next-Wave-of-Digitization.pdf. Accessed August 14, 2017.
Gøtze, J. (2013). The changing role of the enterprise architect. In J. Gøtze (ed) *The changing role of the enterprise architect* (pp. 319–326). IEEE.
Gray, G. (2014). Chief enterprise architect as transformational and transactional leader. *Journal of Enterprise Architecture, 10*, 28–35.
Helfferich, C. (2011). Die Qualität qualitativer Daten: Manual für die Durchführung qualitativer Interviews, 4. Auflage. VS Verlag für Sozialwissenschaften/Springer Fachmedien Wiesbaden GmbH Wiesbaden, Wiesbaden.
Henderson, J. C., & Venkatraman, H. (1993). Strategic alignment: Leveraging information technology for transforming organizations. *IBM Systems Journal, 32*, 472–484. https://doi.org/10.1147/sj.382.0472.
Jonkers, H., Lankhorst, M. M., ter Doest, H. W. L., Arbab, F., Bosma, H., & Wieringa, R. J. (2006). Enterprise architecture: Management tool and blueprint for the organization. *Information Systems Frontiers, 8*, 63–66. https://doi.org/10.1007/s10796-006-7970-2.
Kreutzer, R., & Land, K.-H. (2015). *Digital darwinism*. Berlin Heidelberg, Berlin, Heidelberg: Springer.
Kuckartz, U. (2014). Qualitative Inhaltsanalyse: Methoden, Praxis, Computerunter-stützung (2., durchgesehene Auflage). Grundlagentexte Methoden. Weinheim, Basel: Beltz Juventa.
Levine, A. (2014). The Architect as a salesman within the enterprise. *Journal of Enterprise Architecture, 10*, 36–41.
Levy, Y., & Ellis, T. J. (2006) A Systems approach to conduct an effective literature review in support of information systems research. *Informing Science Journal*, 181–212.
Manwani, S., & Bossert, O. (2016). The challenges and responses for enterprise architects in the digital age. *Journal of Enterprise Architecture, 12*, 6–9.
Mayring, P. (2014). *Qualitative content analysis: Theoretical foundation, basic procedures and software solution*. Klagenfurt: Open Access Repository.
McClure, M. (2007). *Framing a Collaborative Enterprise Architecture Governance Program within the Context of Service-Oriented Software Systems Development*. https://scholarsbank.uoregon.edu/xmlui/.../2007-mcclure.pdf. Accessed July 31, 2017.
Nsubuga, W. M., Magoulas, T., & Pessi, K. (Eds.). (2014). *Understanding the roles of enterprise architects in a proactive enterprise development context*.
Opt' Land, M., Proper, E., Waage, M., Cloo, J., & Steghuis, C. (2009). *Enterprise architecture*. Berlin Heidelberg, Berlin, Heidelberg: Springer.
Pütter, C. (2016). Wie der CIO den Enterprise Architect unterstützen muss. Retrieved from https://www.cio.de/a/wie-der-cio-den-enterprise-architect-unterstuetzen-muss,3260697, Accessed July 25, 2017.
Roeleven, S. (2010). *Why two thirds of enterprise architecture projects fail: An explanation for the limited success of architecture projects*. https://www.cio.com.au/whitepaper/370709/why-two-thirds-of-enterprise-architecture-projects-fail/download/. Accessed August 1, 2017.

Saint-Louis, P., & Lapalme, J. (2016). Investigation of the lack of common understanding in the discipline of enterprise architecture: A systematic mapping study. In *2016 IEEE 20th International Enterprise Distributed Object Computing Workshop (EDOCW)* (pp. 1–9). IEEE.

Scheibenreif (2016) *Top business and sociocultural macro trends enterprise architects need to follow now*. https://www.gartner.com/binaries/content/assets/events/keywords/enterprise-architecture/ea19/top-business-and-sociocultural-macro-trends-enterprise-architects-need-to-follow-now.pdf, Accessed July 20, 2017.

Steghuis, C., & Proper, E. (2008). Competencies and responsibilities of enterprise architects. In W. van der Aalst, J. Mylopoulos, N. M. Sadeh, M. J. Shaw, C. Szyperski, J. L. G. Dietz, A. Albani, & J. Barjis (Eds.), *Advances in enterprise engineering I* (Vol. 10, pp. 93–107). Berlin, Heidelberg: Springer.

Strano, C., & Rehmani, Q. (2007). The role of the enterprise architect. *Information Systems and e-Business Management: ISeB, 5*, 379–396. https://doi.org/10.1007/s10257-007-0053-1.

The Open Group. (2011). *TOGAF® 9.1 > Part VII: Architecture capability framework > architecture skills framework*. http://pubs.opengroup.org/architecture/togaf9-doc/arch/chap52.html. Accessed July 21, 2017.

Uludag, Ö., Kleehaus, M., Xu, X., & Matthes, F. (eds). (2017). *Investigating the role of architects in scaled agile frameworks*.

Walker, M. (2007). *A day in the life of an Enterprise Architect*. https://msdn.microsoft.com/en-us/library/bb945098.aspx. Accessed July 9, 2017.

Webster, J., & Watson, R. T. (2002). *Analyzing the past to prepare for the future: Writing a literature review*. MIS Quarterly, 13–23.

Witzel, A. (2000). The Problem-centered interview. *Forum Qualitative Sozialforschung/Forum: Qualitative Social Research, 1*(1). In *Qualitative research: National, disciplinary, methodical and empirical examples*. http://dx.doi.org/10.17169/fqs-1.1.1132.

A Hierarchical Analysis of Internet Adoption and Usage by the Seniors

Elias Gounopoulos, Ioannis Kazanidis, Stavros Valsamidis and Sotirios Kontogiannis

Abstract The seniors are a large socially vulnerable population group in Greece, and the Internet can help them improve their quality of life. However, they do not take advantage of the technology and prefer to stay offline. Our study examined Internet adoption, usage and the digital skills of seniors in Greece. We analysed the micro-data of the annual national survey on the use of ICT by Greek households for the year 2015. We conducted hierarchical regressions to assess in three stages the influence of the socioeconomic factors to: (a) the decision of the seniors to access and use the Internet, (b) the extent and frequency of Internet use and (c) seniors' digital skills. According to the results, social inequalities are important determinants of seniors' decision to access and use the Internet. The seniors' educational level and gender are very important factors leading to an accumulated advantage, since older men and well-educated seniors use more extensively the Internet and are more digitally skilled. This work emphasizes the need not to treat the elderly as a single group. The Greek state should implement smart policies to address the seniors' digital divide, highlighting the benefits and promoting the technology with training seminars.

Keywords Digital divide · Internet use · Digital skills · Seniors

---

E. Gounopoulos (✉)
Department of Business Administration, University of Western Macedonia, Grevena, Greece
e-mail: egounopoulos@uowm.gr

I. Kazanidis · S. Valsamidis
Department of Accounting and Information Systems, International Hellenic University, Kavala, Greece
e-mail: kazanidis@teiemt.gr

S. Valsamidis
e-mail: svalsam@teiemt.gr

S. Kontogiannis
Department of Mathematics, University of Ioannina, Ioannina, Greece
e-mail: skontog@cc.uoi.gr

M. Janowicz-Lomott et al. (eds.), *Economic and Financial Challenges for Balkan and Eastern European Countries*, Springer Proceedings in Business and Economics,
https://doi.org/10.1007/978-3-030-39927-6_17

1 Introduction

The seniors (aged 65 + years old) or elderly, are a big population group and are considered being socially vulnerable, since most of them are low-educated and do not work, while many of them may face social isolation and health problems.

Using new technologies and the Internet may be very useful for seniors and ensure independent living. It may reduce social isolation (Sum et al. 2008) and provide new opportunities, services and valuable information about health issues (Chaffin and Maddux 2007). The importance of the use of the Information and Communication Technologies (ICTs) from the seniors is substantiated by the emergence of a new scientific discipline which is called gerotechnology. This new field combines gerontology and technology and refers to technology that may fulfil the most important needs of an aging society such as good health, full social participation and independent living based on scientific knowledge about the aging process (Harrington and Harrington 2000).

However, the elderly have a negative attitude toward the use of new technologies and the Internet (Reisdorf et al. 2012) and tend to use it less, compared to young people. They prefer not to use the Internet for many reasons, such as lack of interest or need, lack of skills (Reisdorf 2011) and lack of knowledge (Zickuhr 2013). This variation may represent seniors' several disadvantages at various levels (Helsper and Reisdorf 2013).

According to the Greek national statistics (Hellenic Statistics Authority 2012), the seniors are a very large population group (19.5%) in Greece. The research of Dyken and Kaklamani (2013) showed that despite the inflow of foreigners, this figure is expected to increase further in the next years both in rural and in urban areas. This conclusion is in accordance with other estimations (Global AgeWatch 2016), which predict that in 2030 almost one in three Greeks will be over 60 years old. Moreover, the seniors in Greece have a low quality of life, mainly because of the prolonged economic crisis. According to the Global AgeWatch Index which evaluates the quality of life for older people (Global AgeWatch 2016), Greece is ranked 79th out of 96 countries for the year 2016 and is the lowest-ranked country in Western Europe.

However, Greek seniors do not make use of technology to enhance their quality of life. Age is one of the most important predictors for staying offline in Greece (Gounopoulos et al. 2018). During the year 2014, only 12% of older people (65–74 years) used the Internet at least once a week, compared to 38% of the older people in other European countries (EU28) (Eurostat 2015). They used it less extensively compared to the Greek Internet users and older people in other European countries (Eurostat 2015).

The aim of this paper is to assess hierarchically on three levels the influence of the socioeconomic and geographic level factors to Internet adoption, usage and the digital skills of the seniors in Greece. We conducted hierarchical logistic and linear regressions to the micro-data of the nationwide survey (Use of the ICT's from the Greek households and individuals), which was held by the Hellenic Statistical

Authority for the year 2015. Research results may help the Greek State to design more effective and diversified policy actions in order to help the elderly access and use the Internet.

2 Seniors and New Technologies

By not exploiting effectively the technology, the elderly are not only digitally but also socially excluded. According to many scholars (Norris 2001), this digital exclusion or digital divide is a dynamic, complex and multidimensional phenomenon, which needs to be explored in terms of access and usage in a micro (individuals), meso (social environment) and macro (geographic areas) level (König et al. 2018).

In the micro-level, the perception and the attitude of the elderly about Internet use may be related to their socioeconomic status (Dutton et al. 2013). Various socioeconomic factors such as age, educational level, gender (Helsper and Reisdorf 2013), income and occupation (Lelkes 2013) are related to their decision to use the Internet. The elderly face difficulties in the adoption of new technologies because of: (a) age and education-related factors such as cognitive ability, memory, health and (b) physical barriers (Carpenter and Buday 2007), such as the hand–eye coordination. According to Smith (2014), memory is a predictor of digital skills in video and mobile phone interfaces. In addition, older seniors show low levels of interest, low control and confidence and higher technology anxiety (Jung et al. 2010). The educational level is considered a valid predictor of Internet adoption and use (Reisdorf 2011; Gounopoulos et al. 2018). In particular, the elderly's negative attitude may be because of their inadequate education and information. Based on a national survey in Switzerland ($n = 1105$), Friemel (2016) found that the elderly consider as the most important obstacles the complexity of Internet use and the great effort at the beginning. As a result, the elderly saw no clear benefit from using the Internet. Language may also be an important barrier for them, since most seniors speak only Greek and may face more difficulties getting online (Troulos et al. 2012). The gender is also considered an important factor, since there are distinct differences on the use of the Internet between men and women. Older women are more likely to have Internet access in their homes without using it (Van Deursen and Helsper 2015). This differentiation may be because of their previous work experience, since women are less preferred in technology-related professions. Although there may be no significant differences between women and men, women tend to underestimate their Internet skills (Van Deursen and Van Dijk 2010). The income is associated with the ability to afford telecommunication costs and equipment, although some researchers (Eastman and Lyer 2004) argue that the cost is not an important factor. However, the elderly's occupation which is closely associated with their income, is also related to their experience using the Internet at work.

On the meso level, the composition of the household and the social environment may act as a motivational factor to use the Internet (Schreuers et al. 2017). If their social network comprises technology literate adults, it may be a good support system providing them with help and affecting their attitude and self-efficacy (Gatto and Tak 2008). The elderly can get help from their wider social environment in many ways such as encouragement, motivation to use support from other sources, make the Internet more attractive to learn, and provide them with second-hand access (Friemel 2016). The elderly may have a strong incentive to use the Internet and get help from other people, if their social network comprises young people, grandchildren and friends (Gatto and Tak 2008). According to interviews with older adults which was held in Canada (Schreuers et al. 2017), the seniors prefer to turn to their children, grandchildren, spouse and friends to help them learn how to use technology. However, sometimes the social environment may prevent seniors from using the Internet. This happens when their tech-savvy relatives or friends act as proxy users and use it on behalf of them (Dutton et al. 2013).

On the macro level, rural areas of residence have a poor ICT infrastructure and are thinly populated. This may even be observed in developed countries with a high Internet rate, such as Germany (Doh et al. 2015).

We have formed five research questions to assess hierarchically the influence of the micro (individuals), meso (social environment) and macro (geographic areas) level factors to Internet access, Internet use and the seniors' digital skills.

The first research question (RQ1) examined the most important factors related to Internet home access, which is important but not a necessary condition for using the Internet. The second research question (RQ2) examined the main factors related to Internet use. The third research question (RQ3) examined the most important factors which may influence the decision of older people who have access to the Internet from their home not to use it. In order to assess Internet use by the elderly, we have examined the most important factors related to the frequency and the extent of use (RQ4). The extent of use refers to the diversity of Internet use. The greater the extent of use, the more opportunities and benefits may emerge for Internet users (Wei 2012). Finally, we have examined the most important factors associated with the digital skills of the elderly (RQ5).

The five research questions are as follows:

RQ1. Which are the most important micro, meso and macro factors which may affect the decision of the older people to have access to the Internet from their home?
RQ2. Which are the most important micro, meso and macro factors affecting the decision of the elderly to use the Internet?
RQ3. Which are the micro, meso and macro factors related to the decision of the elderly not to use the Internet, although they have access from their home?
RQ4. Which are the micro, meso and macro factors related to the frequency and extent of Internet use by the elderly?
RQ5. Which are the micro, meso and macro factors related to the digital skills of the elderly?

3 Methodology

3.1 Data

We conducted hierarchical multiple regressions using the micro-data of the nation-wide survey for the year 2015, which aims to investigate the use of ICTs by Greek households.

Our research examined the most important micro, meso and macro factors affecting the adoption and usage of the Internet by the seniors in Greece (Table 1).

The primary sampling unit of the Hellenic Statistical Authority Survey was one or more building blocks, the secondary unit was the household, and the final unit was a randomly selected individual aged 16–74 years. In total, 4667 persons participated in the survey, of which 973 were 65–74 years old (Hellenic Statistics Authority 2016). The majority of older people (844 people) did not use the Internet during the last three months.

3.2 Variables

The binary-dependent variable examining the access to the Internet from home (RQ1) was based on the question: Do you or anyone in your household have access to the Internet at home? (1: yes, 0: no). The binary variable examining Internet use (RQ2) was based on the question: When did you last use the Internet? (1: during the last three months, 0: more than three months or never used it). The binary-dependent variable examining Internet nonuse from people living in households with Internet access (RQ3) was based on the answers of the two previous questions. The binary-dependent variable examining the frequency of Internet use (RQ4) was based on the question: How often on average did you use the Internet in the last 3 months? (1: every day or almost every day, 0: at least once a week (but not every day) or less than a week).

The extent of Internet use (RQ4) was estimated out of a list of 12 activities, by the number of Internet activities carried out by individuals who have used the Internet in the last three months. It is based on the diversification index estimated by Eurostat (European Commission 2016). In order to evaluate the Internet skills of the elderly (RQ5), we used a binary-dependent variable (1: individuals with above basic or basic skills, 0: individuals with low skills level or no skills). The estimation of the elderly's digital skills was based on the European Commission's DigComp framework (2013), which evaluates digital skills in different areas (information, communication, content creation, security and problem solving).

The independent variables of our analysis are continuous (age), dichotomous (gender, the number of household members, household composition), nominal (employment status, the region of residence (Code NUTS 1)) and ordinal (household income, educational level, degree of urbanisation).

Table 1 Demographic characteristics of people aged 65–74

Factors	*N*	Percentage
Micro factors		
Age (65–74 years old)	973	100
Gender		
Man	388	39.9
Woman	585	60.1
Household income		
Lowest quartile	275	28.2
Second lowest quartile	504	51.8
Second highest quartile	167	17.2
Highest quartile	27	2.8
Educational level		
Primary education (ISCEDD 0, 1 or 2)	713	73.3
Upper secondary and post-secondary non-tertiary education (ISCEDD 3 or 4)	155	15.9
Tertiary education (ISCEDD 5, 6, 7 or 8)	105	10.8
Employment status		
Employee or self-employed	21	2.2
Domestic tasks	153	15.7
In retirement or early retirement or given up business	782	80.4
Other inactive person	17	1.7
Meso Factors		
Number of household members		
One member	204	21.0
At least two members	769	79.0
Household composition		
Household without any children	950	97.6
Household with at least one child	23	2.4
Macro factors		
Region of residence (code NUTS 1)		
Attiki (Attica)	346	35.6
Nisoi Aigaiou, Kriti (Aegean Islands and Crete)	88	9.0
Voreia Hellas (Northern Greece)	278	28.6
Kentriki Hellas (Central Greece)	261	26.8
Degree of urbanization		
Urban area	267	
Semi-urban area	573	58.9
Rural area	133	13.7

Data Source Authors calculations based on the Hellenic Statistical Authority Survey on the use of ICTs from the Greek households, 2015. Base: Individuals aged 65–74 years old, ($n = 973$)

3.3 Data Analysis

We carried out hierarchical logistic and linear regressions to the micro-data of the Hellenic Statistical Authority Survey, on the use of Information and Communication Technologies by households and individuals, for the year 2015.

Hierarchical regression is a statistical method that explores in stages the relationships of a dependent and many grouped independent variables. This method helps us evaluate the contribution (i.e., total variation accounted or R^2) of a group of independent variables to the regression model. In order to separately assess the contribution of the three groups (micro, meso and macro level factors), the corresponding variables were entered into the hierarchical regression at three stages. We entered the micro factors at the first stage. The meso factors were entered at stage two and the macro factors at stage three.

We present the results with the use of odds' ratios, except the results of the extent of Internet use in RQ4, where we use linear regression to estimate the influence of the factors related to the extent of Internet use by the elderly. If an odds ratio is greater than 1.0, it represents an increased chance relative to the reference group (Montagnier and Wirthmann 2011).

We analysed the data using the SPSS statistical analysis software (version 21).

4 Results

According to the results of the first research question (RQ1) (Table 2), older people with a low income and low educational level who are living alone with no children in the household and those living in rural areas are more likely not to have Internet access at home. The micro factors are the most important, while the meso and macro factors have a rather minor influence.

Older people with a low educational level who are not working (i.e., those who are in retirement, inactive or do domestic tasks) (Table 3) are more likely not to use the Internet at home. The meso and macro factors have no effect on the decision of the elderly not to use the Internet (RQ2).

Most of the older people who live in households with Internet access do not use it ($n = 262$). These people are more likely to have a lower educational level, be professionally inactive or to deal with domestic tasks, and not to live alone (Table 4). The micro factors are important, while the meso factors have a rather small influence (RQ3).

Table 2 Odds' ratios of logistic regressions for having Internet access at home

Factors	b	Exp (B)
Micro factors		
Age (65–74 years old)	−0.108***	0.898
Gender (reference woman)		
Man	0.326	1.385
Household income (reference lowest quartile)		
Second lowest quartile	0.407	1.502
Second highest quartile	0.815**	2.260
Highest quartile	1.367*	3.924
Educational level (reference: primary education)		
Upper secondary and post-secondary non-tertiary education (ISCEDD 3 or 4)	0.852***	2.344
Tertiary education (ISCEDD 5, 6, 7 or 8)	1.664***	5.279
Employment status (reference: employee or self-employed)		
Domestic tasks	−1.028	0.358
In retirement or early retirement or given up business	−0.596	0.551
Other inactive person	0.421	1.524
Meso factors		
Number of household members—reference: one member		
At least two members	0.556**	1.743
Household composition—reference: household without any children		
Household with at least one child	2.146***	8.550
Macro factors		
Region of residence—reference: Kentriki Hellas (Central Greece)		
Attiki (Attica)	0.338	1.403
Nisoi Aigaiou. Kriti (Aegean Islands and Crete)	0.228	1.255
Voreia Hellas (Northern Greece)	0.122	1.129
Degree of urbanization—reference: rural area		
Urban area	0.491*	1.633
Semi-urban area	0.170	1.186
Constant	5.109**	165.45

	Stage 1: micro factors	Stage 2: meso factors	Stage 3: macro factors
R^2	0.241	0.269	0.283
ΔR^2	–	0.028	0.014

Data Source Authors calculations based on Hellenic Statistical Authority Survey on the use of ICTs from the Greek households, 2015. Base: 65–74 years old people ($n = 973$)
Significance levels: $^{*}p < 0.05$; $^{**}p < 0.01$; $^{***}p < 0.001$

Table 3 Odds' ratios of logistic regressions, for using the Internet at home

Factors	b	Exp (B)
Micro factors		
Age (65–74 years old)	-0.092^{*}	0.912
Gender (reference woman)		
Man	0.196	1.216
Household income (reference: lowest quartile)		
Second lowest quartile	0.307	1.360
Second highest quartile	0.531	1.701
Highest quartile	0.717	2.049
Educational level (reference: primary education)		
Upper secondary and post-secondary non-tertiary education (ISCEDD 3 or 4)	1.684^{***}	5.384
Tertiary education (ISCEDD 5, 6, 7 or 8)	2.319^{***}	10.165
Employment status (reference: employee or self-employed)		
Domestic tasks	-2.266^{**}	0.104
In retirement or early retirement or given up business	-1.544^{**}	0.213
Other inactive person	-2.523^{*}	0.080
Meso factors		
Number of household members—reference: one member		
At least two members	−0.055	0.946
Household composition—reference: household without any children		
Household with at least one child	−0.041	0.960
Macro factors		
Region of residence—reference: Kentriki Hellas (Central Greece)		
Attiki (Attica)	0.506	1.659
Nisoi Aigaiou. Kriti (Aegean Islands and Crete)	0.559	1.748
Voreia Hellas (Northern Greece)	−0.053	0.948
Degree of urbanization—reference: rural area		
Urban area	0.152	1.164
Semi-urban area	−0.042	0.958
Constant	4.472	87.488

	Stage 1: micro factors	Stage 2: meso factors	Stage 3: macro factors
R^2	0.295	0.296	0.307
ΔR^2	–	0.01	0.011

Data Source Authors calculations based on Hellenic Statistical Authority Survey on the use of ICTs from the Greek households, 2015. Base: 65–74 years old people ($n = 973$)
Significance levels: $^{*}p < 0.05$; $^{**}p < 0.01$; $^{***}p < 0.001$

Table 4 Odds' ratios of logistic regressions for having Internet access at home and using the Internet within the last three months

Factors	b	Exp (B)
Micro factors		
Age (65–74 years old)	−0.006	0.994
Gender (reference woman)		
Man	0.112	1.118
Household income (reference lowest quartile)		
Second lowest quartile	0.504	1.655
Second highest quartile	0.488	1.630
Highest quartile	0.611	1.842
Educational level (reference: primary education)		
Upper secondary and post-secondary non-tertiary education (ISCEDD 3 or 4)	1.812^{***}	6.121
Tertiary education (ISCEDD 5, 6, 7 or 8)	1.866^{***}	6.645
Employment status (reference: employee or self-employed)		
Domestic tasks	-2.888^{*}	0.056
In retirement or early retirement or given up business	−2.107	8.227
Other inactive person	-3.871^{*}	0.021
Meso factors		
Number of household members—reference: at least two members		
One member	1.360^{**}	3.896
Household composition—reference: household without any children		
Household with at least one child	1.160	3.191
Macro factors		
Region of residence—reference: Kentriki Hellas (Central Greece)		
Attiki (Attica)	−0.504	0.604
Nisoi Aigaiou. Kriti (Aegean Islands and Crete)	−0.808	0.446
Voreia Hellas (Northern Greece)	−0.121	0.886
Degree of urbanization—reference: rural area		
Urban area	0.141	1.152
Semi-urban area	0.322	1.380
Constant	−2.966	0.052

	Stage 1: micro factors	Stage 2: meso factors	Stage 3: macro factors
R^2	0.286	0.329	0.341
ΔR^2	–	0.043	0.013

Data Source Authors calculations based on Hellenic Statistical Authority Survey on the use of ICTs from the Greek households, 2015. Base: 65–74 years old people with Internet access at home ($n = 262$)

Significance levels: $^{*}p < 0.05$; $^{**}p < 0.01$; $^{***}p < 0.001$

The elderly who use the Internet are a rather small group (13.2% of the total sample). Those who use it frequently (RQ4) (i.e., every day or almost every day) are more likely to be women, lower-educated and living in Central Greece (Table 5). The micro and macro factors are important, while the meso factors have no influence.

Men and higher-educated seniors use more extensively the Internet (Table 6). We found no statistically significant difference between people living in various geographical areas or areas with different urbanisation (RQ4).

According to the results of the fifth research question (RQ5), the seniors who are more digitally skilled are more likely to be men, have a high educational level and live at the Aegean Islands and Crete (Table 7). The micro factors are important while the macro factors have a sufficient influence.

5 Discussion

According to the results, socioeconomic inequalities may be an important reason for the decision of the elderly not to access and use the Internet.

Age is an important determinant, since older seniors do not access and use the Internet. Similar to other countries (Peacock and Künemund 2007), the senior's age may affect negatively their decision to use the Internet and their attitude toward new technologies (Czaja and Lee 2007). Greeks adopt a negative attitude toward the Internet, because they think the Internet is a medium that requires new skills and may bring changes to their lifestyle (Tsatsou 2011).

The educational level is a very important determinant not only for the Internet adoption and use by the elderly, but also for their digital skills level leading to a Matthew effect of increased advantage. The well-educated seniors are more skilled and use the Internet more extensively, while the lower-educated seniors do not use it even when they have access at their home. Moreover, the elderly in Greece as in other European countries have higher illiteracy and lower educational attainment, compared to younger age groups (Kinsella and Taeuber 1993).

The household income is a factor which affects only their decision to access the Internet, but it is not an important factor since there is no influence in their decision to use the Internet. We therefore assume that the elderly who have Internet access at home may afford the necessary equipment and telecommunication costs.

There is no difference between elderly men and women in their decision to access and use the Internet. However, there are differences in the way they use it. Women use it more frequently, while men use it more extensively and are more digitally skilled. We assume that most of the older women are engaged in housework and have no experience with ICTs, while most of the men were working and are more acquainted with the Internet. Seniors who are still working are more experienced and confident with computers and may easily integrate the use of the Internet into their daily lives.

According to the results, the immediate social environment of the seniors (living with other people and children) may have a small positive influence on their decision to access the Internet from their household. However in the survey, almost one in

Table 5 Odds' ratios of logistic regressions for the frequent use of the Internet

Factors	b	Exp (B)
Micro factors		
Age (65–74 years old)	−0.001	0.999
Gender (reference man)		
Woman	1.533*	4.663
Household income (reference lowest quartile)		
Second lowest quartile	0.395	1.485
Second highest quartile	0.371	1.450
Highest quartile	2.106	8.218
Educational level (reference: primary education)		
Upper secondary and post-secondary non-tertiary education (ISCEDD 3 or 4)	0.202	1.224
Tertiary education (ISCEDD 5, 6, 7 or 8)	−2.020*	0.133
Employment status (reference: employee or self-employed)		
Domestic tasks	−0.031	0.969
In retirement or early retirement or given up business	−0.273	0.761
Other inactive person	−22.135	0.000
Meso factors		
Number of household members—reference: at least two members		
One member	0.160	1.173
Household composition—reference: household without any children		
Household with at least one child	−2.157	0.116
Macro factors		
Region of residence—reference: Kentriki Hellas (Central Greece)		
Attiki (Attica)	−1.385	0.250
Nisoi Aigaiou. Kriti (Aegean Islands and Crete)	−2.157*	0.116
Voreia Hellas (Northern Greece)	−1.353	0.258
Degree of urbanization—reference: rural area		
Urban area	−0.999	0.368
Semi-urban area	0.914	2.495
Constant	−1.533	0.216

	Stage 1: micro factors	Stage 2: meso factors	Stage 3: macro factors
R^2	0.240	0.248	0.363
ΔR^2	–	0.08	0.115

Data Source Authors calculations based on Hellenic Statistical Authority Survey on the use of ICTs from the Greek households, 2015. Base: 65–74 years old people who are using the Internet during the last three months ($n = 129$)
Significance levels: $^{*}p < 0.05$; $^{**}p < 0.01$; $^{***}p < 0.001$

Table 6 Linear regression standardized coefficients for the extent of Internet use

Factors	β	t
Micro factors		
Age (65–74 years old)	−0.010	−0.115
Gender (reference man)		
Woman	−0.219*	−2.279
Household income (reference lowest quartile)		
Second lowest quartile	0.046	0.346
Second highest quartile	0.137	0.951
Highest quartile	0.121	1.002
Educational level (reference: primary education)		
Upper secondary and post-secondary non-tertiary education (ISCEDD 3 or 4)	0.163	1.454
Tertiary education (ISCEDD 5, 6, 7 or 8)	0.322*	2.553
Employment status (reference: employee or self-employed)		
Domestic tasks	0.310	0.262
In retirement or early retirement or given up business	−0.110	−0.096
Other inactive person	−0.840	−0.908
Meso factors		
Number of household members—reference: at least two members		
One member	0.125	1.373
Household composition—reference: household without any children		
Household with at least one child	0.111	1.295
Macro factors		
Region of residence—reference: Kentriki Hellas (Central Greece)		
Attiki (Attica)	0.376	−2.663
Nisoi Aigaiou. Kriti (Aegean Islands and Crete)	0.156	1.549
Voreia Hellas (Northern Greece)	0.239	2.008
Degree of urbanization—reference: rural area		
Urban area	−0.386	−2.881
Semi-urban area	−0.083	−0.728
Constant	17.672	0.914

	Stage 1: micro factors	Stage 2: meso factors	Stage 3: macro factors
R^2	0.154	0.184	0.269
ΔR^2	–	0.030	0.085

Data Source Authors calculations based on Hellenic Statistical Authority Survey on the use of ICTs from the Greek households, 2015. Base: 65–74 years old people who are using the Internet during the last three months ($n = 129$)
Significance levels: $^{*}p < 0.05$; $^{**}p < 0.01$; $^{***}p < 0.001$

Table 7 Odds' ratios of logistic regressions for the digital skills of people 65–74 years old

Factors	b	Exp (B)
Micro factors		
Age (65–74 years old)	0.061	1.063
Gender (reference woman)		
Man	1.968**	7.153
Household income (reference lowest quartile)		
Second lowest quartile	0.211	1.235
Second highest quartile	0.460	1.584
Highest quartile	1.732	5.652
Educational level (reference: primary education)		
Upper secondary and post-secondary non-tertiary education (ISCEDD 3 or 4)	3.895*	49.163
Tertiary education (ISCEDD 5, 6, 7 or 8)	4.856**	128.530
Employment status (reference: employee or self-employed)		
Domestic tasks	1.684	5.388
In retirement or early retirement or given up business	0.104	1.110
Other inactive person	−21.069	0.000
Meso factors		
Number of household members—reference: at least two members		
One member	−0.405	0.667
Household composition—reference: household without any children		
Household with at least one child	1.908	6.738
Macro factors		
Region of residence—reference: Kentriki Hellas (Central Greece)		
Attiki (Attica)	1.068	2.908
Nisoi Aigaiou, Kriti (Aegean Islands and Crete)	2.430*	11.359
Voreia Hellas (Northern Greece)	−0.983	0.374
Degree of urbanization—reference: rural area		
Urban area	1.955	7.066
Semi-urban area	0.528	1.696
Constant	−9.943	0.000

	Stage 1: micro factors	Stage 2: meso factors	Stage 3: macro factors
R^2	0.367	0.387	0.494
ΔR^2	–	0.020	0.107

Data Source Authors calculations based on Hellenic Statistical Authority Survey on the use of ICTs from the Greek households, 2015. Base: 65–74 years old people who are using the Internet during the last three months ($n = 129$)

Significance level: $^{*}p < 0.05$; $^{**}p < 0.01$; $^{***}p < 0.001$

two seniors who had access to the Internet at home did not use it. These people were not socially isolated, since most of them (92.6%) were not living alone. We assume that this contradiction is because the elderly may prefer not to use it, because another person may act as a proxy user and help them whenever they wish to. This choice may be more convenient for them (Reisdorf et al. 2012).

However, there is no influence of the immediate social environment (meso factors) on the way seniors use the Internet and on their digital skills.

There is no significant difference in Internet use by seniors who live in various geographic areas of residence and areas with a different degree of urbanisation. However, there is a difference in Internet access. Seniors living in urban areas are more likely to access the Internet compared to seniors living in rural areas. We presume that there are other reasons for this difference such as attitude, since the vast majority of the Greek households (99.7%) have access to a digital subscriber line (DSL) (European Commission 2016).

According to the results of our study, seniors should not be considered as a homogeneous group. The political interventions should not only address the socioeconomic inequalities, but also the different skills and motivations of the older people (Reisdorf and Groselj 2014) and the geographic discrepancies. Nonuse of the Internet should not be stigmatised, but on the contrary, we should highlight the benefits for the elderly.

The Greek government should adopt a policy framework that will emphasise the perceived benefits, such as that proposed by Wang et al. (2011). They suggested policy measures aimed at increasing technology acceptance by the elderly, focusing on improving their daily lives. According to their framework (Wang et al. 2011), the government should promote the technology with the following actions: (i) training seminars and educational material, (ii) advertise the benefits of using technology, (iii) create a business model and collaborations and (iv) provide support for the users.

5.1 *Future Research*

According to the results, the adoption of the technology by the seniors may be examined as a multilevel and dynamic phenomenon which requires analysis in terms of access, usage and digital skills.

In the present study, the R^2 coefficients that estimate the percentage of total variability interpreted by the six models (Tables 1, 2, 3, 4, 5 and 6) are between 26.9% and 49.4%. This means that in a future study, we should examine more factors including attitudes and personal factors, such as health problems and experience with ICT.

A qualitative research will also help us understand more efficiently the attitudes and needs of the elderly about the Internet and the real impact of the social environment to their decision to use effectively the Internet.

References

Carpenter, B. D., & Buday, S. (2007). Computer use among older adults in a naturally occurring retirement community. *Computers in Human Behavior, 23*(6), 3012–3024.

Chaffin, A. J., & Maddux, C. D. (2007). Accessibility accommodations for older adults seeking e-health information. *Journal of Gerontological Nursing, 33*(3), 6–12.

Czaja, S. J., & Lee, C. C. (2007). The potential influence of the internet on the transition to older adulthood. *New dynamics in old age* (pp. 239–252). London: Routledge.

Doh, M., Schmidt, L. I., Herbolsheimer, F., Jokisch, M., & Wahl, H. W. (2015). Patterns of ICT use among "senior technology experts": The role of demographic variables, subjective beliefs and attitudes. In *International Conference on Human Aspects of IT for the Aged Population*, pp. 177–188, Cham: Springer.

Dutton, W. H., Blank, G. & Groselj, D. (2013). *Cultures of the Internet: the Internet in Britain.* Oxford Internet Survey 2013 report. Oxford: Oxford Internet Institute, University of Oxford.

Dyken, M., & Kaklamani S. (2013). The new historical context of population aging. *Journal of Demographic News (EDKA),* Retrieved from: https://www.gerolib.gr/index.php?option=com_k2&view=item&id=974:the-new-historical-context-of-population-aging&Itemid=290&lang=en. Accessed February 2018.

Eastman, J. K., & Lyer, R. (2004). The elderly's uses and attitudes towards the internet. *Journal of Consumer Marketing, 21*(3), 208–220.

European Commission. (2013). *JRC Scientific and Policy Reports: DIGCOMP: A Framework for Developing and Understanding Digital Competence in Europe*. Retrieved from: https://ec.europa.eu/jrc/sites/default/files/lb-na-26035-enn.pdf. Accessed February 2018.

European Commission. (2016). *Digital Agenda Scoreboard key indicators—Digital Agenda Scoreboard*, Retrieved from: https://digital-agenda-data.eu/datasets/digital_agenda_scoreboard_key_indicators/visualizations. Accessed February 2018.

Eurostat. (2015). *People in the EU: who are we and how do we live? statistical books. [online].* Retrieved from: http://ec.europa.eu/eurostat/documents/3217494/7089681/KS-04-15-567-EN-N.pdf/8b2459fe-0e4e-4bb7-bca7-7522999c3bfd. Accessed February 2018.

Friemel, T. N. (2016). The digital divide has grown old: Determinants of a digital divide among seniors. *New Media and Society, 18*(2), 313–331.

Gatto, S. L., & Tak, S. H. (2008). Computer, internet, and e-mail use among older adults: Benefits and barriers. *Educational Gerontology, 34*(9), 800–811.

Global AgeWatch. (2016). *Global AgeWatch Index 2015 Insight report*. Retrieved from https://www.ageinternational.org.uk/Documents/Global_AgeWatch_Index_2015_HelpAge.pdf. Accessed January 2018.

Gounopoulos, E., Kokkonis, G., Valsamidis, S., & Kontogiannis, S. (2018). Digital Divide in Greece-A Quantitative Examination of Internet Nonuse. In *Economy, finance and business in southeastern and central Europe* (pp. 889–903). Cham: Springer.

Harrington, T. L., & Harrington, M. K. (2000). *Gerontechnology: Why and how*. Maastricht, The Netherlands: Shaker.

Hellenic Statistics Authority. (2012). *Permanent Population by age, gender and marital status Total country, Regions*. Retrieved from: http://www.statistics.gr/statistics/-/publication/SAM03/2011. Accessed December 2017.

Hellenic Statistics Authority. (2016). *Quality Report on the Use of Information and Communication Technologies by Households, year 2015*.

Helsper, E. J., & Reisdorf, B. C. (2013). A quantitative examination of explanations for reasons for internet non use. *Cyberpsychology, Behavior, and Social Networking, 16,* 94–99.

Jung, Y., Peng, W., Moran, M., Jin, S. A. A., McLaughlin, M., Cody, M., et al. (2010). Low-income minority seniors' enrollment in a cybercafé: psychological barriers to crossing the digital divide. *Educational Gerontology, 36*(3), 193–212.

Kinsella, K., & Taeuber, C. M. (1993). An aging world II. US Bureau of the census. *International Population Reports, 195,* 92–93.

König R., Seifert A. & Doh M. (2018). Internet use among older Europeans: An analysis based on SHARE data. *Universal Access in the Information Society*, pp. 1–13.

Lelkes, O. (2013). Happier and less isolated: internet use in old age. *Journal of Poverty and Social Justice, 21*(1), 33–46.

Montagnier, P., & Wirthmann, A. (2011). *Digital Divide: from Computer Access to Online Activities-A Micro Data Analysis*, OECD Digital Economy Working Papers no. 189, OECD.

Norris, P. (2001). *Digital divide: Civic engagement, information poverty, and the Internet worldwide*. Cambridge: Cambridge University Press.

Peacock, S. E., & Künemund, H. (2007). Senior citizens and Internet technology. *European Journal of Ageing, 4*(4), 191–200.

Reisdorf, B. C. (2011). Non-adoption of the internet in Great Britain and Sweden: A cross-national comparison. *Information, Communication and Society, 14*(3), 400–420.

Reisdorf, B. C. & Groselj, D. (2014). For what it's worth: Digital inequalities, attitudes and a typology of internet (non-) users. In *Proceedings of the 2014 ACM conference on Web science* (pp. 263–264). ACM.

Reisdorf, B. C., Axelsson, A. S., & Söderholm, H. (2012). *Living Offline-A Qualitative Study of Internet Non-Use in Great Britain and Sweden*, (Selected Papers of Internet Research, 2). Available at: http://spir.aoir.org/index.php/spir/article/view/10. Accessed February 2018.

Schreuers, K., Quan-Haase, A., & Martin, K. (2017). Problematizing the digital literacy paradox in the context of older adults' ICT use: Aging, media discourse, and self-determination. *Canadian Journal of Communication, 42*(2), 45–67.

Smith, A. (2014). *Older adults and technology use*. Available at: http://www.pewinternet.org/2014/04/03/older-adults-and-technology-use/. Accessed January 2018.

Sum, S., Mathews, R. M., Hughes, I., & Campbell, A. (2008). Internet use and loneliness in older adults. *CyberPsychology and Behavior, 11*(2), 208–211.

Troulos, C., Demian, E. & Tsakanikas, A. (2012). *Making the Internet thrive in Greece: Social and Economic Barriers*. Foundation for Economic and Industrial Research (IOBE): Athens.

Tsatsou, P. (2011). Why Internet use? A quantitative examination of the role of everyday life and Internet policy and regulation. *Technology in Society, 33*(1–2), 73–83.

Van Deursen, A. J., & Helsper, E. J. (2015). A nuanced understanding of Internet use and non-use among the elderly. *European journal of communication, 30*(2), 171–187.

Van Deursen, A. J., & Van Dijk, J. A. (2010). Measuring internet skills. *International Journal of Human-Computer Interaction, 26*(10), 891–916.

Wang, A., Redington, L., Steinmetz, V., & Lindeman, D. (2011). The ADOPT model: Accelerating diffusion of proven technologies for older adults. *Ageing International, 36*(1), 29–45.

Wei, L. (2012). Number matters: The multimodality of Internet use as an indicator of the digital inequalities. *Journal of Computer-Mediated Communication, 17*(3), 303–318.

Zickuhr, K. (2013). *Who's not online and why*. Available at http://www.pewinternet.org/2013/09/25/main-report-2/Zickuhr. Accessed February 2018.

What Happened in Turkey After Booking.com Limitation: Sentiment Analysis of Tweets via Text Mining

Ekin Akkol, Serkan Alici, Can Aydin, and Cigdem Tarhan

Abstract Twitter is one of the most popular applications for sharing feelings and opinions. Sentiment analysis also known as opinion mining is basically used to classify text into three or more categories: positive, negative and neutral sentiments. In this study, sentiment analysis is tested on tweets about www.booking.com in Turkey after the court decided to stop the activities of Booking.com. Moreover, after the date that Booking.com stops its services, traffic data of other major Web sites serving in this sector has been obtained and how they are influenced by this activity is also interpreted. As a result of the literature, sentiment analysis on English texts is a highly popular and well-studied topic; however, it has been observed that the study of text mining in Turkish language is limited. The data is obtained on Twitter from starting the date that Booking.com closures in Turkey. The Twitter messages in Turkish were manually obtained from the Internet because of being expensive of old tweet data. The data has been passed through the preprocessing, attribute selection and classification stages. At the end of these processes, the data is analyzed using various text mining algorithms so the success rates achieved are compared and interpreted.

Keywords Booking.com · Sentiment analysis · Twitter · Text mining · Machine learning · Turkish tweet

1 Introduction

In the twenty-first century, social media platforms offer powerful tools that people can easily share their feelings and opinions about various topics with large crowds. Therefore, the social media usage has become an important part of daily routine in our lives (Gaál et al. 2015; Anstead and O'Loughlin 2015; Chen et al. 2011). Sentiment analysis is known as opinion mining or emotion artificial intelligence in the literature (Yang and Lin 2018; Appel et al. 2018; Öztürk and Ayvaz 2018;

E. Akkol · S. Alici · C. Aydin · C. Tarhan (✉)
Department of Management Information Systems, Dokuz Eylul University, Izmir, Turkey
e-mail: cigdem.tarhan@deu.edu.tr

M. Janowicz-Lomott et al. (eds.), *Economic and Financial Challenges for Balkan and Eastern European Countries*, Springer Proceedings in Business and Economics,
https://doi.org/10.1007/978-3-030-39927-6_18

Zheng et al. 2018; Houlihan and Creamer 2017; El-Masri et al. 2017; Geetha et al. 2017; Ma et al. 2017). It is based on the usage of natural language processing, text analysis, computational linguistics and biometrics to systematically identify, extract, quantify and study affective states and subjective information (Antonio et al. 2018; Hameed et al. 2018; Ruan et al. 2018).

Information technology (IT)-based social media data analysis has affected a company's ability to discover their social media intelligence (Lee 2018). As an example of this type of studies, sentiment analysis is performed to customers' online or written reviews and survey responses. It has a wide range area for different disciplines, especially for marketing (Abdi et al. 2018; Li 2018; Ruan et al. 2018). Sentiment analysis is classifying the polarity of a given text at the document, sentence or feature/aspect level—whether the expressed opinion in a document, a sentence or an entity feature/aspect is positive, negative or neutral (Daniel et al. 2017; Oscar et al. 2017; Nguyen and Jung 2017).

Almost 70% of adult Internet users use social media, and this percentage is increasing (Pew-Research 2018). Twitter is one of the most popular applications for sharing feelings and opinions (Mondal et al. 2017; Chappel et al. 2017; LaPoe et al. 2017; Sul et al. 2016). According to the 'Digital in 2017 Global Overview,' 48 million people use social media actively in Turkey (Digital in 2017 Global Overview 2018). Therefore, social media is an important source of data to analyze people's feelings about the events that create the country's agenda. The main reason for this is the intensive use of social media, and there is a great deal of power to spread the news about the agenda directly from social media. Figure 1 shows the social media statis-

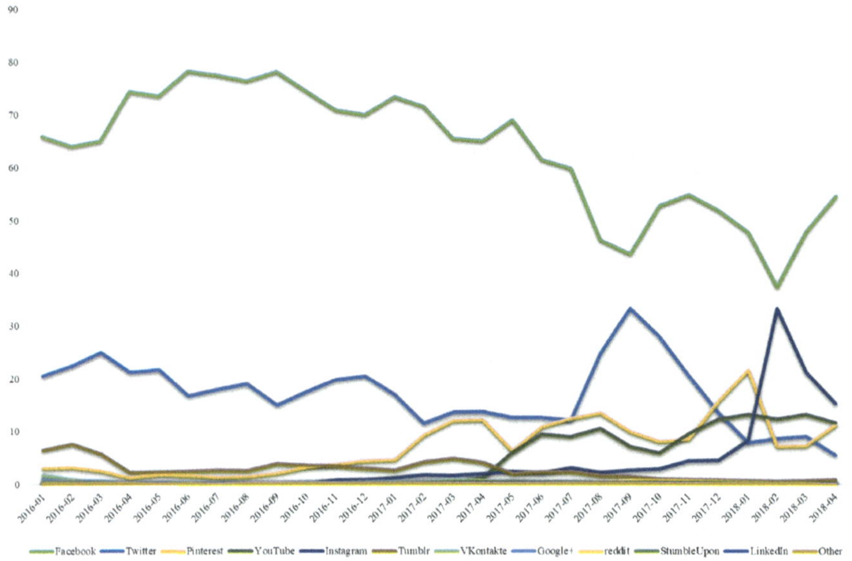

Fig. 1 Social media statistics of Turkey from January 2016 to April 2018 (StatCounter—GlobalStats 2018)

tics of Turkey from January 2016 to April 2018. According to the statistics, Twitter is the second social media platform used in Turkey with 17.67% ratio.

With the increasing popularity of the Internet, tourism facilities have become more digital with increased interconnections between customers, suppliers and firms (Zhou et al. 2014; Philips et al. 2016; Podnar and Javernik 2012; Filieri and McLeay 2013). Therefore, in order to understand why customers choose a product or a service, social media data analysis plays an important role in competitive advantage (Brooks et al. 2014). At this point, Booking.com is an example of IT-based tourism facilities. Booking.com firm was established in 1996 in Amsterdam and has grown from a small Dutch start-up to one of the largest travel e-commerce companies in the world. Now, the firm employs more than 15,000 employees in 198 offices in 70 countries worldwide. The Booking.com Web site and mobile apps are available in over 40 languages, offer 1,742,015 properties and cover 130,452 destinations in 227 countries and territories worldwide. Each day, more than 1,550,000 room nights are reserved on its platform (Booking 2018). Moreover, the firm has long-term relationship with more than 560,000 hotels worldwide, 40,000,000+ guest reviews, 750,000 rooms booked per day, # 1 most visited travel site by traffic, 100+ million visits a month and access to over 180 countries (DPO 2018).

In 2017, an Istanbul court ordered the suspension of the activities of the Web site (www.booking.com) in Turkey on March 29, citing accusations of unfair competition, following a lawsuit filed by the Association of Turkish Travel Agencies (TURSAB). At the end of the lawsuit, it has been concluded to limit www.booking.com's services for the hotel search and booking in Turkey since 2017. The Web site, which had around 13,000 hotel members from Turkey, halted selling rooms in Turkey to Turkish users on March 30, one day after the court decided to block the Web site in the country. The Web site can still be used from foreign countries to make reservations for Turkish hotels and from Turkey to make reservations abroad (Figs. 2 and 3). According to a sector player, Turkey's city hotels take around 35% of their reservations via Web

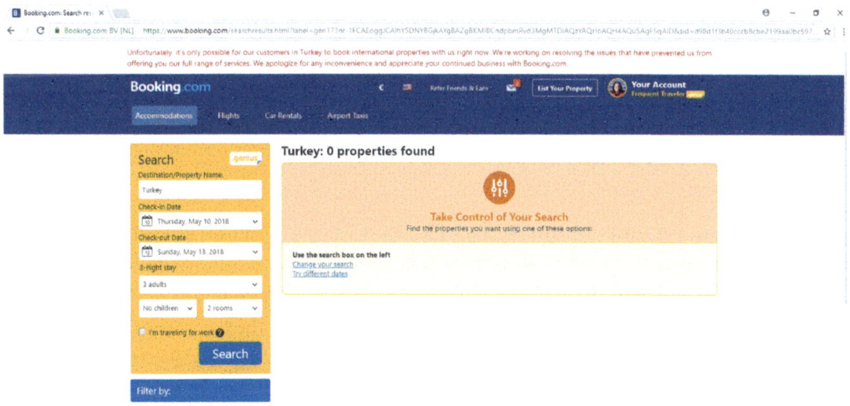

Fig. 2 Booking.com Web site homepage in Turkey

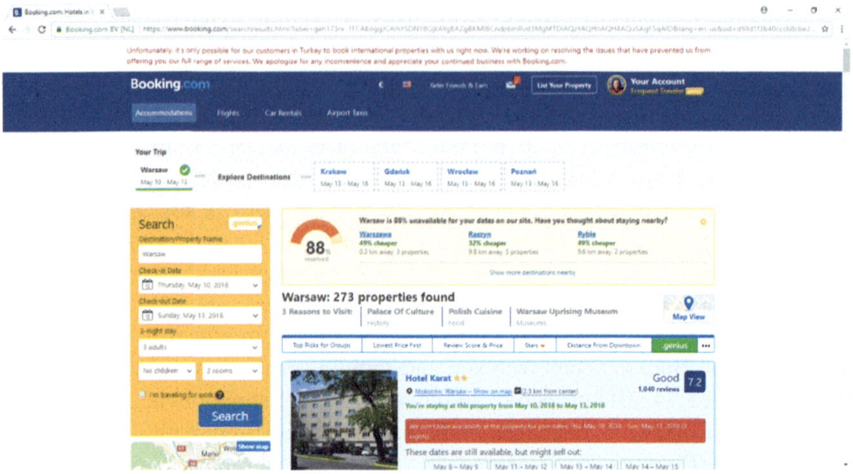

Fig. 3 Booking.com Web site search example for Warsaw

sites, with Booking.com taking a large share of this total (Independent 2018; Hotel Management 2018; Hurriyet 2018).

In this study, sentiment analysis is tested on Turkish tweets about www.booking.com in Turkey after the court decided to stop the activities of Booking.com. Moreover, after the date that Booking.com stops its services, traffic data of other major Web sites serving in this sector has been obtained and how they are influenced by this activity is also interpreted. The data is obtained on Twitter from starting the date that Booking.com closures in Turkey. The Twitter messages in Turkish were manually obtained from the Internet because of being expensive of old tweet data. The data has been passed through the preprocessing, feature selection and classification stages. At the end of these processes, the data is analyzed using various text mining algorithms so the success rates achieved are compared and interpreted.

2 Web Traffic of Online Reservation in Turkey After Booking.com Limitation

There are two main aims in this study. The first one is to determine the emotional analysis of the customers after Booking.com in Turkey; the other one is to analyze how other companies in the same sector are affected by this activity. According to Turkish media reports, up to 30% increase in sales of other companies has been observed after stopping the activities of Booking.com (Posta 2018). In order to be able to determine how other companies in the sector are affected, traffic data of the Web pages of the other companies with a high market share in Turkey was obtained from www.semrush.com Web site.

The numbers of 'unique visitors' of the pages are taken into account and interpreted. The number of unique visitors is the number of entries on the same rope over a given period of time, counted as a single entry. The data obtained before and after stopping the activities of Booking.com was analyzed. The company has ceased its activities in Turkey on March 29, 2017. Table 1 shows the traffic analytics of unique visitors between April 2016 and October 2017 (k).

Traffic data shows (Fig. 4) that the density of the Web pages of other companies has started to increase visibly from April 2017. Although this is thought to be related to the opening of the summer season and many other factors, it is observed that there is an increase in the number of unique visitors compared to the data in the summer of 2017, which appears in the graphs. Therefore, stopping the activities of Booking.com has led users to intensively refer to the sites of other holiday agencies, which has a favorable effect on other agencies. Figure 4, shown, represents the other firms' Web traffic starting from April 2016 to October 2017. According to the statistics, the firms called 'ETS Tur, Jolly Tur, Neredekal.com, Tatilbudur.com, tatilsepeti.com, Tatil.com, trivago and Anı Tur' have increased their unique visitor numbers.

3 Sentiment Analysis of Turkish Tweets via Text Mining

In this study, the data set has been generated from Twitter messages about Booking.com after stopping its activities in Turkey. The data was obtained manually, filtering from Twitter in Turkish. The reason for the manual acquisition of the data is the need for tweet in the past and in large quantities, which leads to huge costs. In the tweets obtained, the parts that are not used in the study such as user name and liking are separated and only a data set consisting of messages is created. Messages in the generated data set are grouped into three categories: positive, negative and neutral. After text preprocessing—cleaning step, the data set of the study is composed of 2000 tweets. The results show that 382 of 2000 tweets are positive, 1274 of them are negative and 344 of them are neutral opinions.

Firstly, the typing mistakes in the data set and the correction of the marking mistakes have been corrected. In addition to this step, the abbreviation is made when the tweet is thrown, and the letter repetition made to emphasize the written word is also corrected. RapidMiner software was used for further preprocessing, machine learning, classification and analysis phases. With the RapidMiner, all letters in the data set are converted to lowercase, clearing of unnecessary characters such as @ and #, clearing of punctuation marks, clearing of words with more or less than a certain number of characters, clearing of stall words that do not make sense in working according to the generated stall word dictionary, identification of roots, disintegration of data. The Snowball library, which was developed for the Turkish language, was used to determine the roots of the words. N-gram model was used for feature selection process. Then, the term frequency weighting method was applied to determine how many times a term has passed in the data set. The supervised learning technique of the machine learning method is used in the study.

Table 1 Traffic analytics: unique visitor table—April 2016–October 2017 (k)

	ETS Tur	Jolly Tur	Neredekal.com	Tatilbudur.com	tatilsepeti.com	Tatil.com	trivago.com	anitur.com.tr
April 2016	100	50	40	70	70	70	50	25
May 2016	90	40	35	50	60	60	40	20
June 2016	105	60	40	55	70	70	50	35
July 2016	100	40	38	55	60	60	55	20
August 2016	98	45	36	60	70	70	55	30
September 2016	90	30	30	50	50	50	40	20
October 2016	80	40	35	60	50	50	45	24
November 2016	90	80	180	110	90	90	200	40
December 2016	230	75	150	115	100	100	220	40
January 2017	220	110	140	120	130	130	200	70
February 2017	260	140	145	120	200	150	260	90
March 2017	300	150	140	115	130	130	240	60
April 2017	250	110	170	125	250	180	350	75
May 2017	450	180	190	280	350	300	600	120
June 2017	700	270	250	290	350	350	650	110
July 2017	650	250	260	310	330	300	700	40
August 2017	675	260	300	280	300	280	600	30
September 2017	575	240	250	170	150	150	280	20
October 2017	300	120	180	100	140	140	260	20

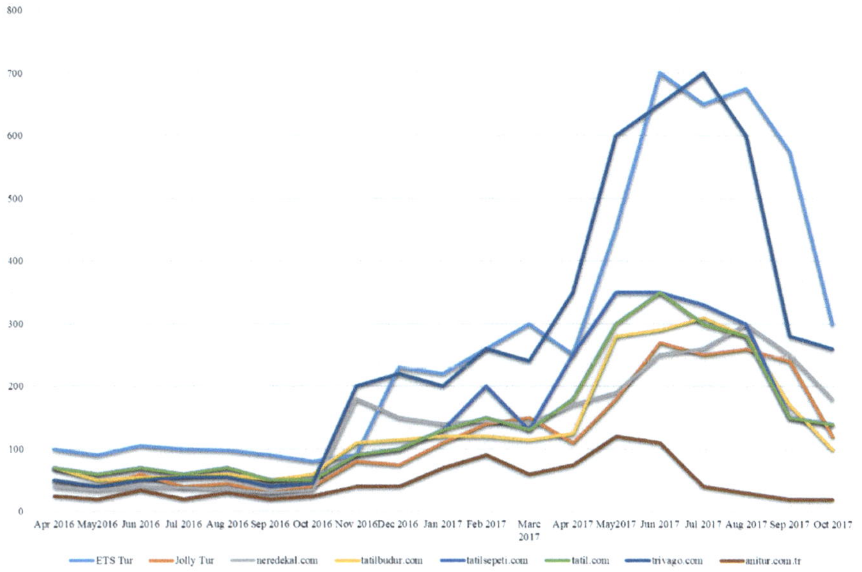

Fig. 4 Traffic analytics: unique visitor chart—April 2016–October 2017 (k)

After all these steps have been completed, experimental results have been obtained by Naive Bayes (kernel), gradient boosted tree, Naive Bayes, k-nearest neighbors (KNNs), sequential minimal optimization (SMO), random forest, decision tree (J48) algorithms. For each algorithm, training data set was selected as shuffled sampling at 0.7, 0.5 and 0.3 ratios and analyzed separately. The success rates obtained as a result of the analyses made are compared. Figure 5 shows the accuracy rate.

4 Conclusion

Turkish tweet sentiment problem is a challenging problem with the fact that the Turkish expressions are short and contain different interpretations in terms of semantics. At the classification stage, the attributes were tested in three different ways for the N-gram model: 2, 3 and 4 grams. The best result is observed from 3-gram model. The success rates of the study were affected from the out of balance of the data set. The existing negative sentences in the data set cause increase in the success rates predicted by negative cues. In this study, machine learning-based approaches were used for sentiment analysis. The highest success rate with 79.29% was obtained with sequential minimal optimization (SMO) algorithm. It was also seen that the highest success rate was always obtained when 0.7 training sets were selected. It is obviously determining that the success rates of the Naive Bayes (kernel) algorithm are almost the same as the SMO algorithm. Among the algorithms used in the study, the KNN algorithm is the most unsuccessful algorithm because of giving unsuccessful results.

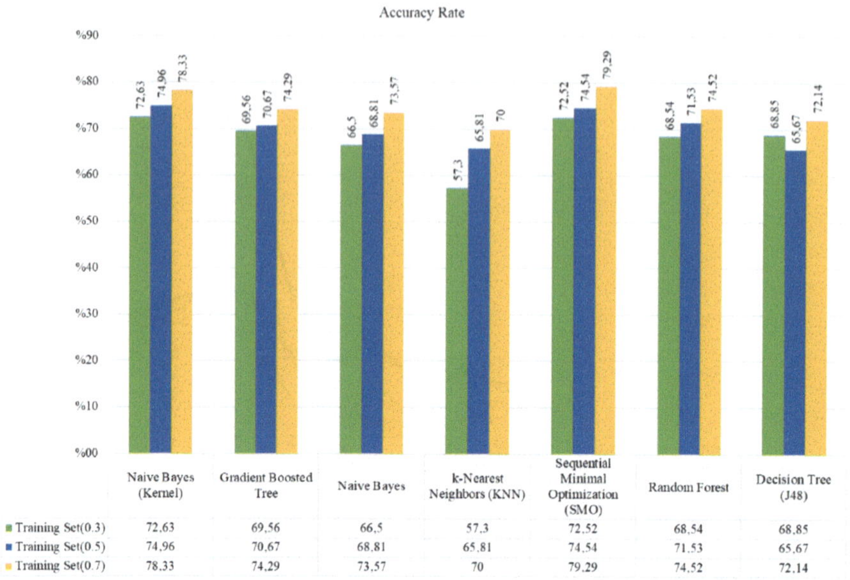

Fig. 5 Accuracy rate

In addition to the accuracy rate, the kappa statistical results obtained are also compared. The kappa statistic ranges from +1 to −1, but gives the relationship between the observed compliance and the chance-based compliance among the classes. When kappa statistic is equal to individual, full harmony is mentioned, while if it is greater than zero, harmony observed is greater or equal to harmony depending on chance. If the kappa statistic is less than zero, it is understood that the classification is not reliable (Aha and Kibler 1991; Nizam and Akın 2014). Table 2 shows the kappa statistical results of the algorithms used in the study. The kappa statistic of sequential minimal optimization, which is the most successful algorithm, was measured as 0.583. This value is an indicator that the classification is reliable.

Table 2 Kappa statistical values

	0.3	0.5	0.7
Naive Bayes (kernel)	0.478	0.520	0.577
Gradient boosted tree	0.343	0.356	0.391
Naive Bayes	0.353	0.409	0.487
k-nearest neighbors (KNNs)	0.301	0.389	0.451
Sequential minimal optimization (SMO)	0.455	0.491	0.583
Random forest	0.285	0.372	0.416
Decision tree (J48)	0.339	0.317	0.407

It is known that the training data used in the classification run and the attributes extracted from the data set are direct effects. For this reason, in the future studies, it is considered to construct a data set consisting of samples with much better discriminability. It is also contemplated to apply additional semantic and mathematical methods in order to increase the size of the data by increasing the number of messages, thereby increasing the ability of the classifiers to generalize, and extracting attributes with better distinguishing characteristics at the feature extraction stage.

References

Abdi, A., Shamsuddin, S. M., & Aliguliyev, R. M. (2018). QMOS: Query-based multi-documents opinion-oriented summarization. *Information Processing and Management, 54,* 318–338.

Aha, D., & Kibler, D. (1991). Instance-based learning algorithms. *Machine Learning, 6*(1).

Anstead, N., & O'Loughlin, B. (2015). Social media analysis and public opinion: The 2010 UK general election. *Journal of Computer-Mediated Communication, 20,* 204–220.

Antonio, N., Almedia, A., Nunes, L., Batista, F., & Ribeiro, R. (2018). Hotel online reviews: Different languages, different opinions. *Information Technology & Tourism, 18*(1–4), 157–185. https://doi.org/10.1007/s40558-018-0107-x.

Appel, O., Chiclana, F., Carter, J., & Fujita, H. (2018). Successes and challenges in developing a hybrid approach to sentiment analysis. *Applied Intelligence, 48*(5), 1176–1188. https://doi.org/10.1007/s10489-017-0966-4.

Booking. (2018). Retrieved January 18, 2018, from http://www.booking.com.

Brooks, G., Heffner, A., & Henderson, D. (2014). A SWOT analysis of competitive knowledge from social media for a small startup business. *Review of Business Information Systems, 8*(1), 23–34.

Chappel, P., Tse, M., Zhang, M., & Moore, S. (2017). Using GPS geo-tagged social media data and geodemographics to investigate social differences: A Twitter pilot study. *Sociological Research Online, 22*(3), 38–56. https://doi.org/10.1177/1360780417724065.

Chen, Y., Fay, S., & Wang, Q. (2011). The role of marketing in social media: How online consumer reviews evolve. *Journal of Interactive Marketing, 25,* 85–94.

Daniel, M., Neves, R. F., & Horta, N. (2017). Company event popularity for financial markets using Twitter and sentiment analysis. *Expert Systems with Applications, 71,* 111–124. https://doi.org/10.1016/j.eswa.2016.11.022.

Digital in 2017 Global Overview. (2018). Retrieved January 18, 2018, from https://wearesocial.com/special-reports/digital-in-2017-global-overview.

DPO. (2018). Retrieved January 18, 2018, from http://blog.directpay.online/booking-com.

El-Masri, M., Altrabsheh, N., & Mansour, H. (2017). Successes and challenges of Arabic sentiment analysis research: A literature review. *Social Network Analysis Mining, 7,* 54. https://doi.org/10.1007/s13278-017-0474-x.

Filieri, R., & McLeay, F. (2013). E-WOM and accommodation an analysis of the factors that influence travelers' adoption of information from online reviews. *Journal of Travel Research, 53*(1), 44–57.

Gaál, Z., Szabó, L., Obermayer-Kovács, N., & Csepregi, A. (2015). Exploring the role of social media in knowledge sharing. *The Electronic Journal of Knowledge Management, 13*(3), 185–197.

Geetha, M., Singha, P., & Sinha, S. (2017). Relationship between customer sentiment and online customer ratings for hotels—An empirical analysis. *Tourism Management, 61,* 43–54.

Hameed, M., Tahir, F., & Shahzad, M. A. (2018). Empirical comparison of sentiment analysis techniques for social media. *International Journal of Advanced and Applied Sciences, 5*(4), 115–123.

Hotel Management. (2018). Retrieved January 18, 2018, from https://www.hotelmanagement.net/development/why-turkey-s-hotels-are-uniting-behind-booking-com.

Houlihan, P., & Creamer, G. G. (2017). Can sentiment analysis and options volume anticipate future returns? *Computational Economics, 50,* 669–685. https://doi.org/10.1007/s10614-017-9694-4.

Hurriyet. (2018). Retrieved January 18, 2018, from http://www.hurriyetdailynews.com/open-branch-in-turkey-to-avoid-ban-association-tells-bookingcom–111663.

Independent. (2018). Retrieved January 18, 2018, from https://www.independent.co.uk/travel/news-and-advice/bookingcom-turkey-priceline-hotels-court-istanbul-ankara-ban-competition-authority-a7658251.html.

LaPoe, V. L., Olson, C. C., & Eckert, S. (2017). Linkedin is my office; Facebook my living room, Twitter the neighborhood bar. *Journal of Communication Inquiry, 41*(3), 185–206. https://doi.org/10.1177/0196859917707741.

Lee, I. (2018). Social media analytics for enterprises: Typology, methods, and processes. *Business Horizons, 61,* 199–210. https://doi.org/10.1016/j.bushor.2017.11.002.

Li, L. (2018). Sentiment-enhanced learning model for online language learning system. *Electronic Commerce Research, 18,* 23. https://doi.org/10.1007/s10660-017-9284-5.

Ma, B., Yuan, H., & Wu, Y. (2017). Exploring performance of clustering methods on document sentiment analysis. *Journal of Information Science, 43*(1), 54–74.

Mondal, M., Messias, J., Ghosh, S., Gummadi, K. P., & Kate, A. (2017). Managing longitudinal exposure of socially shared data on the Twitter social media. *International Journal of Advances in Engineering Sciences and Applied Mathematics, 9,* 238. https://doi.org/10.1007/s12572-017-0196-3.

Nguyen, H. L., & Jung, J. E. (2017). Statistical approach for figurative sentiment analysis on social networking services: A case study on Twitter. *Multimedia Tools and Applications, 76,* 8901–8914. https://doi.org/10.1007/s11042-016-3525-9.

Nizam, H., & Akın, S. S. (2014). Sosyal medyada makine öğrenmesi ile duygu analizinde dengeli ve dengesiz veri setlerinin performanslarının karşılaştırılması. In *XIX. Türkiye'de İnternet Konferansı.*

Oscar, N., Fox, P. A., Croucher, R., Wernick, R., Keune, J., & Hooker, K. (2017). Machine learning, sentiment analysis, and tweets: An examination of Alzheimer's disease stigma on Twitter. *The Journals of Gerontology: Series B, 72*(5), 742–751. https://doi.org/10.1093/geronb/gbx014.

Öztürk, N., & Ayvaz, S. (2018). Sentiment analysis on Twitter: A text mining approach to the Syrian refugee crisis. *Telematics and Informatics, 35,* 13–147.

Pew-Research. (2018). Retrieved January 18, 2018, from http://www.pewinternet.org/fact-sheet/social-media/.

Philips, P., Barnes, S., Zigan, K., & Schegg, R. (2016). Understanding the impact of online reviews on hotel performance: An empirical analysis. *Journal of Travel Research, 56*(2), 235–249. https://doi.org/10.1177/0047287516636481.

Podnar, K., & Javernik, P. (2012). The effect of word of mouth on consumers' attitudes toward products and their purchase probability. *Journal of Promotion Management, 18*(2), 145–168.

Posta. (2018). Retrieved January 18, 2018, from http://www.posta.com.tr/booking-com-yasagi-rakiplerine-yaradi-haberi-1292278.

Ruan, Y., Durresi, A., & Alfantouk, L. (2018). Using Twitter trust network for stock market analysis. *Knowledge-Based Systems, 145,* 207–218.

StatCounter—GlobalStats. (2018). Retrieved January 18, 2018, from http://gs.statcounter.com/social-media-stats/all/turkey/#monthly-201601-201804-bar.

Sul, K. S., Dennis, A. R., & Yuan, L. I. (2016). Trading on Twitter: Using social media sentiment to predict stock returns. *Decision Sciences, 48*(3), 454–488.

Yang, H. L., & Lin, Q. F. (2018). Opinion mining for multiple types of emotion-embedded products/services through evolutionary strategy. *Expert Systems with Applications, 99,* 44–55.

Zheng, L., Wang, H., & Gao, S. (2018). Sentimental feature selection for sentiment analysis of Chinese online reviews. *International Journal of Machine Learning and Cybernetics, 9,* 75–84.

Sentiment Analysis of How Turkish Customers Affected by PayPal Closure

Serkan Alici, Ekin Akkol, Can Aydin, and Cigdem Tarhan

Abstract In this study, sentiment analysis is realized about PayPal activities from 2016 till today. Twitter is one of the easiest ways to share opinions via texting, and there are approximately 20 million Twitter users in Turkey. The data set is obtained from Twitter. The Twitter messages in Turkish were manually obtained from the Internet because of being expensive of old tweet data. The data has been passed through the preprocessing, attribute selection and classification stages. At the end of these processes, the data is analyzed using various text mining algorithms, so the success rates achieved are compared and interpreted. Moreover, starting from the PayPal closure, the Web traffic of other Web sites (3pay.com, bkmepress.com.tr, enpara.com, ininal.com, ipara.com.tr, iyzico.com, papara.com, payu.com.tr, troyodeme.com) operating in Turkey was obtained in the same industry with PayPal. This paper also addressed how these companies were affected by this period.

Keywords PayPal · Sentiment analysis · Twitter · Machine learning · Turkish tweet · Online payment system

1 Introduction

PayPal firm in 2016 due to various regulation operations in Turkey have been stopped. PayPal is an environment where you can shop with thousands of businesses that support PayPal at home or abroad, just by emailing and typing, without sharing your financial information with the merchant. PayPal was first launched money transfer operations in Turkey in 2009. At the end of 2012, sales of Turkish companies abroad with PayPal increased by 22%. By 2015, this number has increased to 84%. According to SimilarTech, over 4193 Web sites and 2 million users exist in which connect from Turkish IP in Turkey. It is estimated that there are 8 million people shopping online in Turkey. In this context, it can be said that one of the people who experienced e-commerce has used PayPal. According to PayPal's 2015 figures, 179 million active

S. Alici · E. Akkol · C. Aydin · C. Tarhan (✉)
Department of Management Information Systems, Dokuz Eylul University, Izmir, Turkey
e-mail: cigdem.tarhan@deu.edu.tr

M. Janowicz-Lomott et al. (eds.), *Economic and Financial Challenges for Balkan and Eastern European Countries*, Springer Proceedings in Business and Economics,
https://doi.org/10.1007/978-3-030-39927-6_19

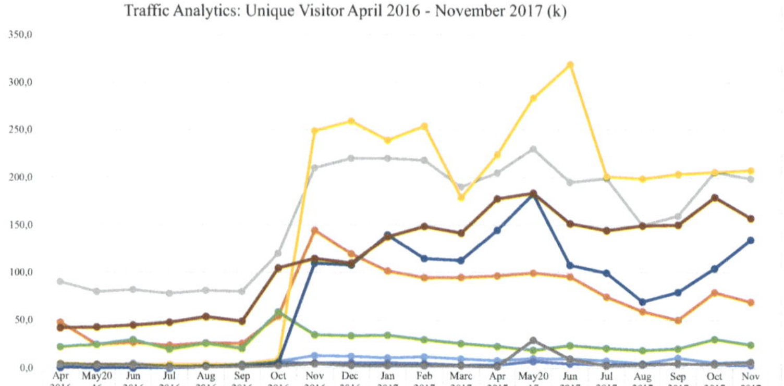

	Apr 2016	May2016	Jun 2016	Jul 2016	Aug 2016	Sep 2016	Oct 2016	Nov 2016	Dec 2016	Jan 2017
3pay.com	4,6	2	5,2	3	2,8	2,5	7	13	12,2	10,8
bkmexpress.com.tr	48	25	27	24	26,5	26	55	145	120	102
enpara.com	90	80	82	78	81	80	120	210	220	220
ininal.com	5	4,5	4,4	4,6	4,7	4,8	10	250	260	240
ipara.com.tr	0	0	0	0	1	3,5	5,8	5,2	5,5	5,3
iyzico.com	22	25	30	20	26	20,5	59	35	34	34,5
papara.com	0	0	0	0	2	1	5	110	108	140
payu.com.tr	42	43	45	48	54	49	105	115	110	138
troyodeme.com	3,5	3,4	3,4	1,4	1	1,2	2,2	4,3	2,2	2,1

	Feb 2017	Marc 2017	Apr 2017	May2017	Jun 2017	Jul 2017	Aug 2017	Sep 2017	Oct 2017	Nov 2017
3pay.com	11,8	9,6	8	10,1	10	7,8	5	11	6	7,0
bkmexpress.com.tr	95	95,3	97	100	96	75	60	51	80	70,0
enpara.com	218	190	205	230	195	199	150	160	206	199,0
ininal.com	255	180	225	285	320	202	200	205	207	209,0
ipara.com.tr	4,8	3	3,2	7,1	4,7	3,7	4,6	4,5	4,0	3,7
iyzico.com	30	26	23	19	24	21	19	20,8	30,8	25,0
papara.com	115	113	145	183	108	100	70	80	105	135,0
payu.com.tr	149	142	178	184	152	145	150	151	180	158,0
troyodeme.com	2,1	2,1	1,2	29	9	2,3	3,4	4,7	4	6

Fig. 1 Online payment Web site traffic between April 2016–October 2017

members and 1.4 billion transactions are made. Turkey is seen as a small market for PayPal but is likely to occur with higher utilization rates in the future (Webrazzi 2018). After 2016, e-commerce companies have turned to alternative payment systems with the closing of PayPal in line with the numbers examined (Fig. 1). In this context, other websites serving in the same sector were established instead of paypal such as 3pay.com, bkmepress.com.tr, enpara.com, ininal.com, ipara.com.tr, iyzico.com, papara.com, payu.com.tr, troyodeme.com.

Twitter data which has 20 million users in Turkey was used for measuring sentimental reactions to closure of PayPal. Sentimental analysis was applied to tweets obtained from Twitter from 2016 until today in Turkey. Unique visitors represent entries on the same IP over a site. The graphics were obtained from www.semrush.com. Figure 1 shows preferred alternative online payment systems after PayPal closure. Besides, it has been observed in the changes of user numbers of alternative firms. According to Fig. 1, the number of unique visitors is highest in online payment systems, respectively, ininal.com, enpara.com, payu.com. The number of unique visitors in these firms has increased considerably in 2017, especially in April-May-June compared to 2016. In addition, the great difference between the rates of unique visitors in April–June 2016 and 2017 is striking. PayPal suspended its activities in Turkey for this reason. Because users are forced to use alternative online payment systems to meet the needs of online payment systems after PayPal closure (Fig. 2). As a result, PayPal's closure has increased the number of users of Turkish online payment companies and has had a positive impact.

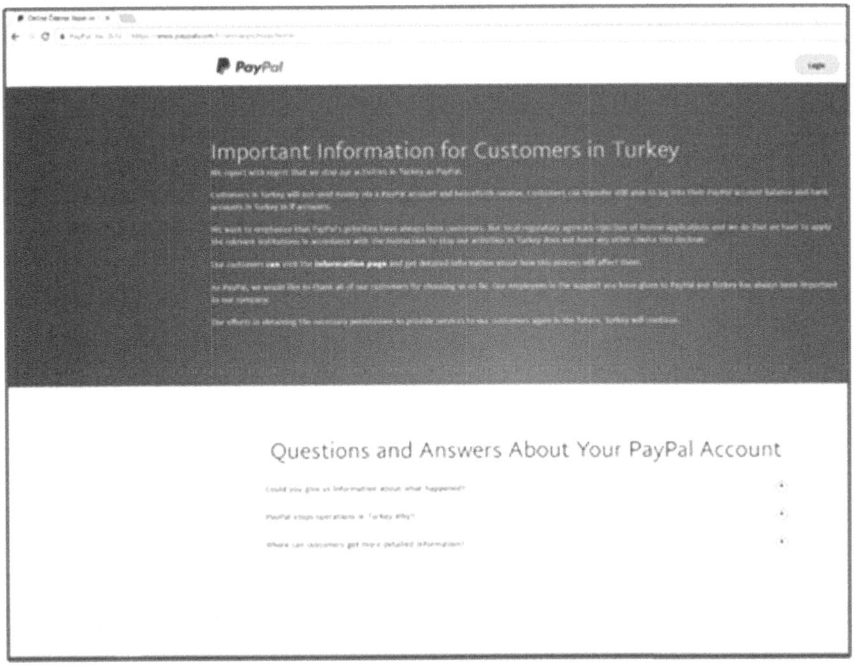

Fig. 2 PayPal Web site disclosure in Turkey

Tweets are basically classified as positive, negative or neutral feelings. Within this scope, tweets related to the closing of PayPal were thrown, and the tweets taken were passed through preprocessing, feature selection and classification stages and analyzed using text mining methods. Text mining is a technology that analyzes a large number of documents for the purpose of discovering previously unknown and important information (Karadağ and Takçı 2010). Text classification is widely used among text mining methods. Text classification is a process of determining which of a predetermined number of categories to include in a document based on its properties (Amasyalı et al. 2006). This method has been used in many different problem areas in the literature. The automatic classification of academic documents (Núñez and Ramos 2012), modeling and predicting political views from Web media data are the examples of these studies (Sobkowicz et al. 2012).

Achieved success rates are compared and interpreted. In addition to this, PayPal has been investigating the traffic of Web pages of alternative payment systems as well as the closure of the payment systems.

2 Literature Review

Within the scope of the study, sentimental analysis was carried out using the text mining method, which is related to PayPal. Tweets have been taken since 2016 and classified as positive, negative and no idea. In addition to using text mining method on social media data, it is used in many different applications. Sentimental analysis studies use approaches such as natural language processing, machine learning, computational linguistics and symbolic techniques (Zhang et al. 2018; Ma et al. 2017; Yang and Lin 2018; Houlian and Creamer 2017; Appel et al. 2018; Öztürk and Ayvaz 2018; El-Masri et al. 2017; Geetha et al. 2017).

Naive Bayes (NB), Random Forest (RF), Sequential Minimal Optimization (SMO), Decision Tree (J48) and 1-Nearest Neighbors (IB1) classification algorithms were used. The best performing classification algorithm was SMO with an average accuracy success rate of 72.33%. Two data sets were used, consisting of balanced and unbalanced tweets of various products of different companies in the food sector. The first data set consists of a total of 824 data, 1113 in the positive class, 277 in the negative class and 610 data in the neutral class, a total of 2000, the second data set, 257 in the positive class, 277 in the negative class and 290 in the neutral class. The balanced data set has been more successful (Nizam and Akın 2018).

In another study, Naive Bayes, RF, SMO, IBK, DT, J48 algorithms were tested separately from the machine learning algorithms via the dermatology data set. Also, SMO algorithm yields the best result in this study again. In the study of analyzing online comments with text mining, Foursquare application was selected as a data source. Foursquare is an application having total number of check-ins, number of individual users and score information. The study used the secret Dirichlet Batch method using Mallet software (Sönmez 2017).

Beyhan in 2014; their position in the GSM industry sector still has investigated the status of the company in Turkey and sentimental analysis methods using data from Twitter. Application stages: Data reading–Fragmentation–Changing parts–Converting to lowercase parts–Parts–Filtering–Clustering-Measuring performance (Beyhan 2014).

Another study is aimed to determine whether the comments made on the digital platforms about the films that are being watched contain emotion according to the content and whether this feeling is positive or negative. In the study, a data set containing 2000 film interpretations was used. Using machine learning methods, Naive Bayes, Center-Based Classifier, Multilayer Artificial Neural Networks and Support Vector Machines classification algorithms were used in MATLAB. Preliminary processing steps were applied before the data set training and classification process. After the pretreatment stage, a vector space model consisting of TF and IDF values was obtained. For all classification algorithms, 75% of the data set is reserved for education and the remaining 25% is used for testing purposes (Kaynar et al. 2016).

Personality type analysis was conducted using text mining methods and Twitter data. In the study, Naive Bayes, Random Tree and Gradient Boosted Tree algorithms were used. No results were obtained from SVN K-NN, ID3, Decision Tree, Decision Stump, Neural Net and SVN algorithms (Bastem and Şeker 2017).

A study was conducted using text mining to determine customer satisfaction. K-NN algorithm, Decision Tree, K-Means, SVM and Naive Bayes algorithms are used in the study (Kuzucu 2015).

In another study, while sentimental analysis on Twitter was performed, the analysis was performed using the bag of words method and n-gram method. The bag of words method is to compare the words with a dictionary of positive, negative and neutral words that can support three different emotion classes. Another method is the n-gram method for finding the repetition rate in a given sequence. In this study, the data was classified as 2, 3 and 4 g (Akgül et al. 2016).

SVN, Naive Bayes, Multinomial Naive Bayes, K-NN algorithms were also used in the sentimental analysis study of Twitter messages in Turkish. The n-gram and bag of words methods are discussed during the preprocessing of the data. The algorithm that yields the best results is the Multinom Naive Bayes algorithm (Çoban et al. 2015).

In the study of classification of social media shares by sentimental analysis method, classification of users' categorization (news, politics, culture) according to contents of users' shares was performed by using Naive Bayes algorithm (Baykara and Gültürk 2017).

Go et al. (2009) analyzed a data set of 1,600,000 tweets, 800,000 positive tweets and 800,000 negative tweets. They did this study for English texts and analyzed the tweets by combining unigram, bigram and unigram with bigram. According to the experimental results, unigram has the accuracy of 82.2% SVM algorithm and bigram has the accuracy of 81.6% Naive Bayes algorithm. As a result of the use of the combination of the maximum entropy algorithm with 83% accuracy showed the best performance (Go et al. 2009).

The aim of Turkmen and Cemgil studies (2014) is to estimate whether there is a tendency and political relevance of the tweets sent during the Gezi Park protests in Istanbul in 2013 with the SVM and Random Forest classification approach. In order to facilitate the classification of 1351 Twitter messages, which are manually marked, they have labeled "demonstration pro", "anti-demonstration" and "neutral" messages and benefited from the chi-square method for attribute selection. In addition to the accuracy criterion, the classification's success was determined by taking the f-criterion which is the harmonic mean of the precision and recall criteria and obtained more efficient results than the SVM algorithm in estimation of relevance (Türkmen and Cemgil 2014).

Nikfarjam et al. (2015) investigated the negative thoughts of the patients about the side effects of drugs by applying the effect analysis on the comments on Twitter and health-related forums. In practice, ADRMine method based on machine learning, which uses conditional random fields, was used to extract the concepts in the drug field. The data set was used as a health site with DailyStrength and Twitter's 6279 and 1784 comments. When the results were examined, it was observed that the ADRMine method was found to be more successful than the MetMap methods with 82.1% SVM and a classifier used in the field of health (Nikfarjam et al. 2015).

As a result of the literature review, the text mining process was carried out in five sections; process data set determination, data preprocessing, feature selection, classification and evaluation. Naive Bayes (NB), Naive Bayes (Kernel), K-Nearest Neighbor (K-NN) and Gradient Boosted Tree and SMO algorithms are tested from text mining algorithms. When the results are examined, the best result is found as the Naive Bayes algorithm. During the data preprocessing phase, both word of bags and n-grams were applied and 4 g gave good results.

3 Methodology

The text mining process used in this section is included in this section. Text mining process is covered under five main headings: data collection, text preprocessing, feature selection, classification and evaluation. The flowchart of these steps is shown in Fig. 3.

Data Set: The data set consists of Turkish Twitter messages about PayPal from 2016 till today. User messages for PayPal's closing are manually retrieved via Twitter. The reason for the manual acquisition is that the cost of retrieving past tweeter messages is very high. In order to prepare the training data, the Twitter messages were manually tagged based on three different classes: positive, negative and neutral.

Text Preprocessing: First, the spelling errors in the texts have been corrected. The next steps in the text preprocessing phase were performed with the Rapid Miner. At this stage, the text has been passed through the RapidMiner program for the purpose of extracting properties that have no effect on the analysis and classification stage. These actions:

- All texts are converted to lowercase and the letter that repeats is deleted.
- The feelings' symbols are cleaned.
- All punctuation marks, digits and unnecessary characters have been cleared.
- URLs, hashtags, usernames and terms with fewer than four characters have been cleared.
- The feature was extracted using the n-gram model. N-gram model is preferred as a model. This is why the bag of words method, which handles the texts

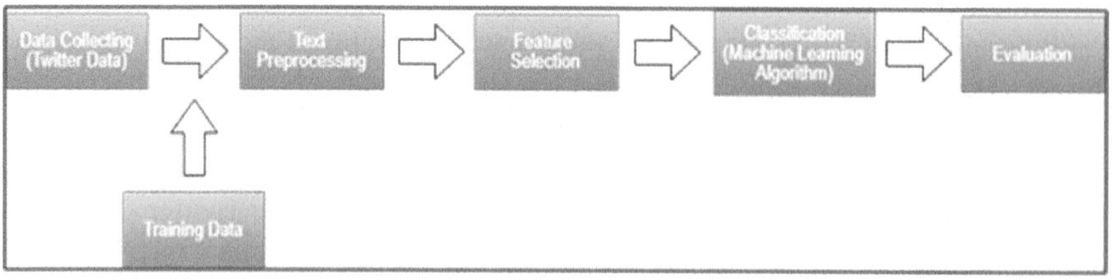

Fig. 3 Text mining methodology

without order and lacks grammatical knowledge, causes high information loss. While many of the words do not contain enough information about how they are handled individually, n-grams can contain higher-level and meaningful information when they come together as compound words and phrases.
- In addition, TF (term frequency) weighting method is used for weighting the attributes.

Feature Selection: It is aimed to reduce the size of attribute by eliminating the effectless data in the emotion analysis in the attribute selection. For this reason, the stand-alone words that do not make any sense at this stage have been removed from the data set. In addition, the words have been separated into roots.
Classification: All experiments were performed using the RapidMiner program. Sequential Minimal Optimization (SMO), Naive Bayes (NB), Naive Bayes Kernel, K-Nearest Neighbors (K-NN), Gradient Boosted Tree, Random Forest and Decision Tree (J48) machine learning algorithms were used on the training data set.
Evaluation of Results: As a result of the analysis, the success rates of the machine learning algorithms are compared. Tweets were modeled by training the machine learning method with Naive Bayes (NB), Naive Bayes (Kernel), Sequental Minimal Optimization (SMO), Decision Tree (J48), K-Nearest Neighbor (K-NN), Random Forest and Gradient Boosted Trees classification algorithms using supervised learning approach. Performance was measured according to model performance measures and kappa statistics used in the comparison of classification algorithms with tweets included in the test data set. The performance of the classification algorithms on the unbalanced data set, which has a total of 1215 tweets, 381 for the positive class, 574 for the negative class and 260 for the neutral class, are shown in Fig. 3.
Accuracy Rate: The most popular and simple method used to measure model success is the accuracy of the model. The ratio of the number is the classified samples to the total number of samples. The accuracy rate is calculated as:

$$\text{Accuracy} = \frac{Tp + Tn}{Tp + Fp + Fn + Tn}$$

$Tp + Tn$ Number of correctly classified samples
$Fp + Fn$ Number of incorrectly classified samples.

According to the accuracy measure (Fig. 4), Naïve Bayes (Kernel) algorithm showed the best result, and other algorithms can be sorted according to this measure as SMO, Random Forest, Gradient Boosted Trees and Naïve Bayes.

Kappa Statistics
The kappa test (Fig. 5) is a statistical method that measures the reliability of fit between two or more observers (Kılıç 2015). The kappa coefficient varies between -1 and $+1$. When full compliance is concerned, $K = 1$. If the observed fit is equal to or greater than the fit due to chance, then $K \geq 0$; if the observed fit is less than the fit

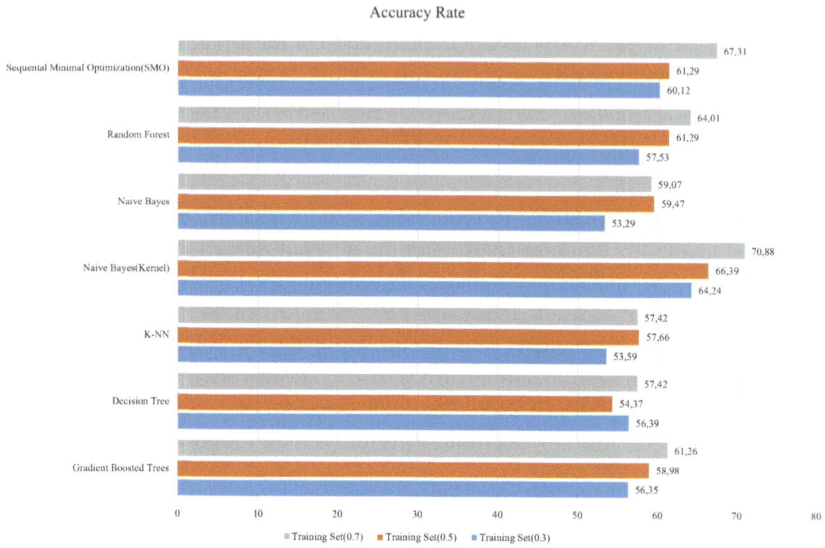

Fig. 4 Accuracy rate of algorithms on training set

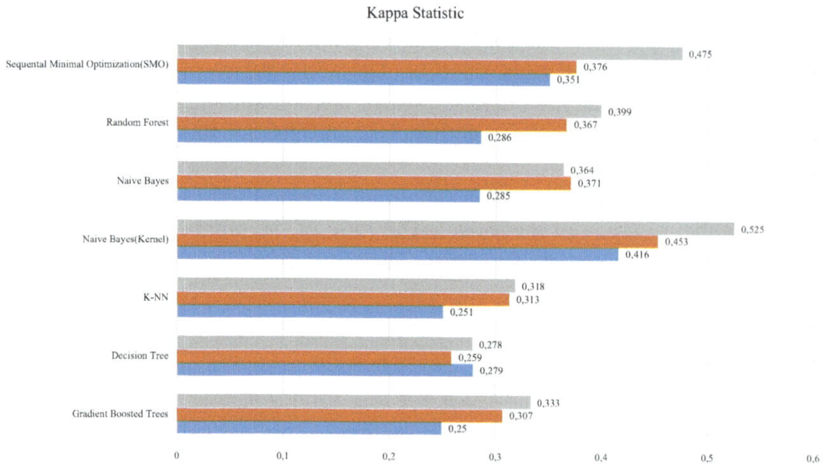

	Gradient Boosted Trees	Decision Tree	K-NN	Naive Bayes(Kernel)	Naive Bayes	Random Forest	Sequential Minimal Optimization(SMO)
Training Set(0.7)	0,333	0,278	0,318	0,525	0,364	0,399	0,475
Training Set(0.5)	0,307	0,259	0,313	0,453	0,371	0,367	0,376
Training Set(0.3)	0,25	0,279	0,251	0,416	0,285	0,286	0,351

Fig. 5 Kappa statistics result via algorithms

due to chance, then $K < 0$. The interpretable range of the kappa coefficient is between 0 and +1, and negative ($K < 0$) values have no meaning in terms of reliability. If the kappa score is above 0.4, it indicates a reasonable agreement. The kappa value is calculated as:

$$K = \frac{(Po - Pc)}{1 - Pc}$$

Po accepted ratio,
Pc expected ratio.

In general, when we evaluate the results, the results of the model performance criteria have increased in accordance with the results that we have already obtained. The best performing classification algorithm is Naive Bayes (Kernel) with an average accuracy success rate of 70.88%.

4 Conclusion

This study was conducted according to the tweet that sentiment analysis works in 2016, because of PayPal's stopping people at its operations in Turkey. Machine learning technique and supervised learning approach from machine learning methods are used on the data sets. The performance comparison of the classification algorithms on the data set is made according to the model performance criterion and kappa statistic values. SMO, Random Forest, Naive Bayes, Naive Bayes (Kernel), K-NN, J48, Gradient Boosted Tree classification algorithms are used in RapidMiner library. It was seen that the data distributions in the classes affected the success on the classification algorithms. The best performing classification algorithm is Naive Bayes (Kernel) with an average accuracy success rate of 70.88%. In this study, the algorithms were compared using the training data set at 0.70, 0.50 and 0.30 at different ratios. According to the results obtained, the accuracy ratio and the kappa coefficient vary according to the usage rates of the training data set in each algorithm. When the use rate of training data set is 0.70, the success rate is high. For this reason, determining the usage rates of the training data set is also important in terms of the analysis results.

As a result of this study, the amount of data is small, and the data classified in the data set is unevenly distributed, causing the accuracy rates to be low. In the total data set, the sample rate in the positive class is 31.36%, the negative class sample rate is 47.24%, and the neutral class sample rate is 21.40%. This unbalanced distribution is not a suitable distribution for text mining and therefore has adversely affected the accuracy rate and kappa coefficient and reduced the success rate. In future studies, it is planned to obtain more data and to increase the rates by creating a balanced data set.

References

Akgül, E., Ertano, C., & Diri, B. (2016). Twitter verileri ile duygu analizi. *Pamukkale Univ Muh Bilim Dergisi, 22*(2), 106–110.

Amasyalı, M. F., Diri, B., & Türkoğlu, F. (2006). Farklı özellik vektörleri ile türkçe dokümanların yazarlarının belirlenmesi. *15. Türkiye Yapay Sinir Ağları Sempozyumu*, Muğla.

Appel, O., Chiclana, F., Carter, J., & Fujita, H. (2018). Successes and challenges in developing a hybrid approach to sentiment analysis. *Applied Intelligence, 48*(5), 1176–1188. https://doi.org/10.1007/s10489-017-0966-4.

Bastem, K., & Şeker, Ş. (2017). Veri madenciliği yöntemleri ile twitter üzerinden MBTI kişilik tipi analizi. *YBS Ansiklopedi.*

Baykara, M., & Gürtürk, U. (2017). Sosyal medya paylaşımlarının duygu analizi yöntemiyle sınıflandırılması. *2nd International conference on computer science and engineering.*

Beyhan, H. (2014). Sosyal medya üzerinden metin madenciliği ve duygu analizi ile pazar değerlendirme. *İstanbul Teknik Üniversitesi Yüksek Lisans Tezi.*

Çoban, Ö., Özyer, B., & Özyer, G. (2015). Türkçe twitter mesajlarının duygu analizi. *23th Signal Processing and Communications Applications Conference (SIU)*, Malatya, Turkey.

El-Masri, M., Altrabsheh, N., & Mansour, H. (2017). Successes and challenges of arabic sentiment analysis research: a literature review. *Social Network Analysis Mining, 7,* 54. https://doi.org/10.1007/s13278-017-0474-x.

Geetha, M., Singha, P., & Sinha, S. (2017). Relationship between customer sentiment and online customer ratings for hotels—an empirical analysis. *Tourism Management, 61,* 43–54.

Go, A., Richa, B., & Lei, H. (2009). Twitter sentiment classification using distant supervision. *CS224N Project Report*, Stanford: 1–12.

Houlihan, P., & Creamer, G. G. (2017). Can sentiment analysis and options volume anticipate future returns? *Computational Economics, 50,* 669–685. https://doi.org/10.1007/s10614-017-9694-4.

Karadağ, A., & Takçı, H. (2010). *Metin madenciliği ile benzer haber tespiti.* Muğla Üniversitesi: Akademik Bilişim Konferansı Bildirileri.

Kaynar, O., Yıldız, M., Görmez, Y., & Albayrak, A. (2016). Makine öğrenmesi yöntemleri ile duygu analizi. *International Artificial Intelligence and Data Processing Symposium.*

Kılıç, S. (2015). Kappa Testi. *Journal of Mood Disorders, 5*(3), 142–144.

Kuzucu, K. (2015). Müşteri memnuniyeti belirlemek için metin madenciliği tabanlı bir yazılım aracı. *Maltepe Üniversitesi Yüksek Lisans Tezi.*

Ma, B., Yuan, H., & Wu, Y. (2017). Exploring performance of clustering methods on document sentiment analysis. *Journal of Information Science, 43*(1), 54–74.

Nikfarjam, A., Sarker, A., O'Connor, K., Ginn, R., & Gonzalez, G. (2015). Pharmacovigilance from social media: mining adverse drug reaction mentions using sequence labeling with word embedding cluster features. *Journal of the American Medical Informatics Association, 22*(3), 671–681.

Nizam, H., & Akın, S. (2018). Sosyal medyada makine öğrenmesi ile duygu analizinde dengeli ve dengesiz veri setlerinin performanslarının karşılaştırılması. *14. Türkiye'de İnternet Konferansı Bildirileri. Yaşar Üniversitesi* İzmir.

Núñez, H., & Ramos, E. (2012). Automatic classification of academic documents using t mining techniques. *In Informatica (CLEI) XXXVIII Conferencia Latinoamericana*, Medelin-Colombia.

Öztürk, N., & Ayvaz, S. (2018). Sentiment analysis on twitter: a text mining approach to the syrian refugee crisis. *Telematics and Informatics, 35,* 13–147.

Sobkowicz, P., Kaschesky, M., & Bouchard, G. (2012). Opinion mining in social media: modeling, simulating, and forecasting political opinions in the web. *Government Information Quarterly, 29,* 470–479.

Sönmez, N. (2017). Çevrimiçi yorumların metin madenciliği ile analizi: istanbuldaki alışveriş merkezleri üzerine bir çalışma. *İstanbul Teknik Üniversitesi Yüksek Lisans Tezi.*

Türkmen, A. C., & Cemgil A. T. (2014). Political interest and tendency prediction from microblog data. *2014 22nd Signal Processing and Communications Applications Conference (SIU), IEEE.*

Webrazzi. Retrieved January 18, 2018, from https://webrazzi.com/2016/05/31/dunden-bugune-rakamlarla-paypal-turkiye/.

Yang, H. L., & Lin, Q. F. (2018). Opinion mining for multiple types of emotion-embedded products/services through evolutionary strategy. *Expert Systems with Applications, 99*(2018), 44–55.

Zheng, L., Wang, H., & Gao, S. (2018). Sentimental feature selection for sentiment analysis of Chinese online reviews. *International Journal of Machine Learning and Cybernetics, 9*, 75–84.

What Is the Priority of the Political Rhetoric of the Russian Presidents: Growth of Bureaucracy or Economic Freedom?

Valery Okulich-Kazarin, Andrej Goloborodko and Olga Kravets

Abstract The paper's purpose is to check the most important political instrument of influence on economic processes in the largest country in the world. Two alternative priorities were examined in the research:

(1) growth of bureaucracy;
(2) growth of economic freedom.

Key main research technique is a content analysis of some government sources. The study shows new scientific results—the priority of the political rhetoric of Russian Presidents is growth of bureaucracy. The results are very highly statistically significant (0.1%). That is why, the results suggest that the decision will be correct in approximately 99.9% of the cases and incorrect in 0.1% of cases only. In this regard, authors have the decision-making process with accurate, controlled probability. The result is really important for Government members, economists, businessmen of many European countries, etc.

Keywords Economic freedom · Public administration · Russian President · Political rhetoric · Growth of the bureaucracy

1 Introduction

Russia had and has a very strong influence on economic and social processes not only in Eastern Europe, but all over the world.

V. Okulich-Kazarin (✉)
Institute of Law, Administration and Economics, Pedagogical University of Cracow, Ul. Podchorążych 2, 30-084 Kraków, Poland
e-mail: v-kazarin@yandex.ru

A. Goloborodko · O. Kravets
Taganrog Institute of Rostov State University of Economics, Rostov Region, Ul. Initsiativnaya D. 48, 347936 Taganrog, Russia
e-mail: goloborodko@tgpi.ru

M. Janowicz-Lomott et al. (eds.), *Economic and Financial Challenges for Balkan and Eastern European Countries*, Springer Proceedings in Business and Economics,
https://doi.org/10.1007/978-3-030-39927-6_20

All the major science and innovation activity indicators for Russia have remained largely unchanged over the past 10–15 years (Dezhina 2018). Expenditures on research and development (R&D) have stayed at the low level.

Macroeconomic indicators of the Russian banking sector, including banking sector assets, capital, loans, securities and household deposits as percent to GDP, revealed a rising trend. Return on assets (ROA), return on equity (ROE) and non-performing loans (NPL) are the main drivers of profitability. At the same time, the trend shows a low growth rate in ROA and equity and high growth rate in NPL, which are of major concern for banking system health (Yadav 2014).

The article of Mirkin et al. (2013) demonstrates that, in comparison with other emerging markets, the financial depth of the Russian economy may be characterized as inadequate. In the Russian financial market potential for growth is combined with exceptionally high risks. Insufficient depth of the financial system undermines its long-term competitiveness and exacerbates its exposure to shocks at the international market.

Zhuplev (2008) examines the background conditions, trends and scenarios of Russian economic internationalization. In the context of globalization, Russia is stepping up efforts to re-establish itself as a regional and global power. Despite recent progress in domestic economic development, Russia's comparative ratings in major international surveys remain modest or low. And many indicators of political rights and civil liberties in Russia demonstrate worsening trends. Russia still lags behind other countries on many of the criteria measuring economic freedom, market attractiveness, globalization, corruption, opacity and competitiveness.

One more article describes the measures taken by government officials to aid Russia's economy in emerging from the depths of the financial crisis. The authors describe the complexity of this task by focusing on how objective policy-making is complicated by the personal interests of Russian political and business leaders (Drobyshevskaya and Zhavoronkov 2009). The political considerations involved in Russian recapitalisation schemes serve as the main political focus in the creation of the desirable recovery strategy.

So, we see that Russian economy is not developing for last ten years. Russian economy needs investments. The investment climate plays a decisive role in the economic development of a society (Cárdenas-García 2014). The investment without first solving the issues affecting the investment climate will lead to the failure of such investment.

And we see that Russian economy is under the influence of political forces.

2 Literature Review

The modern political process in Russia actualizes the problems of social, political and economic transformations which are reflected in political texts and political rhetoric of the political elite.

The influence of rhetoric on people's behavior and their fate has been studied by a number of scientists.

Firstly, the authors (Cichocka et al. 2016) found that more conservative US Presidents used greater proportions of nouns in major speeches.

The author (Walter 2016) joins together recent work in rhetorical political analysis with methodological advances made in intellectual history to prospect the historical and linguistic approach to public reason and deliberation. According to the author's idea, the rhetorical approach studies standards of deliberation that is endogenous to a society instead of imposing them on the basis of one form of philosophical reason or another.

In the studies (Sevincer 2014), the computerized content analysis of historical documents to investigate the relations between positive rhetoric about the future and economic development was used. The more weekly newspaper articles in the economy page of USA Today contained positive thinking about the future, the more the Dow Jones Industrial Average declined. Next paper analyzes how a case for institutional change is made through rhetoric in an individual text (Brown et al. 2012).

The essay (Ihlen 2011) takes stock of the analytical building blocks that can be found in the public relations research and addresses the question raised in the introduction to this special issue: Can external organizational rhetoric help to make society a good place to live? Such analysis can form a basis for the critical discussion of whether organizational rhetoric helps to improve society.

Further, in the work (Grogger 2011), the author studied the influence of rhetoric of different people on the level of their salaries.

As it was shown by Dryzek (2010) that the deliberative democracy requires a deliberative system with multiple components, the linkage of which often needs rhetoric. The appreciation of these aspects of democracy exposes the limitations of categorical tests for the admissibility of particular sorts of rhetoric. The prioritization of bridging over bonding rhetoric is a step in the right direction, while producing misleading results sometimes.

Just recently, in the work of Idan et al. (2018), the authors drew on psycholinguistic research on the role of language in generation of emotions to explore a novel, extremely subtle means of intervention. Specifically, they hypothesized that phrasing conflict-relevant policies in noun form (vs. verb form) would reduce anger and impact of policy support correspondingly.

One more study aims to understand better how various Russian news outlets present stories pertaining to Russia's recent economic downturn and future economic outlook (Cooley and Stokes 2018). This study analyzed over 1500 Russian broadcast TV and online news stories. The strategic and policy implications are discussed at length in the paper.

The official political discourse is the set of norms, values and theories which are used by the political elite. The studying of such discourse is based on the search of the opportunities to distinguish the regularities from unobvious and separate elements which are contained in speeches, performances and written statements of the subject of policy (Levintova n.d.).

This review has shown that rhetoric is a powerful tool for influence on various aspects of life, including political.

The aim of the study is to analyze the priorities of public administration in the political rhetoric of the Russian Presidents.

The question under study is priorities of the political rhetoric of Russian Presidents. That is why, the analysis of governance priorities in Presidential Addresses to the Federal Assembly of the Russian Federation has been undertaken. The authors have analyzed the documents throughout the whole period of the existence of this political tool.

In accordance to the aim of the research, which is to reveal the priorities of the political rhetoric of Russian Presidents, the authors have carried out the content analysis of the Presidential Addresses to the Federal Assembly of the Russian Federation over the period of 20 years.

After the conversion of results of the content analysis, the verification of statistical hypotheses has been carried out. The verification of statistical hypotheses has shown that strengthening of the state was a priority of the political rhetoric of Russian Presidents for 24 years.

As a matter of fact, public administration in itself contains potential opportunity for corruption. According to the survey, the following factors have been attributed as causes of corruption (Dimant and Tosato 2017):

(1) High levels of bureaucracy and inefficient administrative structures;
(2) low levels of democracy, weak civil participation and low political transparency;
(3) low press freedom;
(4) low economic freedom.

For this reason, it was essential to identify clearly the issues to be addressed and prioritize them. The authors had examined two alternative issues in the research:

(1) growth of bureaucracy;
(2) growth of economic freedom.

The results of the study can be used for further scientific analysis and adjustment of economic cooperation between European countries and Russian business.

3 Body of Paper

3.1 Data and Methods

The methods of analysis which are used in the research are validated and well-documented. All methods are economically justified.

There are the key research techniques: literature review, scrupulous content analysis of government sources, graphical reflection of results, formation and verification of statistical hypotheses and drawing of conclusions. Besides, the scientific method has been used to search the relationships between the statistical data. The authors welcome alternative and non-traditional approaches of researchers.

The stages of the research are the following:

Firstly, the authors define the problem for study.

Secondly, they carry out a literature review. It was a selective review of publications in journals indexed in the databases Scopus and Web of Science for the last ten years. In total, over 50 scientific sources on a targeted topic have been analyzed, and the most relevant ones have been thoroughly examined.

Thirdly, they carry out a scrupulous content analysis of 23 government sources. After that, the priorities of the political rhetoric of the Russian Presidents were shown graphically.

The next stage is the formation of statistical hypotheses.

Finally, the verification of statistical hypotheses comes, which is the explanation of the situation based on what is currently known from the content analysis.

One of the simplest cases of checking the statistical hypothesis is checking the equality between average of population and a preset value. The target represents a fixed number μ_0, received not from sample data.

The hypotheses can be presented as the following (BUS_9641_3, 2009, p. 73).

Null hypothesis $H_0 : \mu = \mu_0$.

The null hypothesis holds that the unknown average of population μ is equal to a preset value μ_0.

Alternative hypothesis $H_1 : \mu \neq \mu_0$.

The alternative hypothesis holds that the unknown average of population μ is not equal to a preset value μ_0.

Both hypotheses are based on the results of the analysis of the selection of the Presidential Addresses to the Federal Assembly of the Russian Federation (Russia President 1994–2016) throughout the whole period of the existence of this political tool.

The method of bilateral checking of hypothesis is that about the average of population consists in calculating *t*-statistics according to formulas from the textbook (BUS_9641_3, 2009, p. 83).

In the theory of statistical hypotheses testing, the decision on the correctness of H_0 or H_1 is taken on the basis of the observed realization of the random vector *X* (Cramér 1946). From a practical point of view, the most interesting are the so-called non-randomized tests, which critical functions take only two values: 0 and 1. The decision principle used in taking the decision "the hypothesis Hi is correct" ($i = 0$; 1) is called a statistical test.

In the study, we started the verification of statistical hypotheses by calculation of average error ${}_{\dot{X}}\dot{S}$:

$$ {}_{\dot{X}}\dot{S} = \delta_{\dot{X}} / \sqrt{n}, \tag{1}$$

n—the size of a sample

δ_x—the standard deviation for the sample.

Next, we obtained the actual value of the statistical criterion t_{stat}:

$$t_{\text{stat}} = (\dot{X} - \mu_0) / {}_{\dot{X}}\dot{S}, \quad (2)$$

$\dot{X}$—the expected value,

μ_0—the preset value.

Further, authors compare the deduced value of t_{stat} to the suitable critical value from the standard table of critical values (e.g., t_{table}) to define which of the hypotheses should be accepted.

If the value of t_{stat} in absolute magnitude is less than the value from t_{table}, then the null hypothesis is accepted. If the value of t_{stat} in absolute magnitude is more than the value from t_{table}, then the null hypothesis is rejected and the alternative hypothesis is accepted.

After the interpretation of the data, the authors are able to draw conclusions.

3.2 Scrupulous Content Analysis of Government Sources

For the implementation of the statistical analysis, the authors have employed a number of transformations. They have assigned 0 value (null) for the year when the Address of the Russian President to the Federal Assembly of the Russia was focused on the development of democracy, civil participation, freedom and economic freedom (growth of economic freedom). And they have assigned 1 value (one) for the year when the Address of the Russian President has been focused on the strengthening of the state.

The authors have assigned 0.5 value (zero point five) in the cases when the Address of the Russian President contained two priorities: the development of democracy, civil participation, freedom and economic freedom and the strengthening of the state.

The priorities of each Presidential Address to the Federal Assembly of the Russia (Russia President 1994–2016), overall, years of the existence of this political tool, are reflected in Table 1.

Table 1 shows the priorities of the political rhetoric of all Russian Presidents in four stages. The table shows that Presidents Yeltsin and Medvedev had two priorities. President Putin had only one priority.

Referring to the table, the authors can calculate an average of selection $\dot{X}_i$, a standard statistical deviation for selection $\delta_{x,}$ a standard statistical deviation for population $\delta_{x\text{-}1}$ and a standard mistake ${}_{\dot{X}}\dot{S}$.

Thus, we have the basic data:

- the total amount of selection of $n = 23$,
- the average of selection $\dot{X} = 0.91$,
- the standard statistical deviation for selection $\delta_i = 0.19$.
- the standard statistical deviation for population $\delta_{x-1} = 0.20$.
- the standard mistake ${}_{\dot{X}}\dot{S} = 0.04$.

Table 1 Priorities of the political rhetoric reflected in the Addresses of the Russian President to the Federal Assembly of Russia (from 1994 till 2017) and assigned values

№	Year	Priorities of the political rhetoric	Value
President of the Russian Federation B. Yeltsin			
1	1994	0. Development of democracy, civil participation, freedom and economic freedom (the development of the market reforms) 1. Strengthening of the state (the integrity of the state) (Russian President 1994)	0.5
2	1995	1. Strengthening of the state (development of the federalism and local government bodies) (Russian President 1995)	1.0
3	1996	0. Development of democracy, civil participation, freedom and economic freedom (establishing of foundations of the market economy) 1. Strengthening of the state (Russian President 1996)	0.5
4	1997	1. Strengthening of the state (the order in the power and in the state) (Russian President 1997)	1.0
5	1998	1. Strengthening of the state (effective interaction between the executive and legislative powers) (Russian President 1998)	1.0
6	1999	1. Strengthening of the state (efficiency of the future parliament) (Russian President 1999)	1.0
President of the Russian Federation V. Putin			
7	2000	1. Strengthening of the state (turning Russia into strong and effective state) (Russian President 2000)	1.0
8	2001	1. Strengthening of the state (the division of powers between federal and regional authorities) (Russian President 2001)	1.0
9	2002	1. Strengthening of the state (enhancing of competitiveness of Russia in the world) (Russian President 2002)	1.0
10	2003	1. Strengthening of the state (reduction of the functions of the state agencies) (Russian President 2003)	1.0
11	2004	1. Strengthening of the state (safety of Russia) (Russian President 2004)	1.0
12	2005	1. Strengthening of the state (strengthening of the Federation) (Russian President 2005)	1.0
13	2006	1. Strengthening of the state (confronting external threats) (Russian President 2006)	1.0
14	2007	1. Strengthening of the state (by complex modernization of the country) (Russian President 2007)	1.0
President of the Russian Federation D. Medvedev			
15	2008	1. Strengthening of the state (defense and safety) (Russian President 2008)	1.0

(continued)

Table 1 (continued)

№	Year	Priorities of the political rhetoric	Value
16	2009	0. Development of democracy, civil participation, freedom and economic freedom (modernization of industry and fight against corruption) 1. Strengthening of the state (retaining the status of the world power by Russia) (Russian President 2009)	0.5
17	2010	0. Development of democracy, civil participation, freedom and economic freedom (creation of the innovative economics) 1. Strengthening of the state (new standards in the functioning of the national public administration) (Russian President 2010)	0.5
18	2011	0. Development of democracy, civil participation, freedom and economic freedom (modernization of the economy) 1. Strengthening of the state (development of the country political system) (Russian President 2011)	0.5
President of the Russian Federation V. Putin			
19	2012	1. Strengthening of the state (Russia has to be a sovereign and influential country) (Russian President 2012)	1.0
20	2013	1. Strengthening of the state (strengthening of the armed forces) (Russian President 2013)	1.0
21	2014	1. Strengthening of the state (Russia is a sovereign and strong country) (Russian President 2014)	1.0
22	2015	1. Strengthening of the state (national security) (Russian President 2015)	1.0
23	2016	1. Strengthening of the state (increasing the role of the State Duma, national security) (Russian President 2016)	1.0
–	2017	The President of Russia did not make the presidential address to the Federal Assembly of Russia (Russian President 2017)	–

3.3 *Graphical Reflecting of Results*

Figure 1 shows the priorities of the political rhetoric of the Russian Presidents since 1994 till 2017.

We see that (Fig. 1):

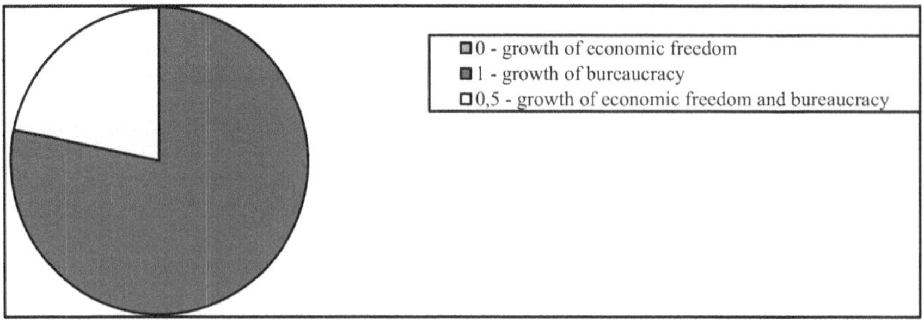

Fig. 1 Priorities of the political rhetoric of the Russian Presidents since 1994 till 2017

1. the growth of bureaucracy as a priority occupies a large part of political rhetoric,
2. the simultaneous growth of economic freedom and bureaucracy is a priority of less than 25%,
3. growth of economic freedom is not a priority.

For obtaining the reasonable answer to the question: what priority of the political rhetoric of the Russian Presidents dominated—the statistical hypotheses have been created and checked.

3.4 Results: Verification of Statistical Hypotheses

Check 1

The null hypothesis: the priority of the political rhetoric of the Russian Presidents is growth of economic freedom.

The authors write down the null hypothesis as follows: $\mu_0 = 0.0$.

The alternative hypothesis: the priority of the political rhetoric of the Russian Presidents is not growth of economic freedom.

The alternative hypothesis is registered: $\mu_0 \neq 0.0$.

Authors calculate t_{stat}:

$t_{\text{stat}} = (0.91 - 0.0)/0.04 = 22.75$,

Further, we carry out a bilateral testing at the level of check of 0.1%. We accept t_{table} from Table 9.1.1 (BUS_9641_3, 2009, p. 42) a value which is equal to 3.792. As the t_{stat} (22.75) is more in absolute magnitude than the value t_{table} from Table 9.1.1 (3.792), the observed difference between the statistical average $\dot{X}$ and the preset value $\mu_0 = 0.0$ cannot be caused only by accident. We reject the null hypothesis and accept the alternative hypothesis: the priority of the political rhetoric of the Russian Presidents is not growth of economic freedom.

Therefore, at the check level (0.1%) of statistical hypotheses, the priority of the political rhetoric of the Russian Presidents is not growth of economic freedom. The result is very highly statistically significant.

Check 2

The null hypothesis: growth of bureaucracy is the priority of the political rhetoric of the Russian Presidents.

Authors write down the null hypothesis as follows: $\mu_0 = 1.0$.

The alternative hypothesis: growth of bureaucracy is not the priority of the political rhetoric of the Russian Presidents.

The alternative hypothesis is registered: $\mu_0 \neq 1.0$.

Authors calculate t_{stat}:

$t_{\text{stat}} = (0.91 - 1.00)/0.04 = 2.25$,

Further, we carry out a bilateral testing at the level of check of 0.1%. We accept t_{table} from Table 9.1.1 (BUS_9641_3, 2009, p. 42) a value which is equal to 3.792. As the t_{stat} (2.25) is less in absolute magnitude than the value t_{table} from Table 9.1.1

(3.792), the observed difference between the statistical average $\dot{X}$ and the preset value $\mu_0 = 1.00$ can be caused by accident. And we accept the null hypothesis: growth of bureaucracy is the priority of the political rhetoric of the Russian Presidents. The result is very highly statistically significant (0.1%).

4 Discussion

Can you trust the results of the research?

Every researcher has a right to try to disprove results. To do this, he needs to get the result more highly statistically significant. This means that he needs to explore additional sources several times more than in the study. And it does not guarantee that the results will be different.

This research was focused on the most important political instrument of influence on economic processes in the largest country in the world-political rhetoric of the Russian Presidents.

The objectives, that were set, have been achieved through a complex of the conducted studies. The research methods are the following: content analysis of the Presidential Addresses to the Federal Assembly of Russia (Russia President 1994–2016) and verification of statistical hypotheses. They have shown priorities of the political rhetoric of the Russian Presidents.

The results are very highly statistically significant (0.1%). That is why, the results suggest that the decision will be correct in approximately 99.9% of the cases and incorrect in 0.1% of the cases only. In this regard, the authors have the decision-making process with accurate, controlled probability.

The publication "Country of officials" (2018) and two statistical reports (Russian statistical yearbook 2005; Russian statistical yearbook 2017) showed growing the number of officials in 1.6 times. It was since 2005 till 2017. Thus, economic practice additionally confirmed the results of our scientific research.

It is well known that the increase in the number of officials increases the burden on the state budget. The growth of bureaucracy increases the burden on business and slows down economic growth. There are two negative impacts of the Presidential priorities, reflected in political rhetoric, to the economic development of Russia.

5 Conclusion

The authors have found the answer to the question: what priorities of the political rhetoric of the Russian Presidents expressed in the Addresses to the Federal Assembly of Russia.

(1) The results of content analysis of 23 government documents have been turned by the authors into rigorous scientific knowledge.

It is proved that the growth of bureaucracy is a priority of the political rhetoric of all Russian Presidents for 24 years. It is proved that the growth of economic freedom is not the priority of the political rhetoric of the Russian Presidents.

The received results are very highly statistically significant (0.1%).

(2) We got clean results without any comments and recommendations. Our results are the basis for comments and recommendations from experts in politics, business, economics, etc.

The result is really important for the government members, economists, businessmen of many European countries, etc. Now heads of state and of international companies can plan economic and other contacts with Russian business and Russian government.

(3) The results of the study—growth of bureaucracy—give us the following hypothesis: corruption in Russia is growing. This is a purpose for further research.

Acknowledgements The research is supported by the International Scientific Group (Belarus, Poland, Serbia, Russia, Ukraine) and the Scientific project: "WPl_BS_Uwarunkowania rozwoju gospodarczego i społecznego krajów Unii Europejskiej, Europy Wschodniej, Azji Centralnej i Azji Wschodniej—czynniki rozwoju (endogeniczne i egzogeniczne), bariery i perspektywy," Pedagogical University of Cracow, Poland, 2018.

The authors would like to thank the reviewers for their insightful comments on draft of this manuscript.

References

Brown, A., Ainsworth, S., & Grant, D. (2012). The rhetoric of institutional change. *Organization Studies, 33*(3), 297–321.

BUS_9641_3. (2009). *Business Statistics. Textbook for the Program «Masters of Business Administration»* (p. 122). USA, NY: Kingston University.

Cárdenas-García, P. J., & Pulido-Fernández, J. I. (2014). Does the investment climate determine the transformation of tourism growth into economic development? *Tourism Economics, 20*(4), 669–694.

Cichocka, A., et al. (2016). On the grammar of politics—or why conservatives prefer nouns. *Political Psychology, 37,* 799–815.

Cooley, S. C., & Stokes, E. C. (2018). Manufacturing resilience: An analysis of broadcast and web-based news presentations of the 2014–2015 Russian economic downturn. *Global Media and Communication, 14*(1), 123–139.

Country of officials: Russia breaks records for the number of civil servants. https://citifox.ru/2017/06/28/strana-chinovnikov-rossiya-bet-rekord, 21.09.2018.

Cramér, H. (1946). *Mathematical methods of statistics*. Princeton Univ. Press.

Dezhina, I. (2018). Innovation policy in Russia and the development of university–industry linkages. *Industry and Higher Education, 32*(4), 245–252.

Dimant, E., Tosato, G. (2017). Causes and effects of corruption: What has past decade's empirical research taught us? survey. *Journal of Economic Surveys*. n/a–n/a. https://doi.org/10.1111/joes.1219.

Drobyshevskaya, T., & Zhavoronkov, S. (2009). The Russian economy and the current crisis. *European View, 8*(2), 319–324.
Dryzek, J. (2010). Rhetoric in democracy: A systemic appreciation. *Political Theory, 38*(3), 319–339.
Grogger, J. (2011). Speech patterns and racial wage inequality. *The Journal of Human Resources, 46*(1), 1–25.
Idan, O., et al. (2018). A Rose by any other name? A subtle linguistic cue impacts anger and corresponding policy support in intractable conflict. *Psychological Science, 29*(6), 972–983.
Ihlen, Ø. (2011). On barnyard scrambles: Toward a rhetoric of public relations. *Management Communication Quarterly, 25*(3), 455–473.
Levintova, E., n.d. Russian intellectual elite and its discourse. Retrieved from www.irex.ru. Access February 15, 2016.
Mirkin, Y., Kuznetsova, O., & Kuznetsov, A. (2013). The financial depth of emerging markets: The case of Russia. *Competition & Change, 17*(2), 156–175.
RUSSIA President. (1994). Poslanie Prezidenta Rossiiskoi Federatsii Federalnomu sobraniiu Rossiiskoi Federatsii. Moskva, Russia, FGUP Izd-vo "Izvestiia".
RUSSIA President. (1995). Poslanie Prezidenta Rossiiskoi Federatsii Federalnomu sobraniiu Rossiiskoi Federatsii. Moskva, Russia, FGUP Izd-vo "Izvestiia".
RUSSIA President. (1996). Poslanie Prezidenta Rossiiskoi Federatsii Federalnomu sobraniiu Rossiiskoi Federatsii. Moskva, Russia, FGUP Izd-vo "Izvestiia".
RUSSIA President. (1997). Poslanie Prezidenta Rossiiskoi Federatsii Federalnomu sobraniiu Rossiiskoi Federatsii. Moskva, Russia, FGUP Izd-vo "Izvestiia".
RUSSIA President. (1998). Poslanie Prezidenta Rossiiskoi Federatsii Federalnomu sobraniiu Rossiiskoi Federatsii. Moskva, Russia, FGUP Izd-vo "Izvestiia".
RUSSIA President. (1999). Poslanie Prezidenta Rossiiskoi Federatsii Federalnomu sobraniiu Rossiiskoi Federatsii. Moskva, Russia, FGUP Izd-vo "Izvestiia".
RUSSIA President. (2000). Poslanie Prezidenta Rossiiskoi Federatsii Federalnomu sobraniiu Rossiiskoi Federatsii. Moskva, Russia, FGUP Izd-vo "Izvestiia".
RUSSIA President. (2001). Poslanie Prezidenta Rossiiskoi Federatsii Federalnomu sobraniiu Rossiiskoi Federatsii. Moskva, Russia, FGUP Izd-vo "Izvestiia".
RUSSIA President. (2002). Poslanie Prezidenta Rossiiskoi Federatsii Federalnomu sobraniiu Rossiiskoi Federatsii. Moskva, Russia, FGUP Izd-vo "Izvestiia".
RUSSIA President. (2003). Poslanie Prezidenta Rossiiskoi Federatsii Federalnomu sobraniiu Rossiiskoi Federatsii. Moskva, Russia, FGUP Izd-vo "Izvestiia".
RUSSIA President. (2004). Poslanie Prezidenta Rossiiskoi Federatsii Federalnomu sobraniiu Rossiiskoi Federatsii. Moskva, Russia, FGUP Izd-vo "Izvestiia".
RUSSIA President. (2005). Poslanie Prezidenta Rossiiskoi Federatsii Federalnomu sobraniiu Rossiiskoi Federatsii. Moskva, Russia, FGUP Izd-vo "Izvestiia".
RUSSIA President. (2006). Poslanie Prezidenta Rossiiskoi Federatsii Federalnomu sobraniiu Rossiiskoi Federatsii. Moskva, Russia, FGUP Izd-vo "Izvestiia".
RUSSIA President. (2007). Poslanie Prezidenta Rossiiskoi Federatsii Federalnomu sobraniiu Rossiiskoi Federatsii. Moskva, Russia, FGUP Izd-vo "Izvestiia".
RUSSIA President. (2008). Poslanie Prezidenta Rossiiskoi Federatsii Federalnomu sobraniiu Rossiiskoi Federatsii. Moskva, Russia, FGUP Izd-vo "Izvestiia".
RUSSIA President. (2009). Poslanie Prezidenta Rossiiskoi Federatsii Federalnomu sobraniiu Rossiiskoi Federatsii. Moskva, Russia, FGUP Izd-vo "Izvestiia".
RUSSIA President. (2010). Poslanie Prezidenta Rossiiskoi Federatsii Federalnomu sobraniiu Rossiiskoi Federatsii. Moskva, Russia, FGUP Izd-vo "Izvestiia".
RUSSIA President. (2011). Poslanie Prezidenta Rossiiskoi Federatsii Federalnomu sobraniiu Rossiiskoi Federatsii. Moskva, Russia, FGUP Izd-vo "Izvestiia".
RUSSIA President. (2012). Poslanie Prezidenta Rossiiskoi Federatsii Federalnomu sobraniiu Rossiiskoi Federatsii. Moskva, Russia, FGUP Izd-vo "Izvestiia".

RUSSIA President. (2013). Poslanie Prezidenta Rossiiskoi Federatsii Federalnomu sobraniiu Rossiiskoi Federatsii. Moskva, Russia, FGUP Izd-vo "Izvestiia".

RUSSIA President. (2014). Poslanie Prezidenta Rossiiskoi Federatsii Federalnomu sobraniiu Rossiiskoi Federatsii. Moskva, Russia, FGUP Izd-vo "Izvestiia".

RUSSIA President. (2015). Poslanie Prezidenta Rossiiskoi Federatsii Federalnomu sobraniiu Rossiiskoi Federatsii. Moskva, Russia, FGUP Izd-vo "Izvestiia".

RUSSIA President. (2016). Poslanie Prezidenta Rossiiskoi Federatsii Federalnomu sobraniiu Rossiiskoi Federatsii. Moskva, Russia, FGUP Izd-vo "Izvestiia".

Russian statistical yearbook. (2017). http://www.gks.ru/free_doc/doc_2017/year/year17.pdf, 22.09.2018.

Russian statistical Yearbook. (2005). http://www.gks.ru/bgd/regl/b05_13/IssWWW.exe/Stg/02-02.htm, 22.09.2017.

Sevincer, A., et al. (2014). Positive thinking about the future in newspaper reports and presidential addresses predicts economic downturn. *Psychological Science, 25*(4), 1010 1017.

Walter, R. (2016). Rhetoric or deliberation? The case for rhetorical political analysis. *Political Studies, 65*(2), 300–315.

Yadav, R. (2014). Twenty five years of Russian banking system: Trends and analysis. *International Studies, 51*(1–4), 101–117.

Zhuplev, A. (2008). Economic internationalization of Russia: Roots, trends, and scenarios. *International Political Science Review, 29*(1), 99–119.

The Determination of Food Preferences with PROMETHEE Multi-criteria Decision-Making Method: A Web-Based Application

Tolga Pelitli, Emre Karagöz, and Kaan Yaralioğlu

Abstract People do not give enough importance to how to be fed healthily in the rush of a daily life. More and more, some diseases occur based on bad nutrition. In nutrition and survival struggle, the healthiest and only nutrient that contains all the nutritional values is mother's milk. A child who gives up the mother's milk struggles to meet his or her physiological needs for the rest of human life. Throughout history, people also have experienced various decision-making processes. However, the increase in the number of decision criteria leads to a multi-criteria decision-making process. Therefore, the aim of this study is to develop an application that aids in finding the optimal food for people to keep a healthy living. This application was developed to change negative food preferences and to continue a healthier, happier, and more peaceful life for people. Food problem choice was solved using multi-criteria decision-making method called PROMETHEE on a web-based platform. Some of the criteria used in the study are fat content, protein content, carbohydrate content, salinity, and cholesterol. Having a different perspective to increase knowledge, awareness levels and living standards of people about nutritional values reveals the most important way of the study.

Keywords Web-based program · Multi-criteria decision-making · PROMETHEE · Choice of food

T. Pelitli (✉) · K. Yaralioğlu
Department of Management Information System, Dokuz Eylül University, Izmir, Turkey
e-mail: tolgapelitli@hotmail.com

K. Yaralioğlu
e-mail: k.yaralioglu@deu.edu.tr

E. Karagöz
Department of Econometrics, Dokuz Eylül University, Izmir, Turkey
e-mail: emre.karagoz@deu.edu.tr

M. Janowicz-Lomott et al. (eds.), *Economic and Financial Challenges for Balkan and Eastern European Countries*, Springer Proceedings in Business and Economics,
https://doi.org/10.1007/978-3-030-39927-6_21

1 Introduction

People are in need of nutrition in their mother's womb, when they are born and throughout their lives. Since the earliest times, societies have shaped their feeding according to many factors, such as geographical conditions, climatic conditions, wars, socioeconomic conditions, beliefs, lifestyles, environmental factors, technology. In this nutrition and survival struggle, the healthiest and only nutrient that contains all nutritional values is mother's milk. A child who gives up the mother's milk struggles to meet his or her physiological needs for the rest of his life. Nobody can live a healthy life until the end of their life by consuming a single food ingredient.

While globalization and technological developments are increasing in today's world, nutritional disorders affecting human life are also increasing. Unhealthy nutrition, physical inactivity, smoking, and alcohol use can be the factors that cause chronic diseases. (Verhagen et al. 2010). The main reason for this is unbalanced, inadequate, and unhealthy forms of nutrition. Health is the most important building block of human life. The greatest factor in the protection of human health concerns the individual feeds. If people make decisions about food choices correctly, healthier societies are created. The most important way to achieve this is to increase people's nutritional awareness and to ensure that they are fed in a balanced, adequate, and healthy manner.

Every living creature in the world is involved in the act of storing and replicating the nutrients that they obtain to sustain their lives using scarce resources. Throughout history, people have experienced various decision-making processes. If the criteria for problem in the decision-making process are one, it is easy for this decision-maker. However, the increase in the number of decision criteria leads to a multi-criteria decision-making process. Multi-criteria decision-making is the process of reaching the optimal result by evaluating multiple criteria from multiple alternatives for the decision to be taken.

This study aims to help people make their nutritional decisions correctly. Because the most important need for human life is the concept of nutrition. The main structure of the work constitutes how people can help them by using technology and science in the selection of food items. In the realization phase of this work, an application platform was developed using web-based technologies.

As a result of the literature review, many topics using multi-criteria decision-making techniques have been found. Some of those, using the analytic hierarchy process an application has been implemented so that the human resources department can select an effective staff (Özbek 2018). In another study, a web-based application was developed using the analytic hierarchy process to optimize site selection for businesses (Mutlutürk 2016). In another study conducted in 2015, a decision support system was developed to compare the surgical methods used in obesity treatment (Karacan 2015). In a study conducted in 2011, a study was carried out on the application of the PROMETHEE method to investment project evaluation and production sector (Aygün 2011). Zhai et al. examined the relationship between various factors via DANP method, and also they developed that promoted PROMETHEE method by introducing the concept of expectation level into the preference function (Zhai et al. 2017). Sennaroglu and Celebi research that location select problem via multiple criteria. They used AHP, PROMETHEE, and VIKOR method to solve problem. Weights of criteria are determined by AHP. Then ranking and selection processes of four alternatives are carried out using PROMETHEE and VIKOR methods (Sennaroglu and Celebi 2018). Silas and Rajsingh research health service conditions and selection process for the right person right hospital. They compared results between electra, PROMETHEE, and AHP. Finally, they reached that PROMETHEE is the best solution for this problem (Silas and Rajsingh 2016). Gul et al. researched the material selection problem via fuzzy PROMETHEE method, and then compared solution results with the fuzzy TOPSIS, fuzzy ELECTRE, and fuzzy VIKOR. Finally, they recommend a generic fuzzy MCDM methodology that can be practically implemented to material selection problem (Gul et al. 2018). Sarı and Timor research supplier evaluation and selection process for business conditions. They used ANP multi-criteria method and then compared ANP and PROMETHEE methods (Sarı and Timor 2016).

2 Methods

2.1 PROMETHEE

The Preference Ranking Organization Method for Enrichment of Evaluation (PROMETHEE) was developed by Jean-Pierre Brans and was first introduced in 1982 in two different models as a conference PROMETHEE I (partial ordering of alternatives) and PROMETHEE II (full order of alternatives) in Quebec, Canada. After few years of PROMETHEE method PROMETHEE III (sorting based on intervals), PROMETHEE IV (for continuous situations), Brans and Mareschall were presented other versions of PROMETHEE V (containing partitioning constraints) and PROMETHEE VI (representing the human brain).

Multi-criteria decision-making problems are classified into three main topics such as selection, classification, and sorting problems (Vassilev et al. 2005). PROMETHEE method is used in sorting problems and selection problems. PROMETHEE is a method of prioritization.

2.1.1 Steps to PROMETHEE Method

PROMETHEE method consists of seven steps. These steps and formulas are given below.

Step 1: Alternatives and criteria are defined. The weights indicating the importance ratings of the alternatives are determined. The data set is created. Table 1 shows that PROMETHEE method data set.

Table 1 PROMETHEE method data set

	Evaluation factors					
		f(1)	*f*(2)	*f*(3)	…	*fk*
Alternatives	A	$f1(a)$	$f2(a)$	$f3(a)$	…	$fk(a)$
	B	$f1(b)$	$f2(b)$	$f3(b)$	…	$fk(b)$
	C	$f1(c)$	$f2(c)$	$f3(c)$	…	$fk(c)$
	…	…	…	…	…	…
Weights	wi	$w1$	$w2$	$w3$	…	wk

Step 2: Preference functions indicating the internal relations of the criteria are determined. There are six preference functions. PROMETHEE compares criteria in a binary form.

q: The value of indifference
p: Definite preference value
s: It is defined as intermediate value or standard deviation between p and q. For which criterion, it is decided by the choice of which preference function to use, by looking at the distribution of the alternate data that is determined by the decision-maker. The value d is the difference between the values of the two alternatives in terms of a criterion.

An important advantage of the PROMETHEE method over other multi-criteria decision methods is that it allows the decision-maker to make a choice for an alternative using the preference functions or to limit the alternative to the values determined by the decision-maker.

- If the decision-maker has no preference in terms of the relevant alternatives, the first choice (ordinary) preference function is used for those alternatives.
- If the decision-maker is to be used for a value with a value above its own value in terms of the relevant criterion, then the preference function should be second type (Type U).
- If the decision-maker wishes to use the preference for alternatives with a value above the mean for any criterion and does not want to ignore the values below this mean, then the preference function to be selected must be the third type (V Type) preference function.
- If the decision-maker chooses a preference in terms of a certain value range, the preference function to be used should be the fourth type preference function.
- If a decision criterion is to be used for alternatives with a value above the median, the preference function to be used must be the fifth type (linear) preference function.
- If, in the decision-maker's preference, the deviation values of their values are used in terms of the relevant criteria, the preference function to be selected will be the Gaussian preference function.

Step 3: Binary comparisons of alternatives for each criterion are made taking into account, and the preference functions and common preference functions are determined. In the form, the common preference function is shown, in which the alternatives are shown by A and B. In binary comparison of alternatives, care should be taken that the criteria are maximization direction or minimization direction.
Step 4: Preference indexes for alternatives compared using common preference functions are calculated.
Step 5: Positive and negative superiority values are calculated for the alternatives. Here are the formulas to use for these calculations. Here, in both forms, x symbolizes other alternatives outside A.
Step 6: The partial ranking between the alternatives is calculated with PROMETHEE 1. Binary comparisons of negative and positive superiority values of alternatives are made. There are three possible situations that may arise in the face of the decision-maker.

1. Another alternative superiority of an alternative

$$\Phi^+(A) > \Phi^+(B) \text{ and } \Phi^-(A) < \Phi^-(B)$$
$$\text{or}$$
$$\Phi^+(A) > \Phi^+(B) \text{ and } \Phi^-(A) = \Phi^-(B)$$
$$\text{or}$$
$$\Phi^+(A) = \Phi^+(B) \text{ and } \Phi^-(A) < \Phi^-(B)$$

2. Alternatives are no different

$$\Phi^+(A) = \Phi^+(B)\ ve\ \Phi^-(A) = \Phi^-(B)$$

3. Inability to compare alternatives

$$\Phi^+(A) > \Phi^+(B) \text{ and } \Phi^-(A) > \Phi^-(B)$$
$$\text{or}$$
$$\Phi^+(A) < \Phi^+(B) \text{ and } \Phi^-(A) < \Phi^-(B)$$

Step 7: PROMETHEE II determines the exact order of alternatives. Priority values for the exact order of the alternatives are calculated by using the following formula and make a sorting. These values are sorted from large to small.

$$\Phi(A) = \Phi^+(A) - \Phi^-(A)$$

$$\Phi(A) > \Phi(B) \quad \Phi(A) = \Phi(B)$$

According to the result obtained, if Φ $(A) >$ Φ (B) for A and B alternatives, then alternative A is over B alternative. If Φ $(A) =$ Φ (B), then the alternative A is no different from the alternative B (Yaralıoğlu 2010).

3 Application

The application was first started by identifying the nutrients in the food groups to be selected and collecting the data from these nutrients. Based on the price criterion, the table of Consumer Price Index (TUFE) of the year 2017 and the average item prices table are used at the point of evaluation of foods. Then the Turkish National Composition Database was used for the nutritional values of the food types covered by the decision points identified as red meat, white meat (chicken and fish), vegetables and pulses. Calories, carbohydrates, fat, protein, salt, calcium, and also the cooking and digestion times of the foods that they contain are the criteria of the alternatives to apply.

The practice in this study was developed using the PROMETHEE method, which is a multi-criteria decision-making method. Individuals are a web-based platform that offers food on their own terms. Especially web-based technology was used to build the platform and programming was done in this direction. The program is web-based, providing the advantages of being able to connect from any media in which the Internet is located and to easily perform the update operations. While developing the platform, HTML5, PHP, and Javascript programming languages were used. MySQL is used as database. Android Studio was used to transform the platform into a mobile interface and making it suitable for all platforms.

This platform consists of three parts according to the user's classification. The first is the customer–user interface, the second is the digital table showing the order follow-up at a restaurant, and the third is the interface that will be used by the person who made the order for the customer. Figure 1 shows these interfaces in general.

Customer–user interface consists of two parts. Among these, the "Ready List" field and the "Decision Support" field are the other. The thoughtful scenario takes place as follows you click on any of these categories, the food belonging to that category will be listed. Besides these foods.

Step 1: User (Customer) comes to a restaurant. Sits at a desk and sees a customer card with a square code in front of it. With the help of the mobile device, it reads the square code and the platform user interface comes in front of it.

Step 2: The customer can choose the food to be ordered directly from the "Ready List." When entering the Ready List section, there are categories. These categories have been indicated throughout the study in four formats as Red Meat, White Meat, Vegetable, and Pulses. When there are two buttons called "Review" and "Order." The client can view the properties of any food by clicking on the "review" button. This information is Food Name, Food Category, Food Price, Calorie Value, Protein Value,

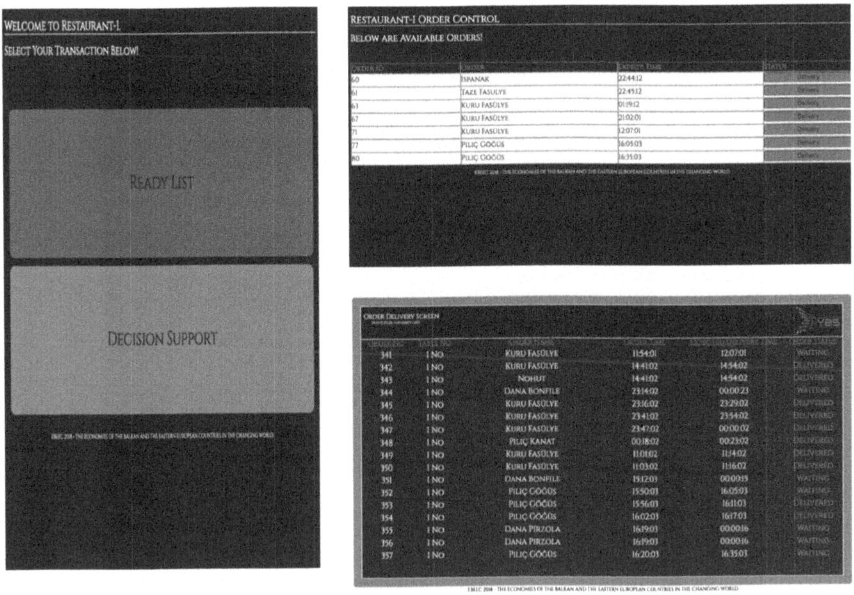

Fig. 1 İnt all user interfaces (customer, general, order)

Oil Value, Carbohydrate Value, Salt Value, Calcium Value, B-12 Value, Potassium Value, Cholesterol Value, Baking Time, Digestion Time.

In the opened window, after the food is examined, the order button can be printed or it can be processed from the "Order" section without examining. These processes are shown in Fig. 2.

Step 3: If the customer does not prefer the "Ready Menu" part, the system offers an alternative to the preferences by selecting the "Decision Support" part. The system performs the processes of PROMETHEE 1 and PROMETHEE 2. When the customer chooses the "Decision Support" part, the new screen will show "Products to be compared" and 8 questions. Comparable product categories are Red Meat, White Meat, Vegetables, and Pulses as mentioned in the first part. These categories constitute alternatives or decision points. The system asks the customer to answer 8 questions. These 8 questions are about the variables to be used in the PROMETHEE process. The variables and decision points to be used are shown in Table 2.

When prompted by customer questions, a new screen opens and displays 6 preference functions used to implement the PROMETHEE method. This field represents the options that the client wishes to express about the variable. These options are shown below:

I have no choice!
For me the values on … are the reason for preference!
For me the values on the average are the reason for preference!

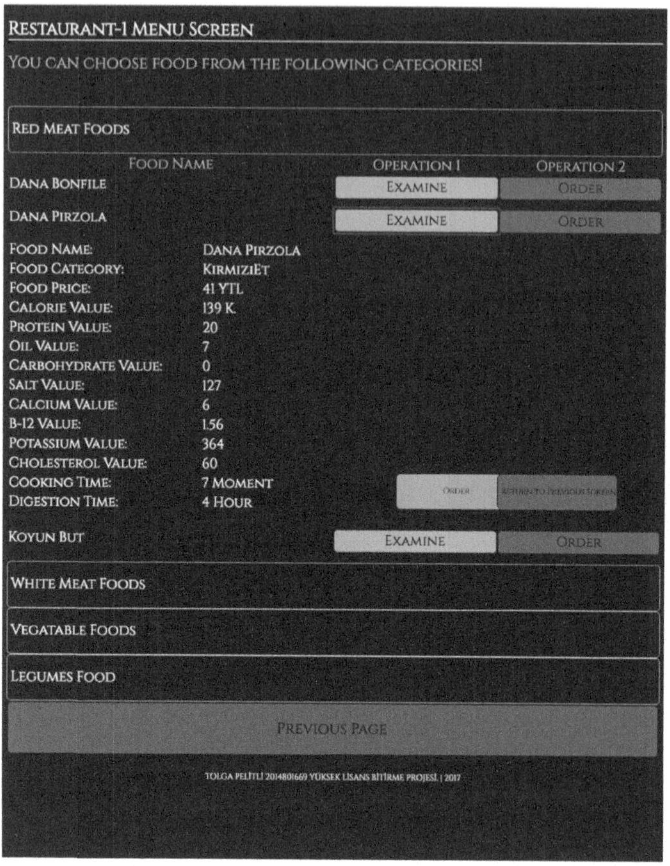

Fig. 2 Ready list functions

Table 2 Decision points, variables, variable weight values

Decision points (alternatives)	Variables (criteria)	Variable weights
Red meat	Price	0.125
White meat	Calorie ratio	0.125
Vegetables	Protein ratio	0.125
Legumes	Fat rate	0.125
	Carbohydrate	0.125
	Cholesterol	0.125
	Cooking time	0.125
	Duration of digestion	0.125

For me, the values between … and … are the reasons for preference!
For me, values between … and … are the reason for preference!
Standard deviations are the reason for preference!

Figure 3 shows the interfaces where these operations are performed.

Step 4: After completing this process for all variables, the customer can click on the "View Results" button to view the best option offered to him, as well as the worst option. On the new arrivals screen, the proposed category and the food options under that category are presented to the customer. On this screen, food can also be inspected and ordered. When the "Order" button is clicked on this screen, the following message is displayed to the customer: "Your order was received at 01:06:12. Expected order delivery time is 01:19:12 dır. In order to be able to serve you better, please give us your opinion about your meal in points!" The warning in this area concerns the customer's

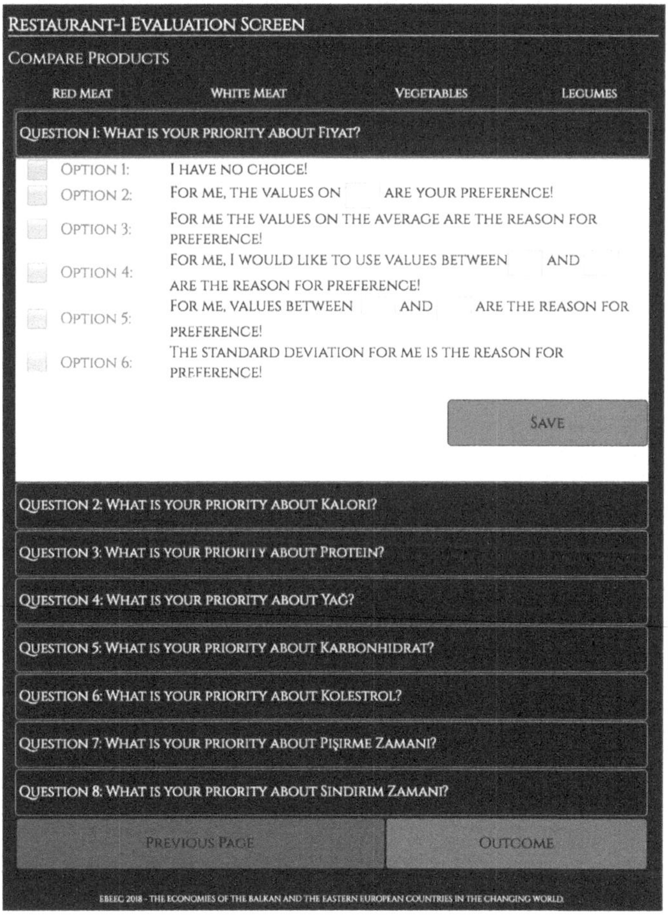

Fig. 3 Decision-making questions and preferences screen

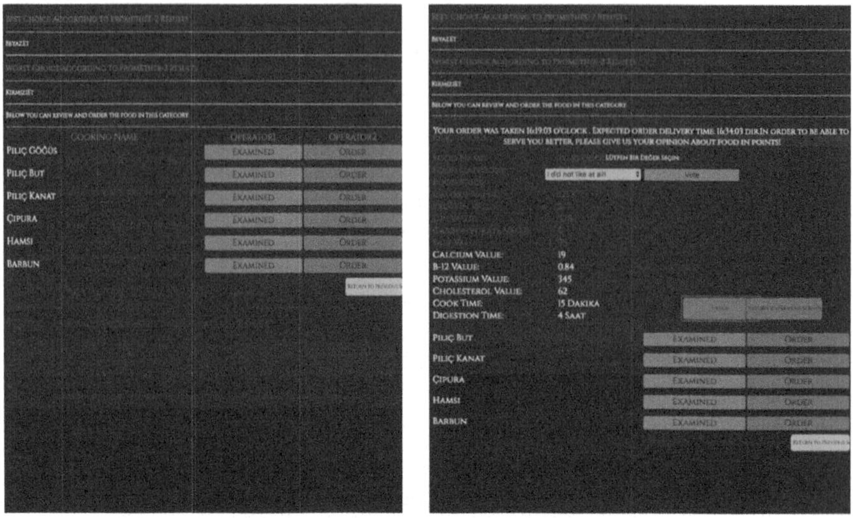

Fig. 4 Decision support result screen

comment on the incoming order. This value constitutes one of the two benchmarks to be used in a general productivity assessment on the chief who prepared the order. The client will make the selection based on the 5-point Likert scale answers. Figure 4 shows this process.

When ordered by the customer, the following values are displayed on a screen in the restaurant.

- Order number
- Table Number
- Order Name
- Ordered Time
- Expected Delivery Time
- Order status.

Figure 5 shows this screen.

In addition to the customer's order information, the chief's order delivery information is also displayed on this screen. All of this information is extracted from the database.

Finally, the chief user interface that prepares the order will be used to update the data in the main tablature. In addition, this interface plays an important role in the chief's productivity evaluation. The process is proceeding as follows.

Step 5: The customer makes the selection and the order button succeeds. Later, the time value ordered by the customer is regarded as the starting time for the concerned chef. Information about the food ordered is drawn from the table in the database.

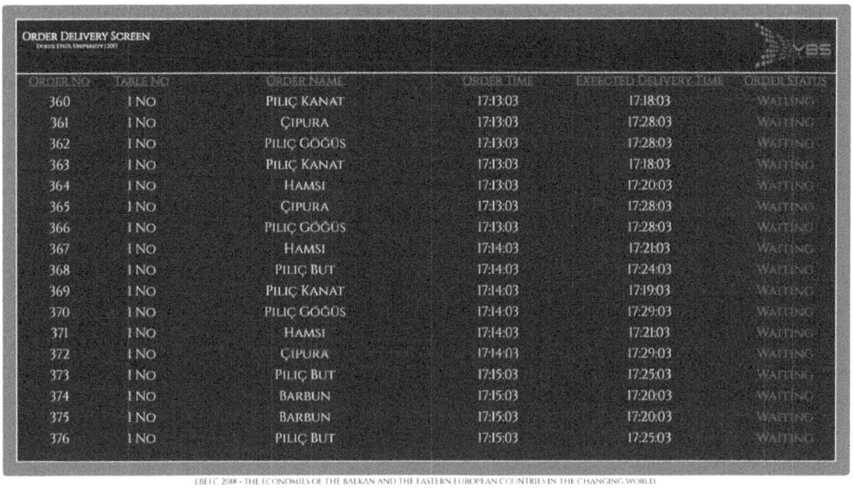

Fig. 5 General order delivery screen

As there is an average completion time for each order, this time is collected by the first order and the expected delivery time is determined. Once the relevant chef completes the submission process, he/she will push the corresponding order delivery button from his/her interface and the order delivery status will be indicated on the general screen. The second criterion in measuring the efficiency value of the chief, which is related to each of these times, is realized. Interpretation of the customer's order is also the first criterion.

The most important fact that people need to exist throughout history is nutrition. People may face many negative factors when they do not fulfill their nutritional needs adequately. These adverse factors can go as far as an avalanche and progress to societal impact. History has witnessed many times to the immigration, wars, and extinctions of an ethnocentric country or its origin due to the scarcity of food resources in the geographical region. Nutrition is so important that today's people are suffering from many chronic illnesses based on malnutrition. Today, one of the greatest causes of obesity, diabetes, cancer, heart diseases, and many other diseases is not enough having balanced and healthy nutrition.

Nowadays, most people do not have a plan of eating habits in their life struggle, so that the nutritional remedies cannot be done correctly. Many people are unaware of the effects of nutrients on their bodies, and how they may face future problems. In this study, it was tried to increase the usage of mobile devices which are indispensable for people of all ages to human health and to have high importance for nutrition values for everyone as well as how price and time are very important in the rush of daily life while people are making food choices. The nutritional values and other variable data of the food group determined in the web-based application created in this direction were established, and the solution was tried to be found by using the PROMETHEE multi-criteria decision-making method.

When you started work, a restaurant scenario was created. In the created scenario, the customer comes to the restaurant and a card with the data matrix on it is extended instead of the menu. In the created scenario, the customer comes to the restaurant and a card with the data matrix on it is extended instead of the menu. The user who reads the matrix gives an access to the application with the aid of the mobile device. Within the established restaurant scenario, the user can enter the decision support section of the application to which has access and easily select the desired food according to the desired PROMETHEE. In addition, since the application is web-based, it provides the possibility to use in any environment where the Internet connection is available, but it is not required in any installation.

It is aimed to improve the awareness and knowledge level of the users about the nutritional values of the users to increase the number of alternatives for the people by taking more food in practice, to gather more information about the factors affecting the preferences of the users, and to collect more data about them, and it will be moved.

4 Conclusion

The most important fact that people need to exist throughout history is nutrition. People may face many negative factors when they do not fulfill their nutritional needs adequately. These adverse factors can go as far as an avalanche and progress to societal impact. History has witnessed many times to the immigration, wars, and extinctions of an ethnocentric country or its origin due to the scarcity of food resources in the geographical region. Nutrition is so important that today's people are suffering from many chronic illnesses based on malnutrition. Today, one of the greatest causes of obesity, diabetes, cancer, heart diseases, and many other diseases is not enough having balanced and healthy nutrition.

Nowadays, most people do not have a plan of eating habits in their life struggle, so that the nutritional remedies cannot be done correctly. Many people are unaware of the effects of nutrients on their bodies, and how they may face future problems. In this study, it was tried to increase the usage of mobile devices which are indispensable for people of all ages to human health and to have high importance for nutrition values for everyone as well as how price and time are very important in the rush of daily life while people are making food choices. The nutritional values and other variable data of the food group determined in the web-based application created in this direction were established, and the solution was tried to be found by using the PROMETHEE multi-criteria decision-making method.

When you started work, a restaurant scenario was created. In the created scenario, the customer comes to the restaurant and a card with the data matrix on it is extended instead of the menu. In the created scenario, the customer comes to the restaurant and a card with the data matrix on it is extended instead of the menu. The user who reads the matrix gives access to the application with the aid of the mobile device. Within the established restaurant scenario, the user can enter the decision support section of the application to which has access and easily select the desired food according to the desired PROMETHEE. In addition, since the application is web-based, it provides the possibility to use in any environment where the internet connection is available, but it is not required in any installation.

In this study, it is aimed to improve the awareness and knowledge level of the users about the nutritional values of the users to increase the number of alternatives for the people by taking more food in practice, to gather more information about the factors affecting the preferences of the users, and to collect more data about them, and it will be moved.

References

Aygün, F. (2011). *Promethee Sıralama Yöntemi ile Yatırım Projesi Değerlendirme ve Üretim Sektöründe Uygulanması* Ankara: Gazi Üniversitesi Fen Bilimleri Enstitüsü.

Gül, M., et al. (2018). A fuzzy logic based PROMETHEE method for material selection problems. *Beni-Suef University Journal of Basic and Applied Sciences, 7*, 68–79.

Karacan, İ. (2015). *A new hybrid decision support tool and an application to health technology selection.* Deniz Harp Okulu Komutanlığı Deniz Bilimleri ve Mühendisliği Enstitüsü.

Mutlutürk, M. E. (2016). *Mobil/Web Tabanlı Bilgi Yönetim Sistemi*. İzmir: Dokuz Eylül Üniversitesi Sosyal Bilimler Enstitüsü.

Özbek, D. (2018). *Çok Kriterli Karar Verme Yöntemi Analitik Hiyerarşi Prosesi (AHP) ile Etkin Personel Seçimine Yönelik Web Tabanlı Bir Uygulama*. İzmir: Dokuz Eylül Üniversitesi Sosyal Bilimler Enstitüsü.

Sarı, T., & Timor, M. (2016). Integrated supplier selection model using Anp, Taguchi loss function and Promethee methods. *Journal of Applied Quantitative Methods, 11*(1).

Sennaroglu, B., & Celebi, G. (2018). A military airport location selection by AHP integrated PROMETHEE and VIKOR methods. *Transportation Research Part D, 59*, 160–173.

Silas, S., & Rajsingh, E.B. (2016). Performance analysis on algorithms for selection of desired healthcare services 2213-0209/© 2016 Elsevier GmbH.

Vassilev, V., Genova, K., & Vassileva, M. (2005). A brief survey of multicriteria decision making methods. *Bulgarian Academy of Sciences Cybernetics and Information Technologies, 5*(1), 4.

Verhagen, H., Vos, E., Francl, S., Heinonen, M., & van Loveren, H. (2010). Status of nutrition and health claims in Europe. *Archives of Biochemistry and Biophysics, 501*(1), 6–15.

Yaralıoğlu, K. (2010). *Karar Verme Yöntemleri*. Ankara: Detay Yayıncılık.

Zhai, Y., et al. (2017). Identification of key factors in health service adoption based on Internet of things and empirical test. 978-1-5090-4657-7/17 IEEE.

The Role of Financial Education in Additional Saving for Retirement

Sylwia Pieńkowska-Kamieniecka

Abstract Financial security in old age depends on individual choices and decisions made on the basis of the possessed financial expertise. Its scope depends on financial knowledge, which strongly influences the possessed savings for old age. There has been a growing interest in many countries concerning the subject of financial education for increasing the financial knowledge and expertise. The aim of this chapter is to present that without proper and serious retirement education and financial education, it will be difficult to achieve the effect of a larger engagement of the society in additional saving for retirement. To present to what extent the level of knowledge and education affects saving for old age, this chapter used the data from the research Social Diagnosis. In 2015 for this research 11.7 thousand households in Poland were tested. In order to realize the research aim the model of logistic regression was used. The studies conducted indicated, that level of financial literacy in Poland is low and only a small percentage of Poles save additionally for retirement. Besides, financial education should particularly focus on people with low degree of education who do not display any financial competence and have low willingness to save.

Keywords Additional pension schemes · Financial education · Knowledge · Saving

1 Introduction

The need for financial education is broadly recognized around the world (Norman 2010; Lusardi and Mitchell 2014; Mandell and Klein 2009; McCormick 2009; Clark et al. 2003). Proper financial education along with financial protection and financial inclusion constitutes a key element of financial empowerment of individuals and is essential to reinforce the whole financial system (Atkinson and Messy 2013; Lewis and Messy 2012). The ability to properly evaluate one's material status depends

S. Pieńkowska-Kamieniecka (✉)
University of Warmia and Mazury, Oczapowskiego 4, 10-720 Olsztyn, Poland
e-mail: sylwia.pienkowska@uwm.edu.pl

M. Janowicz-Lomott et al. (eds.), *Economic and Financial Challenges for Balkan and Eastern European Countries*, Springer Proceedings in Business and Economics,
https://doi.org/10.1007/978-3-030-39927-6_22

on their literacy and financial competence. As a result, they can assure their financial safety, particularly in the period of lower income during retirement (Singh 2014; Jacobs-Lawson and Hershey 2005; Lusardi and Mitchell 2007; Skinner 2007). Moreover, according to "win-win" strategy presented by Messy (2009), proper financial education implemented in three areas, such as: improving the standard of living, increasing the effectiveness of financial markets and competitiveness as well as reducing public expenditures, accompanies economic growth. Therefore, financial education is important not only for parties on the financial market, but also for the whole society.

Many governments around the world try to encourage their citizens to save. Simultaneously, common low financial literacy and awareness of financial issues (Klapper et al. 2015; Valant 2015) cause low willingness to save in general, but also low willingness to save for retirement which is crucial to maintain consumption on the same level as during professional activity (Alessie et al. 2011; Olsen and Whitman 2007). In the view of decreasing level of benefits from public pension schemes and complexity of products aimed at long-term saving, financial education focused on retirement protection (retirement education) is particularly required (OECD 2008a).

The aim of the present chapter is to prove that it may be difficult to achieve greater social engagement in additional retirement saving without serious and proper financial education on retirement. Consequently, the scale and saving possibilities of Poles were presented and it was shown how financial literacy determines saving and investing in Poland as compared with other countries. It was also investigated how the very level of education impacts the willingness to save, particularly for retirement.

2 Determinants of Financial Literacy and Education in the Retirement System

In recent years, there has been a growing interest in financial literacy. International Network on Financial Education (INFE) at OECD defines financial literacy as a fusion of literacy, awareness, skills, attitude and behaviour which are essential to undertake decisions in order to reach financial well-being (OECD/INFE 2011) in every stage of life.

Results of numerous research indicate that the social level of financial literacy and retirement awareness is low (Benartzi and Thaler 2007; OECD 2015; Klapper et al. 2015; Mandell and Klein 2009; Lusardi and Mitchell 2014; Czapiński and Góra 2016). It has become a serious problem since financial literacy is a significant determinant of financial planning, which increases the chances of saving (Alessie et al. 2011). Therefore, the society needs financial information and education in the scope of public as well as additional part of retirement system.

In order to be effective, this form of education must improve literacy so that it broadens financial competence and skills of financial planning which, in turn, lead to a change in financial behaviours (Fig. 1).

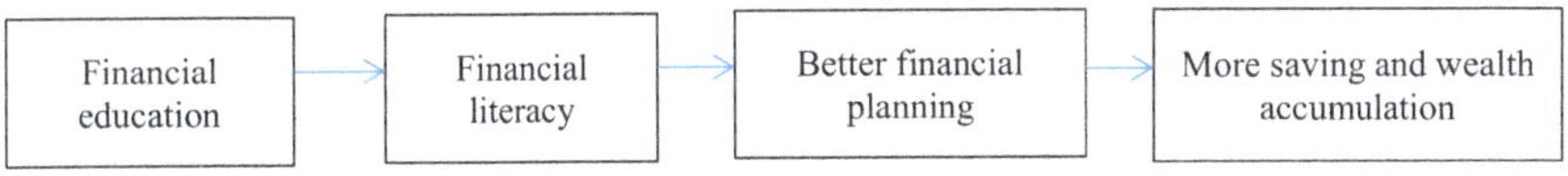

Fig. 1 Impact of financial education on the change of financial behaviours. *Source* Own elaboration based on de Meza et al. (2008)

Table 1 Determinants of the need and intensity of financial education

Level of public pension	High level of individual decisions and choices	Limited/no individual decisions and choices
Substantial public pension	Medium financial education required	Less financial education required
Limited public pension	Extensive financial education required	Medium financial education required

Source OECD (2008b)

Therefore, it may be concluded that a higher level of literacy and financial skills increases long-term savings, including retirement savings. In particular, there is a growing need for retirement literacy which constitutes a key element of financial literacy and contains all the information which is essential to comprehend all issues associated with the pension scheme (Olejnik and Białowąs 2015).

The role and intensity of financial education, with a closer look at its retirement aspect, need to be considered with respect to the construction and characteristics of the pension scheme, particularly the level of retirement protection provided by the public scheme. As societies receive lower benefits from the base part of the pension scheme due to a lowering replacement rate, it is each individual's own responsibility to assure higher standard of living while on pension. In pension schemes with defined contribution, financial protection during retirement depends on individual choices and decisions (Clark et al. 2003) based on one's literacy and financial competence. Such a situation in many countries implies the validity and need for broad education regarding financial and retirement systems, which is illustrated in Table 1.

As a result, it may be concluded that in Poland, where the level of benefits offered from the base (public) system will be lowering and the rate of pension will be highly dependent on individual choices and decisions of future pensioners (by additional pension protection), financial education, particularly retirement education, is greatly required.

3 Methodology and Data

In the research, literature and comparative methods were used along with the data from Polish and abroad research institutes. As for presenting the impact of education and literacy on saving for retirement, the chapter uses the data of the representative nationwide research Social Diagnosis.[1] In 2015, 11.7 thousand of Polish households with 35.3 thousand members took part in this study. In each household, the household head as the major decision-maker provided replies to the research queries. In order to realize the research aim the model of logistic regression was used.

In the chapter the following dependent variables were assumed in the construction of particular logit models: Y_1—saving in general, ($M1$ model), Y_2—saving for retirement ($M2$ model).

Dependent variables in particular models were dichotomous variables, i.e. zero-one. The variables took on the following form:

$$Y = \begin{cases} 1, & \text{if it occured} \\ 0, & \text{if it did not occur} \end{cases}$$

Verification of the correctness of models considered in this chapter was conducted with the use of the Hosmer–Lemeshow test. Its high values allow concluding that the models were correct.

4 Scale and Possibilities of Saving in General and Saving for Retirement

Many countries worldwide face the issue of low savings and savings for retirement. In Poland, this issue is particularly urgent. The results of Social Diagnosis 2015 indicate that only about 43% of interviewed households in Poland have some savings, and barely every third household declared that savings collected by them are aimed at financial protection for retirement (Table 2).

Although the awareness of worse financial situation during retirement among Poles is relatively high (almost 75% of Poles claim that pension provided by the public system does not allow to satisfy basic needs during retirement) (Polska 2016), yet approximately 40% of professionally active Poles do not think of ways to improve this situation (Czapiński and Góra 2016). Nonetheless, it needs to be stressed that

Table 2 Owing savings by households and savings for retirement as a saving goal

Specification	Savings		Savings for retirement	
	Number	In %	Number	In %
Yes	5052	43.1	2341	31.4
No	6666	56.9	5103	68.6
Total	11,718	100.0	7444	100.0

Source Own study based on the Social Diagnosis (2015)

[1] It is a complex study on conditions and quality of life of Poles in their own perspective, conducted cyclically since 2000.

knowledge of the rules of retirement system as well as of financial products aimed at long-term saving for retirement in Poland is low (Table 3).

Meanwhile, opportunities for additional saving, also for retirement, are growing. In recent years, income and expenditures of households have been rising systematically; nonetheless, the share of expenditures in income has decreased, which signals an expanding area for additional saving. Moreover, Poles perceive their material status more positively (Fig. 2).

Despite the aforementioned positive tendencies, the willingness of Poles to save for retirement remains on a low level. Households accumulate savings foremostly for unexpected circumstances (approximately 64% of saving households).

Table 3 Knowledge of institutionalized forms of saving for retirement in Poland and the actual level of their use

Specification	Awareness of particular form, in %	Using a particular form of saving at the end of 2016	
		Number, in thous.	% of total employed
Individual retirement accounts	27	902.6	5.2
Individual retirement security accounts	14	643.1	3.2
Employee pension schemes	6	395.6	2.4

Source Own elaboration based on TNS Polska (2016), data of the Polish Financial Supervision Authority and Rutecka et al. (2014)

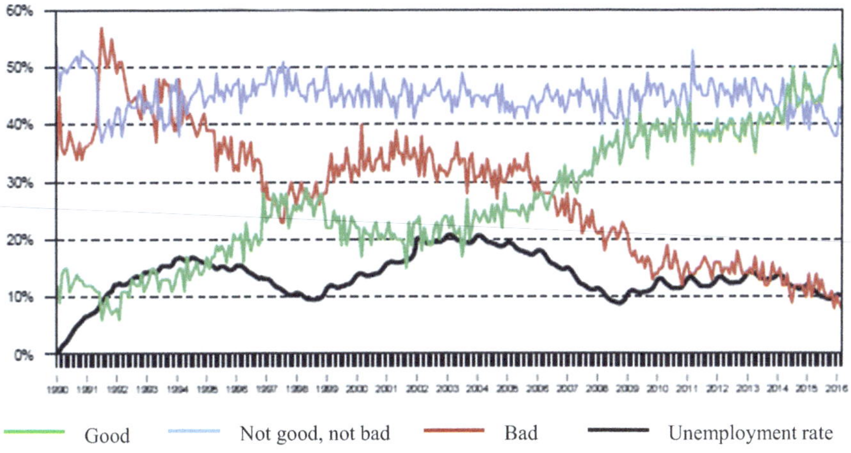

Fig. 2 Evaluation of one's material status among Polish households. *Source* CBOS (2016)

5 Factors of Saving in General and Saving for Retirement

The decision to save additionally for retirement by households is affected by numerous factors which are of economic as well as non-economic character (Kolasa and Liberda 2014; van Erp et al. 2013). One of them is education. Research of Cole and Shastry (2007) indicates that individuals with low level of education are likely to have lower income and wealth. Simultaneously, well-educated individuals are more likely to report income from retirement savings.

The analysis of logistic regression conducted within the nationwide research Social Diagnosis 2015 shows that saving and particularly saving for retirement are not determined by the same variables. For instance, gender impact can be noticed only in the case of saving in general where men have nearly 40% greater chances for saving. Saving for retirement turns out to be determined by a greater number of variables. For saving in general of significance are socio-professional status, place of residence and the number of hours spent on reading press (Table 4).

Although education generally has influence on the willingness to save and save for retirement, its role is much greater in the case of saving for retirement. People with higher education have almost 80% greater chances of saving for retirement than those with elementary education (the difference is around 73% as for saving in general). Consequently, it may be concluded that the chances of saving for retirement increase with greater education and literacy. The results of the present research indicate there is an impact of the number of volumes at home and number of hours spent on reading press weekly on saving behaviours. In houses with over 500 volumes, the chances of household head for saving for retirement are higher by approximately 31% than in houses where the number of volumes is lower (26–50 volumes). In the case of saving for retirement of significance (not present for saving in general) is also the effect of knowledge gained from reading press. It appears that every additional hour weekly devoted to reading press increases the chances of saving for retirement by 2.7%. Higher levels of education correspond to higher wages (Baum 2014). Therefore, income, as a derivative of education, also influences the willingness to save in general as well as saving for retirement (though income impact is in this case weaker). Income growth by 1 thousand PLN increases the chances of savings in general by approximately 24% and by 9% of additional retirement savings. Moreover, on the basis of the results one may conclude that the length of education, the fact of holding a managerial position or the number of hours spent on using the Internet are of no significance to any form of saving.

6 The Impact of Literacy and Financial Education on Saving

Planning and saving for retirement are closely connected with literacy which has a strong impact on accumulating wealth for old age (Pieńkowska-Kamieniecka and

Table 4 Estimates of parameters of logistic regression for saving in general and saving for retirement

Variable		Savings Exp(B) $M1$	Savings for retirement Exp(B) $M2$
Gender	$K = 0, M = 1$	1.398***	–
Age	Aged 65 and over (base)	*	***
	Up to 24	0.550	0.066*
	25–34 years	0.520*	0.190***
	35–44 years	0.590*	0.298***
	45–59 years	0.681	0.491*
	60–64 years	0.866	0.821
Socio-professional status	Unemployed and professionally passive (base)	–	***
	Employees of public sector	–	0.750
	Employees of private sector	–	0.990
	Private entrepreneurs	–	1.450
	Farmers	–	1.558
	Pensioners and retirees	–	1.211
	Pupils and students	–	–
Place of residence	Rural area (base)	–	*
	Cities with population over 500 thousand	–	1.457*
	Cities with population 200–500 thousand	–	1.175
	Cities with population 100–200 thousand	–	1.508*
	Cities with population 20–100 thousand	–	0.905
	Cities with population under 20 thousand	–	1.146
Level of education	Higher (base)	***	***
	Elementary and lower	0.269***	0.202**
	Lower secondary and vocational	0.413***	0.682*
	Secondary	0.558***	0.697**
Number of book volumes at home	Over 500 volumes (base)	***	*
	None	0.612	0.973

(continued)

Table 4 (continued)

Variable		Savings Exp(*B*) *M*1	Savings for retirement Exp(*B*) *M*2
Gender	$K = 0, M = 1$	1.398***	–
	Up to 25	0.749	0.721
	26–50 volumes	0.928	0.638*
	51–100 volumes	1.152	0.884
	101–500 volumes	1.250	1.010
Number of years of education	Continuous variable	–	–
Does the person hold a managerial position?	No (base)	–	–
Income	Continuous variable	1.236***	1.092***
Number of hours weekly spent on reading press	Continuous variable	–	1.027*
Number of hours spent on using the Internet last week?	Continuous variable	–	–
Constant		1.196	0.883
Cox-Snell's *R*-squared		0.105	0.094
Nagelkerke's *R*-squared		0.141	0.135
Hosmer–Lemeshow (*p*-value)		0.161	0.238
Log-likelihood		3.834555	2.459860
N		3.013	2.259

Note ***$p < 0.001$, **$p < 0.01$, *$p < 0.05$
Source Own study based on the Social Diagnosis (2015)

Walczak 2016). Research on financial competence reflecting the level of financial literacy is of key role to indicate the need for financial education across the population (Financial Literacy 2013). Studies conducted in many countries worldwide, both developed and developing, are aimed at not only evaluating financial literacy, but the skill of putting it into practice. In order to test the level of financial knowledge, a number of queries regarding key financial concepts are used. OECD/INFE study, conducted in 14 countries, utilized a set of eight questions which have been chosen to cover a range of financial topics, none of which were excessively complex and required expert knowledge. It concerned the following issues: division, time-value of money, interest paid on a loan, calculation of interest plus principal, compound interest, risk and return, definition of inflation and diversification (OECD/INFE 2013). It turned out that the level of financial knowledge differed significantly between countries. The best knowledge was observed among respondents from Hungary and Estonia where accordingly 69% and 61% of subjects provided correct answers to at least ¾ of the queries (reaching the so-called high score). In Poland, the percentage of people with high score amounted to 49%.

The results evidently show that the level of financial literacy has impact on saving (Fig. 3).

While comparing average financial literacy scores between the group of respondents having any savings or investment product and those without, it may be observed that the respondents with such a product were typically more financially literate than those without. In-depth analyses indicate that the issue of low financial literacy and consequent need for greater education concern mainly women, young and elderly people (with age the curve of financial competence takes on the shape of "∩") (Xu and Zia 2012), those with low income and low degree of education.

As for retirement protection, the impact of education and financial literacy is also visible in the respondents' view on who is responsible for material status during retirement. It turns out that well-educated people with greater economic literacy do not claim that it is the state's responsibility to provide for their pension (Table 5). Evidently, this results from their greater knowledge regarding the functioning of the retirement system: they are aware that in the face of lowering replacement rates from the public system, it is the future pensioner's responsibility to assure resources for this period of life. Consequently, they understand better the necessity to accumulate additional retirement savings.

The situation is similar in the case of people who participated in various forms of financial education and also had talks on economy and finances in childhood in their family home. Also Kempson and Finney (2009) argue that encouraging to save since early childhood shapes pro-saving behaviours in adult life.

The aforementioned research reports confirm that education and gained knowledge have positive influence on comprehension of financial and retirement issues and, as a result, willingness to save additionally for retirement. It seems crucial when

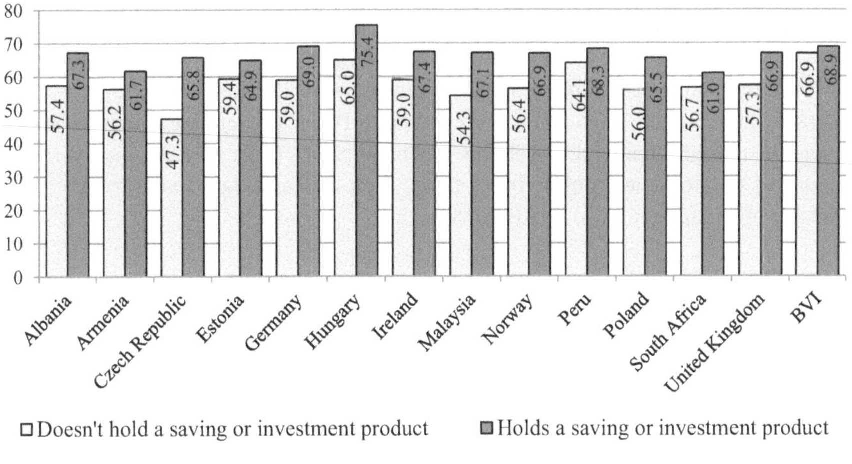

Fig. 3 Average financial literacy by saving and investing, in %. *Source* OECD/INFE (2013)

Table 5 Opinions on who should be responsible for material status on retirement, in %

Specification	The state	Jointly the state and future pensioner	Everyone should rely on themselves; we cannot count, that state will provide pension
Level of education			
Primary	59	17	24
Vocational	64	19	17
Secondary	50	24	26
Higher	47	26	27
Index (level) of financial literacy			
Low	59	22	19
Medium	57	22	28
High	50	22	28
The need for greater economic literacy			
Unnecessary	62	14	24
Necessary	51	26	23
Share in economic education at and outside school			
Yes	39	26	35
No	61	20	18
Talks on economy and finances in childhood in family home			
Never	61	15	24
Rarely	52	26	22
Regularly	42	31	27

Source Own elaboration based on NBP (2015)

taking into consideration the results of the research conducted by Narodowy Bank Polski (2015), i.e. the central bank of the Republic of Poland which has shown that Poles feel the need to expand their literacy and skills regarding saving for retirement (54%). Other important topics include: management of household budget (44%), insurances (44%) and taxes (42%). According to Poles, the leading role in financial education should be played by schools and universities (56%), media (press, radio, Internet, TV) (46%) and public institutions, such as Narodowy Bank Polski or the Ministry of Finances (31%) (NBP 2015).

7 Conclusions

Financial literacy in Poland is low and accompanied by a low level of financial competence, which leads to insufficient activity regarding the process of long-term saving. Despite a constantly growing awareness of the need to save and greater financial opportunities, still only a small percentage of Poles save additionally for retirement. The results of the present research signal an immense role of education in the perception of saving in general and saving for retirement (not taking into consideration the field of education). Financial education should particularly focus on people with low degree of education who do not display any financial competence and have low willingness to save. In the face of negative demographic tendencies and lowering level of retirement protection provided by the state of key role ought to be retirement education, particularly due to the fact that Poles see the need for greater education in this aspect. It should be conducted since early childhood, and its main apostles should be schools and universities, though the society would like to be fully informed also by the media or public institutions.

All in all, the society needs to have access to adequate information and financial education on retirement which will improve the level of economic literacy and retirement awareness of Poles.

References

Alessie, R., van Rooij, M., & Lusardi, A. (2011). Financial literacy, retirement preparation and pension expectations in the Netherlands. *DNB Working Paper*, No. 289.

Atkinson, A., & Messy, F. A. (2013). Promoting financial inclusion through financial education. *OECD Working Papers on Finance, Insurance and Private Pensions*, No. 34. OECD Publishing.

Atkinson, A., Messy, F.A., Rabinovich, L., Yoong, J. (2015). Financial education for long-term savings and investments. Review of research and literature. *OECD Working Papers on Finance, Insurance and Private Pensions*, No. 39 (p. 3). OECD.

Baum, S. (2014). *Higher education earnings premium. Value, variation, and trends* (p. 1). Urban Institute

Benartzi, S., & Thaler, R. H. (2007). Heuristics and biases in retirement savings behavior. *Jorunal of Economic Pespectives, 3*(21), 99.

CBOS. (2016). *Material status of poles* (p. 64). No: Research Report.

Clark, R. L., d'Ambrosio, M. B., McDermed, A. A., & Sawant, K. (2003). Financial education and retirement savings. *Paper Presented at Sustainable Community Development: What Works, What Doesn't, and Why,* Washington DC.

Cole, S., & Shastry, G. K. (2007). If you are so smart, why aren't you rich? The effects of education, financial literacy and cognitive ability on financial market participation (p. 26). Available at: www.people.hbs.edu/scole/webfiles/savings.pd. Accessed March 30, 2017.

Czapiński, J., & Góra, M. (2016). Świadomość „emerytalna" Polaków. Raport z badania ilościowego. *Publikacje Europejskiego Kongresu Finansowego*, Warszawa.

De Meza, D., Irlenbusch, B., & Reyniers, D. (2008). Financial capability: A behavioural economics perspective. Financial services authority. *Consumer Research, 69*, 16.

Jacobs-Lawson, J. M., & Hershey, D. A. (2005). Influence of future time perspective, financial knowledge, and financial risk tolerance on retirement saving behaviors. *Financial Services Review, 14*(4), 331–344.

Klapper, L., Lusardi, A., van Oudheusden, P. (2015). Financial literacy around the world: insights from the standard and poor's ratings services global financial literacy survey. Available at: http://gflec.org/wpcontent/uploads/2015/11/Finlit_paper_16_F2_singles.pdf. Accessed 28 March 2017.

Kemspon, A., & Finney, A. (2009). *Saving in lower income households: A review of the evidence* (p. 20). Personal Finance Research Centre, Bristol.

Kolasa, A., & Liberda, B. (2014). Determinants of saving in Poland: Are they different in other OECD countries? *Working Paper*, No. 13, University of Warsaw, Faculty of Economic Sciences.

Lewis, S., & Messy, F. A. (2012). Financial education, savings and investments. *OECD Working Papers on Finance, Insurance and Private Pensions*, N. 22, OECD Publishing.

Lusardi, A. & Mitchell, O. S. (2007). Financial literacy and retirement preparedness: Evidence and implications for financial education. *Business Economics*, 35–44.

Lusardi, A., & Mitchell, O. S. (2014). The economic importance of financial literacy: Theory and evidence. *Journal of Economic Literature, 52*(1), 5–44.

Mandell, S., & Klein, L. S. (2009). The impact of financial literacy education on subsequent financial behavior. *Journal of Financial Counseling and Planning, 20*(1), 15–24.

McCormick, M. H. (2009). The effectiveness of youth financial education: A review of the literature. *Journal of Financial Counseling and Planning, 20*(1), 70–83.

Messy, F. A. (2009). OECD financial education principles and best practices. *OECD-IOPS Mena Workshop on Pension Regulation and Supervision*. Available at: http://www.iopsweb.org/principlesguidelines/42155019.pdf. Accessed March 30, 2017.

NBP(2015). Stan wiedzy i świadomości ekonomicznej Polaków 2015, Konsorcjum Pracownia Badań i Innowacji Społecznych „Stocznia" i Grupa IQS dla Departamentu Edukacji i Wydawnictw NBP.

Norman, A. S. (2010). Importance of financial education in making informed decision on spending. *Journal of Economics and International Finance, 2*(10), 199–207.

OECD. (2008a). *Improving financial education and awareness on insurance and private pensions.*

OECD. (2008b). *Financial education and saving for retirement*. Available at: http://www.oecd.org/finance/private-pensions/39197801.pdf. Accessed March 30, 2017.

OECD/INFE. (2011). *Measuring financial literacy: Questionnaire and guidance notes for conducting an internationally comparable survey of financial literacy* (p. 3). Paris.

OECD/INFE. (2013). *Financial literacy and inclusion: Results of OECD/INFE survey across countries and by gender* (p. 81). Paris.

OECD. (2015). *Improving financial literacy. Analysis of issues and policies* (p. 12).

Olejnik, I. & Białowąs, S. (2015). Pension literacy and Consumers' decisions in the context of pension system reform. *Problemy Polityki Społecznej, 29*(2), 14.

Olsen, A., & Whitman, K. (2007). Effective retirement savings programs: Design features and financial education. *Social Security Bulletin, 67*(3), 63–72.

Pieńkowska-Kamieniecka, S., & Walczak, D.(2016). Willingness of Polish Households to Save for Retirement. *European Financial Systems 2016, Proceedings of the 13th International Scientific Conferences*, Brno, June 27–28.

Rutecka, J., Bielawska, K., Petru, R., Pieńkowska-Kamieniecka, S., Szczepański, M., & Żukowski, M. (2014). *Dodatkowy system emerytalny w Polsce – diagnoza i rekomendacje zmian*. TEP, Warszawa.

Singh, U. (2014). Financial literacy and financial stability are two aspect of efficiency economy. *Journal of Finance, Accounting and Management, 5*(2), 59–76.

Skinner, J. (2007). Are you sure you're saving enough for retirement? *Journal of Economic Perspectives, 21*(3), 59–80.

TNS Polska. (2016). *Skłonność Polaków do dodatkowego oszczędzania na emeryturę – mit czy rzeczywistość?* (p. 7). Available at: http://www.tnsglobal.pl/coslychac/files/2016/03/Sklonnosc-do-oszczedzania-na-emeryture-2016–03-04.pdf. Accessed March 25, 2017.

Valant, J. (2015). Improving the financial literacy of European consumers. *EPRS*, European Commission.

Van Erp, F., Vermeer, N., & van Vuuren, D. (2013). Non-financial determinants of retirement. *Netspar Panel Paper, 34*.

Xu, L., & Zia, B. (2012). Financial literacy around the world. An overview of the evidence with practical suggestions for the way forward. *Policy Research Working Paper* (p. 9). The World Bank, No. 61707.

The manufacturer's authorised representative in the EU is Springer Nature Customer Service Centre GmbH, Europaplatz 3, 69115 Heidelberg, Germany. If you have any concerns regarding our products, please contact ProductSafety@springernature.com

Printed and bound by CPI Group (UK) Ltd, Croydon, CR0 4YY
30/09/2026
02225648-0013